Taste of Home
Baking
Classics

Taste of Home
B O O K S

REIMAN MEDIA GROUP, INC. • GREENDALE, WISCONSIN

A TASTE OF HOME/READER'S DIGEST BOOK

© 2008 Reiman Media Group, Inc.
5400 S. 60th St., Greendale WI 53129
All rights reserved.

Editor: Janet Briggs
Art Director: Edwin Robles, Jr.
Layout Designer: Catherine Fletcher
Proofreader: Linne Bruskewitz
Project Indexer: Jean Duerst
Recipe Asset Management System: Coleen Martin, manager;
Sue A. Jurack, specialist
Editorial Assistant: Barb Czysz
Food Director: Diane Werner RD
Recipe Testing and Editing: Taste of Home Test Kitchen
Food Photography: Reiman Photo Studio
Cover Photo Photographer: Rob Hagen
Cover Food Stylist: Suzanne Breckenridge
Cover Set Stylist: Stephanie Marchese

Senior Editor/Books: Mark Hagen
Creative Director: Ardyth Cope
Vice President, Book Marketing: Dan Fink
Chief Marketing Officer: Lisa Karpinski
Vice President, Executive Editor/Books: Heidi Reuter Lloyd
Senior Vice President, Editor in Chief: Catherine Cassidy
President, Consumer Marketing: Dawn Zier
President, Food & Entertaining: Suzanne M. Grimes
President and Chief Executive Officer: Mary G. Berner

Pictured on front cover (clockwise from top): Ozark Mountain Berry Pie (p.113), Cinnamon Raisin Bread (p. 88), Chocolate Cupcakes (p. 205) and Fancy Peanut Butter Cookies (p. 319).
Pictured on spine: Toffee Cranberry Crisps (p. 313).
Pictured on back cover (from left to right): Orange Chocolate Chip Bread (p. 16), Colonial Oat Bread (p. 53) and Raspberry Delights (p. 363).

International Standard Book Number (10): 0-89821-612-5
International Standard Book Number (13): 978-0-89821-612-7

Library of Congress Control Number: 2008925632

For other Taste of Home books and products, visit tasteofhome.com.
For more Reader's Digest products and information, visit rd.com (in the United States)
rd.ca (in Canada)

Printed in China
1 3 5 7 9 10 8 6 4 2

Table of Contents

10 Tips for *Baking Success*

First read the entire recipe.

The aroma and fantastic flavor of fresh-baked breads, cakes and cookies just can't be beat. Let baking be one of your secret pleasures while your family and friends think you're pampering them with sensational creations. Included in this extensive collection of **655 fabulous recipes** are chip-packed cookies, gooey brownies, delectable cakes, fruity pies, tender yeast breads and so much more! To get you started, we've shared the following 10 essential baking pointers so you can bake with confidence.

1 Reading Is Fundamental
Read the entire recipe before you begin. If you are not familiar with a technique or term, refer to a cooking reference or search for information on the Internet. Visit **tasteofhome.com** for how-to videos, articles and tips on baking.

2 Check Out Ingredients
Gather all the ingredients before you begin. If you're missing an ingredient, look at the Ingredient Substitutions chart on the inside back cover of this book. You may have a substitution. If not, a trip to the store will be necessary.

Assemble all of the ingredients for the recipe.

3 Prep Ingredients Before Mixing
Prepare all the ingredients. Let butter soften, separate eggs, chop nuts, etc.

Too firm—butter is too hard to cream.

Softened just right.

4 Select and Prep Pans
Use the type of pan and the size of pan stated in the recipe. Generally pans are filled two-thirds to three-fourths full.

Use an 8-in. x 4-in. x 2-in. loaf pan filled two-thirds plus muffin pan for extra batter, a larger 9-in. x 5-in. x 3-in. loaf pan or several 5-3/4-in. x 3-in. x 2-in. loaf pans.

Pan is too full.

Grease and flour pan if recipe directs. For yeast breads, prepare pans before shaping the dough.

Grease pan as recipe directs with shortening or cooking spray.

5 Get the Oven Ready
Position the oven rack so the baking pan will be in center of the oven or position the oven rack as the recipe directs. Preheat oven. For yeast breads, preheat during the final rise time.

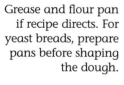
Position oven rack before preheating the oven.

Measure with Precision

Accurately measure the ingredients. Use a liquid measuring cup for wet ingredients, such as milk, honey, molasses, corn syrup, water, juice or oil. Before measuring sticky ingredients like molasses or corn syrup, coat the inside of the measuring tool with cooking spray. This will make cleanup easier.

Check level of liquid at your eye level.

Dry measuring cups allow ingredients to be measured right to the rim of the cup. They are used to measure dry and packable ingredients, like flour, sugar, chocolate chips, nuts, shortening and sour cream.

Fill dry ingredients to the rim and sweep off excess with the flat edge of a metal spatula or knife.

Measuring spoons are used to measure both liquid and dry ingredients. It's nice to have two sets when baking. Use one set for measuring the liquid ingredients and the other for dry.

Wet and dry ingredients should be filled to the rim of the spoon.

Mix it Up

Follow the mixing directions as they are written. Altering the method may affect how the final baked good looks and/or tastes.

Cream until light and fluffy.

Fold lighter weight ingredients into heavier ones with a rubber spatula.

Use a sturdy wooden spoon to stir chips, nuts and dried fruit into heavy batters.

Start the Timer

Most recipes give a range for the baking time. Set a kitchen timer for the low end of the time range immediately after the food has been placed in the oven.

Set the timer for the shortest time given in the recipe.

The toothpick is clean; the cake is done.

The toothpick has crumbs on it; the cake needs more baking time.

Check Doneness

Check for doneness at the shortest time given in the recipe using the stated doneness test. If the baked good does not test done, continue baking and check again.

Take Time to Cool Off

A wire rack is used for cooling baked goods because it allows air to circulate around the food, which prevents moist, soggy spots. Many cookies can be immediately removed from the baking pan to a wire rack.

Carefully transfer to wire rack to cool.

Other foods like cakes and quick bread loaves need to rest for 10 minutes in their pan. The resting time helps prevent these items from crumbling when they are removed. Still other items—angel food cakes and chiffon cakes baked in tube pans—are cooled completely in their pan. Some baked goods are delicious warm, but others need to be cooled completely for frosting or easy slicing.

Cool most baked goods for 10 minutes before removing from pan.

pg. 28

Quick Breads

pg. 20

pg. 30

pg. 31

Best Cheese Bread

Joanie Elbourn, Gardner, Massachusetts

*My husband and I often make a meal of bread and salad.
We enjoy the garlic, dill and cheddar flavors in this savory
bread. We think it's best served fresh from the oven.*

3-3/4   cups all-purpose flour
2-1/2   cups (10 ounces) shredded cheddar cheese
    5   teaspoons baking powder
  1/2   teaspoon garlic powder
  1/2   teaspoon dill weed
    2   eggs
1-1/2   cups milk
  1/3   cup canola oil
    3   tablespoons honey

In a large bowl, combine the flour, cheese, baking powder,
garlic powder and dill. In another bowl, whisk eggs, milk,
oil and honey. Stir into flour mixture just until moistened.

Pour into a greased 9-in. x 5-in. x 3-in. loaf pan. Bake at
350° for 55-65 minutes or until a toothpick inserted near
the center comes out clean (top will have an uneven
appearance). Cool for 10 minutes before removing from
pan to a wire rack. Serve warm. Store in the refrigerator.
Yield: 1 loaf (16 slices each).

Best Bran Muffins

Karen Hill, Sheridan, Oregon

These hearty muffins were a staple with my twin sister and me all through high school. Raisins or dried cranberries can make a nice addition.

- 1-1/2 cups old-fashioned oats
- 1 cup All-Bran
- 1 cup boiling water
- 2-1/2 cups all-purpose flour
- 1/2 cup sugar
- 1/2 cup packed brown sugar
- 1/4 cup toasted wheat germ
- 2-1/2 teaspoons baking soda
- 1/2 teaspoon salt
- 2 eggs, beaten
- 2 cups buttermilk
- 1/2 cup butter, melted

Place oats and cereal in a bowl; cover with boiling water. Let stand for 5 minutes. In a large bowl, combine the flour, sugars, wheat germ, baking soda and salt. In another bowl, combine the eggs, buttermilk, butter and oat mixture. Stir into flour mixture just until moistened.

Fill greased muffin cups two-thirds full. Bake at 375° for 18-20 minutes or until a toothpick inserted near the center comes out clean. Cool for 5 minutes before removing from pans to wire racks. Serve warm. **Yield:** 2 dozen.

Poppy Seed Pound Cake Muffins

Glenda York, Wichita, Kansas

Muffins are one of my favorite foods, and these are so good! I enjoy making several varieties of muffins at one time to have on hand for breakfast or lunch.

- 1-1/2 cups butter, softened
- 1 cup sugar
- 2 eggs
- 1 cup (8 ounces) plain yogurt
- 1 teaspoon vanilla extract
- 2 cups all-purpose flour
- 1 tablespoon poppy seeds
- 1/2 teaspoon salt
- 1/4 teaspoon baking soda

In a large bowl, cream butter and sugar until light and fluffy. Beat in the eggs, yogurt and vanilla. Combine the flour, poppy seeds, salt and baking soda. Stir into creamed mixture just until moistened.

Fill paper-lined muffin cups two-thirds full. Bake at 400° for 20-25 minutes or until a toothpick inserted near the center comes out clean. Cool for 5 minutes before removing from pans to wire racks. **Yield:** 14 muffins.

Cinnamon Chip Raisin Scones

Mary Ann Morgan, Cedartown, Georgia

This creative recipe features raisins and homemade cinnamon chips to produce rich, mouthwatering scones. I think they're best served warm with lemon curd.

CINNAMON CHIPS:
- 3 tablespoons sugar
- 3 teaspoons ground cinnamon
- 2 teaspoons shortening
- 2 teaspoons corn syrup

SCONES:
- 1-2/3 cups bread *or* all-purpose flour
- 2 tablespoons sugar
- 2 teaspoons baking powder
- 1/2 teaspoon salt
- 1/3 cup cold butter
- 1/2 cup evaporated milk
- 1/2 cup raisins
- Additional evaporated milk

In a large bowl, combine the sugar, cinnamon, shortening and corn syrup with a fork until crumbly and evenly blended. Spread onto a foil-lined baking sheet. Bake at 250° for 30-40 minutes or until melted and bubbly. Cool completely; break into small pieces.

In a large bowl, combine the flour, sugar, baking powder and salt. Cut in butter until the mixture resembles coarse crumbs. Stir in milk just until moistened. Gently stir in raisins and cinnamon chips.

Turn onto a lightly floured surface. Roll to 1/2-in. thickness; cut with a floured 2-in. biscuit cutter.

Line a baking sheet with foil and grease the foil. Place scones 1 in. apart on foil. Brush tops lightly with additional milk. Bake at 400° for 14-16 minutes or until golden brown. Serve warm. **Yield:** 15 scones.

Chocolate Mini Loaves

Elizabeth Downey, Evart, Michigan

The moist texture of these mini loaves resembles a pound cake. Each bite is rich and succulent, making this perfect for dessert as well as snacking.

- 1/2 cup butter, softened
- 2/3 cup packed brown sugar
- 1 cup (6 ounces) semisweet chocolate chips, melted and cooled
- 2 eggs
- 2 teaspoons vanilla extract
- 2-1/2 cups all-purpose flour
- 1 teaspoon baking powder
- 1 teaspoon baking soda
- 1-1/2 cups applesauce
- 1/2 cup miniature semisweet chocolate chips
- GLAZE:
- 1/2 cup semisweet chocolate chips
- 1 tablespoon butter
- 5 teaspoons water
- 1/2 cup confectioners' sugar
- 1/4 teaspoon vanilla extract
- Dash salt

In a large bowl, cream butter and brown sugar until light and fluffy. Add the melted chocolate chips, eggs and vanilla; mix well. Combine the flour, baking powder and baking soda; add to creamed mixture alternately with applesauce. Fold in miniature chocolate chips.

Divide batter among five greased 5-3/4-in. x 3-in. x 2-in. loaf pans, about 1 cup in each. Bake at 350° for 30-40 minutes or until a toothpick inserted near the center comes out clean. Cool for 10 minutes before removing from pans to wire racks to cool completely.

For glaze, combine the chocolate chips, butter and water in a saucepan; cook and stir over low heat until chocolate is melted. Remove from the heat; stir in the confectioners' sugar, vanilla and salt until smooth. Drizzle over cooled loaves. **Yield:** 5 mini loaves (5 slices each).

Spicy Sausage Muffins

Shirley Glaab, Hattiesburg, Mississippi

Ready for a change of pace? This muffin has a terrific spicy flavor with a good blend of herbs, sausage and cheese. It's very different from other savory muffins.

- 1/2 pound bulk hot pork sausage
- 1/4 cup chopped green onions
- 1/4 cup chopped sweet red pepper
- 3/4 cup all-purpose flour
- 1/2 cup cornmeal
- 1 tablespoon minced fresh cilantro
- 1 teaspoon baking soda
- 1/2 teaspoon salt
- 3/4 teaspoon minced fresh thyme *or* 1/4 teaspoon dried thyme
- 1 egg, lightly beaten
- 1 cup buttermilk
- 3/4 cup shredded sharp cheddar cheese

In a large skillet, cook the sausage, onions and red pepper over medium heat until meat is no longer pink; drain and set aside. In a large bowl, combine the flour, cornmeal, cilantro, baking soda, salt and thyme.

In another bowl, combine egg and buttermilk. Stir into flour mixture just until moistened. Fold in cheese and sausage mixture.

Fill greased muffin cups two-thirds full. Bake at 375° for 25-30 minutes or until a toothpick inserted near the center comes out clean. Cool for 5 minutes before removing from pan to a wire rack. Serve warm. Store in the refrigerator. **Yield:** 1 dozen.

Broccoli Corn Bread

Colleen Goodwin, Livingston, Texas

This tender bread with a sweet corn flavor can be served as a side dish with any meaty entree. The broccoli and cottage cheese combination is delicious.

- 2 packages (8-1/2 ounces *each*) corn bread/muffin mix
- 4 eggs
- 1-1/2 cups (12 ounces) 4% cottage cheese
- 3/4 cup butter, melted
- 3 cups frozen chopped broccoli, thawed
- 1 large onion, chopped

In a large bowl, combine corn bread mixes. In another bowl, beat the eggs, cottage cheese and butter. Stir into corn bread mixes just until moistened. Fold in broccoli and onion.

Transfer to a greased 13-in. x 9-in. x 2-in. baking pan. Bake at 350° for 40-45 minutes or until a toothpick inserted near the center comes out clean. Let stand for 10 minutes before cutting. Serve warm. Store in the refrigerator. **Yield:** 12-15 servings.

Aunt Betty's Blueberry Muffins

Sheila Raleigh, Kechi, Kansas

My Aunt Betty bakes many items each Christmas, but I look forward to these mouthwatering muffins the most.

- 1/2 cup old-fashioned oats
- 1/2 cup orange juice
- 1 egg
- 1/2 cup canola oil
- 1/2 cup sugar
- 1-1/2 cups all-purpose flour
- 1-1/4 teaspoons baking powder
- 1/2 teaspoon salt
- 1/4 teaspoon baking soda
- 1 cup fresh *or* frozen blueberries

TOPPING:
- 2 tablespoons sugar
- 1/2 teaspoon ground cinnamon

In a large bowl, combine oats and orange juice; let stand for 5 minutes. Beat in the egg, oil and sugar until blended. Combine flour, baking powder, salt and baking soda; stir into oat mixture just until moistened. Fold in blueberries.

Fill greased or paper-lined muffin cups two-thirds full. Combine topping ingredients; sprinkle over tops. Bake at 400° for 20-25 minutes or until a toothpick inserted near the center comes out clean. Cool for 5 minutes before removing from pan to a wire rack. Serve warm. **Yield:** about 1 dozen.

Editor's Note: If using frozen blueberries, do not thaw before adding to batter.

Dutch Apple Loaf

Gladys Meyer, Ottumwa, Iowa

Being of Dutch descent, I knew I had to try this recipe for a fruity quick bread. It freezes well, so I often have a loaf on hand for church bazaars.

- 1/2 cup butter, softened
- 1 cup sugar
- 2 eggs
- 1/4 cup buttermilk
- 1 teaspoon vanilla extract
- 2 cups all-purpose flour
- 1 teaspoon baking soda
- 1/2 teaspoon salt
- 2 cups diced peeled tart apples
- 1/2 cup chopped walnuts

TOPPING:
- 1/4 cup sugar
- 1/4 cup all-purpose flour
- 2 teaspoons ground cinnamon
- 1/4 cup cold butter, cubed

In a large bowl, cream butter and sugar until light and fluffy. Add eggs, one at a time, beating well after each addition. Beat in buttermilk and vanilla. Combine the flour, baking soda and salt; gradually add to creamed mixture. Fold in apples and walnuts. Pour into a greased 9-in. x 5-in. x 3-in. loaf pan.

For topping, combine the sugar, flour and cinnamon. Cut in butter until mixture resembles coarse crumbs. Sprinkle over batter. Bake at 350° for 55-60 minutes or until a toothpick inserted near the center comes out clean. Cool for 10 minutes before removing from pan to a wire rack. **Yield:** 1 loaf (16 slices).

Almond Apricot Bread

Kathy Cary, Wildwood, Missouri

My mother, who is a big apricot and almond fan, inspired me to create this tempting quick bread. The teachers at our children's school look forward to me making these pretty loaves each Christmas.

2-1/2   cups all-purpose flour
  1/2   cup sugar
  1/2   cup packed brown sugar
    3   teaspoons baking powder
    1   teaspoon salt
    1   package (7 ounces) apricots with mixed fruit baby food, *divided*
    1   egg
  3/4   cup plus 1 teaspoon milk, *divided*
    3   tablespoons canola oil
1-1/8   teaspoons almond extract, *divided*
  2/3   cup sliced almonds, coarsely chopped
  1/2   cup diced dried apricots
  1/2   cup confectioners' sugar

In a large bowl, combine the flour, sugars, baking powder and salt. Set aside 1 tablespoon baby food for glaze. In another bowl, beat the egg, 3/4 cup milk, oil, 1 teaspoon almond extract and remaining baby food. Stir into flour mixture just until moistened. Fold in almonds and apricots.

Pour into a greased 9-in. x 5-in. x 3-in. loaf pan. Bake at 350° for 55-65 minutes or until a toothpick inserted near the center comes out clean. Cool for 10 minutes before removing from the pan to a wire rack to cool completely.

For glaze, combine the confectioners' sugar, reserved baby food, and remaining milk and extract until smooth. Drizzle over bread. **Yield:** 1 loaf (16 slices).

Removing a Loaf Bread from the Pan To easily remove a quick bread from a loaf pan, line the greased pan with a piece of parchment or waxed paper that just fits the bottom of the pan. Grease the paper and make sure there are no crinkles in the paper. (Any crinkles will make grooves in the bottom of the bread.) When the bread is removed from the pan, gently peel off the paper and turn the bread top side up to cool.

Mom's Buttermilk Biscuits

Judith Rush, Katy, Texas

Rich buttermilk biscuits baking in the oven will bring back warm memories of your own mom's kitchen. These have a classic old-fashioned flavor that's stood the test of time. You can make them with little effort.

- 2   cups all-purpose flour
- 2-1/4 teaspoons baking powder
- 3/4 teaspoon salt
- 1/4 teaspoon baking soda
- 1/3 cup shortening
- 3/4 cup buttermilk

In a large bowl, combine the flour, baking powder, salt and baking soda. Cut in shortening until mixture resembles coarse crumbs. Stir in buttermilk just until moistened.

Turn onto a lightly floured surface. Roll to 1/2-in. thickness; cut with a floured 2-1/2-in. biscuit cutter. Place 1 in. apart on an ungreased baking sheet. Bake at 450° for 8-10 minutes or until golden brown. Serve warm. **Yield:** 1 dozen.

Confetti Muffins

Nancy Piram, St. Cloud, Minnesota

These savory herb and vegetable muffins are a nice break from the usual sweet muffins. Serve them with soups, barbecued entrees or main-dish salads.

- 1-1/2 cups all-purpose flour
- 2   tablespoons sugar
- 2   teaspoons baking powder
- 1/2 teaspoon baking soda
- 1/2 teaspoon salt
- 1/2 teaspoon dried basil
- 1/4 teaspoon dried tarragon
- 1/3 cup chopped green onions
- 1/3 cup chopped sweet red pepper
- 1/4 cup chopped green pepper
- 1/2 cup butter, cubed
- 1/4 cup minced fresh parsley *or* 4 teaspoons dried parsley flakes
- 2   eggs
- 2/3 cup sour cream
- 1   tablespoon Dijon mustard

In a large bowl, combine the flour, sugar, baking powder, baking soda, salt, basil and tarragon; set aside. In a skillet, saute onions and peppers in butter until tender. Stir in parsley; cook for 10 minutes.

In a large bowl, beat the eggs, sour cream and mustard. Add onion mixture. Stir into flour mixture just until moistened.

Fill greased or paper-lined muffin cups two-thirds full. Bake at 400° for 15-20 minutes or until a toothpick inserted near the center comes out clean. Cool for 5 minutes before removing from pan to a wire rack. Serve warm or at room temperature. Store in the refrigerator. **Yield:** 1 dozen.

Barbecued Corn Muffins

Shawn Roland, Madison, Mississippi

When I was growing up on a farm in Mississippi, I was encouraged to bake by my grandmother and mother. I rarely use written recipes, but this one is a classic.

- 1/2 pound ground beef
- 1/4 cup packed brown sugar
- 1/4 cup ketchup
- 1   tablespoon Worcestershire sauce
- 1   teaspoon prepared mustard
- 1/2 teaspoon salt
- 1/4 teaspoon pepper
- 1/4 teaspoon garlic powder
- 1   package (8-1/2 ounces) corn bread/muffin mix
- 2/3 cup shredded cheddar cheese

In a large skillet, cook beef over medium heat until no longer pink; drain and place in a bowl. Add the brown sugar, ketchup, Worcestershire sauce, mustard, salt, pepper and garlic powder.

Prepare corn bread mix according to package directions. Fill greased muffin cups with a scant 2 tablespoons of batter. Top each with 2 tablespoons beef mixture; sprinkle with cheese. Top with remaining corn bread mix.

Bake at 400° for 12-15 minutes or until a toothpick inserted in the corn bread comes out clean. Cool for 5 minutes before removing from pan to a wire rack. Serve warm. Store in the refrigerator. **Yield:** 1 dozen.

Ham 'n' Cheese Muffins

Kati DeLaurier, Pine Mountain Club, California

While living in Oregon, I frequented a local restaurant that served these muffins. They wouldn't share the recipe, so I came up with my own creation.

1-3/4 cups all-purpose flour
2-1/2 teaspoons baking powder
1 teaspoon ground mustard
1/2 teaspoon ground cumin
2 eggs
1 cup buttermilk
2 cups diced fully cooked ham
2 cups (8 ounces) shredded cheddar cheese, *divided*

In a large bowl, combine the flour, baking powder, mustard and cumin. In another bowl, whisk eggs and buttermilk. Stir into flour mixture just until moistened. Fold in ham and 1-1/4 cups cheese.

Fill greased muffin cups two-thirds full. Sprinkle with remaining cheese. Bake at 375° for 20-25 minutes or until a toothpick inserted near the center comes out clean. Cool for 5 minutes before removing from pans to wire racks. Serve warm. Store in the refrigerator. **Yield:** 1-1/2 dozen.

Peanut Butter Pumpkin Bread

Anita Chicke, Frisco, Texas

My husband brought this recipe home from the office many years ago. Each fall, I bake several of these lovely loaves to share with family and friends. Pumpkin and peanut butter are a unique, delicious combination.

3-1/2 cups all-purpose flour
3 cups sugar
2 teaspoons baking soda
1-1/2 teaspoons salt
1 teaspoon ground cinnamon
1 teaspoon ground nutmeg
1 can (15 ounces) solid-pack pumpkin
4 eggs
1 cup canola oil
3/4 cup water
2/3 cup peanut butter

In a large bowl, combine the flour, sugar, baking soda, salt, cinnamon and nutmeg. In another bowl, combine the pumpkin, eggs, oil, water and peanut butter. Stir into flour mixture just until moistened.

Pour into two greased 9-in. x 5-in. x 3-in. loaf pans. Bake at 350° for 60-70 minutes or until a toothpick inserted near the center comes out clean. Cool for 10 minutes before removing from pans to wire racks. **Yield:** 2 loaves (16 slices each).

Editor's Note: Reduced-fat or generic brands of peanut butter are not recommended for this recipe. Six 5-3/4-in. x 3-in. x 2-in. loaf pans may be used; bake for 40-45 minutes.

Cheesy Drop Biscuits

Milly Heaton, Richmond, Indiana

I wanted to capture the flavor of cheese biscuits I enjoyed when dining out. So I took my favorite buttermilk biscuit recipe and added to it.

2 cups all-purpose flour
2 teaspoons baking powder
1 teaspoon salt
1/4 teaspoon baking soda
1/4 teaspoon garlic powder
1 cup (4 ounces) shredded cheddar cheese
1/4 cup grated Parmesan cheese
2/3 cup buttermilk
1/3 cup canola oil
Additional Parmesan cheese, optional

In a large bowl, combine the flour, baking powder, salt, baking soda and garlic powder. Add the cheeses. In a small bowl, combine buttermilk and oil. Stir into flour mixture just until moistened.

Drop by 1/4 cupfuls 2 in. apart onto a greased baking sheet. Sprinkle with additional Parmesan cheese if desired. Bake at 450° for 10-12 minutes or until golden brown. Serve warm. Store in the refrigerator. **Yield:** about 1 dozen.

Northwoods Muffins

Kay Englund, Ham Lake, Minnesota

Even those who aren't fond of wild rice rave about these golden muffins flecked with colorful blueberries and cranberries. They're a terrific take-along treat.

- 2 cups all-purpose flour
- 1/2 cup sugar
- 3 teaspoons baking powder
- 1/2 teaspoon salt
- 2 eggs
- 3/4 cup buttermilk
- 1/4 cup butter, melted
- 1 cup cooked wild rice
- 1/2 cup fresh *or* frozen blueberries
- 1/2 cup fresh *or* frozen cranberries

In a large bowl, combine the flour, sugar, baking powder and salt. In another bowl, whisk the eggs, buttermilk and butter. Stir in flour mixture just until moistened. Fold in the rice, blueberries and cranberries.

Fill greased or paper-lined muffin cups two-thirds full. Bake at 375° for 20-25 minutes or until a toothpick inserted near the center comes out clean. Cool for 5 minutes before removing from pans to wire racks. Store in the refrigerator. **Yield:** 16 muffins.

Editor's Note: If using frozen blueberries or cranberries, do not thaw before adding to batter.

Filling Muffin Cups Using a spoon to fill muffin cups with batter can get messy. To quickly place batter into muffin cups with little mess, use an ice cream scoop with a quick release, or pour the batter from a measuring cup.

Orange Chocolate Chip Bread

Luene Byers, Salt Lake City, Utah

The classic combination of flavors in this recipe reminds me of the orange and chocolate candy my grandmother made for the holidays. We like to snack on this bread.

  4   teaspoons grated orange peel (about 1 medium orange)
Boiling water
1/3   cup orange juice
  2   cups all-purpose flour
  1   cup sugar
  1   teaspoon baking powder
1/2   teaspoon baking soda
1/2   teaspoon salt
  1   egg
  2   tablespoons butter, melted
  1   teaspoon vanilla extract
  1   cup (6 ounces) semisweet chocolate chips

Place orange peel in a small bowl. Add enough boiling water to orange juice to measure 1 cup. Pour over orange peel; let stand for 10 minutes.

Meanwhile, in a large bowl, combine the flour, sugar, baking powder, baking soda and salt. In another bowl, beat egg, butter, vanilla and reserved orange mixture. Stir into flour mixture just until moistened. Fold in chocolate chips.

Pour into a greased 8-in. x 4-in. x 2-in. loaf pan. Bake at 350° for 55-65 minutes or until a toothpick inserted near the center comes out clean. Cool for 10 minutes before removing from pan to a wire rack. **Yield:** 1 loaf (16 servings).

The Perfect Cut Use a sawing motion and a thin sharp knife to cut quick bread loaves. Use a serrated knife for breads with fruits and/or nuts.

Rhubarb Muffins

Alma Hansen, New Denmark, New Brunswick

A cousin in Maine gave me this recipe. I take these slightly tart treats to meetings where lunch is being served and always come home with an empty plate. It's a good way to use up plentiful rhubarb.

      2-1/2 cups all-purpose flour
          1 cup packed brown sugar
          1 teaspoon baking powder
          1 teaspoon baking soda
        1/2 teaspoon salt
        1/4 teaspoon ground nutmeg
          1 egg
          1 cup buttermilk
        1/2 cup canola oil
          2 teaspoons vanilla extract
          2 cups diced fresh *or* frozen rhubarb

In a large bowl, combine the flour, brown sugar, baking powder, baking soda, salt and nutmeg. In another bowl, whisk the egg, buttermilk, oil and vanilla. Stir into flour mixture just until moistened. Fold in rhubarb.

Fill paper-lined muffin cups two-thirds full. Bake at 350° for 22-25 minutes or until a toothpick inserted near the center comes out clean. Cool for 5 minutes before removing from pans to wire racks. Serve warm. **Yield:** 16 muffins.

Editor's Note: If using frozen rhubarb, measure rhubarb while still frozen, then thaw completely. Drain in a colander, but do not press liquid out.

Cheddar Puff Biscuits

Mary Burrows, Rome, New York

This is one of my favorite biscuit recipes because it's fast, simple and doesn't require any special ingredients. I sometimes freeze some baked puffs, then reheat in foil.

        1/2 cup milk
          2 tablespoons butter
        1/2 cup all-purpose flour
          2 eggs
        1/2 cup shredded cheddar cheese
        1/4 cup chopped onion
        1/4 teaspoon garlic powder
        1/4 teaspoon pepper

In a small saucepan, bring milk and butter to a boil. Add flour all at once and stir until a smooth ball forms. Remove from the heat; let stand for 5 minutes. Add eggs, one at a time, beating well after each addition. Add the cheese, onion, garlic powder and pepper; beat until mixture is smooth and shiny.

Drop by rounded teaspoonfuls 2 in. apart onto greased baking sheets. Bake at 350° for 25-30 minutes or until golden brown. Serve warm. Store in the refrigerator. **Yield:** about 2 dozen.

Olive Pepperoni Snack Muffins

Dorothy Swanson, St. Louis, Missouri

Savory Italian-flavored treats will delight the sports fans in your family while they watch their favorite game. Try them as a perfect partner to a hot bowl of soup.

          3 cups all-purpose flour
          2 tablespoons sugar
      1-1/2 teaspoons baking powder
      1-1/2 teaspoons salt
        1/2 teaspoon dried oregano
        1/4 teaspoon baking soda
          1 package (8 ounces) cream cheese, softened
          2 eggs
          1 cup plus 2 tablespoons milk
        1/4 cup canola oil
          1 package (3-1/2 ounces) pepperoni, diced
        1/4 cup chopped stuffed olives

In a large bowl, combine the flour, sugar, baking powder, salt, oregano and baking soda. In another bowl, beat the cream cheese, eggs, milk and oil until smooth. Stir into flour mixture just until moistened. Fold in pepperoni and olives.

Fill greased or paper-lined muffin cups three-fourths full. Bake at 375° for 20-25 minutes or until a toothpick inserted near the center comes out clean. Cool for 5 minutes before removing from pans to wire racks. Serve warm. Store in the refrigerator. **Yield:** 22 muffins.

Leavening Power Does your baking powder and baking soda give disappointing results? Are your quick breads and muffins not as high as you expected? Check the expiration date on the leavening container. If it's past the date on the package, toss it out and replace it with a fresh one.

Potato Drop Biscuits

Roberta Strohmaier, Lebanon, New Jersey

When you don't have time to make biscuit dough from scratch and cut out the biscuits, you can rely on this four-ingredient recipe.

2-1/4   cups biscuit/baking mix
   1/3   cup mashed potato flakes
   2/3   cup milk
      2   tablespoons sour cream

In a large bowl, combine biscuit mix and potato flakes. In a small bowl, whisk milk and sour cream. Stir into the biscuit mix mixture just until moistened.

Drop by heaping tablespoonfuls onto a greased baking sheet. Bake at 400° for 10-12 minutes or until tops begin to brown. Serve warm. **Yield:** 1 dozen.

Cherry Chip Granola Bread

Pat Habiger, Spearville, Kansas

Buttermilk makes this colorful bread moist and delicious while granola and almonds add special crunch. We like to snack on slices around the clock.

1-1/3   cups all-purpose flour
   1/3   cup sugar
      1   teaspoon baking soda
   1/2   teaspoon salt
      1   egg
      1   cup buttermilk
   1/4   cup canola oil
      1   teaspoon vanilla extract
      1   cup granola without raisins
   1/2   cup chopped almonds
   1/2   cup semisweet chocolate chips
   1/2   cup chopped red candied cherries

In a large bowl, combine the flour, sugar, baking soda and salt. In another bowl, whisk the egg, buttermilk, oil and vanilla. Stir into flour mixture just until moistened. Fold in the remaining ingredients.

Pour into two greased 5-3/4-in. x 3-in. x 2-in. loaf pans. Bake at 350° for 30-35 minutes or until a toothpick inserted near the center comes out clean. Cool for 10 minutes before removing from pans to wire racks. **Yield:** 2 mini loaves (5 slices each).

Cranberry Streusel Loaf

Lois McAtee, Oceanside, California

I relied on this foolproof recipe when teaching our children to bake. Each slice is dotted with plump cranberries and flecks of orange peel.

   1/3   cup packed brown sugar
      3   tablespoons all-purpose flour
      2   tablespoons cold butter
   3/4   cup finely chopped pecans
BREAD:
      2   cups all-purpose flour
   3/4   cup sugar
1-1/2   teaspoons baking powder
   1/2   teaspoon ground nutmeg
   1/2   teaspoon ground allspice
   1/4   teaspoon salt
      1   egg
   3/4   cup orange juice
      3   tablespoons butter, melted
      2   tablespoons grated orange peel
      1   cup fresh *or* frozen cranberries
   1/2   cup golden raisins

In a bowl, combine brown sugar and flour. Cut in butter until crumbly. Stir in pecans; set aside.

In a large bowl, combine the flour, sugar, baking powder, nutmeg, allspice and salt. In another bowl, whisk the egg, orange juice, butter and orange peel. Stir into flour mixture just until moistened. Fold in cranberries and raisins.

Transfer half of the batter to a greased 9-in. x 5-in. x 3-in. loaf pan. Sprinkle with half of the streusel; repeat layers. Bake at 350° for 65-70 minutes or until a toothpick inserted near the center comes out clean. Cool for 10 minutes before removing from pan to a wire rack. **Yield:** 1 loaf (16 slices).

Roasted Red Pepper Muffins

Fancheon Resler, Bluffton, Indiana

In 1998, I was the chairman of the 4-H committee designated to assemble a cookbook. This recipe was submitted by an 11-year-old boy, who used it for one of his baking projects.

- 1 teaspoon cornmeal
- 1-3/4 cups all-purpose flour
- 3 tablespoons sugar
- 2 teaspoons baking powder
- 1/2 teaspoon coarsely ground pepper, *divided*
- 1/4 teaspoon salt
- 1 egg
- 3/4 cup buttermilk
- 1/4 cup canola oil
- 2/3 cup chopped roasted sweet red peppers
- 1/2 cup shredded part-skim mozzarella cheese

Grease muffin cups and sprinkle with the cornmeal; set aside. In a large bowl, combine the flour, sugar, baking powder, 1/4 teaspoon pepper and salt. In another bowl, beat the egg, buttermilk and oil. Stir into flour mixture just until moistened. Fold in red pepper and cheese.

Fill prepared muffin cups two-thirds full. Sprinkle with remaining pepper. Bake at 400° for 20-25 minutes or until a toothpick inserted near the center comes out clean. Cool for 5 minutes before removing from pan to a wire rack. Serve warm. Store in the refrigerator. **Yield:** 1 dozen.

Coconut Bread

Janis Hoople, Stanton, Michigan

Sprinkling sugar on top of this bread before baking gives it a delectable crunch. The flavor from almond extract pairs nicely with the coconut.

- 1/4 cup butter, softened
- 1 cup sugar
- 1 egg
- 1/2 teaspoon vanilla extract
- 1/2 teaspoon almond extract
- 2 cups all-purpose flour
- 3 teaspoons baking powder
- 1/4 teaspoon salt
- 1 cup milk
- 3/4 cup flaked coconut

Additional sugar

In a large bowl, cream butter and sugar until light and fluffy. Beat in the egg and extracts. Combine the flour, baking powder and salt; add to creamed mixture alternately with milk. Fold in coconut.

Pour into a greased 9-in. x 5-in. x 3-in. loaf pan. Sprinkle with sugar. Bake at 350° for 50-55 minutes or until a toothpick inserted near the center comes out clean. Cool for 10 minutes before removing from pan to a wire rack. **Yield:** 1 loaf (16 slices).

Lemon Blueberry Drop Scones

Jacqueline Hendershot, Orange, California

I enjoy serving these fruity scones for baby and bridal showers. They're a bit lower in fat than other scone recipes.

- 2 cups all-purpose flour
- 1/3 cup sugar
- 2 teaspoons baking powder
- 1 teaspoon grated lemon peel
- 1/2 teaspoon baking soda
- 1/4 teaspoon salt
- 1 cup (8 ounces) lemon yogurt
- 1 egg
- 1/4 cup butter, melted
- 1 cup fresh *or* frozen blueberries

GLAZE:
- 1/2 cup confectioners' sugar
- 1 tablespoon lemon juice
- 1/2 teaspoon grated lemon peel

In a large bowl, combine the flour, sugar, baking powder, lemon peel, baking soda and salt. In another bowl, combine the yogurt, egg and butter. Stir into flour mixture just until moistened. Fold in blueberries.

Drop by heaping tablespoonfuls 2 in. apart onto a greased baking sheet. Bake at 400° for 15-18 minutes or until lightly browned. Combine glaze ingredients; drizzle over warm scones. **Yield:** 14 scones.

Editor's Note: If using frozen blueberries, do not thaw before adding to batter.

Carrot Cheesecake Muffins

Joyce Brash, New Richmond, Quebec

With a rich cream cheese filling and flecks of carrots, raisins and nuts, these moist muffins will certainly bring compliments to the cook.

  4 ounces cream cheese, softened
  2 tablespoons sugar
1-1/2 teaspoons grated orange peel
BATTER:
  1/3 cup butter, softened
  1/2 cup packed brown sugar
    2 eggs
  1/2 cup evaporated milk
    2 tablespoons orange juice
1-1/2 cups all-purpose flour
    1 teaspoon baking powder
  1/2 teaspoon baking soda
  1/2 teaspoon ground cinnamon

1-1/4 cups finely grated carrots (about 3 medium)
  1/2 cup raisins
  1/2 cup chopped walnuts

In a small bowl, beat the cream cheese, sugar and peel until blended; set aside. In another small bowl, cream butter and brown sugar until light and fluffy. Add the eggs, milk and orange juice; mix well. Combine the flour, baking powder, baking soda and cinnamon; stir into creamed mixture just until moistened. Stir in the carrots, raisins and walnuts.

Fill greased muffin cups with 2 tablespoons batter. Top each with 2 teaspoons filling; top with remaining batter. Bake at 350° for 23-25 minutes or until a toothpick inserted near the comes out clean. Cool for 5 minutes before removing from pan to a wire rack to cool. Store in the refrigerator. **Yield:** 1 dozen.

Chocolate Muffins

Nellie Million Wimmer, Portage, Michigan

This recipe originally called for applesauce, but one time in a pinch, I substituted sour cream...it worked! Chocolate lovers can't resist these rich cake-like muffins.

2-2/3　cups all-purpose flour
1-1/2　cups sugar
　1/2　cup baking cocoa
1-1/2　teaspoons baking soda
　1/2　teaspoon salt
　　3　eggs
　　1　cup (8 ounces) sour cream
　1/2　cup water
　1/2　cup milk
　1/2　cup canola oil
　　1　teaspoon vanilla extract
　1/2　cup semisweet chocolate chips

In a large bowl, combine the flour, sugar, cocoa, baking soda and salt. In another bowl, whisk the eggs, sour cream, water, milk, oil and vanilla. Stir into flour mixture just until moistened. Fold in chocolate chips.

Fill greased or paper-lined muffin cups two-thirds full. Bake at 325° for 20-25 minutes or until a toothpick inserted near the center comes out clean. Cool for 5 minutes before removing from pans to wire racks. **Yield:** 2 dozen.

Irish Soda Bread

Sandra Linder, Blue Springs, Nebraska

Each bite of this traditional loaf is dotted with raisins. My family considers this my best-ever bread recipe.

　　2　cups all-purpose flour
　　2　tablespoons sugar
　　1　teaspoon baking powder
　　1　teaspoon baking soda
　1/2　teaspoon salt
　　3　tablespoons cold butter
　　1　cup buttermilk
　1/2　cup raisins
Additional melted butter
Additional flour

In a bowl, combine the flour, sugar, baking powder, baking soda and salt. Cut in butter until crumbly. Stir in buttermilk just until moistened. Fold in raisins.

Knead on a floured surface for 8-10 times. Shape into a 7-in. round loaf; place on a greased baking sheet. With a sharp knife, cut a 1/4-in.-deep cross on top of the loaf.

Bake at 375° for 25-35 minutes or until golden brown. Remove from pan to a wire rack. Brush with additional butter. Cool. Dust with additional flour. **Yield:** 1 loaf.

Cheese-Filled Gingerbread

Michelle Smith, Running Springs, California

I very rarely make special trips to the store for one or two forgotten groceries. I prefer to wing it in the kitchen. It was during one of those baking experiments that I created this variation of honey nut bread.

　　1　package (8 ounces) cream cheese, softened
　　1　cup sugar
　1/3　cup all-purpose flour
　　1　egg
BATTER:
　　3　cups all-purpose flour
　1/2　cup sugar
1-1/2　teaspoons baking soda
1-1/2　teaspoons salt
　　1　teaspoon ground ginger
　　2　eggs
　3/4　cup milk
　3/4　cup canola oil
　1/2　cup molasses
1-1/2　cups chopped walnuts
GLAZE:
　　1　cup confectioners' sugar
　　1　to 2 tablespoons milk

In a large bowl, beat the cream cheese, sugar, flour and egg until smooth; set aside. In a large bowl, combine the flour, sugar, baking soda, salt and ginger. In another bowl, beat the eggs, milk, oil and molasses until smooth. Stir into flour mixture just until moistened. Fold in walnuts.

Spoon a third of the batter into a greased and floured 10-in. fluted tube pan. Top with the reserved cream cheese mixture. Carefully spoon remaining batter over filling. Bake at 350° for 40-50 minutes or until a toothpick inserted near the center comes out clean. Cool for 10 minutes before removing from pan to a wire rack.

For glaze, combine confectioners' sugar and enough milk to achieve desired consistency. Drizzle over bread. Store in the refrigerator. **Yield:** 16-20 servings.

Lemon Raspberry Jumbo Muffins

Carol Thoreson, Rockford, Illinois

These are my all-time favorite muffins because they can be made with blueberries instead of raspberries with the same delicious results.

    2   cups all-purpose flour
    1   cup sugar
    3   teaspoons baking powder
  1/2   teaspoon salt
    2   eggs
    1   cup half-and-half cream
  1/2   cup canola oil
    1   teaspoon lemon extract
    1   cup fresh *or* frozen unsweetened raspberries

In a large bowl, combine the flour, sugar, baking powder and salt. In another bowl, combine the eggs, cream, oil and extract. Stir into flour mixture just until moistened. Fold in the raspberries.

Fill greased jumbo muffin cups two-thirds full. Bake at 400° for 22-25 minutes or until a toothpick inserted near the center comes out clean. Cool for 5 minutes before removing from pan to a wire rack. Serve warm. **Yield:** 8 jumbo muffins.

Editor's Note: If using frozen raspberries, do not thaw before adding to batter. Sixteen regular-size muffin cups may be used; bake for 18-20 minutes.

Monkey Bread

Charlene Wilson, Williamsburg, Ohio

The dear friend who gave me this recipe has since passed away, but I think of her every time I prepare this sweet bread. Maple syrup provides a saucy caramel flavor.

    2   tubes (7-1/2 ounces *each*) refrigerated buttermilk biscuits
    1   cup packed brown sugar
    1   teaspoon ground cinnamon
    1   teaspoon ground nutmeg
  1/2   cup butter, melted
  1/2   cup chopped nuts
  1/2   cup maple syrup

Cut each biscuit into quarters. In a small bowl, combine the brown sugar, cinnamon and nutmeg. Dip biscuits in butter, then roll in sugar mixture. Layer half the biscuits in a 10-in. fluted pan; sprinkle with half the nuts. Repeat layers. Pour syrup over top.

Bake at 350° for 25-30 minutes or until golden brown. Immediately invert onto a serving platter. Serve warm. Store in the refrigerator. **Yield:** 1 loaf.

Onion Shortcake

Helen Greenleaf, Chehalis, Washington

My dear friend, Barbara, is asked to bring this bread for just about every type of gathering. She was kind enough to share the recipe with me.

    1   package (8-1/2 ounces) corn bread/muffin mix
  1/3   cup milk
  1/4   cup canola oil
    1   egg
    1   large onion, chopped
    1   can (8-1/2 ounces) cream-style corn
1-1/2   cups (6 ounces) shredded cheddar cheese, *divided*
    1   cup (8 ounces) sour cream
  1/2   cup mayonnaise
    1   teaspoon salt
    2   drops hot pepper sauce

In a bowl, combine the corn bread mix, milk, oil and egg. Spread in a greased 9-in. square baking pan. In another bowl, combine the onion, corn, 1 cup cheddar cheese, sour cream, mayonnaise, salt and hot pepper sauce.

Spoon over batter. Top with remaining cheese. Bake at 425° for 25-30 minutes or until golden brown. Cool for 15 minutes before cutting. Store in the refrigerator. **Yield:** 12 servings.

Editor's Note: Reduced-fat or fat-free mayonnaise is not recommended for this recipe.

Sage Cornmeal Biscuits

Mary Kincaid, Bostic, North Carolina

My family loves these outstanding savory biscuits with eggs and sausage at breakfast or with meats at dinner. They bake up light and tender and have just the right amount of sage.

1-1/2   cups all-purpose flour
  1/2   cup cornmeal
    3   teaspoons baking powder
  1/2   to 3/4 teaspoon rubbed sage
  1/2   teaspoon salt
  1/3   cup shortening
  3/4   cup milk

In a bowl, combine the flour, cornmeal, baking powder, sage and salt. Cut in shortening until mixture resembles coarse crumbs. Stir in milk just until moistened.

Turn onto a lightly floured surface. Roll to 3/4-in. thickness; cut with a floured 2-in. biscuit cutter. Place 2 in. apart on an ungreased baking sheet. Bake at 450° for 10-12 minutes or until browned. Serve warm. **Yield:** 10 biscuits.

Tender Biscuits When working with biscuit dough, use a light touch. Overhandling, kneading too long or using too much flour can make the biscuits tough and/or dry.

Peppery Hush Puppies

Carolyn Griffin, Macon, Georgia

For our family, a good fish dinner just isn't complete without these zesty hush puppies. You can also serve them alone as a satisfying snack.

- 2 cups cornmeal
- 1 cup plus 3 tablespoons all-purpose flour
- 2 teaspoons baking powder
- 1-1/2 teaspoons sugar
- 1 teaspoon salt
- 1/2 teaspoon baking soda
- 1 egg
- 2/3 cup water
- 1/2 cup buttermilk
- 1/2 cup butter, melted
- 1 cup grated onion
- 2 jalapeno peppers, seeded and chopped
- 1 small green pepper, chopped

Oil for deep-fat frying

In a large bowl, combine the cornmeal, flour, baking powder, sugar, salt and baking soda. In another bowl, whisk the egg, water, buttermilk and butter. Stir in the onion, jalapenos and green pepper. Stir into cornmeal mixture just until moistened.

In an electric skillet or deep-fat fryer, heat oil to 375°. Drop batter by teaspoonfuls, a few at a time, into hot oil. Fry until golden brown on both sides. Drain on paper towels. Serve warm. **Yield:** 6 dozen.

Editor's Note: When cutting hot peppers, disposable gloves are recommended. Avoid touching your face.

Keep Them Hot Here's how to keep the first few batches of Hush Puppies warm while you finish frying the rest of the batter. After the Hush Puppies have drained on the paper towels, place them on a baking sheet in a 200° oven. This way, the entire batch will have that fresh-from-the-fryer taste.

Almond Pear Muffins

Frances Finegan, Gaithersburg, Maryland

I always bake muffins on the weekends and freeze them for breakfasts or snacks during the week. I take a few out in the morning, and they thaw by the time I get to work.

- 1 cup all-purpose flour
- 1 cup whole wheat flour
- 1/2 cup sugar
- 1 teaspoon baking powder
- 1 teaspoon baking soda
- 1 teaspoon ground cinnamon
- 1/4 teaspoon salt
- 1/4 teaspoon ground nutmeg
- 1/4 teaspoon ground cloves
- 2 eggs
- 1/2 cup plain yogurt
- 1/2 cup milk
- 1/2 cup canola oil
- 1 teaspoon almond extract
- 1 cup chopped peeled pear (about 1 medium)
- 1/2 cup chopped almonds

In a large bowl, combine the first nine ingredients. In another large bowl, beat the eggs, yogurt, milk, oil and extract. Stir into flour mixture just until moistened. Fold in pear and almonds.

Fill greased or paper-lined muffin cups two-thirds full. Bake at 400° for 12-15 minutes or until a toothpick inserted near the center comes out clean. Cool for 5 minutes before removing from pans to wire racks. Serve warm. **Yield:** 15 muffins.

Baking Powder Drop Biscuits

Sharon Evans, Rockwell, Iowa

One day I had company coming and realized I had run out of biscuit mix. I'd never made biscuits from scratch before, but I decided to give this recipe a try...and it was fabulous. Now this is the only way I make them!

- 2 cups all-purpose flour
- 2 tablespoons sugar
- 4 teaspoons baking powder
- 1/2 teaspoon cream of tartar
- 1/2 teaspoon salt
- 1/2 cup shortening
- 2/3 cup milk
- 1 egg

In a large bowl, combine the flour, sugar, baking powder, cream of tartar and salt. Cut in shortening until the mixture resembles coarse crumbs. In a small bowl, whisk milk and egg. Stir into crumb mixture just until moistened.

Drop by heaping spoonfuls 2 in. apart onto an ungreased baking sheet. Bake at 450° for 10-12 minutes or until golden brown. Serve warm. **Yield:** 1 dozen.

Pumpkin Cranberry Nut Bread

Darlene Conger, Greenville, Texas

This bread has a terrific combination of flavors that's perfect for the holidays. I like to make and freeze loaves to share with friends and neighbors.

- 3/4 cup butter, softened
- 2 cups sugar
- 3 eggs
- 1 can (15 ounces) solid-pack pumpkin
- 1-1/2 teaspoons grated orange peel
- 3-1/2 cups all-purpose flour
- 2 teaspoons ground cinnamon
- 1 teaspoon salt
- 1 teaspoon baking soda
- 1/2 teaspoon baking powder
- 1 cup chopped walnuts
- 1 cup chopped fresh *or* frozen cranberries

In a large bowl, cream butter and sugar until light and fluffy. Add eggs, one at a time, beating well after each addition. Beat in pumpkin and orange peel (mixture will appear curdled). Combine the flour, cinnamon, salt, baking soda and baking powder; add to pumpkin mixture just until moistened. Fold in walnuts and cranberries.

Pour into two greased 8-in. x 4-in. x 2-in. loaf pans. Bake at 350° for 65-75 minutes or until a toothpick inserted near the center comes out clean. Cool for 10 minutes before removing from pans to wire racks. **Yield:** 2 loaves (12 slices each).

Apple Streusel Muffins

Michele Olsen, Wessington Springs, South Dakota

Pieces of tender apples appear in every bite of these moist, pretty muffins. The streusel topping adds a touch of sweetness.

- 2 cups all-purpose flour
- 1 cup sugar
- 3 teaspoons baking powder
- 1-1/4 teaspoons ground cinnamon
- 1/2 teaspoon baking soda
- 1/2 teaspoon salt
- 2 eggs
- 1 cup (8 ounces) sour cream
- 1/4 cup butter, melted
- 1-1/2 cups chopped peeled tart apples

TOPPING:
- 1/4 cup sugar
- 3 tablespoons all-purpose flour
- 1/4 teaspoon ground cinnamon
- 2 tablespoons cold butter

In a large bowl, combine the flour, sugar, baking powder, cinnamon, baking soda and salt. In another bowl, beat the eggs, sour cream and butter. Stir into flour mixture just until moistened. Fold in apples. Fill greased or paper-lined muffin cups two-thirds full.

For topping, combine the sugar, flour and cinnamon. Cut in butter until mixture resembles coarse crumbs. Sprinkle a rounded teaspoonful over each muffin.

Bake at 400° for 18-20 minutes or until a toothpick inserted near the center comes out clean. Cool for 5 minutes before removing from the pans to wire racks. Serve warm. **Yield: 16 muffins.**

Tomato-Cheese Snack Bread

Karen Farruggia, West Winfield, New York

My family is fond of cheese, so I have many recipes calling for that delectable ingredient. This rich bread is a great way to showcase garden-fresh tomatoes. Serve it as a snack or with your favorite grilled meats.

- 2 cups biscuit/baking mix
- 2/3 cup milk
- 3 medium tomatoes, peeled and cut into 1/4-inch slices
- 1 medium onion, finely chopped
- 2 tablespoons butter
- 1 cup (4 ounces) shredded cheddar cheese
- 3/4 cup sour cream
- 1/3 cup mayonnaise
- 3/4 teaspoon salt
- 1/4 teaspoon pepper
- 1/4 teaspoon dried oregano

Paprika

In a bowl, combine biscuit mix and milk just until moistened. Turn onto a floured surface; knead 10-12 times. Press onto the bottom and 1 in. up the sides of a greased 13-in. x 9-in. x 2-in. baking dish. Arrange tomato slices over top.

In a skillet, saute onion in butter until tender; remove from the heat. Stir in cheese, sour cream, mayonnaise, salt, pepper and oregano. Spoon over tomatoes. Sprinkle with paprika.

Bake at 400° for 20-25 minutes or until browned. Let stand for 10 minutes before cutting. Serve warm. Store in the refrigerator. **Yield: 12-15 servings.**

Parmesan Butter Dips

Ruby Seaman, Bonners Ferry, Idaho

I always get compliments when I serve these breadsticks with homemade soup. They're quick and easy to make, even for folks who've never tried their hand at baking homemade bread.

- 2-1/4 cups all-purpose flour
- 2 tablespoons sugar
- 3 teaspoons baking powder
- 1 teaspoon salt
- 1 cup milk
- 1/2 cup butter, melted
- 1/4 cup grated Parmesan cheese

In a bowl, combine the flour, sugar, baking powder and salt. Stir in milk just until moistened. Turn onto a floured surface; divide into 18 pieces. Roll each into a 5-in. rope.

Pour butter into a shallow pan. Dip ropes in butter. Place 2 in. apart on greased baking sheets. Sprinkle with Parmesan cheese. Bake at 400° for 12-15 minutes or until golden brown. Serve warm. **Yield: 1-1/2 dozen.**

Peanut Butter Mini Muffins

Connie Barz, San Antonio, Texas

These bite-size muffins are perfect to send in our kids' lunches for snacktime. I make regular-size muffins for church functions and watch them disappear.

1-3/4   cups all-purpose flour
  2/3   cup packed brown sugar
2-1/2   teaspoons baking powder
  1/4   teaspoon salt
    1   egg
  3/4   cup milk
  2/3   cup chunky peanut butter
  1/4   cup canola oil
1-1/2   teaspoons vanilla extract
  2/3   cup miniature semisweet chocolate chips

In a large bowl, combine the flour, brown sugar, baking powder and salt. In another bowl, combine the egg, milk, peanut butter, oil and vanilla. Stir into flour mixture just until moistened. Fold in chocolate chips.

Fill greased or paper-lined miniature muffin cups two-thirds full. Bake at 350° for 15-17 minutes or until a toothpick inserted near the center comes out clean. Cool for 5 minutes before removing from pans to wire racks. **Yield:** 4 dozen.

Editor's Note: Reduced-fat or generic brands of peanut butter are not recommended for this recipe. Twelve regular-size muffin cups may be used; bake for 22-25 minutes.

Banana Bran Muffins

Shelley Mitchell, Baldur, Manitoba

Our four daughters love these spiced moist muffins. With a little help from myself or my mom, the girls are all learning to be great cooks.

1-1/2 cups all-purpose flour
1/2 cup whole wheat flour
1 cup oat bran
3 teaspoons ground cinnamon
2 teaspoons baking powder
2 teaspoons baking soda
1/2 teaspoon ground nutmeg
1/4 teaspoon allspice
2 eggs
1 cup orange juice
1/2 cup sugar
1/2 cup packed brown sugar
1/2 cup canola oil
1 cup mashed ripe bananas (2 to 3 medium)
1/2 cup chopped walnuts

In a bowl, combine the flours, oat bran, cinnamon, baking powder, baking soda, nutmeg and allspice. In another bowl, beat the eggs, juice, sugars and oil. Stir into flour mixture just until moistened. Fold in bananas and nuts.

Fill greased or paper-lined muffin cups two-thirds full. Bake at 400° for 15-18 minutes or until a toothpick inserted near the center comes out clean. Cool for 5 minutes before removing from pans to wire racks. Serve warm. **Yield:** 2 dozen.

Apple Crunch Muffins

Brenda Betz, Oakland, Maryland

These apple-filled muffins taste like little coffee cakes. I sometimes drizzle hot caramel over the muffins and serve them as dessert.

1-1/2 cups all-purpose flour
3/4 cup sugar
2 teaspoons baking powder
1 teaspoon ground cinnamon
1/4 teaspoon baking soda
1/4 teaspoon salt
1/4 teaspoon ground allspice
1/8 teaspoon ground nutmeg
2 eggs
1-1/4 cups sour cream
1/2 cup butter, melted
1 cup diced unpeeled tart apple
TOPPING:
1/2 cup chopped walnuts
1/4 cup all-purpose flour
3 tablespoons sugar
1/4 teaspoon ground cinnamon
1/8 teaspoon ground nutmeg
2 tablespoons cold butter

Sweet 'n' Savory Date Loaves

Diane Card, Hilliard, Ohio

My family and I were thrilled when this bread won "best of show" for quick breads at the state fair a few years ago. I sometimes substitute peach nectar for the apricot nectar with terrific results.

1-1/2 cups apricot nectar
1-1/2 cups chopped dates
1/2 cup chopped dried apricots
1 tablespoon grated orange peel
1-1/4 teaspoons dried rosemary, crushed
1/4 cup butter, softened
1 cup sugar
1 egg
1/3 cup evaporated milk
2-1/4 cups all-purpose flour
1-1/2 teaspoons baking soda

In a large saucepan, bring the apricot nectar, dates and apricots to a boil. Reduce heat; cover and simmer for 5 minutes. Remove from the heat; add peel and rosemary. Cool for 10 minutes.

In a large bowl, cream butter and sugar until light and fluffy. Beat in egg and milk. Combine the flour and baking soda; add to the creamed mixture alternately with the date mixture.

Pour into three greased 5-3/4-in. x 3-in. x 2-in. loaf pans. Bake at 375° for 30-35 minutes or until a toothpick inserted near the center comes out clean. Cool for 10 minutes before removing from pans to wire racks. **Yield:** 3 mini loaves (5 slices each).

In a large bowl, combine the flour, sugar, baking powder, cinnamon, baking soda, salt, allspice and nutmeg. In another bowl, beat the eggs, sour cream and butter. Stir into flour mixture just until moistened. Fold in apple. Fill greased or paper-lined muffin cups one-third full.

For topping, combine the walnuts, flour, sugar, cinnamon and nutmeg. Cut in butter until mixture resembles coarse crumbs. Sprinkle about two-thirds of the topping over batter. Top with remaining batter; sprinkle with remaining topping. Bake at 375° for 20-25 minutes or until a toothpick inserted near the center comes out clean. Cool for 5 minutes before removing from pans to wire racks. **Yield:** 16 muffins.

Little Texas Corn Bread

Mildred Sherrer, Fort Worth, Texas

I love to serve this cheesy corn bread alongside a bowl of heartwarming chili. The green chilies add a nice little kick.

     1 cup cornmeal
     1 cup (4 ounces) shredded cheddar cheese
     1 tablespoon baking powder
     2 eggs
     1 can (8-1/2 ounces) cream-style corn
     1 cup (8 ounces) sour cream
   1/2 cup canola oil
     1 can (4 ounces) chopped green chilies, drained

In a large bowl, combine the cornmeal, cheese and baking powder. In another bowl, combine the eggs, corn, sour cream, oil and chilies. Stir into cornmeal mixture just until moistened.

Pour into a greased 8-in. square baking dish. Bake at 400° for 30-35 minutes or until a toothpick inserted near the center comes out clean. Serve warm. Store in the refrigerator. **Yield:** 8 servings.

Editor's Note: This recipe does not use flour.

Cherry Chip Muffins

Shirley Glaab, Hattiesburg, Mississippi

When Valentine's Day rolls around, I like to bake these cute muffins in small heart-shaped tins. Drizzled with pink icing, they look adorable and taste wonderful.

   1-1/2 cups all-purpose flour
     1/2 cup sugar
       2 teaspoons baking powder
     1/2 teaspoon salt
       1 egg
     1/2 cup milk
     1/4 cup canola oil
       1 jar (10 ounces) red maraschino cherries
     3/4 cup miniature semisweet chocolate chips
     1/2 cup chopped pecans
       1 cup confectioners' sugar
Softened cream cheese, optional

In a large bowl, combine the flour, sugar, baking powder and salt. In another bowl, whisk egg, milk and oil; stir into flour mixture just until moistened. Drain cherries, reserving 2 tablespoons of juice for glaze. Chop cherries; fold chips, pecans and cherries into the batter.

Drop by tablespoonfuls into greased or paper-lined heart-shaped or miniature muffin cups. Bake at 375° for 10-13 minutes or until a toothpick inserted near the center comes out clean. Cool for 10 minutes before removing from pans to wire racks. Combine the confectioners' sugar and the reserved cherry juice to make a thin glaze; drizzle over muffins. Serve with cream cheese if desired. **Yield:** about 4 dozen.

Skillet Sausage Corn Bread

Carolyn Griffin, Macon, Georgia

This unique corn bread is prepared in a skillet. I cut it into wedges and serve it with bacon, eggs and fresh fruit for a hearty breakfast.

       1 pound bulk pork sausage
   1-1/2 cups cornmeal
     1/2 cup all-purpose flour
       4 teaspoons baking powder
       1 tablespoon sugar
       1 egg
       1 cup milk

In a 9-in. ovenproof skillet, cook sausage over medium heat until no longer pink. Drain, reserving 2 tablespoons drippings. In a large bowl, combine the cornmeal, flour, baking powder and sugar. In another bowl, beat egg and milk. Stir into cornmeal mixture just until moistened. Fold in sausage and reserved drippings. Return to skillet.

Bake at 425° for 20-25 minutes or until a toothpick inserted near the center comes out clean. Serve warm. Store in the refrigerator. **Yield:** 8 servings.

Dilly Biscuit Squares

Lorene Corbett, Ringgold, Nebraska

My husband grew up in the South, where biscuits are practically daily fare. So I began adding variety to this ordinary quick bread. These are good with seafood, beef and pasta dishes.

  2 cups all-purpose flour
  4 teaspoons baking powder
  1 tablespoon sugar
1/2 teaspoon salt
  1 cup (4 ounces) shredded cheddar cheese
1/4 cup shortening
3/4 cup plus 1 tablespoon milk

DILL BUTTER:
1/4 cup butter, melted
1/2 teaspoon dill weed
1/8 teaspoon garlic salt

In a large bowl, combine the flour, baking powder, sugar and salt. Stir in the cheese. Cut in shortening until mixture resembles coarse crumbs. Stir in milk just until moistened.

Turn onto a lightly floured surface. Roll out into a 3/4-in.-thick square. Cut into 12 squares. Place 1/8 in. apart on an ungreased baking sheet. Bake at 450° for 10-12 minutes or until golden brown. Combine dill butter ingredients; brush over hot biscuits. Serve warm. Store in the refrigerator. **Yield:** 1 dozen.

Zucchini Cheese Bread

Debi Stile, Efland, North Carolina

This recipe came about when I was trying to make a zucchini bread that didn't call for sugar. I use slices of this attractive bread when making sandwiches.

  3 cups all-purpose flour
  1 teaspoon baking powder
  1 teaspoon baking soda
  1 teaspoon salt
  3 eggs
3/4 cup canola oil
2-1/2 cups shredded unpeeled zucchini (about 2 medium)
  1 cup (4 ounces) shredded cheddar cheese
1/2 cup chopped onion

In a large bowl, combine the flour, baking powder, baking soda and salt. In another bowl, whisk eggs and oil. Stir into flour mixture just until moistened. Fold in zucchini, cheese and onion.

Pour into a greased 9-in. x 5-in. x 3-in. loaf pan. Bake at 375° for 55-65 minutes or until a toothpick inserted near the center comes out clean. Cool for 10 minutes before removing from pan to a wire rack. Serve warm. Store in the refrigerator. **Yield:** 1 loaf (16 slices).

Lemon Loaf

Shelli Aday, Georgetown, Texas

I found this recipe in my files one day when I was looking for a bread that called for ingredients already in my pantry. I gave the loaf to some friends, and it was a hit.

1/3 cup shortening
  1 cup sugar
  2 eggs
1-1/2 cups all-purpose flour
1-1/2 teaspoons baking powder
1/4 teaspoon salt
1/2 cup milk
1/2 cup chopped pecans
  2 teaspoons grated lemon peel

TOPPING:
2/3 cup sugar
1/3 cup lemon juice

In a large bowl, cream shortening and sugar until light and fluffy. Add eggs, one at a time, beating well after each addition. Combine the flour, baking powder and salt; add to creamed mixture alternately with milk. Stir in pecans and lemon peel.

Pour into a greased 9-in. x 5-in. x 3-in. loaf pan. Bake at 350° for 55-65 minutes or until a toothpick inserted near the center comes out clean.

For topping, combine sugar and lemon juice. Spoon over bread while still in pan. Cool for 10 minutes before removing from pan to a wire rack. **Yield:** 1 loaf (16 slices).

Banana Split Bread

Janis Allnatt, Rochester, New York

I developed this recipe in an effort to add pizzazz to my plain banana bread. I was pleased with the results, and so were my family and friends.

2/3	cup shortening
1-1/4	cups sugar
4	eggs
3-1/2	cups all-purpose flour
2-1/2	teaspoons baking powder
1	teaspoon baking soda
1/2	teaspoon salt
1-1/2	cups mashed ripe bananas (about 4 medium)
2	cans (8 ounces *each*) crushed pineapple, drained
2	cups (12 ounces) semisweet chocolate chips
1	jar (10 ounces) red maraschino cherries, chopped and well drained
1	cup chopped walnuts

In a large bowl, cream shortening and sugar until light and fluffy. Add eggs, one at a time, beating well after each addition. Combine the flour, baking powder, baking soda and salt; add to creamed mixture alternately with bananas and pineapple. Fold in the chocolate chips, cherries and walnuts.

Pour into two greased 9-in. x 5-in. x 3-in. loaf pans. Bake at 350° for 60-65 minutes or until a toothpick inserted near the center comes out clean. Cool for 10 minutes before removing from pans to wire racks to cool. **Yield:** 2 loaves (16 slices each).

Storing Quick Breads Wrap the cooled bread in foil or plastic wrap and store at room temperature. For breads with perishable ingredients, such as cream cheese or cheese, store in the refrigerator.

Yeast Breads

pg. 63

pg. 47

pg. 44

Italian Dinner Rolls

Marie Elaine Basinger, Connellsville, Pennsylvania

Over the years, I've added a pinch of this and a dash of that to this recipe until my family agreed it was just right. These rolls are especially good served warm with spaghetti.

3-1/2 to 4 cups all-purpose flour
   2 tablespoons sugar
   2 packages (1/4 ounce *each*) active dry yeast
   2 teaspoons garlic salt
   1 teaspoon onion powder
   1 teaspoon Italian seasoning
   1 teaspoon dried parsley flakes
   1 cup milk
1/2 cup water
   4 tablespoons butter, *divided*
   1 egg
3/4 cup grated Parmesan cheese, *divided*

In a large bowl, combine 1-1/2 cups flour, sugar, yeast and seasonings. In a small saucepan, heat the milk, water and 2 tablespoons butter to 120°-130°. Add to flour mixture; beat until moistened. Add egg; beat on medium speed for 3 minutes. Stir in 1/2 cup cheese and enough remaining flour to form a soft dough.

Turn onto floured surface; knead until smooth and elastic, about 6-8 minutes. Place in a greased bowl, turning once to grease top. Cover and let rest for 15 minutes.

Punch dough down. Turn onto a lightly floured surface; divide into 15 pieces. Shape each into a ball. Melt remaining butter; dip tops of the balls in butter and the remaining cheese.

Place in a greased 13-in. x 9-in. x 2-in. baking pan. Cover and let rest for 10 minutes. Bake at 375° for 20-25 minutes or until golden brown. Remove from pans to wire racks to cool. **Yield:** 15 rolls.

Baking Classics | Yeast Breads

40-Minute Hamburger Buns

Jessie McKenney, Twodot, Montana

Here on our ranch, I cook for three men, who love hamburgers. These fluffy yet hearty buns are just right for their big appetites. I also serve the buns plain with a meal.

    2   tablespoons active dry yeast
    1   cup plus 2 tablespoons warm water (110° to 115°)
  1/3   cup canola oil
  1/4   cup sugar
    1   egg
    1   teaspoon salt
    3   to 3-1/2 cups all-purpose flour

In a large bowl, dissolve yeast in warm water. Add oil and sugar; let stand for 5 minutes. Add the egg, salt and enough flour to form a soft dough.

Turn onto a floured surface; knead until smooth and elastic, about 3-5 minutes. Do not let rise. Divide into 12 pieces; shape each into a ball. Place 3 in. apart on greased baking sheets.

Cover and let rest for 10 minutes. Bake at 425° for 8-12 minutes or until golden brown. Remove from pans to wire racks to cool. **Yield:** 1 dozen.

Mom's Swedish Rye

Kathy Ponton, Delphos, Kansas

I usually double this old-world recipe so I have extra loaves available in the freezer.

    1   package (1/4 ounce) active dry yeast
    2   cups warm water (110° to 115°)
  1/4   cup sugar
  1/4   cup shortening
  1/4   cup molasses
    2   teaspoons salt
  3/4   cup rye flour
    5   to 6 cups all-purpose flour
Melted butter

In a large bowl, dissolve yeast in warm water. Add the sugar, shortening, molasses, salt, rye flour and 3 cups all-purpose flour. Beat until smooth. Stir in enough remaining flour to form a soft dough.

Turn onto a floured surface; knead until smooth and elastic, about 6-8 minutes. Place in a greased bowl, turning once to grease top. Cover and let rise in a warm place until doubled, about 1-1/2 hours.

Punch dough down. Turn onto a lightly floured surface; divide in half. Shape into loaves. Place in two greased 9-in. x 5-in. x 3-in. loaf pans. Cover and let rise until doubled, about 1 hour.

Bake at 350° for 40-45 minutes or until golden brown. Remove from pans to wire racks. Brush with melted butter if desired. Cool. **Yield:** 2 loaves (16 slices each).

Braided Peppery Cheese Rolls

Deborah Amrine, Grand Haven, Michigan

These eye-catching braided rolls are a wonderful accompaniment to any meal. The coarsely ground pepper isn't overpowering. I sometimes like to use the dough when making hamburger buns.

  4-1/4   to 4-3/4 cups all-purpose flour
      3   tablespoons sugar
      2   packages (1/4 ounce *each*) active dry yeast
  1-1/2   teaspoons salt
      1   teaspoon coarsely ground pepper
  1-1/2   cups milk
    1/4   cup butter
      2   eggs
    1/2   cup shredded cheddar cheese

In a large bowl, combine 2 cups flour, sugar, yeast, salt and pepper. In a saucepan, heat milk and butter to 120°-130°. Add to flour mixture; beat on medium speed for 2 minutes. Add 1 egg and 1/2 cup flour; beat 2 minutes longer. Stir in cheese and enough remaining flour to form a soft dough.

Turn onto a floured surface; knead until smooth and elastic, about 6-8 minutes. Place in a greased bowl, turning once to grease top. Cover and let rise in a warm place until doubled, about 30 minutes.

Punch dough down. Turn onto a floured surface; cover and let rest for 15 minutes. Divide into 36 pieces. Shape each into a 6-in. rope. Braid three ropes together. Pinch ends to seal. Repeat with remaining dough. Place on greased baking sheets. Cover and let rise in a warm place until doubled, about 30 minutes.

Beat remaining egg; brush over braids. Bake at 375° for 15-17 minutes or until golden brown. Remove from pan to a wire rack to cool. **Yield:** 1 dozen.

Blue Ribbon White Bread

Pam Goodlet, Washington Island, Wisconsin

For seven consecutive years at our local fair, this recipe took first-place honors. My relatives rave about this bread and its pleasant subtle ginger flavor.

1	package (1/4 ounce) active dry yeast
2-1/2	cups warm water (110° to 115°)
1	cup nonfat dry milk powder
3	tablespoons shortening
2	tablespoons sugar
2	teaspoons salt
1/4	teaspoon ground ginger
6	to 7 cups all-purpose flour

In a large bowl, dissolve yeast in warm water. Add the milk powder, shortening, sugar, salt, ginger and 3-1/2 cups flour. Beat until smooth. Stir in enough remaining flour to form a soft dough.

Turn onto a floured surface; knead until smooth and elastic, about 6-8 minutes. Place in a greased bowl, turning once to grease top. Cover and let rise in a warm place until doubled, about 1 hour.

Punch dough down. Turn onto a lightly floured surface; divide in half. Shape into loaves. Place in two greased 8-in. x 4-in. x 2-in. loaf pans. Cover and let rise until doubled, about 45 minutes.

Bake at 350° for 40-45 minutes or until golden brown and bread sounds hollow when tapped. Remove from pans to wire racks to cool. **Yield:** 2 loaves.

Broccoli Cheese Fan

Jo Groth, Plainfield, Iowa

With broccoli, bacon and cheese, this delectable bread has the taste of a stuffed baked potato. Brunches at our house wouldn't be complete without this pretty bread. Even beginner bakers will soon master this attractive loaf.

3-1/4	to 3-1/2 cups all-purpose flour
1	tablespoon sugar
1	package (1/4 ounce) quick-rise yeast
1	teaspoon salt
1	cup water
1	tablespoon butter, softened
1-1/2	cups finely chopped fresh broccoli, cooked and drained
1	cup (4 ounces) shredded cheddar cheese
5	bacon strips, cooked and crumbled
1	egg
1/2	teaspoon dried minced onion
1/2	teaspoon dried oregano
1	egg white
1	tablespoon cold water

In a large bowl, combine 2-1/4 cups flour, sugar, yeast and salt. In a saucepan, heat water and butter to 120°-130°. Add to flour mixture. Beat on medium speed for 2 minutes. Add eggs and 1/2 cup flour; beat 2 minutes longer. Stir in enough remaining flour to form a soft dough.

Turn onto a floured surface; knead until smooth and elastic, about 4 minutes. Cover and let rest for 10 minutes.

Meanwhile, in a large bowl, combine the broccoli, cheese, bacon, egg, onion and oregano. On a lightly floured surface, roll dough into a 16-in. x 9-in. rectangle with a 16-in. side facing you. Spoon broccoli mixture lengthwise over top two-thirds of dough to within 1 in. of edges.

Starting at the plain long side, fold dough over half of filling; fold over again. Pinch seams to seal and tuck ends under. Place seam side down on a greased baking sheet. With a sharp knife, cut into eight strips to within 1 in. of pinched edge. Separate strips slightly; twist to allow filling to show. Cover and let rise until doubled, about 15 minutes.

Beat egg white and cold water; brush over dough. Bake at 400° for 25 minutes or until golden brown. Remove from pan to a wire rack. Serve warm. Store in the refrigerator. **Yield:** 1 loaf (16 slices).

Soft Oat Rolls

Judiann McNulty, Laramie, Wyoming

An old friend served these rolls when my family went to her house for Sunday dinner several years ago. I made sure I had a copy of the recipe before leaving.

1-1/4	cups boiling water
2/3	cup quick-cooking oats
1/4	cup butter, softened
1/2	teaspoon salt
1/2	cup sugar
1	egg, lightly beaten
1	package (1/4 ounce) active dry yeast
3-1/2	to 4 cups all-purpose flour

In a large bowl, pour boiling water over cereal. Add the butter and salt. Let stand until mixture cools to 110°-115°, stirring occasionally. Add the sugar, egg, yeast and 2 cups flour. Beat until smooth. Stir in enough remaining flour to form a soft dough.

Turn onto a floured surface; knead until smooth and elastic, about 5 minutes. Cover and let rest for 10 minutes.

Roll dough to 1/2-in. thickness. Cut with a floured 2-1/2-in. biscuit cutter. Place 2 in. apart on lightly greased baking sheets. Cover and let rise in a warm place until doubled, about 1 hour.

Bake at 375° for 15-20 minutes or until golden brown. Remove from pans to wire racks. Serve warm. **Yield:** about 1-1/2 dozen.

Braided Pizza Loaf

Debbie Meduna, Plaza, North Dakota

Working women can take the frozen bread dough out in the morning and then prepare this hearty loaf when they get home. It's important to let the filling cool completely before spreading on the dough.

  1 loaf (1 pound) frozen bread dough, thawed
  1 pound ground beef
  1 medium onion, finely chopped
  1 can (8 ounces) tomato sauce
  1 teaspoon salt
  1 teaspoon dried oregano
  1 teaspoon paprika
  1 teaspoon pepper
1/2 teaspoon garlic salt
  1 cup (4 ounces) shredded cheddar cheese
  1 cup (4 ounces) shredded part-skim mozzarella cheese
Melted butter

Place the dough in a greased bowl, turning once to grease top. Cover and let rise in a warm place until doubled, about 1 hour.

Meanwhile, in a large skillet, cook beef and onion over medium heat until meat is no longer pink; drain. Stir in the tomato sauce and seasonings. Bring to a boil. Reduce heat; simmer, uncovered, for 30 minutes, stirring occasionally.

Cool completely. Punch dough down. Turn onto a lightly floured surface; roll into a 15-in. x 12-in. rectangle. Place on a greased baking sheet. Spread filling lengthwise down center third of rectangle. Sprinkle cheeses over filling.

On each long side, cut 1-1/2-in.-wide strips about 2-1/2 in. into center. Starting at one end, fold alternating strips at an angle across filling. Brush with butter.

Bake at 350° for 30-35 minutes or until golden brown. Serve warm. Store in the refrigerator. **Yield:** 1 loaf.

Swiss Onion Bread

Martha Smith, Canton, Ohio

Our granddaughter, Lena, used this recipe as part of her 4-H project, and it was very well received. The slight crunch from poppy seeds pairs well with the creamy Swiss cheese.

    2 packages (1/4 ounce *each*) active dry yeast
1-1/2 cups warm water (110° to 115°), *divided*
    1 teaspoon plus 1/4 cup sugar, *divided*
  1/2 cup butter, melted
    1 medium onion, finely chopped
    1 egg
    2 teaspoons salt
  1/4 teaspoon ground mustard
6-3/4 to 7-1/4 cups bread *or* all-purpose flour
  3/4 cup shredded Swiss cheese
FILLING:
  3/4 cup finely chopped onion
  1/4 cup shredded Swiss cheese
    3 tablespoons butter
    1 tablespoon poppy seeds
    1 teaspoon paprika
  1/2 teaspoon salt
EGG WASH:
    1 egg yolk
    2 teaspoons water
Additional poppy seeds, optional

In a large bowl, dissolve yeast in 1/2 cup warm water. Add 1 teaspoon sugar; let stand for 5 minutes. Add the butter, onion, egg, salt, mustard, 3 cups flour and remaining water and sugar. Beat until smooth. Stir in cheese and enough remaining flour to form a soft dough.

Turn onto a floured surface; knead until smooth and elastic, about 8-10 minutes. Place in a greased bowl, turning once to grease top. Cover and let rise in a warm place until doubled, about 45 minutes.

Punch dough down. Turn onto a lightly floured surface; divide in half. Roll each portion into an 18-in. x 10-in. rectangle. Cut in half lengthwise. Combine filling ingredients; spread to within 1/2 in. of edges. Roll up each jelly-roll style, starting with a long side; pinch seams to seal. Place two ropes side by side on a greased baking sheet. Twist ropes together; pinch ends to seal and tuck under. Repeat with remaining dough.

Cover and let rise in a warm place until doubled, about 45 minutes. Beat egg yolk and water; brush over twists. Sprinkle with additional poppy seeds if desired.

Bake at 375° for 25-35 minutes or until golden brown. Remove from pans to wire racks to cool. Store in the refrigerator. **Yield:** 2 loaves (16 slices each).

Veggie Loaves

Judiann McNulty, Laramie, Wyoming

A vegetable puree lends to this bread's lovely light texture. Made with egg whites, this bread is lower in fat and cholesterol than other breads.

- 2 tablespoons active dry yeast
- 1/2 cup warm water (110° to 115°)
- 2 cups milk
- 1/3 cup canola oil
- 2 egg whites
- 3 tablespoons honey
- 2 cups chopped cabbage
- 2 large carrots, sliced
- 1 large celery rib, cut into chunks
- 1/2 cup cornmeal
- 1 tablespoon salt
- 5 to 6 cups whole wheat flour

In a bowl, dissolve yeast in warm water. In a blender or food processor, combine the milk, oil, egg whites, honey and vegetables. Cover and process until smooth. Add cornmeal, salt and vegetable mixture to yeast mixture; mix well. Stir in enough flour to form a stiff dough.

Turn onto a floured surface; knead until smooth and elastic, about 8-10 minutes. Do not let rise. Divide in half. Shape into two loaves. Place in two greased 9-in. x 5-in. x 3-in. loaf pans. Cover and let rise in a warm place until doubled, about 1 hour.

Bake at 350° for 35-40 minutes or until browned. Remove from pans to wire racks to cool. Store in the refrigerator. **Yield:** 2 loaves (16 slices each).

Dilly Onion Braid

Gail Bailey, Edgewood, Illinois

This delicious recipe, given to me by a neighbor, pairs very well with spaghetti and a crisp salad. Top it off with a fresh fruit bowl for a well-balanced meal.

- 2-1/2 to 3 cups all-purpose flour
- 2 tablespoons sugar
- 1 package (1/4 ounce) active dry yeast
- 1 tablespoon dill seed
- 1 to 2 teaspoons dill weed
- 1-1/2 teaspoons salt
- 1 cup (8 ounces) sour cream
- 1/4 cup water
- 2 tablespoons butter
- 1 egg
- 1/3 cup finely chopped onion
- 1 egg yolk
- 2 teaspoons cold water

In a large bowl, combine 1-1/2 cups flour, sugar, yeast, dill seed, dill weed and salt. In a small saucepan, heat the sour cream, water and butter to 120°-130°; add to flour mixture. Beat on medium speed for 2 minutes. Add the egg, 1/2 cup flour and onion; beat 2 minutes longer. Stir in enough remaining flour to form a firm dough.

Turn onto a floured surface; knead until smooth and elastic, about 6-8 minutes. Place in a greased bowl, turning once to grease top. Cover and let rise in a warm place until doubled, about 1-1/2 hours.

Punch dough down. Turn onto a lightly floured surface; divide dough into thirds. Shape each into a 20-in. rope. Place ropes on a greased baking sheet and braid; pinch ends to seal and tuck under. Cover and let rise until doubled, about 30 minutes.

Beat egg yolk and cold water; brush over braid. Bake at 350° for 30-40 minutes or until golden brown. Remove from pan to a wire rack to cool. **Yield:** 1 loaf (16 slices).

Making a Braid Arrange three ropes of the dough lengthwise on a greased baking sheet, so they are almost touching. Starting in the middle, loosely braid. Turn the pan and repeat braiding from the middle of the pan to the other end. Press each end to seal and tuck ends under.

Easy Crescent Rolls

Ruth Sanford, Wasilla, Alaska

I learned to cook and bake under my mother's fantastic guidance. She always treated the family to home-baked bread, and I've learned to do the same.

- 1 package (1/4 ounce) active dry yeast
- 1 cup warm water (110° to 115°)
- 3 eggs
- 4 to 4-1/2 cups all-purpose flour
- 1/2 cup sugar
- 1 teaspoon salt
- 1/2 cup shortening

In a small bowl, dissolve yeast in warm water. In a small bowl, beat eggs until light. Add to yeast mixture; set aside. In a large bowl, combine 1 cup flour, sugar and salt. Cut in shortening until mixture resembles coarse crumbs. Stir in yeast mixture. Stir in enough remaining flour until dough leaves the side of the bowl and is soft (dough will be sticky). Do not knead. Cover and refrigerate overnight.

Punch dough down. Turn onto a well-floured surface; divide into thirds. Roll each into a 12-in. circle; cut each circle into 12 wedges. Roll up wedges from wide end and place with pointed end down 2 in. apart on greased baking sheets. Curve ends to form a crescent shape. Cover and let rise in a warm place until doubled, about 45 minutes.

Bake at 375° for 10-12 minutes or until light golden brown. Remove from pans to wire racks. **Yield:** 3 dozen.

Taco Bread

Twilla Eisele, Wellsville, Kansas

Taco seasoning and green chilies are the secrets to this bread's slightly spicy flavor. A friend gave me the recipe.

- 3-1/2 cups to 4 cups all-purpose flour
- 1 cup cornmeal
- 1 envelope taco seasoning
- 3 tablespoons sugar
- 2 packages (1/4 ounce *each*) active dry yeast
- 1 tablespoon dried minced onion
- 1 teaspoon salt
- 1 can (10-3/4 ounces) condensed tomato soup, undiluted
- 3/4 cup water
- 2 tablespoons butter
- 1 can (4 ounces) chopped green chilies, drained

In a large bowl, combine 1-1/2 cups flour, cornmeal, taco seasoning, sugar, yeast, onion and salt. In a large saucepan, heat the soup, water and butter to 120°-130°. Add to flour mixture; beat on medium speed for 3 minutes. Stir in chilies and enough remaining flour to form a soft dough.

Turn onto a floured surface; knead until smooth and elastic, about 6-8 minutes. Place in a greased bowl, turning once to grease top. Cover and let rise in a warm place until doubled, about 1 hour.

Punch dough down. Shape into a loaf. Place in a greased 9-in. x 5-in. x 3-in. loaf pan. Cover and let rise in a warm place until doubled, about 45 minutes.

Bake at 350° for 45-50 minutes or until golden brown. Remove from pan to a wire rack. Serve warm. **Yield:** 1 loaf (16 slices).

Cloverleaf Bran Rolls

Marvel Herriman, Hayesville, North Carolina

These tender, delicious rolls are great for a gathering. They're especially good served warm!

- 1 cup All-Bran
- 1 cup boiling water
- 2 packages (1/4 ounce *each*) active dry yeast
- 1 cup warm water (110° to 115°)
- 1 cup shortening
- 3/4 cup sugar
- 1 teaspoon salt
- 2 eggs, beaten
- 6 cups all-purpose flour

In a small bowl, combine bran and boiling water; set aside. In another bowl, dissolve yeast in warm water. In a large mixing bowl, cream shortening, sugar and salt. Add eggs and yeast mixture; mix well. Add bran mixture and 2 cups flour; beat well. Gradually add enough remaining flour to form a soft dough.

Turn onto a lightly floured surface; knead until smooth and elastic, about 6-8 minutes. Place in a greased bowl, turning once to grease top. Cover and let rise until doubled, about 1 hour.

Punch dough down. Turn onto a lightly floured surface. Divide into six portions; divide each into 12 pieces. Shape each into a ball; place three balls in each greased muffin cup. Cover and let rise until doubled, about 1 hour.

Bake at 350° for 15-18 minutes or until lightly browned. Remove from pans to wire racks. **Yield:** 2 dozen.

Cheddar Batter Bread

Deb Keslar, Utica, Nebraska

I love batter breads because I can offer my family delicious homemade bread without the hassle of kneading and shaping the dough. This loaf is terrific with chili.

- 2 cups all-purpose flour
- 2 tablespoons sugar
- 1 package (1/4 ounce) active dry yeast
- 1/4 teaspoon onion powder
- 1/4 teaspoon salt
- 1/4 teaspoon pepper
- 1 cup milk
- 2 tablespoons butter, softened
- 1 egg
- 1/2 cup cornmeal
- 3/4 cup shredded cheddar cheese

Additional cornmeal

In a large bowl, combine 1-1/2 cups flour, sugar, yeast, onion powder, salt and pepper. In a small saucepan, heat milk and butter to 120°-130°. Add to flour mixture; beat until moistened. Add egg; beat on low speed for 30 seconds. Beat on high for 3 minutes. Stir in cornmeal and remaining flour. Stir in the cheese (batter will be thick). Do not knead. Cover and let rise in a warm place until doubled, about 20 minutes.

Stir dough down. Grease an 8-in. x 4-in. x 2-in. loaf pan and sprinkle with additional cornmeal. Spoon batter into prepared pan. Cover and let rise in a warm place until doubled, about 30 minutes.

Bake at 350° for 35-40 minutes or until golden brown. Cool for 10 minutes before removing from pan to a wire rack. Store in the refrigerator. **Yield:** 1 loaf (16 slices).

About Batter Breads Batter breads are not kneaded like most yeast breads and have a coarser texture and rougher look. Batter breads are beaten with an electric mixer to help develop the gluten. Because they are not kneaded, it is important to beat them until the batter comes away from the bowl and appears stringy. Batter breads are best served the day they are made.

Parmesan Loaves

Sue Trotter, Coweta, Oklahoma

I've been making this bread since my college days, when I shared an apartment with five home economics majors. My family likes it best fresh out of the oven, but it also freezes and reheats well.

- 1 package (1/4 ounce) active dry yeast
- 1/4 cup warm water (110° to 115°)
- 2 cups warm milk (110° to 115°)
- 1 cup grated Parmesan cheese
- 2 tablespoons sugar
- 2 tablespoons canola oil
- 2 teaspoons salt
- 1/8 teaspoon cayenne pepper
- 5-1/2 to 6 cups all-purpose flour
- 1/4 cup butter, melted
- 2 teaspoons garlic salt

In a large bowl, dissolve yeast in warm water. Add the milk, cheese, sugar, oil, salt, cayenne and 2 cups flour. Beat until smooth. Stir in enough of the remaining flour to form a soft dough.

Turn onto a floured surface; knead until smooth and elastic, about 6-8 minutes. Place in a greased bowl, turning once to grease top. Cover and let rise in a warm place until doubled, about 1-1/2 hours.

Punch dough down. Turn onto a floured surface; divide in half. Cover and let rest for 10 minutes. Roll each into a 16-in. x 10-in. rectangle. Brush with butter; sprinkle with garlic salt. Cut into four 10-in. x 4-in. rectangles.

Stack butter side up. Cut each stack into five 4-in. x 2-in. strips. Place five strips cut side down in a greased 8-in. x 4-in. x 2-in. loaf pan. Repeat with remaining dough. Cover and let rise in a warm place until doubled, about 1 hour.

Bake at 350° for 40-45 minutes or until golden brown. Remove from pans to wire racks to cool. **Yield:** 2 loaves (16 slices each).

Honey Whole Wheat Braids

Pat Young, Backus, Minnesota

This hearty, wholesome bread has a slightly sweet taste from honey. I grind my own whole wheat for in this recipe.

      1 package (1/4 ounce) active dry yeast
2-1/4 cups warm water (110° to 115°), *divided*
      1 tablespoon sugar
   1/3 cup honey
      3 tablespoons canola oil
   1/2 cup nonfat dry milk powder
1-1/2 teaspoons salt
      6 to 6-1/2 cups whole wheat flour
All-purpose flour
Melted butter

In a large bowl, dissolve yeast in 1/4 cup warm water. Add sugar; let stand for 5 minutes. Add the honey, oil, milk powder, salt, 3 cups whole wheat flour and remaining water; beat for 3 minutes. Stir in enough remaining whole wheat flour to form a soft dough.

Turn onto a surface dusted with all-purpose flour; knead until smooth and elastic, about 8-10 minutes. Place in a greased bowl, turning once to grease top. Cover and let rise in a warm place until doubled, about 2 hours.

Punch dough down. Turn onto a lightly floured surface; divide into six portions. Shape each into a 15-in. rope. Braid three ropes; pinch ends to seal and tuck under. Repeat with remaining dough. Place in two greased 8-in. x 4-in. x 2-in. loaf pans. Cover and let rise until doubled, about 1 hour.

Bake at 350° for 30-35 minutes or until golden brown. Remove from pans to wire racks. Brush with melted butter. Cool. **Yield:** 2 loaves (16 slices each).

Cheddar Flat Bread

Joan Lucia, Gilboa, New York

I work full-time and don't get to spend as much time in the kitchen as I'd like. So I often make an entire meal from scratch on Sunday. This bread is usually on the menu.

1	package (1/4 ounce) active dry yeast
1/4	cup warm water (110° to 115°)
3/4	cup warm milk (110° to 115°)
2	tablespoons butter, softened
1	tablespoon sugar
1-1/2	teaspoons salt
2-1/2	to 3 cups all-purpose flour
1/4	cup butter, melted
2	tablespoons dried minced onion
1/2	teaspoon dried oregano
1/2	teaspoon paprika
1/4	teaspoon garlic salt
1/4	teaspoon celery seed
1	cup (4 ounces) shredded cheddar cheese

In a large bowl, dissolve yeast in warm water. Add the milk, butter, sugar and salt. Beat on medium speed for 3 minutes. Stir in enough remaining flour to form a stiff dough. Turn onto a floured surface; knead until smooth and elastic, about 6-8 minutes. Place in a greased bowl, turning once to grease top. Cover and let rise in a warm place until doubled, about 45 minutes.

Punch dough down. Divide in half. Press each into a greased 9-in. pie plate. In a small bowl, combine melted butter and seasonings; brush over dough. Sprinkle with cheese. Prick dough several times with a fork. Cover and let rise until doubled, about 30 minutes.

Bake at 350° for 20-25 minutes or until golden brown. Remove from pans to wire racks to cool. Store in the refrigerator. **Yield:** 2 loaves (12 slices each).

English Muffin Loaf

Rosemarie Leek, Lake Hopatcong, New Jersey

This simple recipe does not require kneading and calls for just one rising time. Slices are absolutely delicious toasted and topped with butter.

- 3 cups all-purpose flour
- 1 package (1/4 ounce) active dry yeast
- 1-1/2 teaspoons sugar
- 1 teaspoon salt
- 1/8 teaspoon baking soda
- 1 cup milk
- 1/4 cup water
- Cornmeal

In a bowl, combine 2 cups flour, yeast, sugar, salt and baking soda. In a saucepan, heat milk and water to 120°-130°. Add to flour mixture; beat until smooth. Stir in remaining flour (batter will be stiff). Do not knead.

Grease an 8-in. x 4-in. x 2-in. loaf pan and sprinkle with cornmeal. Spoon batter into prepared pan. Cover and let rise in a warm place until doubled, about 45 minutes.

Bake at 400° for 30-35 minutes or until golden brown. Remove from pan to a wire rack to cool. **Yield:** 1 loaf.

Grandpa's Pizza Bread

Barbara Schimke, Etna, New Hampshire

My grandmother made this pan bread often but never wrote down the recipe. Eventually, my dad experimented until he came up with precise measurements. Our kids love Grandpa's Pizza Bread.

- 1 package (1/4 ounce) active dry yeast
- 1-1/2 cups warm water (110° to 115°), *divided*
- 4 teaspoons sugar
- 4 teaspoons plus 2 tablespoons olive oil, *divided*
- 1-1/2 teaspoons salt
- 3-1/2 to 4 cups all-purpose flour
- Salt and coarsely ground pepper to taste

In a large bowl, dissolve the yeast in 1/2 cup warm water. Add sugar; let stand for 5 minutes. Add 4 teaspoons of oil, salt, remaining water and 2 cups flour. Beat until smooth. Stir in enough remaining flour to form a soft dough.

Turn onto a floured surface; knead until smooth and elastic, about 6-8 minutes. Place in a greased bowl, turning once to grease top. Cover and let rise in a warm place until doubled, about 1 hour.

Punch dough down. Brush a 13-in. x 9-in. x 2-in. baking pan with 1 tablespoon oil. Press dough into pan. Brush with remaining oil and sprinkle with salt and pepper. Cover and let rise in a warm place until doubled, about 45 minutes.

Bake at 375° for 20-25 minutes or until lightly browned. Cut in squares; serve warm, or at room temperature. **Yield:** 16-20 servings.

Potato Bread

Martha Clayton, Utopia, Texas

The firm crust of this loaf is reminiscent of old-fashioned breads. Using some of the potato cooking water provides even more flavor.

- 1 medium potato, peeled and diced
- 1-1/2 cups water
- 2 packages (1/4 ounce *each*) active dry yeast
- 1/2 cup warm water (110° to 115°)
- 1 cup warm milk (110° to 115°)
- 2 tablespoons butter, softened
- 2 tablespoons sugar
- 2 teaspoons salt
- 6-1/2 to 7-1/2 cups all-purpose flour
- Additional all-purpose flour

Place potato and 1-1/2 cups water in a small saucepan. Bring to a boil. Reduce heat; cover and simmer until very tender. Drain, reserving 1/2 cup liquid. Mash potatoes (without added milk or butter); set aside.

In a large bowl, dissolve yeast in warm water. Add the milk, butter, sugar, salt, 4 cups flour, potatoes and reserved cooking liquid; beat until smooth. Stir in enough remaining flour to form a stiff dough.

Turn onto a floured surface; knead until smooth and elastic, about 6-8 minutes. Place in a greased bowl, turning once to grease top. Cover and let rise in a warm place until doubled, about 1 hour.

Punch dough down. Turn onto a lightly floured surface; divide in half. Shape into loaves. Place in two greased 9-in. x 5-in. x 3-in. loaf pans. Cover and let rise until doubled, about 30 minutes.

Sprinkle lightly with additional flour. Bake at 375° for 35-40 minutes or until golden brown. Remove from pans to wire racks to cool. **Yield:** 2 loaves (16 slices each).

Buttery Herb Loaves

Rhoda Coffey, Oklahoma City, Oklahoma

A succulent herb butter is the secret to this bread's irresistible richness. These lovely loaves disappear quickly.

    2   packages (1/4 ounce *each*) active dry yeast
  1/4   cup warm water (110° to 115°)
    1   cup warm milk (110° to 115°)
    2   eggs
  1/3   cup shortening
  1/4   cup sugar
    1   tablespoon salt
4-1/2   to 5 cups all-purpose flour
HERB BUTTER:
  1/2   cup butter, softened
    1   garlic clove, minced
  1/2   teaspoon dried basil
  1/2   teaspoon dried minced onion
  1/2   teaspoon caraway seeds
  1/4   teaspoon dried oregano
  1/8   teaspoon cayenne pepper
Melted butter
Sesame *or* poppy seeds

In a large bowl, dissolve yeast in warm water. Add milk, eggs, shortening, sugar, salt and 1 cup flour. Beat until smooth. Stir in enough remaining flour to form a soft dough.

Turn onto a floured surface; knead until smooth and elastic, about 6-8 minutes. Place in a greased bowl, turning once to grease the top. Cover and let rise in a warm place until doubled, about 1-1/2 hours.

Punch dough down. Turn onto a lightly floured surface; divide in half. Roll each portion to 1/16-in. thickness; cut out ten 5-in. circles from each. Combine the butter, garlic, basil, onion, caraway seeds, oregano and cayenne; spread over dough. Fold circles in half; set half aside.

For each loaf, start with one folded circle on a greased baking sheet with folded edge toward the right. Working from right to left, add another piece with folded edge on right side, overlapping three-fourths of the previous piece. Repeat.

Form a second rectangular loaf from the reserved folded circles. Brush with melted butter; sprinkle with sesame seeds. Cover and let rise in a warm place until doubled, about 30 minutes.

Bake at 350° for 20-25 minutes or until golden brown. Remove from pans to wire racks. Serve warm. **Yield:** 2 loaves (16 slices each).

Soft Italian Bread Twists

Marcia Rand, Adams, Nebraska

Although my heritage is strictly Dutch, my family loves Italian food. These seasoned breadsticks are a great accompaniment to lasagna and pizza.

    1   teaspoon sugar
    1   teaspoon salt, *divided*
    1   package (1/4 ounce) quick-rise yeast
    2   to 2-1/2 cups all-purpose flour
  2/3   cup warm water (120° to 130°)
    1   tablespoon canola oil
    3   tablespoons butter, melted
  1/2   teaspoon garlic powder
  1/4   teaspoon paprika
Italian seasoning *or* grated Parmesan cheese, optional

In a food processor, combine the sugar, 3/4 teaspoon salt, yeast and 2 cups flour. Cover and process for 5-10 seconds. While processing, gradually add warm water and oil in a steady stream. Process for 1 minute or until smooth and elastic. Add 1 to 2 tablespoons of water or flour if needed.

Turn onto a floured surface. Roll into a 15-in. x 12-in. rectangle. Cut into 12 strips. Fold each strip in half lengthwise; twist each strip several times. Pinch ends to seal. Place 2 in. apart on a greased baking sheet.

In a small bowl, combine the butter, garlic powder, paprika and remaining salt. Brush some over dough. Sprinkle with Italian seasoning or Parmesan cheese if desired. Cover and let rise in a warm place until doubled, about 25 minutes.

Bake at 425° for 6-8 minutes or until golden brown. Brush with remaining butter mixture. **Yield:** 1 dozen.

Ham-Stuffed Bread

Lilburne Flohr-Svendsen, Barra Bonita, Brazil

I made this hearty bread for our daughter's wedding years ago. It caught on so well that I now serve it at all of our special-occasion events.

1	tablespoon active dry yeast
1	cup warm milk (110° to 115°)
1	egg
1/2	cup canola oil
1/2	teaspoon salt
2-3/4	to 3-1/4 cups all-purpose flour

FILLING:

1	small onion, chopped
1/3	cup canola oil
2	medium tomatoes, chopped
1	garlic clove, minced

Salt and pepper to taste

1/2	pound fully cooked ham, chopped
1	teaspoon cider vinegar
1/2	teaspoon dried oregano

In a large bowl, dissolve yeast in warm milk. Add the egg, oil and salt and 2 cups of flour. Beat until smooth. Stir in enough remaining flour to form a stiff dough. Place in a greased bowl, turning once to grease top. Cover and let rise in a warm place until doubled, about 1 hour.

Meanwhile, in a large skillet, saute onion in oil until tender. Add the tomatoes, garlic, salt and pepper. Cook over medium heat until liquid is absorbed, about 30 minutes. Remove from the heat. Stir in the ham, vinegar and oregano. Cool.

Punch dough down. Turn onto a lightly floured surface; roll into a 14-in. x 12-in. rectangle. Spread filling over dough to within 1/2 in. of edges. Roll up jelly-roll style, starting with a long side; pinch seam to seal and tuck ends under. Place seam side down on a greased baking sheet. Do not let rise.

Bake at 375° for 18-22 minutes or until golden brown. Remove from pan to a wire rack. Serve warm. Store in the refrigerator. **Yield:** 1 loaf.

Parmesan Butterhorns

Mrs. Bruce Shidler, Plymouth, Indiana

Our youngest daughter, Stephanie, has won several awards with this recipe. These buttery rolls with subtle Parmesan flavor are wonderful served warm or at room temperature.

3-3/4	cups all-purpose flour
1/4	cup sugar
1	teaspoon salt
1	cup cold butter, cubed
1	package (1/4 ounce) active dry yeast
1	cup warm milk (110° to 115°)
1	egg
1/2	cup grated Parmesan cheese

Melted butter

In a large bowl, combine the flour, sugar and salt; cut in butter until mixture resemble fine crumbs. Dissolve yeast in warm milk; stir into flour mixture with egg. Beat until smooth. Do not knead. Cover and refrigerate overnight.

Punch dough down. Turn onto a lightly floured surface; divide into thirds. Roll each into a 12-in. circle. Sprinkle with Parmesan cheese. Cut each circle into 12 wedges.

Roll up wedges from the wide end and place with pointed end down 2 in. apart on ungreased baking sheets. Curve ends to form a crescent shape. Cover and let rise in a warm place until doubled, about 30 minutes.

Bake at 375° for 10-15 minutes or until golden brown. Brush with melted butter. Remove from pans to wire racks to cool. **Yield:** 3 dozen.

Pull-Apart Garlic Buns

Carolina Hofeldt, Lloyd, Montana

My Italian neighbor has passed along many delicious recipes, including this one. The soft, tender buns are easy to pull apart.

2-1/2	to 3 cups all-purpose flour
1	tablespoon sugar
1	package (1/4 ounce) active dry yeast
1	teaspoon salt
1/2	cup milk
1/2	cup water
2	tablespoons shortening
1	egg
1	teaspoon paprika
1/2	teaspoon garlic powder
1/4	cup butter, melted
1	tablespoon sesame seeds

In a large bowl, combine 1-1/2 cups flour, sugar, yeast and salt. In a saucepan, heat the milk, water and shortening to 120°-130°. Add to flour mixture; beat until moistened. Add egg; beat on medium speed for 3 minutes. Stir in enough remaining flour to form a soft dough.

Turn onto a floured surface; knead until smooth and elastic, about 6-8 minutes. Do not let rise.

Divide into 12 pieces. Shape each into a bun. Combine paprika and garlic powder. Dip each bun in melted butter, then in paprika mixture. Place six buns in a greased 9-in. x 5-in. x 3-in. loaf pan; sprinkle with half of sesame seeds. Top with remaining buns and sesame seeds. Cover and let rise in a warm place until doubled, about 45 minutes.

Bake at 375° for 30-35 minutes or until golden brown. Remove from the pan to a wire rack to cool. **Yield:** 1 loaf (12 buns).

Finnish Wheat Rolls

Tarya Mannonen-Cameron, Seattle, Washington

When I came to the United States from Finland for college, I missed the breads from back home. So I came up with this recipe to recapture those fabulous flavors.

2	packages (1/4 ounce *each*) active dry yeast
2	cups warm water (110° to 115°)
1	cup butter, melted
1/4	cup dried parsley flakes
1	tablespoon dried rosemary, crushed
2	teaspoons salt
1	teaspoon rubbed sage
1	teaspoon dried thyme
2-3/4	cups whole wheat flour
3	to 3-1/2 cups all-purpose flour

Additional melted butter

In a large bowl, dissolve yeast in warm water. Add the butter, parsley, rosemary, salt, sage, thyme and whole wheat flour. Beat until smooth. Stir in enough all-purpose flour to form a soft dough.

Turn onto a floured surface; knead until smooth and elastic, about 6-8 minutes. Place in a greased bowl, turning once to grease top. Cover and let rise in a warm place until doubled, about 30 minutes.

Punch dough down. Turn onto a lightly floured surface; divide into 24 pieces. Shape each into a ball. Place 2 in. apart on greased baking sheets. Cover and let rise in a warm place until doubled, about 30 minutes.

Brush with additional melted butter. Bake at 425° for 25-30 minutes or until golden brown. Remove from pans to wire racks. Serve warm. **Yield:** 2 dozen.

No-Fuss Dinner Rolls

Laurie Rice, Butler, Pennsylvania

I really enjoy making these rolls for our son because he loves them and the recipe is so easy. In a little over an hour, you can offer your family oven-fresh rolls.

- 1 package (1/4 ounce) active dry yeast
- 1-1/2 cups warm milk (110° to 115°)
- 1 egg
- 2 tablespoons butter, melted
- 2 tablespoons sugar
- 1 teaspoon salt
- 4 cups all-purpose flour

Melted butter

In a large bowl, dissolve yeast in warm milk. Add the egg, butter, sugar, salt and 2 cups flour. Beat on medium speed for 3 minutes. Stir in remaining flour (batter will be stiff). Do not knead.

Cover and let rest for 15 minutes. Stir dough down. Fill greased muffin cups three-fourths full. Cover and let rise in a warm place until doubled, about 30 minutes.

Bake at 400° for 12-15 minutes or until golden brown. Brush with melted butter. Cool for 1 minute before removing from pans to wire racks. **Yield:** about 15 rolls.

Easy Stromboli

Katie Troyer, Meadville, Pennsylvania

My family prefers this stromboli instead of ordinary pizza. Experiment with different filling ingredients to suit your family's tastes.

- 1 tablespoon active dry yeast
- 1 cup warm water (110° to 115°)
- 3 tablespoons canola oil
- 1/2 teaspoon salt
- 2-3/4 to 3-1/4 cups all-purpose flour
- 1 cup pizza sauce
- 1 pound bulk pork sausage, cooked and drained
- 1 can (4 ounces) mushroom stems and pieces, drained
- 1 package (3-1/2 ounces) sliced pepperoni
- 1 cup (4 ounces) shredded part-skim mozzarella cheese

In a bowl, dissolve yeast in warm water. Add oil, salt and 2 cups flour. Beat until smooth. Stir in enough remaining flour to form a soft dough. Turn onto a floured surface; knead until smooth and elastic, about 6-8 minutes. Cover and let rest for 10 minutes.

Turn onto a lightly floured surface; roll into a 14-in. x 12-in. rectangle. Transfer to a greased 15-in. x 10-in. x 1-in. baking pan. Spoon pizza sauce to within 1/2 in. of edges. Top with sausage, mushrooms, pepperoni and cheese. Roll up jelly-roll style, starting with a long side; pinch seam to seal and tuck ends under.

Bake at 400° for 30-35 minutes or until golden brown. Serve warm. Store in the refrigerator. **Yield:** 1 loaf.

Herbed Onion Focaccia

Krista Frank, Rhododendron, Oregon

This bread is so full of flavor that spreading butter on it is not necessary. I always hear yums, oohs and aahs when guests take their first bite. It's best served warm, and the next day makes the best toast you've ever had!

- 1 cup water (70° to 80°)
- 1/3 cup finely chopped onion
- 1 tablespoon sugar
- 1-1/2 teaspoons salt
- 1 teaspoon grated Parmesan cheese
- 1/2 teaspoon garlic powder
- 1/2 teaspoon dried basil
- 1/2 teaspoon dill weed
- 1/2 teaspoon pepper
- 3 cups all-purpose flour
- 2 teaspoons active dry yeast

TOPPING:
- 1 tablespoon olive oil
- 1/2 teaspoon grated Parmesan cheese
- 1/2 teaspoon dried parsley flakes
- 1/4 teaspoon salt
- 1/8 teaspoon pepper

In bread machine pan, place the first 11 ingredients in order suggested by manufacturer. Select dough setting (check dough after 5 minutes of mixing; add 1 to 2 tablespoons of water or flour if needed).

When cycle is completed, turn dough onto a greased baking sheet and punch down (dough will be sticky). With lightly oiled hands, pat dough into a 9-in. circle. Brush with oil; sprinkle with Parmesan cheese, parsley, salt and pepper. Cover and let rise in a warm place until doubled, about 45 minutes.

Bake at 400° for 18-20 minutes or until golden brown. Cut into wedges; serve warm. **Yield:** 1 loaf (1-1/2 pounds).

Ranch Rolls

Larry Miller, Ashland, Kentucky

After sampling some homemade crackers from friends a few years ago, I was inspired to add some ranch salad dressing mix to my basic roll recipe.

 1 package (1/4 ounce) active dry yeast
1-1/4 cups warm water (110° to 115°), *divided*
 1 teaspoon honey
 1/2 cup canola oil
 1/3 cup sugar
 2 eggs
 2 envelopes ranch salad dressing mix
 2 teaspoons salt
 1 teaspoon dill weed
4-1/2 to 5-1/2 cups all-purpose flour
CHEESE TOPPING:
 2 tablespoons sesame seeds
 2 tablespoons grated Parmesan cheese
 2 tablespoons finely chopped pecans
 1/4 teaspoon dill weed

In a large bowl, dissolve yeast in 1/4 cup warm water. Add honey; let stand for 5 minutes. Add the oil, sugar, 1 egg, salad dressing mix, salt, dill, 1 cup flour and remaining water. Beat until smooth. Stir in enough remaining flour to form a soft dough.

Turn onto a lightly floured surface; knead until smooth and elastic, about 6-8 minutes. Place in a greased bowl, turning once to grease top. Cover and let rise in a warm place until doubled, about 1 hour.

Punch dough down. Turn onto a lightly floured surface; divide into 12 pieces. Place in greased muffin cups. Beat the remaining egg; brush over dough. Combine topping ingredients; sprinkle over rolls. Cover and let rise in a warm place until doubled, about 45 minutes.

Bake at 400° for 15-20 minutes or until golden brown. Remove from pans to wire racks to cool. **Yield:** 1 dozen.

Checking the Dough in a Bread Machine After the bread machine has mixed the dough for about 5 minutes, our recipes recommend that you check the dough. If the dough is lumpy or too dry, add a little more water. If the dough is sticky and won't form a ball, it is too moist. Add a little more flour.

Rosemary Cheddar Bread

Tammy Perrault, Lancaster, Ohio

My husband and I love rosemary- and cheddar-crusted potatoes, so I adapted a potato bread recipe to include our favorite flavors. The bread machine makes this herbed loaf a snap to prepare.

 1 cup water (70° to 80°)
 3 tablespoons olive oil
 1/2 cup mashed potato flakes
7-1/2 teaspoons sugar
 3 teaspoons dried rosemary, crushed
 1 teaspoon salt
 3 cups bread flour
2-1/4 teaspoons active dry yeast
 1-1/4 cups finely shredded cheddar cheese

In bread machine pan, place the first eight ingredients in order suggested by manufacturer. Select basic bread setting. Choose crust color and loaf size if available. Bake according to bread machine directions (check dough after 5 minutes of mixing; add 1 to 2 tablespoons of water or flour if needed).

Just before the final kneading (your machine may audibly signal this), add the cheese. **Yield:** 1 loaf (about 1-1/2 pounds).

Editor's Note: We recommend you do not use a bread machine's time-delay feature for this recipe.

Colonial Oat Bread

Marge Kriner, Bloomsburg, Pennsylvania

My mother baked bread several times a week when I was young, and this was one of our favorites. Now my family enjoys it, especially with homemade soup.

      4   cups whole wheat flour
      1   cup quick-cooking oats
      2   packages (1/4 ounce *each*) active dry yeast
      3   teaspoons salt
  2-1/4   cups water
    1/2   cup honey
    1/4   cup butter, softened
      1   egg
      3   to 3-1/2 cups all-purpose flour
Additional quick-cooking oats, optional

In a large bowl, combine the whole wheat flour, oats, yeast and salt. In a small saucepan, heat the water, honey and butter to 120°-130°. Add to flour mixture; beat just until moistened. Add egg; beat until smooth. Stir in enough remaining flour to form a stiff dough.

Turn onto a floured surface; knead until smooth and elastic, about 6-8 minutes. Place in a greased bowl, turning once to grease top. Cover and let rise in a warm place until doubled, about 1 hour.

Punch dough down. Turn onto a lightly floured surface; divide in half. Shape into round or oval-shaped loaves. Place on two greased baking sheets. Cover and let rise until doubled, about 30 minutes.

With a sharp knife, make several shallow "X-shaped" cuts on the top of each loaf. Sprinkle with additional oats if desired. Bake at 350° for 35-40 minutes or until browned. Remove from pans to wire racks to cool. **Yield:** 2 loaves (16 slices each).

Honey White Loaves

Lois Kamps, Hudsonville, Michigan

When I was searching for a moist bread that wouldn't crumble when thinly sliced, a friend urged me to try her grandmother's age-old recipe. It slices perfectly.

        2   packages (1/4 ounce *each*) active dry yeast
    2-1/2   cups warm water (110° to 115°)
      1/2   cup butter, melted
      1/2   cup honey
        2   eggs
        3   teaspoons salt
        8   to 9 cups all-purpose flour

In a large bowl, dissolve yeast in warm water. Add the butter, honey, eggs, salt and 4 cups flour. Beat on medium speed for 3 minutes. Stir in enough remaining flour to form a soft dough.

Turn onto a floured surface; knead until smooth and elastic, about 6-8 minutes. Place in a greased bowl, turning once to grease top. Cover and let rise in a warm place until doubled; about 1 hour.

Punch dough down. Divide into thirds. Shape into loaves. Place in three greased 8-in. x 4-in. x 2-in. loaf pans. Cover and let rise until doubled, about 30 minutes.

Bake at 375° for 25-30 minutes or until golden brown. Remove from pans to wire racks to cool. **Yield:** 3 loaves (16 slices each).

Greasing the Bowl for Rising Use canola or vegetable oil, or cooking spray to grease the bowl that the yeast dough will rise in. If using oil, add a little to the bowl, then using a paper towel coat the entire inside of the bowl with oil. Cover the dough with plastic wrap or a clean kitchen towel. If using plastic wrap, coat with cooking spray to prevent it from sticking to the dough.

Skillet Rolls

Susan Baughman, Houston, Pennsylvania

Baking these rolls in a skillet makes them soft and tender. I like them best split and spread with butter and berry jelly.

    1   package (1/4 ounce) active dry yeast
    1/4 cup warm water (110° to 115°)
    1   cup warm buttermilk (110° to 115°)
    1/4 cup butter, softened
    1/4 cup sugar
    1   teaspoon salt
    1/4 teaspoon baking soda
    1   egg
    4   to 4-1/2 cups all-purpose flour
    1   tablespoon cornmeal
    1   tablespoon butter, melted

In a large bowl, dissolve yeast in warm water. Add the buttermilk, butter, sugar, salt, baking soda and egg. Beat until blended. Stir in enough flour to form a soft dough.

Turn onto a floured surface; knead until smooth and elastic, about 6-8 minutes. Place in a greased bowl, turning once to grease top. Cover and let rise in a warm place until doubled, about 1 hour.

Punch dough down. Turn onto a lightly floured surface; knead for 5 minutes. Divide into 24 pieces. Shape each into a ball. Grease a 12-in. ovenproof skillet and sprinkle with cornmeal. Place rolls in prepared pan. Cover and let rise until doubled, about 40 minutes.

Drizzle butter over rolls. Bake at 375° for 18-20 minutes or until golden brown. Remove from skillet to a wire rack to cool. **Yield:** 2 dozen.

Editor's Note: Warmed buttermilk will appear curdled.

Rye Breadsticks

Mary Johnston, Fredericktown, Pennsylvania

I love to experiment with bread recipes. My soft breadsticks are delicious with a casserole or hearty bowl of soup.

    1   tablespoon active dry yeast
    1-1/2 cups warm water (110° to 115°), *divided*
    2   tablespoons honey
    2   cups whole wheat flour
    1   cup rye flour
    1   to 1-1/2 cups all-purpose flour

In a large bowl, dissolve yeast in 1/2 cup warm water. Add honey; let stand for 5 minutes. Stir in the remaining water, whole wheat flour, rye flour and enough all-purpose flour to form a soft dough.

Turn onto a floured surface; knead until smooth and elastic, about 6-8 minutes. Do not let rise. Divide dough into 16 pieces. Roll each into a 10-in. rope. Place 2 in. apart on a greased baking sheet. Cover and let rise in a warm place until doubled, about 30 minutes.

Bake at 350° for 20-25 minutes or until golden brown. Serve warm. **Yield:** 16 breadsticks.

Country Herb Bread

Sandy Neukam, Huntingburg, Indiana

I've relied on this traditional recipe for years. Everyone in the family loves the perfectly flavored herb loaves, especially our little boy, who always asks for more brown bread.

    2   cups all-purpose flour
    2   cups whole wheat flour
    1   cup rye flour
    2   packages (1/4 ounce *each*) active dry yeast
    1   tablespoon sugar
    2   teaspoons salt
    1/4   cup dried parsley flakes
    1/4   to 1/2 teaspoon dried marjoram
    1/4   to 1/2 teaspoon dried rosemary, crushed
    1-1/2 cups water
    3   tablespoons butter
    1   egg white
    1   tablespoon cold water

In a large bowl, combine the flours. Place 1-1/2 cups flour in a large bowl; add yeast, sugar, salt and herbs. In a saucepan, heat water and butter to 120°-130°. Add to flour mixture; beat just until moistened. Stir in enough remaining flour mixture to form a stiff dough.

Turn onto a floured surface; knead until smooth and elastic, about 6-8 minutes. Place in a greased bowl, turning once to grease top. Cover and let rise in a warm place until doubled, about 1 hour.

Punch dough down. Let rest for 15 minutes. Turn onto a lightly floured surface; divide in half. Shape into two loaves.

Place in two greased 9-in. x 5-in. x 3-in. loaf pans. With a sharp knife, make four to five diagonal slashes across the top of each loaf, or make a wheat design as shown in photo. Cover and let rise in a warm place until doubled, about 1 hour.

Beat egg white and cold water; brush over loaves. Bake at 375° for 30-35 minutes or until golden brown and bread sounds hollow when tapped. Remove from pans to wire racks to cool. **Yield:** 2 loaves (16 slices each).

Three-Grain Wild Rice Bread

Kim L'Hote, Wausau, Wisconsin

Wild rice really shines in this one-of-a-kind recipe. The first time I made this bread, I knew I'd found a new favorite. Everyone who has tried it since confirms that over and over again! Wild rice takes some time to cook, so plan ahead when you want to make this fabulous bread.

- 1 package (1/4 ounce) active dry yeast
- 1/3 cup warm water (110° to 115°)
- 2 cups warm milk (110° to 115°)
- 2 cups whole wheat flour
- 1/2 cup rye flour
- 1/2 cup quick-cooking oats
- 1/2 cup honey
- 2 tablespoons butter, melted
- 2 teaspoons salt
- 4 to 4-1/2 cups bread *or* all-purpose flour
- 1 cup cooked wild rice, cooled to room temperature
- 1 egg
- 1 tablespoon cold water

In a large bowl, dissolve yeast in warm water. Add the milk, whole wheat flour, rye flour, oats, honey, butter, salt and 2 cups bread flour. Beat until smooth. Stir in wild rice and enough remaining bread flour to form a stiff dough.

Turn onto a floured surface; knead until smooth and elastic, about 8-10 minutes. Place in a greased bowl, turning once to grease top. Cover and let rise in a warm place until doubled, about 1-1/2 hours.

Punch dough down. Turn onto a lightly floured surface; divide in half. Shape into loaves. Transfer to two greased 9-in. x 5-in. x 3-in. loaf pans. Cover and let rise until doubled, about 30 minutes.

Beat egg and cold water; brush over loaves. Bake at 375° for 35-40 minutes or until golden brown. Remove from pans to wire racks to cool. **Yield:** 2 loaves (16 slices each).

Quick Calzones

Clarice Brender, North Liberty, Iowa

These individual stuffed pizzas taste delectable with or without the sauce on the side. Prepare half of the calzones with ham and the other half with pepperoni to satisfy all of the diners at your event.

- 2 cups (8 ounces) shredded part-skim mozzarella cheese
- 1 carton (15 ounces) ricotta cheese
- 6 ounces diced fully cooked ham *or* sliced pepperoni
- 1 teaspoon garlic powder
- 2 loaves (1 pound *each*) frozen bread dough, thawed

Warmed spaghetti *or* pizza sauce, optional

In a large bowl, combine the cheeses, ham and garlic powder. Divide each loaf into eight pieces.

On a floured surface, roll each portion into a 5-in. circle. Place filling in the center of each circle. Bring dough over filling; pinch seams to seal.

Place seam side down on greased baking sheets. Bake at 375° for 30-35 minutes or until golden brown. Serve warm with sauce if desired. Store in the refrigerator. **Yield:** 16 servings.

Sunflower Bread

Marianne Segall, Cody, Wyoming

I do the cooking at our family-owned guest ranch. I use thick slices of this nutty bread as an accompaniment to soup in winter and as sandwich bread in summer. Visitors can't resist it.

- 4 cups all-purpose flour
- 1 cup whole wheat flour
- 1 cup salted sunflower kernels, toasted
- 2 packages (1/4 ounce *each*) active dry yeast
- 2 teaspoons salt
- 1-1/4 cups water
- 1/2 cup milk
- 1/3 cup honey
- 3 tablespoons butter

Additional salted sunflower kernels, optional

In a large bowl, combine 2 cups all-purpose flour, whole wheat flour, sunflower kernels, yeast and salt. In a saucepan, heat the water, milk, honey and butter to 120°-130°. Add to flour mixture. Beat until smooth. Stir in enough remaining all-purpose flour to form a soft dough.

Turn onto a floured surface; knead until smooth and elastic, about 6-8 minutes. Place in a greased bowl, turning once to grease top. Cover and let rise in a warm place until doubled, about 1 hour.

Punch dough down. Turn onto a lightly floured surface; divide in half. Shape into loaves. Roll loaves in additional sunflower kernels if desired. Place in two greased 8-in. x 4-in. x 2-in. loaf pans. Cover and let rise until doubled, about 45 minutes.

Bake at 375° for 35-40 minutes or until golden brown. Remove from pans to wire racks to cool. **Yield:** 2 loaves (12 slices each).

Kaiser Rolls

Loraine Meyer, Bend, Oregon

These rolls can be enjoyed with soup or used for sandwiches. I make them at least once a month. This recipe earned me a blue ribbon at the county fair.

- 2 packages (1/4 ounce *each*) active dry yeast
- 2 cups warm water (110° to 115°), *divided*
- 4 tablespoons sugar, *divided*
- 1/3 cup canola oil
- 2 teaspoons salt
- 6 to 6-1/2 cups all-purpose flour
- 1 egg white
- 2 teaspoons cold water

Poppy *and/or* sesame seeds

In a large bowl, dissolve yeast in 1/2 cup warm water. Add 1 tablespoon sugar; let stand for 5 minutes. Add the oil, salt, remaining warm water and sugar and 4 cups flour. Beat until smooth. Stir in enough remaining flour to form a soft dough.

Turn onto a floured surface; knead until smooth and elastic, about 6-8 minutes. Place in a greased bowl, turning once to grease top. Cover and let rise in a warm place until doubled, about 1 hour.

Punch dough down. Turn onto a lightly floured surface; divide into 16 pieces. Shape each into a ball. Place 2 in. apart on greased baking sheets. Cover and let rise until doubled, about 30 minutes.

Beat egg white and cold water; brush over rolls. Sprinkle with poppy and/or sesame seeds. With scissors, cut a 1/4-in.-deep cross on tops of rolls.

Bake at 400° for 15-20 minutes or until golden brown. Remove from pans to wire racks to cool. **Yield:** 16 rolls.

Tender Herb Dinner Rolls

Ruth Campbell, Staunton, Virginia

A blend of herbs makes these mouthwatering rolls stand out from all others. They're especially tasty with poultry and fish.

- 3-1/2 to 4 cups all-purpose flour
- 3 tablespoons sugar
- 1 package (1/4 ounce) active dry yeast
- 2 teaspoons dried basil
- 1 teaspoon salt
- 1 teaspoon celery seed
- 1 teaspoon rubbed sage
- 1 teaspoon dried thyme
- 1/8 teaspoon ground ginger
- 1-1/4 cups milk
- 1/4 cup shortening
- 1 egg

In a large bowl, combine 1-1/2 cups flour, sugar, yeast and seasonings. In a saucepan, heat milk and shortening to 120°-130°. Add to flour mixture; beat until moistened. Beat in egg until smooth. Stir in enough remaining flour to form a soft dough. Do not knead. Cover and refrigerate for 2 hours.

Punch dough down. Turn onto a floured surface; divide into 24 pieces. Shape each into a ball. Place 2 in. apart on greased baking sheets. Cover and let rise in a warm place until doubled, about 1 hour.

Bake at 400° for 12-14 minutes or until golden brown. Remove from pans to wire racks to cool. **Yield:** 2 dozen.

Easy Bread Squares

Elsie Harms, Nokomis, Illinois

There's no kneading or rolling out dough in this extra-easy yeast recipe. I like to serve generous slices alongside spaghetti.

- 3-1/2 cups all-purpose flour
- 1 tablespoon sugar
- 1 package (1/4 ounce) active dry yeast
- 1 teaspoon salt
- 1-1/2 cups warm water (120° to 130°)
- 2 tablespoons shortening

Melted butter

In a large bowl, combine 1-1/2 cups flour, sugar, yeast and salt. Add water and shortening. Beat on medium speed for 3 minutes. Stir in the remaining flour (batter will be stiff). Do not knead. Cover and let rise in a warm place for 30 minutes.

Stir dough down. Spread evenly into a greased 13-in. x 9-in. x 2-in. baking pan. Cover and let rise until doubled, about 40 minutes.

Bake at 375° for 30-35 minutes or until golden brown. Cool for 10 minutes before removing from pan to a wire rack. Brush with melted butter. Cut into squares. **Yield:** 12-15 servings. **Yield:** 2 dozen.

In a large bowl, dissolve yeast in warm water. Add the wheat flour, brown sugar, oil, salt and ground sunflower kernels. Beat until smooth. Stir in enough all-purpose flour to form a firm dough.

Turn onto a floured surface; knead until smooth and elastic, about 5-7 minutes. Place in a greased bowl, turning once to grease top. Cover and let rise in a warm place until doubled, about 1 hour.

Punch dough down. Turn onto a floured surface; knead 10 times. Divide in half; let rest for 5 minutes. Sprinkle 3 tablespoons of sunflower kernels over the bottom and sides of two greased 8-in. x 4-in. x 2-in. loaf pans. Shape dough into loaves; place in pans. Press remaining kernels into top of dough. Cover and let rise until doubled, about 45 minutes.

Beat egg and cold water; brush over dough. Bake at 375° for 40-45 minutes or until golden brown. Remove from pans to wire racks to cool. **Yield:** 2 loaves (12 slices each).

Bacon Onion Breadsticks

Michelle Buerge, Ithaca, Michigan

With a delicious blend of bacon, butter and onion, these soft breadsticks are hard to resist. Our family enjoys them with soup and salad.

> 2 tablespoons active dry yeast
> 2 cups warm milk (110° to 115°), *divided*
> 1 teaspoon sugar
> 1/2 cup butter, melted
> 1-1/4 teaspoons salt, *divided*
> 5-1/2 to 6 cups all-purpose flour
> 1 pound sliced bacon, diced
> 1 medium onion, chopped
> 1/4 teaspoon pepper
> 1 egg, beaten
> Coarse salt

In a large bowl, dissolve yeast in 1 cup warm milk. Add sugar; let stand for 5 minutes. Add butter, 1 teaspoon salt and remaining milk. Beat until smooth. Stir in enough flour to form a soft dough.

Turn onto a floured surface; knead until smooth and elastic, about 6-8 minutes. Place in a greased bowl, turning once to grease top. Cover and let rise in a warm place until doubled, about 1-1/2 hours.

Meanwhile, in a large skillet, saute bacon and onion until bacon is crisp; drain. Add pepper and remaining salt. Cool completely. Punch dough down. Turn onto a floured surface; knead bacon mixture into dough.

Roll dough into a 14-in. square. Brush with egg; sprinkle with coarse salt. Cut dough in half lengthwise and in thirds widthwise. Cut each section into six strips. Place 2 in. apart on greased baking sheets. Cover and let rise in a warm place until doubled, about 30 minutes.

Bake at 375° for 15-20 minutes or until golden brown. Remove from pans to wire racks to cool. **Yield:** 3 dozen.

Toasted Sunflower Bread

Caroline Kunkel, St. Joseph, Missouri

Although I found this recipe in an old cookbook, the hearty flavor appeals to all generations. It's a nice alternative to ordinary whole wheat bread.

> 1-1/4 cups sunflower kernels, *divided*
> 1 tablespoon soy sauce
> 1 tablespoon active dry yeast
> 3 cups warm water (110° to 115°)
> 4 cups whole wheat flour
> 1 tablespoon brown sugar
> 1 tablespoon canola oil
> 2 teaspoons salt
> 2 to 2-1/2 cups all-purpose flour
> 1 egg
> 1 tablespoon cold water

In a small skillet over medium heat, cook and stir 1 cup of sunflower kernels until lightly browned, about 6 minutes; remove from the heat. Stir in soy sauce until kernels are evenly coated. Cool, stirring several times. Transfer to a blender or food processor; cover and process until ground.

Tomato Spinach Bread

Avanell Hewitt, North Richland Hills, Texas

I've been making these savory swirled loaves for many years. The colors really add to the festive feel of Christmas dinner at our house.

- 1 package (1/4 ounce) active dry yeast
- 1 cup warm water (110° to 115°)
- 4 teaspoons butter, melted
- 1 teaspoon salt
- 2-3/4 to 3 cups bread flour

SPINACH DOUGH:
- 1/4 cup cold water
- 1 package (10 ounces) frozen chopped spinach, thawed and squeezed dry
- 1 package (1/4 ounce) active dry yeast
- 3/4 cup warm water (110° to 115°)
- 4 teaspoons butter, melted
- 1 teaspoon salt
- 3-1/4 to 3-1/2 cups bread flour

TOMATO DOUGH:
- 1 package (1/4 ounce) active dry yeast
- 1 cup warm water (110° to 115°)
- 4 teaspoons butter, melted
- 1 teaspoon salt
- 1 can (6 ounces) tomato paste
- 3-1/4 to 3-3/4 cups bread flour
- 1 egg white
- 1 teaspoon cold water

For plain dough, in a large mixing bowl, dissolve yeast in warm water. Add butter, salt and 2 cups flour; beat until smooth. Add enough remaining flour to form a firm dough.

Turn onto a lightly floured surface; knead until smooth and elastic, about 6-8 minutes. Place in a greased bowl, turning once to grease top. Cover and refrigerate overnight.

For spinach dough, puree cold water and spinach in a food processor. In a large mixing bowl, dissolve yeast in warm water. Add butter, salt, 2 cups flour and spinach mixture; beat until smooth. Add enough remaining flour to form a firm dough. Turn onto a lightly floured surface. With lightly floured hands, knead until smooth and elastic, about 6-8 minutes. Place in a greased bowl, turning once to grease top. Cover and refrigerate overnight.

For tomato dough, in a large mixing bowl, dissolve yeast in warm water. Add butter, salt, tomato paste and 2 cups flour; beat until smooth. Add enough remaining flour to form a firm dough. Turn onto a lightly floured surface. With lightly floured hands, knead until smooth and elastic, about 6-8 minutes. Place in a greased bowl, turning once to grease top. Cover and refrigerate overnight.

Punch down each dough and divide in half; cover. On a lightly floured surface, roll out one portion of each dough into a 10-in. x 8-in. rectangle. Place a rectangle of spinach dough on plain dough; top with tomato dough. Roll into a 12-in. x 10-in. rectangle. Roll up jelly-roll style, starting with a long side; pinch seams to seal and tuck ends under. Place seam side down on a greased baking sheet. Repeat with remaining dough.

Cover and let rise in a warm place until doubled, about 30 minutes. With a sharp knife, make three shallow diagonal slashes across the top of each loaf. Beat egg white and cold water; brush over loaves. Bake at 350° for 35-45 minutes or until loaves are golden brown. Remove to wire racks to cool. **Yield:** 2 loaves.

Rich Cheese Bread

Linda Bamber, Bolivar, Missouri

Our two sons always request this cheesy bread during the holidays. It's a favorite to serve with soup or to use for making sandwiches.

- 5 to 6 cups bread flour
- 1/2 cup cornmeal
- 1 package (1/4 ounce) active dry yeast
- 1/2 teaspoon salt
- 2 cups water
- 1/2 cup molasses
- 2 tablespoons butter
- 8 ounces process cheese (Velveeta), cut into 1/2-inch cubes

Additional cornmeal

In a large bowl, combine 2 cups flour, cornmeal, yeast and salt. In a large saucepan, heat the water, molasses and butter to 120°-130°. Add to flour mixture; beat just until moistened. Stir in enough of the remaining flour to form a soft dough.

Turn onto a floured surface; knead until smooth and elastic, about 6-8 minutes. Cover and let rise in a warm place until doubled, about 1 hour.

Punch dough down. Turn onto a lightly floured surface; divide in half. Work half of the cheese cubes into each portion of dough. Shape into round loaves.

Place in two greased 9-in. round baking pans. Sprinkle with additional cornmeal. Cover and let rise in a warm place until doubled, about 1 hour.

Bake at 350° for 45-50 minutes or until golden brown. Remove from pan to wire racks to cool. Store in the refrigerator. **Yield:** 2 loaves (16 slices each).

Jalapeno Garlic Bread

Natalie Ann Gallagher, Clovis, California

My mother loves spicy foods, so I created this crusty, rustic loaf just to suit her taste. Now my whole family enjoys its zesty flavor and asks for it often.

    1   cup warm fat-free milk (70° to 80°)
  1/2   cup egg substitute
    2   tablespoons butter, melted
    1   teaspoon salt
    2   cups bread flour
    2   cups whole wheat flour
  1/4   cup sugar
    2   teaspoons active dry yeast
FILLING:
  3/4   cup chopped seeded jalapeno peppers
    3   garlic cloves, minced
    5   teaspoons butter, softened, *divided*
    1   teaspoon garlic salt
    3   tablespoons grated Parmesan cheese, *divided*

In bread machine pan, place the first eight ingredients in order suggested by manufacturer. Select dough setting (check dough after 5 minutes of mixing; add 1 to 2 tablespoons of water or flour if needed).

In a small bowl, combine the jalapenos and garlic; set aside. When cycle is completed, turn dough onto a lightly floured surface. Divide dough in half.

For each loaf, roll one portion of dough into a 14-in. x 9-in. rectangle. Spread with 1-1/2 teaspoons butter. Sprinkle with 1/2 teaspoon garlic salt, 1 tablespoon Parmesan cheese and 1/3 cup jalapeno mixture. Roll up jelly-roll style, starting with a short side; pinch seam to seal. Place in a 9-in. x 5-in. x 3-in. loaf pan coated with cooking spray. Cover and let rise in a warm place until doubled, about 40 minutes.

Melt remaining butter; brush over loaves. Sprinkle with remaining Parmesan cheese and jalapeno mixture. Bake at 350° for 40-50 minutes or until golden brown. Remove from pans to wire racks to cool. **Yield:** 2 loaves (12 slices each).

Editor's Note: When cutting hot peppers, disposable gloves are recommended. Avoid touching your face.

Mom's Dinner Rolls

Patricia Collins, Imbler, Oregon

My mother was always experimenting with recipes. She had a knack for combining the right ingredients. This is one of my most treasured recipes she shared with me.

  1/4   cup finely chopped onion
    4   garlic cloves, minced
  1/4   cup butter, cubed
    1   teaspoon dried basil
    1   teaspoon dried oregano
  1/2   teaspoon *each* dried marjoram, tarragon and
         parsley flakes
    1   package (1/4 ounce) active dry yeast
  3/4   cup warm water (110° to 115°)
    1   teaspoon sugar
    1   teaspoon salt
    2   cups all-purpose flour
    1   egg, lightly beaten

In a small skillet, saute onion and garlic in butter until tender. Stir in herbs; cool. In a food processor, dissolve yeast in warm water. Add the sugar, salt and onion mixture. Add flour; cover and process until dough forms a smooth ball.

Turn onto a floured surface; knead until smooth and elastic, about 6-8 minutes. Place in a greased bowl, turning once to grease top. Cover and let rise in a warm place until doubled, about 1 hour.

Punch dough down. Turn onto a floured surface; divide into 24 pieces. Shape each into a ball. Place 2 in. apart on greased baking sheets. Cover and let rise in a warm place until doubled, about 30 minutes.

Brush with egg. Bake at 350° for 20-25 minutes or until golden brown. Remove from pans to wire racks. Serve warm. **Yield:** 2 dozen.

Kansas Whole Wheat Bread

Linda Pauls, Buhler, Kansas

This lightly textured wheat bread won an award at the Celebrate Kansas Wheat Bake-Off several years ago.

2-1/2   cups whole wheat flour
1/2   cup quick-cooking oats
1/4   cup toasted wheat germ
2   packages (1/4 ounce *each*) active dry yeast
2   teaspoons salt
1   cup water
1   cup (8 ounces) 4% cottage cheese
1/2   cup mashed potatoes (without added milk *or* butter)
1/4   cup butter, softened
1/4   cup milk
1/4   cup honey
2   tablespoons molasses
2   eggs
3   to 4 cups all-purpose flour

In a large bowl, combine the whole wheat flour, oats, wheat germ, yeast and salt. In a saucepan, heat the water, cottage cheese, potatoes, butter, milk, honey and molasses to 120°-130°. Add to flour mixture; beat just until moistened. Add eggs; beat until smooth. Stir in enough all-purpose flour to form a soft dough. Turn onto a floured surface; knead until smooth and elastic, about 8-10 minutes.

Place in a greased bowl, turning once to grease top. Cover and let rise in a warm place until doubled, about 1 hour.

Punch dough down. Turn onto a lightly floured surface; divide in half. Shape into two flattened balls. Place on two greased baking sheets. Cover and let rise until doubled, about 45 minutes.

With a sharp knife, make a shallow "X-shaped" cut in the top of each loaf. Bake at 350° for 35-40 minutes. Cover loosely with foil if top browns too quickly. Remove from pans to wire racks to cool. **Yield:** 2 loaves (12 slices each).

Savory Wheat Crescents

Martha Larson, Great Falls, Montana

Parmesan cheese and garlic salt give these hearty crescent rolls a scrumptious, savory flavor.

1   package (1/4 ounce) active dry yeast
1/2   cup warm water (110° to 115°)
8-1/2   teaspoons honey, *divided*
2   cups whole wheat flour
3/4   cup warm milk (110° to 115°)
6   tablespoons butter, softened, *divided*
1   egg
1   teaspoon salt
1-3/4   to 2-1/4 cups all-purpose flour
1/4   cup grated Parmesan cheese
1/4   teaspoon garlic salt

In a large bowl, dissolve yeast in warm water. Stir in 2 teaspoons honey; let stand for 5 minutes. Add the whole wheat flour, milk, 2 tablespoons butter, egg, salt, remaining honey and 1 cup all-purpose flour. Beat on medium speed for 3 minutes. Stir in enough remaining all-purpose flour to form a soft dough.

Turn onto a floured surface; knead until smooth and elastic, about 6-8 minutes. Place in a greased bowl, turning once to grease top. Cover and let rise in a warm place until doubled, about 1 hour.

Punch dough down. Knead on a floured surface for 30 seconds. Roll into a 12-in. circle. Melt remaining butter; brush over dough. Combine Parmesan cheese and garlic salt; sprinkle over dough.

Cut into 16 wedges. Roll up wedges from the wide end and place with pointed end down on greased baking sheets. Curve ends to form a crescent shape. Cover and let rise in a warm place until doubled, about 20 minutes.

Bake at 400° for 12-15 minutes or until golden brown. Remove from pans to wire racks to cool. **Yield:** 16 rolls.

60-Minute Mini Breads

Holly Hill, Franklin, Texas

When I was 11 years old, I entered this bread at our county fair. It beat out more than 90 food entries to win Junior Grand Champion and Best of Show! Sometimes I make one large loaf instead of two mini loaves.

3   cups all-purpose flour
1   tablespoon sugar
1   teaspoon salt
1   package (1/4 ounce) quick-rise yeast
3/4   cup water
1/4   cup milk
2   tablespoons butter

In a large bowl, combine 2 cups flour, sugar, salt and yeast. In a saucepan, heat the water, milk and butter to 120°-130°. Add to flour mixture. Beat on medium speed for 2 minutes. Add 1/2 cup flour; beat 2 minutes longer. Stir in enough remaining flour to form a soft dough.

Turn onto a floured surface; knead until smooth and elastic, about 6-8 minutes. Do not let rise. Divide in half. Roll each portion into an 8-in. x 5-in. rectangle.

Roll up jelly-roll style, starting with a short side; pinch seam to seal. Place seam side down in two greased 5-in. x 3-in. x 2-in. loaf pans. Fill a 13-in. x 9-in. x 2-in. baking pan with 1 in. of hot water. Set loaf pans in water.

Cover and let rise for 15 minutes. Remove loaf pans from the water bath. Bake at 400° for 20-25 minutes or until golden brown. Remove from pans to wire racks to cool. **Yield:** 2 mini loaves (4 slices each).

Caraway Puffs

Glennis Endrud, Buxton, North Dakota

Our daughter took these light-as-a-feather rolls to a 4-H event and came home with a Grand Champion ribbon! We think they're especially good served straight from the oven.

    1   package (1/4 ounce) active dry yeast
  1/4   cup warm water (110° to 115°)
    1   cup (8 ounces) warm 4% cottage cheese (110° to 115°)
    2   tablespoons sugar
    1   tablespoon butter, softened
    2   teaspoons caraway seeds
    1   teaspoon salt
  1/4   teaspoon baking soda
2-1/3   cups all-purpose flour
    1   egg

In a large bowl, dissolve yeast in warm water. Add the cottage cheese, sugar, butter, caraway seeds, salt, baking soda and 1-1/3 cups flour. Beat on medium speed for 3 minutes. Add egg and 1/2 cup flour; beat 2 minutes longer. Stir in enough remaining flour to form a firm dough (batter will be stiff). Do not knead. Cover and let rise in a warm place until doubled, about 45 minutes. Stir dough down.

Spoon into greased muffin cups. Cover and let rise in a warm place until doubled, about 35 minutes.

Bake at 400° for 12-14 minutes or until golden brown. Cool in pan for 1 minute. Serve immediately. **Yield:** 1 dozen.

Stromboli Ladder Loaf

Chrystie Wear, Greensboro, North Carolina

My bread maker is the key for this tasty filled pizza. For variation, add veggies to the filling or make it a Rueben with salad dressing, corned beef, sauerkraut and Swiss cheese.

1-1/2 cups water (70° to 80°)
   2 tablespoons canola oil
   1 teaspoon lemon juice
   2 tablespoons nonfat dry milk powder
   2 tablespoons sugar
   1 teaspoon salt
   4 cups bread flour
   3 teaspoons active dry yeast
FILLING:
 3/4 cup pizza sauce
   1 package (3-1/2 ounces) sliced pepperoni
   2 cups (8 ounces) shredded part-skim mozzarella cheese
 1/2 cup grated Parmesan cheese
   1 egg white
   1 tablespoon water

In bread machine pan, place the first eight ingredients in order suggested by manufacturer. Select dough setting (check dough after 5 minutes of mixing; add 1-2 tablespoons of water or flour if needed). When cycle is completed, turn dough onto a floured surface. Roll into a 15-in. x 12-in. rectangle. Place on a greased baking sheet.

Spread pizza sauce in a 3-in. strip lengthwise down the center of dough to within 2 in. of short ends. Arrange pepperoni over sauce; sprinkle with cheeses. On each long side, cut 1-in.-wide strips about 2-1/2 in. into center. Starting at one end, fold alternating strips at an angle across filling. Pinch ends to seal.

Beat egg white and water; brush over dough. Bake at 425° for 20-25 minutes or until golden brown. Let stand for 10 minutes before cutting. **Yield:** 1 loaf (2 pounds).

Editor's Note: We recommend you do not use a bread machine's time-delay feature for this recipe.

Overnight Whole Wheat Rolls

Denise Fidler, Syracuse, Indiana

I love to bake and even have a small business selling bread. Making rolls and bread from scratch is an art easily mastered with practice. The swirled shape of these rolls is very attractive.

    2   packages (1/4 ounce *each*) active dry yeast
1-1/4   cups warm water (110° to 115°)
  3/4   cup butter, melted, *divided*
  1/2   cup honey
    2   teaspoons salt
    3   eggs
    2   cups whole wheat flour
    3   cups all-purpose flour
Additonal melted butter

In a large bowl, dissolve yeast in warm water. Add 1/2 cup butter, honey, salt, eggs, whole wheat flour and 1/2 cup all-purpose flour. Beat until smooth. Stir in enough remaining all-purpose flour to form a soft dough.

Do not knead. Place in a greased bowl, turning once to grease top. Cover and let rise in a warm place until doubled, about 1 hour. Punch dough down. Cover and refrigerate overnight.

Punch dough down. Turn onto a lightly floured surface; divide in half. Roll each into a 15-in. x 8-in. rectangle. Brush with remaining butter to within 1/2 in. of edges. Roll up jelly-roll style, starting with a long side; pinch seam to seal. Cut each into 15 rolls.

Place rolls cut side up in greased muffin cups. Cover and let rise in a warm place until doubled, about 45 minutes.

Bake at 400° for 8-10 minutes or until golden brown. Remove from pans to wire racks. Brush with additional butter. Cool. **Yield:** 2-1/2 dozen.

Italian Cheese Loaves

Tin Molitor, New Market, Minnesota

This quick-and-easy yeast bread is a favorite of my daughter and my best friend. They could eat an entire loaf!

    2   packages (1/4 ounce *each*) active dry yeast
    3   cups warm water (110° to 115°)
    3   tablespoons shortening
    3   tablespoons sugar
  1/2   teaspoon salt
    7   to 8 cups all-purpose flour
  1/2   cup shredded part-skim mozzarella cheese
  1/4   cup shredded cheddar cheese
  1/4   teaspoon garlic powder
  1/4   teaspoon onion powder

In a large bowl, dissolve yeast in warm water. Add the shortening, sugar, salt and 4 cups flour. Beat until smooth. Add the cheeses, garlic powder and onion powder. Stir in enough remaining flour to form a soft dough.

Turn onto a floured surface; knead until smooth and elastic, about 6-8 minutes. Do not let rise. Divide in half; shape into two loaves.

Place in two greased 9-in. x 5-in. x 3-in. loaf pans. Do not let rise. Bake at 350° for 25-30 minutes or until golden brown. Remove from pans to wire racks to cool. Store in the refrigerator. **Yield:** 2 loaves (16 slices each).

Traditional Pita Bread

Lynne Hartke, Chandler, Arizona

My husband taught me how to make this pita bread when we were first dating. He's always looking out for good recipes.

    1   package (1/4 ounce) active dry yeast
1-1/4   cups warm water (110° to 115°)
    2   teaspoons salt
    3   to 3-1/2 cups all-purpose flour

In a large bowl, dissolve yeast in warm water. Stir in salt and enough flour to form a soft dough. Turn onto a floured surface; knead until smooth and elastic, about 6-8 minutes. Do not let rise.

Divide dough into six pieces; knead each for 1 minute. Roll each into a 5-in. circle. Cover and let rise in a warm place until doubled, about 45 minutes.

Place upside down on greased baking sheets. Bake at 500° for 5-10 minutes. Remove from pans to wire racks to cool. **Yield:** 6 pita breads.

Two-Grain Yeast Rolls

Susan Plumb, Acworth, Georgia

Our weekly menu features these homemade oatmeal-potato rolls at least once. Depending on the meal, I may sprinkle them with cinnamon and brown sugar or brush on garlic butter. The possibilities are endless.

- 1/2   cup cubed peeled potatoes
- 1/2   cup quick-cooking oats
- 1/2   cup butter, softened, *divided*
- 2   packages (1/4 ounce *each*) active dry yeast
- 1   cup warm water (110° to 115°)
- 2   eggs
- 2/3   cup sugar
- 1   teaspoon salt
- 4   cups bread flour
- 1   to 1-1/4 cups whole wheat flour

Poppy seeds *or* sesame seeds, optional

Place potatoes in a small saucepan and cover with water. Bring to a boil; cook until tender. Drain, reserving 3 tablespoons water. Combine oats and reserved water (mixture will be crumbly). In a large bowl, mash the potatoes. Stir in 6 tablespoons butter until blended (potatoes will be very soft). Stir in oat mixture.

In a large bowl, dissolve yeast in warm water. Add the eggs, sugar, salt, 2 cups bread flour and potato mixture. Beat until smooth. Stir in remaining bread flour and enough whole wheat flour to form a stiff dough.

Turn onto a floured surface; knead until smooth and elastic, about 6-8 minutes. Place in a greased bowl, turning once to grease top. Cover and refrigerate overnight.

Punch dough down. Turn onto a lightly floured surface; divide into 32 pieces. Shape each piece into a ball. Place in two greased 9-in. round baking pans. Cover and let rise in a warm place until doubled, about 1 hour.

Bake at 350° for 24-30 minutes or until golden brown. Remove from pans to wire racks. Melt remaining butter; brush over rolls. Sprinkle with poppy or sesame seeds if desired. **Yield:** 32 rolls.

Crusty French Bread

Deanna Naivar, Temple, Texas

A delicate texture makes this bread absolutely wonderful. I sometimes use the dough to make breadsticks, which I brush with melted butter and sprinkle with garlic powder.

- 1   package (1/4 ounce) active dry yeast
- 1   cup warm water (110° to 115°)
- 2   tablespoons sugar
- 2   tablespoons canola oil
- 1-1/2   teaspoons salt
- 3   to 3-1/4 cups all-purpose flour

Cornmeal
- 1   egg white
- 1   teaspoon cold water

In a large bowl, dissolve yeast in warm water. Add the sugar, oil, salt and 2 cups flour. Beat until blended. Stir in enough remaining flour to form a stiff dough.

Turn onto a floured surface; knead until smooth and elastic, about 6-8 minutes. Place in a greased bowl, turning once to grease top. Cover and let rise in a warm place until doubled, about 1 hour. Punch dough down; return to bowl. Cover and let rise for 30 minutes.

Punch dough down. Turn onto a lightly floured surface. Shape into a 16-in. x 2-1/2-in. loaf with tapered ends. Sprinkle a greased baking sheet with cornmeal; place loaf on baking sheet. Cover and let rise until doubled, about 25 minutes.

Beat egg white and cold water; brush over dough. With a sharp knife, make diagonal slashes 2 in. apart across top of loaf. Bake at 375° for 25-30 minutes or until golden brown. Remove from pan to a wire rack to cool. **Yield:** 1 loaf (16 slices).

Making Slashes Slashing or scoring the top of a bread loaf allows steam to vent and helps prevent cracking. When you make slashes in the dough, always use a sharp knife and make the slashes shallow, not too deep.

2 teaspoons celery seed
1-1/2 teaspoons salt
1 teaspoon rubbed sage
1/4 to 1/2 teaspoon ground nutmeg
1 egg
3 to 3-1/2 cups all-purpose flour

In a large bowl, dissolve yeast in warm water. Add the milk, sugar, shortening, celery seed, salt, sage, nutmeg, egg and 2 cups flour. Beat until smooth. Stir in enough remaining flour to form a soft dough.

Turn onto a floured surface; knead until smooth and elastic, about 6-8 minutes. Place in a greased bowl, turning once to grease top. Cover and let rise in a warm place until doubled, about 1-1/2 hours.

Punch dough down. Shape into a round loaf. Place in a greased 8-in. or 9-in. pie plate. Cover and let rise in a warm place until doubled, about 45 minutes.

Bake at 400° for 35-40 minutes or until golden brown and bread sounds hollow when tapped. Remove from pie plate to a wire rack to cool. **Yield:** 1 loaf (16 slices).

Buttermilk Onion Bread

Joan Powers, East Wenatchee, Washington

This oniony bread is a snap to prepare in the bread machine. It's perfect served warm with dinner or when used to make hearty sandwiches. It smells great while baking.

1 cup plus 2 tablespoons warm buttermilk (70° to 80°)
1 tablespoon butter
2-1/2 cups bread flour
1/2 cup whole wheat flour
3 tablespoons sugar
1 tablespoon dried minced onion
1 tablespoon dried parsley flakes
1-1/2 teaspoons salt
1 teaspoon dill weed
2-1/4 teaspoons active dry yeast

In bread machine pan, place all ingredients in order suggested by manufacturer. Select basic bread setting. Choose crust color and loaf size if available. Bake according to bread machine directions (check dough after 5 minutes of mixing; add 1 to 2 tablespoons of water or flour if needed). **Yield:** 1 loaf (1-1/2 pounds, 16 slices).

Country Sage Bread

Norma Round, Sparks, Nevada

A friend gave me this recipe years ago. The unique combination of sage, celery seed and nutmeg makes this bread deliciously different.

1 package (1/4 ounce) active dry yeast
1/4 cup warm water (110° to 115°)
3/4 cup warm milk (110° to 115°)
2 tablespoons sugar
2 tablespoons shortening

Pumpkin Cloverleaf Rolls

Donna Bucher, Tirane, Albania

I came up with this recipe when I was looking for something festive to take to an autumn covered-dish dinner. These rolls were a big hit.

1 package (1/4 ounce) active dry yeast
1/4 cup warm water (110° to 115°)
10 teaspoons brown sugar, *divided*
1 cup warm milk (110° to 115°)
1 cup canned pumpkin
6 tablespoons butter, melted
4-1/2 teaspoons grated orange peel
1 tablespoon salt
4-1/4 to 4-3/4 cups all-purpose flour
1 egg, lightly beaten

In a large bowl, dissolve yeast in warm water. Add 1 teaspoon brown sugar; let stand for 5 minutes. Add the milk, pumpkin, butter, orange peel, salt, remaining sugar and 2 cups flour. Beat on medium speed for 2 minutes. Stir in enough remaining flour to form a soft dough.

Turn onto a floured surface; knead until smooth and elastic, about 10 minutes. Place in a greased bowl, turning once to grease top. Cover and let rise in a warm place until doubled, about 1 hour.

Punch dough down. Turn onto a lightly floured surface; knead until smooth and elastic, about 6-8 minutes.

Divide into six portions. Divide each into 12 pieces. Shape each into a ball; place three balls in each greased muffin cup. Cover and let rise until doubled, about 30 minutes.

Brush rolls with egg. Bake at 400° for 20-25 minutes or until golden brown. Remove from pans to wire racks to cool. **Yield:** 2 dozen.

Soft Pretzels

Lucinda Walker, Somerset, Pennsylvania

Big soft pretzels are all the rage in shopping malls across the country. I think it's worth the time to make them from scratch to get the incomparable homemade taste.

        2   packages (1/4 ounce *each*) active dry yeast
        2   cups warm water (110° to 115°)
    1/2   cup sugar
    1/4   cup butter, softened
        2   teaspoons salt
        1   egg
6-1/2   to 7-1/2 cups all-purpose flour
        1   egg yolk
        2   tablespoons cold water
Coarse salt

In a large bowl, dissolve yeast in warm water. Add the sugar, butter, salt, egg and 2 cups flour. Beat until smooth. Stir in enough remaining flour to form a stiff dough. Place in a greased bowl, turning once to grease top. Cover and refrigerate for 2-24 hours.

Punch dough down. Turn onto a lightly floured surface; divide in half. Cut each into 16 pieces. Roll each piece into a 20-in. rope. Shape into a pretzel.

Place on greased baking sheets. Beat egg yolk and cold water; brush over pretzels. Sprinkle with coarse salt. Cover and let rise in a warm place until doubled, about 25 minutes.

Bake at 400° for 15-20 minutes or until golden brown. Remove from pans to wire racks to cool. **Yield:** 32 pretzels.

Storing Yeast Breads Completely cool unsliced yeast bread before placing in an airtight container or a resealable plastic bag. Yeast bread will stay fresh at room temperature for 2 to 3 days. Bread with cream cheese or other perishable ingredients should be stored in the refrigerator. For longer storage, freeze bread in an airtight container or resealable plastic bag for up to 3 months.

Oatmeal Mini Loaves

Doris Kosmicki, Pinckney, Michigan

I first came across this recipe in an old cookbook. As I became more brave with bread baking, I decided to redo this recipe, changing and adding ingredients to enhance flavor and nutrition.

1-1/2 cups old-fashioned oats
3/4 cup whole wheat flour
1/2 cup packed brown sugar
1/4 cup toasted wheat germ
3 teaspoons salt
1 package (1/4 ounce) active dry yeast
2-1/2 cups water
2 tablespoons butter
5-1/2 to 6 cups all-purpose flour
Melted butter, optional
Additional old-fashioned oats, optional

In a large bowl, combine the oats, whole wheat flour, brown sugar, wheat germ, salt and yeast. In a small saucepan, heat water and butter to 120°-130°. Add to flour mixture just until moistened. Add 3 cups all-purpose flour; beat until smooth. Stir in enough remaining all-purpose flour to form a soft dough.

Turn onto a floured surface; knead until smooth and elastic, about 6-8 minutes. Place in a greased bowl, turning once to grease top. Cover and let rise in a warm place until doubled, about 1 hour.

Punch dough down. Turn onto a lightly floured surface; divide into five portions. Shape each into a loaf. Place in five greased 5-in. x 3-in. x 2-in. loaf pans. Cover and let rise until doubled, about 30 minutes.

Bake at 350° for 30-35 minutes or until golden brown. Remove from pans to wire racks. Brush with melted butter; sprinkle with additional oats if desired. Cool. **Yield:** 5 mini loaves (5 slices each).

Editor's Note: Two greased 9-in. x 5-in. x 3-in. loaf pans may be used; bake for 35-40 minutes.

Hearty Raisin Bread

Maureen Cerza, Wilmington, Illinois

Although I just recently moved to the country, I love from-scratch cooking, and baking bread is a favorite pastime. This rich bread has a delectable cinnamon flavor and is loaded with raisins.

- 2 packages (1/4 ounce *each*) active dry yeast
- 1/2 cup warm water (110° to 115°)
- 1-1/2 cups warm milk (110° to 115°)
- 1/2 cup butter, melted
- 1/4 cup honey
- 2 teaspoons salt
- 1-1/2 teaspoons ground cinnamon
- 2 eggs
- 3 cups whole wheat flour
- 3-1/2 to 4 cups all-purpose flour
- 2 cups raisins
- 1 egg white
- 2 tablespoons cold water

In a bowl, dissolve yeast in warm water. Add the milk, butter, honey, salt, cinnamon, eggs and whole wheat flour. Beat until smooth. Stir in enough all-purpose flour to form a soft dough. Turn onto a floured surface; knead until smooth and elastic, about 8-10 minutes.

Place in a greased bowl, turning once to grease top. Cover and let rise in a warm place until doubled, about 1 hour.

Punch dough down. Turn onto a lightly floured surface; sprinkle with raisins and knead in. Divide in half. Shape into loaves. Place in two greased 9-in. x 5-in. x 3-in. loaf pans. Cover and let rise until doubled, about 45 minutes.

Beat egg white and cold water; brush over dough. Bake at 375° for 35-40 minutes or until golden brown and bread sounds hollow when tapped. Cover loosely with foil if top browns too quickly. Remove from pans to wire racks to cool. **Yield:** 2 loaves (16 slices each).

Potato Casserole Bread

Lisa Powers, Leadore, Idaho

Potatoes make this bread tender and delicious. It freezes well, so you can enjoy one loaf right away and freeze the other to have later.

- 2 packages (1/4 ounce *each*) active dry yeast
- 1/2 cup warm water (110° to 115°)
- 1 can (12 ounces) evaporated milk
- 2 cups mashed potatoes (without added milk *or* butter)
- 8 bacon strips, cooked and crumbled
- 1/4 cup butter, softened
- 2 eggs
- 3 tablespoons sugar
- 2 tablespoons dried minced onion
- 1 tablespoon caraway seeds
- 1 teaspoon garlic salt
- 1 teaspoon salt
- 6-1/4 to 6-3/4 cups all-purpose flour

In a large bowl, dissolve yeast in warm water. Add the milk, potatoes, bacon, butter, eggs, sugar, onion, caraway seeds, garlic salt, salt and 3 cups flour. Beat until smooth. Stir in enough remaining flour to form a soft dough.

Turn onto a floured surface; knead until smooth and elastic, about 6-8 minutes. Place in a greased bowl, turning once to grease top. Cover and let rise in a warm place until doubled, about 1 hour.

Punch dough down. Turn onto a lightly floured surface; divide in half. Shape each into a round loaf. Place in two greased 2-qt. round baking dishes with straight sides. Cover and let rise in a warm place until doubled, about 40 minutes.

Bake at 350° for 40-50 minutes or until golden brown. Remove from baking dishes to wire racks to cool. **Yield:** 2 loaves (16 slices each).

Proofing Yeast To make sure active dry yeast (not quick-rise yeast) is alive and active, you may first want to proof it. To proof, dissolve one package of yeast and 1 teaspoon sugar in 1/4 cup warm water (110° to 115°). Let stand for 5 to 10 minutes. If the mixture foams up, the yeast is alive and active. If it does not foam, the yeast should be discarded.

Coffee Cakes & Sweet Rolls

pg. 87

pg. 81

pg. 88

pg. 79

Giant Upside-Down Pecan Rolls

Janet Miller, Lafayette, Indiana

I like to keep a baked batch of these extra-large sweet rolls in the freezer to surprise my family on weekends. To reheat, thaw in the refrigerator overnight, wrap in foil and bake at 350° for 20 to 30 minutes or until heated through.

- 2 packages (1/4 ounce *each*) active dry yeast
- 1/2 cup warm water (110° to 115°)
- 1-3/4 cups sugar, *divided*
- 2/3 cup warm milk (110° to 115°)
- 3/4 cup butter, softened, *divided*
- 1 teaspoon salt
- 1 egg
- 1 egg yolk
- 4-3/4 to 5-1/4 cups all-purpose flour
- 1 tablespoon ground cinnamon
- 1 cup chopped pecans

BROWN SUGAR-NUT SYRUP:
- 1 cup packed dark brown sugar
- 1/4 cup butter, cubed
- 2 tablespoons water
- 1 cup pecan halves

EGG WASH:
- 1 egg white
- 1 teaspoon water

In a large bowl, dissolve yeast in warm water. Add 3/4 cup sugar, milk, 1/2 cup butter, salt, egg, egg yolk and 3 cups flour. Beat on medium speed for 3 minutes. Stir in enough remaining flour to form a soft dough.

Turn onto a floured surface; knead until smooth and elastic, about 6-8 minutes. Place in a greased bowl, turning once to grease top. Cover and let rise in a warm place until doubled, about 1-1/2 hours.

Punch dough down. Turn onto lightly floured surface. Roll into a 24-in. x 18-in. rectangle. Melt remaining butter; brush over dough. Combine cinnamon and remaining sugar; sprinkle to within 1/2 in. of edges. Sprinkle with pecans. Roll up jelly-roll style, starting with a short side; pinch seam to seal. Cut into six slices.

For syrup, combine the brown sugar, butter and water in a saucepan. Bring to a boil; boil and stir for 1 minute. Pour into a greased 13-in. x 9-in. x 2-in. baking. Arrange pecan halves, flat side up, over syrup. Place rolls cut side down over pecans. Press down gently. Cover and let rise until doubled, about 1 hour.

Beat egg white and water; brush over rolls. Bake at 350° for 35-40 minutes or until golden brown. Immediately invert onto a serving platter. **Yield:** 6 rolls.

Lemon Yogurt Muffins

Nicole Horne, Macon, Georgia

I only had this recipe a short time before it became a personal favorite. Folks like the light and tender texture of these muffins. I'm grateful to my mother, who taught me the goodness of baking from scratch.

- 1-3/4 cups all-purpose flour
- 3/4 cup sugar
- 1 tablespoon grated lemon peel
- 1 teaspoon baking powder
- 3/4 teaspoon baking soda
- 1/4 teaspoon salt
- 1 egg
- 1 cup (8 ounces) lemon *or* plain yogurt
- 6 tablespoons butter, melted
- 1 tablespoon lemon juice

TOPPING:
- 1/3 cup lemon juice
- 1/4 cup sugar
- 1 teaspoon grated lemon peel

In a large bowl, combine the flour, sugar, lemon peel, baking powder, baking soda and salt. In another bowl, whisk the egg, yogurt, butter and lemon juice. Stir into flour mixture just until moistened.

Fill greased or paper-lined muffin cups two-thirds full. Bake at 400° for 20-24 minutes or until a toothpick inserted near the center comes out clean. Cool for 5 minutes; leave muffins in pan.

Using a toothpick, poke 6-8 holes in each muffin. In a saucepan, combine the topping ingredients. Cook and stir over low heat until sugar is dissolved. Spoon over warm muffins. **Yield:** 1 dozen.

Blueberry Streusel Coffee Cake

Eunice Sawatzky, Lowe Farm, Manitoba

My sister-in-law made this coffee cake with the fresh blueberries we picked while our families were vacationing at her cottage one summer. I've used frozen berries at home with wonderful results. Each time I bake this bread, we're reminded of those fun times.

1/2	cup butter, softened
1-3/4	cups sugar
2	eggs
2	teaspoons vanilla extract
3-1/2	cups all-purpose flour
2	tablespoons baking powder
1	teaspoon salt
1-1/2	cups milk
3	cups fresh *or* frozen blueberries

STREUSEL TOPPING:

3/4	cup sugar
1/2	teaspoon ground cinnamon
1/3	cup cold butter

In a large bowl, cream butter and sugar until light and fluffy. Beat in eggs and vanilla until blended. Combine the flour, baking powder and salt; add to creamed mixture alternately with milk, beating well after each addition. Fold in blueberries.

Pour into a greased 13-in. x 9-in. x 2-in. baking dish. For topping, combine sugar and cinnamon. Cut in butter until mixture resembles coarse crumbs. Sprinkle over batter.

Bake at 375° for 35-40 minutes or until a toothpick inserted near the comes out clean. Cool in pan on a wire rack. **Yield:** 12-16 servings.

Editor's Note: If using frozen blueberries, do not thaw before adding to batter.

Change it Up Fresh or frozen cranberries or pitted cherries can be used in place of the blueberries in Blueberry Streusel Coffee Cake. If the cherries are large, you may want to cut them in half.

Mashed Potato Doughnuts

Tammy Evans, Nepean, Ontario

As a special treat in winter, my parents would make a double batch of these doughnuts to welcome us six kids home from school. This recipe from my great-aunt has been handed down through the generations.

- 1 package (1/4 ounce) active dry yeast
- 1 cup warm buttermilk (110° to 115°)
- 1-1/2 cups warm mashed potatoes (without added milk and butter)
- 3 eggs
- 1/3 cup butter, melted
- 3 cups sugar, *divided*
- 4 teaspoons baking powder
- 1-1/2 teaspoons baking soda
- 1 teaspoon salt
- 1 teaspoon ground nutmeg
- 6 cups all-purpose flour
- Oil for deep-fat frying
- 1/2 teaspoon ground cinnamon

In a large bowl, dissolve yeast in warm buttermilk. Add the potatoes, eggs and butter. Add 2 cups sugar, baking powder, baking soda, salt, nutmeg and 3 cups flour. Beat until smooth. Stir in enough remaining flour to form a soft dough. Do not knead. Cover and refrigerate for 2 hours.

Turn onto a floured surface; divide into fourths. Roll each portion to 1/2-in. thickness. Cut with a floured 3-in. doughnut cutter. In an electric skillet or deep-fat fryer, heat oil to 375°. Fry doughnuts, a few at a time, until golden brown on both sides. Drain on paper towels. Combine remaining sugar and cinnamon; roll doughnuts in cinnamon-sugar while warm. **Yield:** about 2 dozen.

Editor's Note: Warmed buttermilk will appear curdled.

Lemon-Glazed Poppy Seed Ring

Betty Hass, Fort Myers, Florida

I like to modify existing recipes to be more interesting. This bread is a combination of three old standbys: the poppy seed kolaches my Ukranian grandmother used to make, the cinnamon rolls I learned to make in Girl Scouts and the lemon glaze from my favorite bundt cake.

- 1 tube (17.3 ounces) large refrigerated biscuits
- 1/2 cup poppy seed filling

GLAZE:
- 1 cup confectioners' sugar
- 2 tablespoons lemon juice

Do not separate biscuits. Place on a greased baking sheet and pat into a 14-in. x 8-in. rectangle. Spread poppy seed filling to within 1/2 in. of edges. Roll up jelly-roll style, starting with a long side; pinch seam to seal. Bring ends together to form a ring; pinch ends to seal.

With scissors, cut from outside edge to two-thirds of the way toward center of ring at 1-in. intervals. Gently stretch ring to form a 4-1/2-in. center. Separate strips slightly; twist to allow filling to show.

Bake at 375° for 15-17 minutes or until golden brown. Remove from pan to a wire rack. Combine glaze ingredients; drizzle over warm coffee cake. Cool. **Yield:** 1 loaf (14 slices).

Pineapple Drop Doughnuts

Deanna Richter, Elmore, Minnesota

These light, cake-like treats warm you up on a cold winter morning. They satisfy your hunger for doughnuts with less effort and time.

- 3 cups all-purpose flour
- 3/4 cup sugar
- 2 tablespoons baking powder
- 3/4 teaspoon salt
- 3 eggs
- 1 cup milk
- 1 can (20 ounces) crushed pineapple, drained
- Oil for deep-fat frying
- Confectioners' sugar

In a large bowl, combine the flour, sugar, baking powder and salt. In another bowl, whisk eggs and milk. Stir in pineapple. Stir into flour mixture just until blended.

In an electric skillet or deep-fat fryer, heat oil to 375°. Drop batter by heaping teaspoonfuls a few at a time, into hot oil. Fry until golden brown, about 1-1/2 minutes on each side. Drain on paper towels. Dust with confectioners' sugar. **Yield:** about 10 dozen.

Editor's Note: Doughnuts may be frozen in an airtight container for up to 1 month. To reheat, place on a microwave-safe plate and microwave on high for 5-10 seconds or until warm. Dust with confectioners' sugar.

Maple Nut Coffee Bread

Deanne Roberts, Orem, Utah

This recipe makes one large coffee cake, so it's great to take to potlucks. The maple flavoring is a nice change from the more common fruit fillings.

- 1 tablespoon active dry yeast
- 1/4 cup warm water (110° to 115°)
- 1 cup warm milk (110° to 115°)
- 1/4 cup shortening
- 1/4 cup sugar
- 1 egg
- 1 teaspoon salt
- 1 teaspoon maple flavoring
- 1/8 teaspoon ground cardamom
- 3-1/2 cups all-purpose flour

FILLING:
- 1 cup packed brown sugar
- 1/3 cup chopped pecans
- 1 teaspoon ground cinnamon
- 1 teaspoon maple flavoring
- 6 tablespoons butter, softened

GLAZE:
- 1-1/2 cups confectioners' sugar
- 1/4 teaspoon maple flavoring
- 2 to 3 tablespoons milk

In a large bowl, dissolve yeast in warm water. Add the milk, shortening, sugar, egg, salt, maple flavoring, cardamom and 2 cups flour. Beat until smooth. Stir in enough remaining flour to form a soft dough.

Turn onto a floured surface; knead until smooth and elastic, about 6-8 minutes. Place in a greased bowl, turning once to grease top. Cover and let rise in a warm place until doubled, about 1 hour.

Meanwhile, grease a baking sheet or 14-in. pizza pan or line with foil. For filling, combine the brown sugar, pecans, cinnamon and maple flavoring; set aside.

Punch dough down. Turn onto a lightly floured surface; divide into thirds. Roll each into a 14-in. circle; place one on prepared pan. Spread with a third of the butter; sprinkle with a third of the filling. Top with a second circle of dough; top with butter and filling. Repeat. Pinch to seal.

Carefully place a glass in center of circle. With scissors, cut from outside edge just to the glass, forming 16 wedges (see Fig. 1). Remove glass; twist each wedge five to six times. Pinch ends to seal and tuck under. Cover and let rise until doubled, about 30 minutes.

Bake at 375° for 25-30 minutes or until golden brown. For glaze, combine the sugar, maple flavoring and enough milk to achieve desired consistency; set aside.

Carefully remove bread from pan by running a metal spatula under it to loosen. Transfer to a wire rack. Drizzle with glaze. Cool completely or serve while slightly warm. **Yield:** 1 loaf.

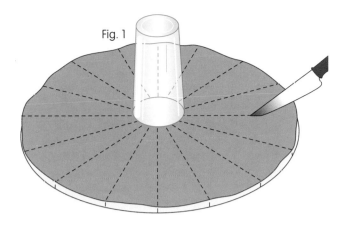

Fig. 1

Apricot Braid

Virginia Adams, Prosser, Washington

Golden raisins and dried apricots give this lovely loaf a nicely sweet flavor, while walnuts add a little crunch.

- 1 package (1/4 ounce) active dry yeast
- 1/4 cup warm water (110° to 115°)
- 1 cup warm milk (110° to 115°)
- 1/2 cup sugar
- 1/4 cup shortening
- 2 teaspoons salt
- 1 egg
- 1/2 cup chopped golden raisins
- 1/2 cup chopped dried apricots
- 1/4 cup chopped walnuts
- 1 teaspoon grated lemon peel
- 4-1/4 to 4-3/4 cups all-purpose flour

VANILLA GLAZE:
- 1 cup confectioners' sugar
- 1/4 teaspoon vanilla extract
- 1 to 2 tablespoons milk

In a large bowl, dissolve yeast in warm water. Add the milk, sugar, shortening and salt; beat until smooth. Add the egg, raisin, apricots, walnuts, lemon peel and 1 cup flour; mix well. Stir in enough remaining flour to form a soft dough.

Turn onto a floured surface; knead until smooth and elastic, about 6-8 minutes. Place in a greased bowl, turning once to grease top. Cover and let rise in a warm place until doubled, about 1-1/4 hours.

Punch dough down. Turn onto a lightly floured surface; divide into five portions. Shape each portion into an 18-in. rope. Place three ropes on a greased baking sheet; braid. Pinch ends to seal and tuck under. Twist the two remaining ropes together. Pinch ends to seal. Place on top of braid; tuck ends under. Cover and let rise until doubled, about 1 hour.

Bake at 350° for 40-45 minutes or until golden brown. Remove from pan to a wire rack to cool. Combine Vanilla Glaze ingredients. Drizzle over braid. **Yield:** 1 loaf.

Cranberry Cinnamon Christmas Tree Rolls

Margery Richmond, Lacombe, Alberta

These festive rolls are sure to spark lively conversations at your holiday brunch. Colorful cranberries make an appetizing addition to ordinary cinnamon rolls.

3-3/4 to 4-1/4 cups all-purpose flour
  1/4 cup sugar
  1 tablespoon active dry yeast
  1 teaspoon salt
  1/2 cup sour cream
  1/2 cup water
  1/4 cup butter, cubed
  2 eggs

FILLING:
  2 cups fresh *or* frozen cranberries
  1/2 cup water
1-1/2 cups packed brown sugar, *divided*
  1 cup chopped pecans
  1/3 cup butter, softened
  1 tablespoon ground cinnamon
  1/4 cup butter, melted

TOPPING:
  1/4 cup corn syrup
  3/4 cup confectioners' sugar
  1 tablespoon milk
Cranberries and red and green candied cherries, halved

In a large bowl, combine 1-1/2 cups flour, sugar, yeast and salt. In a small saucepan, heat the sour cream, water and butter to 120°-130°; add to flour mixture. Beat on medium speed for 2 minutes. Add eggs and 1/2 cup flour; beat 2 minutes longer. Stir in enough remaining flour to form a soft dough.

Turn onto a floured surface; knead until smooth and elastic, about 6-8 minutes. Place in a greased bowl, turning once to grease top. Cover and let rise in a warm place until doubled, about, about 1-1/2 hours.

Meanwhile, in a large saucepan, bring cranberries and water to a boil. Cover and boil gently for 5 minutes. Stir in 1/2 cup brown sugar. Reduce heat; simmer, uncovered, for 5 minutes or until thickened, stirring occasionally. Cool. Combine the pecans, softened butter, cinnamon and remaining brown sugar; set aside.

Punch dough down. Turn onto a lightly floured surface; divide in half. Roll each into a 14-in. x 12-in. rectangle. Brush each with 1 tablespoon melted butter. Spread half of the pecan mixture. Roll up jelly-roll style, starting with a long side; pinch seam to seal. Brush with remaining melted butter.

To form a tree from each log, cut a 2-in. piece from one end for a tree trunk; set aside. Then cut each log into 15 slices. Cover two baking sheets with foil and grease well. Center one slice near the top of each prepared baking sheet.

Arrange slice with sides touching in four more rows, adding one slice for each row, forming a tree. Center the reserved slice lengthwise below the tree for trunk. Cover and let rise until doubled, about 45 minutes.

Bake at 350° for 25-30 minutes or until golden brown. In a saucepan, heat corn syrup over low heat. Transfer foil with trees onto wire racks; brush with corn syrup. Cool for 20 minutes.

In a small bowl, combine the confectioners' sugar and milk. Fill a small pastry or plastic bag; cut a small hole in corner of bag. Pipe on trees for garlands. Garnish with cranberries and candied cherries. **Yield:** 2 trees (16 rolls each).

Rolling Out Yeast Dough You'll notice that yeast dough has a spring to it. When you roll it out, it sometimes springs back. If you're having trouble getting it to stretch to the correct size, let the dough rest for 5 to 10 minutes. Then proceed to roll out to size stated in the recipe.

Chocolate Caramel Braids

Patty Bourne, Owings, Maryland

Candy bars are the chocolate-caramel surprise in this bread. I invented the braid as a way to make my basic yeast sweet bread recipe a little more decadent.

6	to 6-1/2 cups all-purpose flour
1/3	cup sugar
2	packages (1/4 ounce *each*) active dry yeast
1-1/2	teaspoons salt
2	cups (16 ounces) sour cream
1/2	cup water
1/4	cup butter, cubed
2	eggs
48	fun-size Snickers *or* Milky Way candy bars

EGG WASH:

1	egg white
1	tablespoon water

In a large bowl, combine 1-1/2 cups flour, sugar, yeast and salt. In a small saucepan, heat the sour cream, water and butter to 120°-130°; add to flour mixture. Beat on medium speed for 2 minutes. Add eggs and 1/2 cup flour; beat 2 minutes longer. Stir in enough remaining flour to form a soft dough.

Turn onto a floured surface; knead until smooth and elastic, about 6-8 minutes. Place in a greased bowl, turning once to grease top. Cover and let rise in a warm place until doubled, about 1 hour.

Punch dough down; divide into thirds. On a greased baking sheet, roll out one portion into a 16-in. x 10-in. rectangle. Place 16 candy bars lengthwise in two rows down the center third of the rectangle.

On each long side, cut 1-in.-wide strips into the center to within 1/2 in. of candy bars. Starting at one end, fold alternating strips at an angle across candy bars. Pinch ends to seal and tuck under. Repeat with remaining dough and candy bars. Cover and let rise until doubled, about 1 hour.

Beat egg white and water; brush over braids. Bake at 375° for 15-20 minutes or until golden brown. Remove from pans to wire racks to cool. **Yield:** 3 loaves (16 slices each).

Royal Rhubarb Coffee Cake

Lorraine Robinson, Stony Plain, Alberta

For another twist, you can use raspberries and blueberries in place of the rhubarb with equally delicious results.

- 1/3 cup butter, softened
- 1 cup sugar
- 1 egg
- 1 teaspoon vanilla extract
- 2 cups all-purpose flour
- 3 teaspoons baking powder
- 1/2 teaspoon salt
- 1 cup milk
- 3-1/2 cups chopped fresh *or* frozen rhubarb, thawed and drained

TOPPING:
- 3/4 cup packed brown sugar
- 1/4 cup butter, melted
- 1 teaspoon ground cinnamon

In a large bowl, cream butter and sugar until light and fluffy. Add egg and vanilla; beat well. Combine the flour, baking powder and salt; add to creamed mixture alternately with milk.

Transfer to a greased 13-in. x 9-in. x 2-in. baking dish. Spoon rhubarb to within 1/2 in. of edges. Combine topping ingredients; sprinkle over top.

Bake at 350° for 45-55 minutes or until a toothpick inserted near the center comes out clean. Cool on a wire rack. **Yield:** 15 servings.

Editor's Note: If using frozen rhubarb, measure rhubarb while still frozen, then thaw completely. Drain in a colander, but do not press liquid out.

Teddy Bear Bread

Edna Hoffman, Hebron, Indiana

I had lots of fun making this adorable bread with one of our granddaughters. She was so proud of it and kept it in her bedroom! Finally, she reluctantly brought it out to share with her family.

- 1 package (1/4 ounce) active dry yeast
- 1-1/2 cups warm water (110° to 115°)
- 1/2 cup warm milk (110° to 115°)
- 3 tablespoons butter, softened
- 3 tablespoons sugar
- 2 teaspoons salt
- 5-1/4 to 5-3/4 cups all-purpose flour
- 12 raisins
- 1 egg
- 1 tablespoon cold water

Ribbon, optional

In a large bowl, dissolve yeast in warm water. Add the milk, butter, sugar, salt and 3 cups flour. Beat until smooth. Stir in enough remaining flour to form a stiff dough.

Turn onto a floured surface; knead until smooth and elastic, about 6-8 minutes. Place in a greased bowl, turning once to grease top. Cover and let rise in a warm place until doubled, about 1 hour.

Punch dough down. Turn onto a lightly floured surface; divide into four portions. Cut one portion in half; shape into balls. Cut another portion into 14 pieces; shape into balls. Shape remaining two portions into balls.

To form bear body, place each large ball in the center of a greased baking sheet. Place a medium ball above body for head; flatten slightly. Place two small balls on each side of head for ears. Place one small ball in the center of head for nose, and four small balls around body for arms and legs. Cover and let rise until doubled, about 1 hour.

With a sharp knife or scissors, cut slits for ears, eyes, nose and belly button. Insert raisins into slits. Beat egg and cold water; brush over dough.

Bake at 375° for 25-30 minutes or until golden brown. Remove from pans to wire racks to cool. If desired, tie a bow around bear's neck with ribbon. **Yield:** 2 loaves (12 slices each).

Almond Bear Claws

Aneta Kish, La Crosse, Wisconsin

These bear claws are absolutely melt-in-your-mouth delicious! It's impossible to resist the delicate pastry, rich almond filling and pretty fanned tops sprinkled with sugar and almonds. I made yummy treats like this when I worked in a bakery years ago.

1-1/2   cups cold butter, cut into 1/2-inch pieces
    5   cups all-purpose flour
    1   package (1/4 ounce) active dry yeast
1-1/4   cups half-and-half cream
  1/4   cup sugar
  1/4   teaspoon salt
    2   eggs
    1   egg white
  3/4   cup confectioners' sugar
  1/2   cup almond paste, cubed
    1   tablespoon water
Coarse *or* granulated sugar
Sliced almonds

In a bowl, toss butter with 3 cups flour until well coated; refrigerate. In a large bowl, combine yeast and remaining flour. In a saucepan, heat cream, sugar and salt to 120°-130°. Add to yeast mixture with 1 egg. Beat until smooth. Stir in butter mixture just until moistened.

Place dough onto a well floured surface; roll into a 21-in. x 12-in. rectangle. Starting at a short side, fold dough in thirds, forming a 12-in. x 7-in. rectangle. Give dough a quarter turn; roll into a 21-in. x 12-in. rectangle. Fold into thirds, starting with a short side. Repeat, flouring surface as needed. (Do not chill dough between each rolling and folding.) Cover and chill for 4 to 24 hours or until firm.

For filling, in a small bowl, beat egg white until foamy. Gradually add confectioners' sugar and almond paste;

beat until smooth. Cut dough in half widthwise. Roll each portion into a 12-in. square; cut each square into three 12-in. x 4-in. strips. Spread about 2 tablespoons filling down center of each strip. Fold long edges together; seal edges and ends. Cut into three pieces.

Place on greased baking sheets with folded edge facing away from you. With scissors, cut strips four times to within 1/2 in. of folded edge; separate slightly. Repeat with remaining dough and filling. Cover and let rise in a warm place until doubled, about 1 hour. Lightly beat water and remaining egg; brush over dough. Sprinkle with sugar and almonds. Bake at 375° for 15 minutes or until golden brown. Remove from pans to wire racks to cool. **Yield:** 1-1/2 dozen.

Orange Bow Knots

Daphne Blanford, Gander, Newfoundland and Labrador

Baking is my favorite pastime, and I normally have my freezer well-stocked with breads, muffins and cookies. This recipe for rolls with a refreshing orange flavor has been in the family as long as I can remember. We especially enjoy them for breakfast and brunch.

    1   package (1/4 ounce) active dry yeast
  1/4   cup warm water (110° to 115°)
    1   cup warm milk (110° to 115°)
  1/2   cup shortening
  1/3   cup sugar
  1/4   cup orange juice
    2   tablespoons grated orange peel
    1   teaspoon salt
    2   eggs
5-1/4   to 5-3/4 cups all-purpose flour
ICING:
    1   cup confectioners' sugar
    2   tablespoons orange juice
    1   teaspoon grated orange peel

In a large bowl, dissolve yeast in warm water. Add the milk, shortening, sugar, orange juice and peel, salt, eggs and 3 cups flour. Beat until smooth. Stir in enough remaining flour to form a soft dough.

Turn onto a lightly floured surface; knead until smooth and elastic, about 6-8 minutes. Place in a greased bowl, turning once to grease top. Cover and let rise in a warm place until doubled, about 1-1/4 hours.

Punch dough down. Turn onto a lightly floured surface; divide in half. Shape each into 12 balls. Roll each into a 10-in. rope. Tie into a knot and tuck ends under. Place 2 in. apart on greased baking sheets. Cover and let rise until doubled, about 45 minutes.

Bake at 375° for 12-15 minutes or until golden brown. Remove from pans to wire racks. Combine icing ingredients; drizzle over rolls. **Yield:** 2 dozen.

Tangy Lemon Clovers

Judy Jack, Holt, Missouri

Lemon extract and lemon peel lend to the refreshingly different flavor of these rolls.

- 2 packages (1/4 ounce *each*) active dry yeast
- 1-1/2 cups warm water (110° to 115°)
- 1/2 cup sugar
- 1/2 cup nonfat dry milk powder
- 1/2 cup butter-flavored shortening
- 3 eggs
- 1 teaspoon salt
- 1 teaspoon lemon extract
- 1/2 teaspoon ground cinnamon
- 1/2 teaspoon ground nutmeg
- 1/4 teaspoon ground ginger
- 5 to 5-1/2 cups all-purpose flour

TOPPING:
- 1 cup sugar
- 1 teaspoon grated lemon peel
- 1/2 teaspoon ground nutmeg
- 1/4 cup butter, melted

In a large bowl, dissolve yeast in warm water. Add the sugar, milk powder, shortening, eggs, salt, extract, spices and 2 cups flour. Beat until smooth. Stir in enough remaining flour to form a soft dough.

Turn onto a lightly floured surface; knead until smooth and elastic, about 6-8 minutes. Place in a greased bowl; turning once to grease top. Cover and let rise in a warm place until doubled, about 1 hour.

Punch dough down. Turn onto a floured surface; divide in half. Cover and let rest for 15 minutes. Shape each portion into a 16-in. log. Cut each log into 12 pieces; shape each piece into a ball. In a shallow bowl, combine the sugar, peel and nutmeg. Dip tops of balls in butter, then in sugar mixture. Place topping side up in well-greased muffin cups.

Using greased kitchen scissors, cut rolls into quarters, almost to the bottom. Cover and let rise until doubled, about 45 minutes. Brush with remaining butter; sprinkle with remaining sugar mixture.

Bake at 375° for 15-20 minutes or until golden brown. Remove from the pans to wire racks. Serve warm. **Yield:** 2 dozen.

Speedy Cinnamon Rolls

Nicole Weir, Hager City, Wisconsin

On special occasions when we were growing up, my mother would make as many as four batches of these delicious cinnamon rolls to satisfy the appetites of her eight ravenous children. Today this recipe is still a hit.

- 1 loaf (1 pound) frozen bread dough, thawed
- 2 tablespoons butter, melted
- 2/3 cup packed brown sugar
- 1/2 cup chopped walnuts
- 1 teaspoon ground cinnamon
- 1/2 cup heavy whipping cream

On a floured surface, roll dough into an 18-in. x 6-in. rectangle; brush with butter.

In a large bowl, combine the brown sugar, walnuts and cinnamon; sprinkle over dough. Roll up jelly-roll style, starting with a long side; pinch seams to seal. Cut into 16 slices.

Place cut side down in two greased 9-in. round baking pans. Cover and let rise until doubled, about 50 minutes.

Pour 1/4 cup cream over each pan. Bake at 350° for 25-30 minutes or until golden brown. Immediately invert onto serving plates. **Yield:** 1-1/2 dozen.

Christmas Stollen Ring

Dee Beyer, East Bernard, Texas

It's common for German families to gather on Christmas Eve to eat this traditional sweet bread. I've been cooking and baking for more than 40 years and especially enjoy doing so during the holidays.

- 5-1/4 cups all-purpose flour
- 1/4 cup sugar
- 2 packages (1/4 ounce *each*) active dry yeast
- 1 teaspoon salt
- 1 cup butter, softened
- 1 cup milk
- 1/2 cup water
- 2 eggs
- 1/2 cup golden raisins
- 1/2 cup chopped candied fruit
- 1/2 cup chopped walnuts
- 1/2 teaspoon grated lemon peel
- 1/2 teaspoon grated orange peel

FILLING:
- 3 tablespoons butter, softened
- 1/2 cup sugar
- 1 tablespoon ground cinnamon

GLAZE:
- 1 cup confectioners' sugar
- 1/4 teaspoon vanilla extract
- 2 to 3 tablespoons milk

Red and green candied cherries, halved

In a large bowl, combine 1-1/2 cups flour, sugar, yeast and salt. In a small saucepan, heat the butter, milk and water to 120°-130° Add to flour mixture; beat just until moistened. Beat on medium speed for 2 minutes. Add eggs; beat until smooth. Stir in enough remaining flour to form a soft dough. Stir in the raisins, candied fruit, walnuts, and lemon and orange peel. Cover and refrigerate overnight.

Punch dough down. Turn onto a lightly floured surface. Roll into an 18-in. x 12-in. rectangle; spread butter to within 1/2 in. of edges. Combine sugar and cinnamon; sprinkle over dough. Roll up jelly-roll style, starting with a long side; pinch seam to seal.

Place seam side down on a greased baking sheet; pinch ends together to form a ring. With a scissors, cut from outside edge two-thirds of the way toward center of the ring at 1-in. intervals. Separate strips lightly; twist to allow filling to show, slightly overlapping with the previous piece. Cover and let rise in a warm place until doubled, about 1 hour.

Bake at 350° for 25-30 minutes or until golden brown. Remove from pan to a wire rack to cool.

For glaze, combine the sugar, vanilla and enough milk to achieve desired consistency. Drizzle over warm stollen. Decorate with candied cherries. **Yield:** 1 loaf (18 slices).

Bird Rolls

Margaret Fowler, Plainfield, Indiana

I make a point of having these tender bird rolls "fly in" for Easter dinner. With their slightly sweet flavor, the grandchildren can't help but gobble them up.

- 1 package (1/4 ounce) active dry yeast
- 1 cup warm milk (110° to 115°)
- 1/4 cup butter, melted
- 1/4 cup packed brown sugar
- 2 eggs
- 1 teaspoon salt
- 3-1/2 to 4 cups all-purpose flour

TOPPING:
- 1 egg
- 1 tablespoon water
- 16 whole unblanched almonds

In a large bowl, dissolve yeast in warm milk. Add the butter, brown sugar, 2 eggs, salt and 2 cups flour. Beat until smooth. Stir in enough remaining flour to form a soft dough.

Turn onto a floured surface; knead until smooth and elastic, about 6-8 minutes. Place in a greased bowl, turning once to grease top. Cover and let rise in a warm place until doubled, about 1 hour.

Punch dough down. Turn onto a lightly floured surface; divide into 16 pieces. Roll each into a 12-in. rope; tie each into a knot.

To form birds' head, tuck one end back into knots. With a sharp knife or scissors, cut two slits on opposite end to form tail feathers. Place 2 in. apart on greased baking sheets. Cover and let rise until doubled, about 30 minutes.

Beat egg with water; brush over dough. Bake at 350° for 15-20 minutes or until golden brown. Insert an almond into each for beak. Remove from pans to wire racks to cool. **Yield:** 16 rolls.

Honey Pull-Apart Bread

Donna Bittinger, Oakland, Maryland

When I came across this recipe in an old family cookbook, I knew it would be an instant favorite with my family. We enjoy it fresh from the oven, and it disappears in a flash.

- 2 packages (1/4 ounce *each*) active dry yeast
- 1/4 cup warm water (110° to 115°)
- 1 cup warm milk (110° to 115°)
- 1/2 cup shortening
- 1/4 cup sugar
- 2 teaspoons salt
- 2 eggs
- 4-1/2 to 5 cups all-purpose flour

FILLING:
- 2 tablespoons butter, melted
- 1 cup honey
- 1 cup chopped pecans
- 1/2 cup sugar
- 1/4 cup grated orange peel
- 2 tablespoons orange juice
- 2 teaspoons ground cinnamon

GLAZE:
- 1/3 cup honey
- 1/3 cup sugar
- 2 teaspoons grated orange peel
- 1 tablespoon butter

In a large bowl, dissolve yeast in warm water. Add the milk, shortening, sugar, salt, eggs and 2 cups flour. Beat until smooth. Stir in enough remaining flour to form a stiff dough.

Turn onto a floured surface; knead until smooth and elastic, about 6-8 minutes. Place in a greased bowl, turning once to grease top. Cover and let rise in a warm place until doubled, about 1 hour.

Punch dough down. Turn onto a lightly floured surface; divide in half. Roll each into a 16-in. x 12-in. rectangle. Brush with butter. Combine remaining filling ingredients; spread over dough to within 1/2 in. of edges.

Roll up jelly-roll style, starting with a long side. Pinch seam to seal. Cut each into 16 slices. Place cut side down in a greased one-piece 10-in. tube pan. Cover and let rise until doubled, about 45 minutes.

Bake at 350° for 40-45 minutes or until golden brown. Cool in pan for 10 minutes before inverting onto a serving plate. In a small saucepan, combine glaze ingredients; heat until sugar is dissolved. Drizzle over warm bread. **Yield:** 16 servings.

Lemon Candy Canes

Marie Frangpane, Eugene, Oregon

We enjoy looking at these cute candy cane rolls as much as we love eating them! For even more festive fun, I sometimes decorate them with sliced candied cherries.

    1   package (1/4 ounce) active dry yeast
  1/2   cup warm water (110° to 115°)
  1/3   cup sour cream
    1   egg
    3   tablespoons butter, softened
    3   tablespoons sugar
    1   teaspoon salt
2-3/4   to 3 cups all-purpose flour
FILLING:
  1/2   cup finely chopped walnuts *or* pecans
  1/3   cup sugar
    3   tablespoons butter, melted
    1   tablespoon grated lemon peel
LEMON ICING:
    1   cup confectioners' sugar
    1   tablespoon lemon juice
    1   tablespoon water
  1/4   teaspoon vanilla extract

In a large bowl, dissolve yeast in warm water. Add the sour cream, egg, butter, sugar, salt and 1-1/4 cups flour. Beat until smooth. Stir in enough remaining flour to form a soft dough.

Turn onto a floured surface; knead until smooth and elastic, about 6-8 minutes. Place in a greased bowl, turning once to grease top. Cover and let rise in a warm place until doubled, about 1 hour.

Punch dough down. Turn onto a lightly floured surface; divide in half. Let rest for 10 minutes. Roll each into a 12-in. x 8-in. rectangle.

In a small bowl, combine filling ingredients. Spread half of the filling over dough to within 1/2 in. of edges. Fold in half lengthwise; pinch seam to seal. Cut into 12 strips. Holding both ends of strip, twist each strip three or four times.

Place 2 in. apart on greased baking sheets. Curve one end to form a cane. Cover and let rise until doubled, about 30 minutes.

Bake at 375° for 12-14 minutes or until golden brown. Remove from pans to wire racks to cool. Combine icing ingredients; drizzle over rolls. **Yield:** 2 dozen.

Sour Cream Coffee Cake

Doris Rice, Storm Lake, Iowa

This coffee cake is a favorite for breakfast or brunch. I've also taken it to potlucks and served it as dessert. Tender slices feature an appealing crunchy filling.

    1   cup butter, softened
1-1/2   cups sugar
    3   eggs
    1   teaspoon *each* almond, lemon and vanilla extracts
2-1/2   cups all-purpose flour
    2   teaspoons baking powder
    1   teaspoon baking soda
    1   cup (8 ounces) sour cream
FILLING:
  1/3   cup chopped pecans
    3   tablespoons sugar
    1   tablespoon ground cinnamon
GLAZE:
    1   cup confectioners' sugar
    2   tablespoons milk

In a large bowl, cream butter and sugar. Add eggs, one at a time, beating well after each addition. Beat in extracts. Combine the flour, baking powder and baking soda; add to creamed mixture alternately with sour cream.

Spread half of the batter in a greased and floured 10-in. fluted tube pan. Make a well in the center of the batter. Combine filling ingredients; sprinkle into well. Carefully cover with remaining batter.

Bake at 350° for 45-50 minutes or until a toothpick inserted near the center comes out clean. Cool for 10 minutes before removing from pan to a wire rack. Combine glaze ingredients; drizzle over warm cake. **Yield:** 16 servings.

Serve Them Warm Coffee cakes are best with the fresh-from-the-oven flavor. To reheat, wrap unfrosted coffee cake in foil. Reheat at 325° to 350° for 10 minutes or until warm.

Apple Danish

Dorothea Ladd, Ballston Lake, New York

This dough should be refrigerated for at least 2 hours. You can prepare it the night before and bake the rolls fresh in the morning as a special breakfast treat.

    1   package (1/4 ounce) active dry yeast
  1/4   cup warm water (110° to 115°)
    5   cups all-purpose flour
  1/4   cup sugar
    1   teaspoon salt
    1   teaspoon grated lemon peel
    1   cup cold butter, cubed
    1   cup warm milk (110° to 115°)
    2   eggs, lightly beaten
FILLING:
1-1/2   cups chopped peeled tart apples
  3/4   cup chopped walnuts
  1/3   cup sugar
1-1/2   teaspoons ground cinnamon
    2   tablespoons butter, melted
GLAZE:
    2   cups confectioners' sugar
    3   tablespoons milk
  1/2   teaspoon vanilla extract

In a small bowl, dissolve yeast in warm water. In a large bowl, combine the flour, sugar, salt and lemon peel; cut in butter until mixture resembles fine crumbs. Stir in the yeast mixture, milk and eggs until blended.

Turn onto a lightly floured surface; knead about 20 times (dough will be slightly sticky). Cover and refrigerate for at least 2 hours.

For filling, combine the apples, walnuts, sugar and cinnamon; set aside. Punch dough down. Turn onto a lightly floured surface; divide in half. Roll each portion into an 18-in. x 15-in. rectangle; brush with butter. Sprinkle filling to within 1/2 in. of edges.

Starting with a short side, fold a third of the dough over filling; repeat with other side, making a 15-in. x 6-in. rectangle. Pinch seams to seal. Cut each into 15 slices. Twist each slice a few times; pinch ends together, forming a small circle. Place 2 in. apart on greased baking sheets.

Bake at 400° for 12-15 minutes or until golden brown. Remove from pans to wire racks. Combine glaze ingredients; drizzle over warm rolls. **Yield:** 2-1/2 dozen.

Cinnamon Raisin Bread

Joan Ort, Milford, New Jersey

Slices of warm cinnamon bread and a cup of hot tea work wonders for holiday visitors to our home. My mother received this recipe from a friend.

 2 packages (1/4 ounce *each*) active dry yeast
 2 cups warm water (110° to 115°)
 1 cup sugar, *divided*
1/4 cup canola oil
 3 teaspoons salt
 2 eggs
 6 to 6-1/2 cups all-purpose flour
 1 cup raisins
Additional canola oil
 3 teaspoons ground cinnamon

In a large bowl, dissolve yeast in warm water. Add 1/2 cup sugar, oil, salt, eggs and 4 cups flour. Beat until smooth. Stir in enough remaining flour to form a soft dough.

Turn onto a floured surface; knead until smooth and elastic, about 6-8 minutes. Place in a greased bowl, turning once to grease top. Cover and let rise in a warm place until doubled, about 1 hour.

Punch dough down. Turn onto a lightly floured surface; divide in half. Knead 1/2 cup raisins into each; roll each portion into a 15-in. x 9-in. rectangle. Brush with additional oil. Combine cinnamon and remaining sugar; sprinkle to within 1/2 in. of edges.

Tightly roll up jelly-roll style, starting with a short side; pinch seam to seal. Place seam side down in two greased 9-in. x 5-in. x 3-in. loaf pans. Cover and let rise until doubled, about 30 minutes.

Brush with oil. Bake at 375° for 45-50 minutes or until golden brown. Remove from pans to wire racks to cool. **Yield:** 2 loaves (16 slices each).

Pineapple Sweet Rolls

Bernice Morris, Marshfield, Missouri

These sweet rolls are very similar to the kind found in bakeries—only better! Pineapple adds just the right amount of sweetness. My husband can't eat just one.

- 1 package (1/4 ounce) active dry yeast
- 1/4 cup warm water (110° to 115°)
- 1 tablespoon plus 1/4 cup sugar, *divided*
- 1 cup warm milk (110° to 115°)
- 1/2 cup butter, melted, *divided*
- 2 eggs, lightly beaten
- 1 teaspoon salt
- 5 to 5-1/2 cups all-purpose flour

TOPPING:
- 1-1/2 teaspoons cornstarch
- 1 can (8 ounces) crushed pineapple, undrained

GLAZE:
- 1-1/2 cups confectioners' sugar
- 1 teaspoon vanilla extract
- 1 to 2 tablespoons milk

In a large bowl, dissolve yeast in warm water. Add 1 tablespoon sugar; let stand for 5 minutes. Add the milk, 1/4 cup butter, eggs, salt, remaining sugar and 1-1/2 cups flour. Beat until smooth. Stir in enough remaining flour to form a soft dough.

Turn onto a floured surface; knead until smooth and elastic, about 6-8 minutes. Place in a greased bowl, turning once to grease top. Cover and let rise until doubled, about 45 minutes.

Punch dough down. Turn onto a floured surface; divide in half. Roll each into a 12-in. x 8-in. rectangle. Brush with some of the remaining butter. Roll up jelly-roll style, starting with a long side. Pinch seam to seal.

Cut each into 12 slices. Place cut side down 2 in. apart on greased baking sheets. Brush with remaining butter. Cover and let rise until doubled, about 30 minutes.

Meanwhile, in a small saucepan, combine cornstarch and pineapple until blended. Bring to a boil over medium heat; cook and stir for 2 minutes or until thickened. Remove from the heat.

Place a teaspoonful of filling in the center of each roll. Bake at 425° for 12-16 minutes or until golden brown. Remove from pans to wire racks.

For glaze, combine sugar, vanilla and enough milk to achieve desired consistency. Drizzle over warm rolls. **Yield:** 2 dozen.

Long Johns

Twilla Eisele, Wellsville, Kansas

The tattered recipe in my files is a good indication of how popular these doughnuts have been in our family over the years. They disappear in a hurry, so I usually double the recipe.

- 1 package (1/4 ounce) active dry yeast
- 1/4 cup warm water (110° to 115°)
- 1 cup warm milk (110° to 115°)
- 1/4 cup butter, softened
- 1/4 cup sugar
- 1/2 teaspoon salt
- 1 egg
- 3-1/4 to 3-3/4 cups all-purpose flour
- Oil for deep-fat frying

GLAZE:
- 1-1/4 cups confectioners' sugar
- 1 tablespoon brown sugar
- 1 tablespoon water
- 1/2 teaspoon vanilla extract
- 1/8 teaspoon salt

In a large bowl, dissolve yeast in warm water. Add the milk, butter, sugar, salt and egg and 2 cups flour. Beat until smooth. Stir in enough flour to form a soft dough.

Do not knead. Place in a greased bowl, turning once to grease top. Cover and let rise in a warm place until doubled, about 1 hour.

Punch dough down. Turn onto a lightly floured surface; roll into a 12-in. x 8-in. rectangle. Cut into 3-in. x 1-in. rectangles. Place on greased baking sheets. Cover and let rise in a warm place until doubled, about 30 minutes.

In an electric skillet or deep-fat fryer, heat oil to 400°. Fry doughnuts, a few at a time, until golden brown on both sides. Drain on paper towels. Combine glaze ingredients. Dip tops in glaze while warm. **Yield:** 2-1/2 dozen.

Banana Nut Yeast Bread

Elizabeth Zesiger, Oroville, Washington

A friend gave me this recipe many years ago. She liked it because it requires no kneading but has the same terrific taste and aroma of traditional banana bread.

    2   packages (1/4 ounce *each*) active dry yeast
  1/3   cup warm water (110° to 115°)
    1   cup mashed ripe bananas (2 to 3 medium)
  1/2   cup sugar
  1/3   cup warm milk (110° to 115°)
  1/3   cup butter, softened
  1/2   teaspoon salt
    2   eggs
    5   to 5-1/2 cups all-purpose flour
  1/2   cup chopped nuts

In a large bowl, dissolve yeast in warm water. Add the bananas, sugar, milk, butter, salt, eggs and 3 cups flour. Beat on medium speed for 3 minutes. Stir in nuts. Stir in enough remaining flour to form a stiff batter. Do not knead.

Spoon into two greased 9-in. x 5-in. x 3-in. loaf pans. Cover and let rise in a warm place until doubled, about 1-1/2 hours.

Bake at 375° for 25-30 minutes or until golden brown and bread sounds hollow when tapped. Remove from pans to wire racks to cool. **Yield:** 2 loaves (16 slices each).

Mandarin Orange Breakfast Bites

Delores Thompson, Clear Lake, Iowa

These taste like doughnuts without the hassle of rolling out and frying. Our daughter likes me to have them waiting for her and her friends after school.

1-1/2   cups all-purpose flour
  1/2   cup sugar
1-3/4   teaspoons baking powder
  1/2   teaspoon salt
  1/2   teaspoon ground nutmeg
  1/2   cup butter, softened
    1   egg
  1/2   cup milk
    1   teaspoon almond extract
    1   can (11 ounces) mandarin oranges, drained and diced
TOPPING:
  1/3   cup sugar
    1   teaspoon ground cinnamon
  1/2   cup butter, melted

In a large bowl, combine the flour, sugar, baking powder, salt and nutmeg. Cut in butter until mixture resembles coarse crumbs. In another bowl, whisk the egg, milk and extract. Stir into crumb mixture just until moistened. Fold in oranges.

Fill greased or paper-lined miniature muffin cups two-thirds full. Bake at 350° for 15-20 minutes or until a toothpick inserted into the center comes out clean. Cool for 5 minutes before removing from pans to wire racks. Combine sugar and cinnamon. Dip tops of warm muffins in melted butter, then in cinnamon-sugar. **Yield:** 2-1/2 dozen.

Cheese-Filled Coffee Cakes

Shirley Hartman, Colorado Springs, Colorado

I began collecting interesting recipes years ago when I had dreams of owning a bed-and-breakfast. I never met that goal but came away with flavorful recipes like this.

4-1/2   cups all-purpose flour
  1/2   cup sugar
    2   packages (1/4 ounce *each*) active dry yeast
    1   teaspoon salt
    1   cup (8 ounces) sour cream
  1/2   cup butter, cubed
  1/2   cup water
    2   eggs
FILLING:
    2   packages (8 ounces *each*) cream cheese, softened
  3/4   cup sugar
    1   egg
    1   teaspoon almond extract
  1/8   teaspoon salt
GLAZE:
    2   cups confectioners' sugar
    3   tablespoons milk
  1/2   teaspoon vanilla extract

In a large bowl, combine 1-1/2 cups flour, sugar, yeast and salt. In a small saucepan, heat the sour cream, butter and water to 120°-130°; add to flour mixture. Beat on medium speed for 2 minutes. Add eggs and 1/2 cup flour; beat 2 minutes longer. Stir in enough remaining flour to form a firm dough. Do not knead. Cover and refrigerate for 2 hours.

In a small bowl, beat filling ingredients until smooth; set aside. Turn dough onto a lightly floured surface; divide into four pieces. Roll each into a 12-in. x 8-in. rectangle. Spread filling to within 1/2 in. of edges.

Roll up jelly-roll style, starting with a long side; pinch seams to seal and tuck ends under. Place, seams side down, on two greased baking sheets. With a sharp knife, make deep slashes across the top of each loaf. Cover and let rise in a warm place until doubled, about 1 hour.

Bake at 375° for 20-25 minutes or until golden brown. Remove from pans to wire racks. Combine glaze ingredients; drizzle over warm loaves. Cool. Store in the refrigerator. **Yield:** 4 loaves.

Pies

pg. 113

pg. 98

pg. 109

pg. 117

Classic Pie Pastry

Taste of Home Test Kitchen

Just four ingredients are all you need to create a fabulous flaky pie crust. The double-crust recipe should be used when making a lattice-topped pie.

DOUBLE CRUST PASTRY:

2   cups all-purpose flour
3/4   teaspoon salt
2/3   cup shortening
6   to 7 tablespoons cold water

In a large bowl, combine flour and salt; cut in the shortening until crumbly. Gradually add water, tossing with a fork until dough forms a ball (Fig. 1). Divide dough in half so that one ball is slightly larger than the other. Roll out larger ball to fit a 9-in. x 10-in. pie plate (Fig. 2).

Transfer pastry to pie plate. Trim pastry even with edge. Pour desired filling into crust. Roll out remaining pastry to fit top of pie. Place over filling (Fig. 3). Trim, seal and flute edges (Fig. 4). Cut slits in pastry. Bake according to recipe directions. **Yield:** Pastry for double-crust pie (9 or 10 inches).

Single Crust Pastry: Use 1-1/4 cups all-purpose flour, 1/2 teaspoon salt, 1/3 cup shortening and 4 to 5 tablespoons cold water. Proceed as directed, making just 1 ball.

Fig. 1

Fig. 2

Fig. 3

Fig. 4

Candy Bar Pie

Mary Ann Smith, Groton, New York

Here's a very rich and creamy pie that tastes terrific. A small sliver is all most folks can handle.

5   Snickers candy bars (2.07 ounces *each*), cut into 1/4-inch pieces
1   pastry shell (9 inches), baked
12   ounces cream cheese, softened
1/2   cup sugar
2   eggs
1/3   cup sour cream
1/3   cup peanut butter
2/3   cup semisweet chocolate chips
2   tablespoons whipping cream

Place candy bar pieces in the pastry shell; set aside. In a large bowl, beat cream cheese and sugar until smooth. Add the eggs, sour cream and peanut butter; beat on low speed just until combined. Pour into pastry shell. Bake at 325° for 35-40 minutes or until set. Cool on wire rack.

In a small heavy saucepan, melt chocolate chips with cream over low heat; stir until smooth. Spread over filling. Refrigerate for 2 hours or overnight. Cut with a warm knife. **Yield:** 8-10 servings.

Editor's Note: Reduced-fat or generic brands of peanut butter are not recommended for this recipe.

Fall Pear Pie

Ken Churches, San Andreas, California

A wide slice of this festive, fruity pie is a great end to a delicious meal. The mellow flavor of pears is a refreshing alternative to the more common pies for the holidays. It's nice to serve a dessert that's a little unexpected.

    8   cups thinly sliced peeled pears
  3/4   cup sugar
  1/4   cup quick-cooking tapioca
  1/4   teaspoon ground nutmeg
Pastry for double-crust pie (9 inches)
    1   egg, lightly beaten
  1/4   cup heavy whipping cream, optional

In a large bowl, combine the pears, sugar, tapioca and nutmeg. Let stand for 15 minutes. Line a pie plate with bottom crust; add pear mixture. Roll out remaining pastry to fit top of pie. Place over filling; seal and flute edges. Cut large slits in pastry. Brush with egg.

Bake at 375° for 55-60 minutes or until the pears are tender. Remove to a wire rack. Pour cream through slits if desired. Store in the refrigerator. **Yield:** 8 servings.

How Many Pears? Don't know how many pears will make 8 cups thinly sliced pears? One medium pear will yield about 1 cup of slices. When you go shopping, buy about 10 pears. That way you'll have some wiggle room in case you don't get a cup per pear. Any pears left over will make a super snack or a great addition to a tossed salad.

Brownie Pie a la Mode

Beverly Thornton, Cortlandt Manor, New York

This is an easy brownie recipe when you need something good, fancy and chocolaty.

1/2	cup sugar
2	tablespoons butter
2	tablespoons water
1-1/2	cups semisweet chocolate chips
2	eggs
1	teaspoon vanilla extract
2/3	cup all-purpose flour
1/4	teaspoon baking soda
1/4	teaspoon salt
3/4	cup chopped walnuts

FUDGE SAUCE:

1	cup (6 ounces) semisweet chocolate chips
1/2	cup evaporated milk
1/4	cup sugar
1	tablespoon butter

Vanilla ice cream

In a small saucepan, bring the sugar, butter and water to a boil over medium heat. Remove from the heat; stir in chips until melted. Set aside to cool.

In a large bowl, beat eggs and vanilla. Beat in chocolate mixture until blended. Combine the flour, baking soda and salt; add to chocolate mixture. Stir in walnuts.

Pour into a greased 9-in. pie plate. Bake at 350° for 28-30 minutes or until a toothpick inserted near the center comes out clean. Cool on a wire rack.

For fudge sauce, in a small heavy saucepan or microwave, heat the chips, milk, sugar and butter until chocolate and butter are melted; stir until smooth. Drizzle some over pie. Cut into wedges; serve with ice cream and additional fudge sauce. **Yield:** 6-8 servings.

Peach Cream Pie

Denise Goedeken, Platte Center, Nebraska

The sour cream filling and cinnamon crumb topping complement the fruit flavor in this yummy pie.

- 1-1/2 cups all-purpose flour
- 1/2 teaspoon salt
- 1/2 cup cold butter

FILLING:
- 4 cups unsweetened sliced peaches (about 6 medium)
- 1 cup sugar, *divided*
- 2 tablespoons all-purpose flour
- 1 egg
- 1/2 teaspoon vanilla extract
- 1/4 teaspoon salt
- 1 cup (8 ounces) sour cream

TOPPING:
- 1/3 cup sugar
- 1/3 cup all-purpose flour
- 1 teaspoon ground cinnamon
- 1/4 cup cold butter

In a small bowl, combine flour and salt; cut in butter until crumbly. Press into a 9-in. pie plate.

For filling, place peaches in a large bowl; sprinkle with 1/4 cup sugar and toss gently to coat. In another small bowl, combine the flour, egg, vanilla, salt and remaining sugar; fold in sour cream. Stir into peaches.

Pour into crust. Bake at 400° for 15 minutes. Reduce heat to 350°; bake 20 minutes longer.

For topping, in a small bowl, combine the sugar, flour and cinnamon. Cut in butter until crumbly. Sprinkle over top of pie. Increase oven temperature to 400°; bake for 15 minutes or until topping is browned. Cool on a wire rack. Store in the refrigerator. **Yield:** 6-8 servings.

Butterscotch Pumpkin Pie

Elizabeth Fehr, Cecil Lake, British Columbia

When I'm in the mood for something sweet, this is the recipe I reach for. The addition of butterscotch pudding makes this a tasty twist on traditional pumpkin pie.

- 1 cup graham cracker crumbs
- 1/4 cup butter, melted

FILLING:
- 1 cup fat-free milk
- 1 package (.9 ounce) sugar-free instant butterscotch pudding mix
- 1 cup canned pumpkin
- 1 teaspoon ground cinnamon
- 1/2 teaspoon ground nutmeg

TOPPING:
- 1 cup reduced-fat whipped topping
- 1 teaspoon vanilla extract

In a small bowl, combine cracker crumbs and butter; press onto the bottom of a 9-in. pie plate. Bake at 350° for 10 minutes; cool.

For filling, In a small bowl, whisk milk and pudding mix for 2 minutes. Let stand for 2 minutes or until soft-set. Stir in the pumpkin, cinnamon and nutmeg until blended.

Pour into crust. Chill for at least 2 hours. Combine topping ingredients; serve with pie. **Yield:** 8 servings.

Autumn Apple Tart

Grace Howaniec, Waukesha, Wisconsin

Wisconsin has many apple orchards and we enjoy going apple picking. This attractive tart is one of my favorite ways to use this abundant fall fruit.

- 1-1/4 cups all-purpose flour
- 1 tablespoon sugar
- 1 teaspoon baking powder
- 1/2 teaspoon salt
- 1/2 cup cold butter, cubed
- 1 egg, lightly beaten
- 2 tablespoons milk
- 6 medium tart apples, peeled and cut into 1/4-Inch slices

TOPPING:
- 1/3 to 1/2 cup sugar
- 2 tablespoons butter
- 1/2 teaspoon ground cinnamon
- 1/2 teaspoon ground nutmeg
- 1-1/2 tablespoons all-purpose flour

In a large bowl, combine the flour, sugar, baking powder and salt. Cut in butter until mixture resembles fine crumbs. Combine egg and milk; stir into flour mixture until blended.

Press onto the bottom and up the sides of an ungreased 11-in. tart pan with removable bottom. Arrange apple slices over crust.

In a small bowl, combine topping ingredients; sprinkle over apples. Place pan on a baking sheet. Bake at 350° for 50-60 minutes or until apples are tender. Serve warm or cool. **Yield:** 12 servings.

Line with a double thickness of heavy-duty foil. Bake at 450° for 8 minutes or until lightly browned. Remove foil; cool on a wire rack.

For filling, in a small saucepan, combine the sugar, cornstarch, flour and salt. Gradually stir in water. Cook and stir over medium heat until thickened and bubbly, about 2 minutes. Reduce the heat; cook and stir 2 minutes longer. Remove from the heat. Gradually stir 1 cup hot filling into egg yolks; return all to pan. Bring to a gentle boil; cook and stir for 2 minutes. Remove from the heat. Stir in the butter, lemon juice, peel and extract until butter is melted. Pour hot filling into crust.

In a small bowl, beat egg whites and cream of tartar on medium speed until soft peaks form. Gradually beat in sugar, 1 tablespoon at a time, on high until stiff, glossy peaks form and sugar is dissolved. Spread evenly over hot filling, sealing edges to crust.

Bake at 350° for 12-15 minutes or until the meringue is golden brown. Cool on a wire rack for 1 hour. Refrigerate for at least 3 hours before serving. Store in the refrigerator. **Yield:** 6-8 servings.

Lemon Meringue Pie

Susan Jones, Bradford, Ohio

My father loves lemon meringue pie and always wants one for his birthday. I rely on this recipe, which won first place at our county fair. It has a light, flaky crust, refreshing lemon filling and soft meringue with pretty golden peaks.

1-1/2	cups all-purpose flour
1/2	teaspoon salt
1/2	cup shortening
1/4	cup cold water

FILLING:

1-1/2	cups sugar
1/4	cup cornstarch
3	tablespoons all-purpose flour
1/4	teaspoon salt
1-1/2	cups water
3	egg yolks, beaten
2	tablespoons butter
1/3	cup lemon juice
1	teaspoon grated lemon peel
1	teaspoon lemon extract

MERINGUE:

3	egg whites
1/4	teaspoon cream of tartar
6	tablespoons sugar

In a small bowl, combine flour and salt; cut in the shortening until crumbly. Gradually add water, tossing with a fork until dough forms a ball. Roll out pastry to fit a 9-in. pie plate. Transfer pastry to pie plate. Trim pastry to 1/2 in. beyond edge of pie plate; flute edges.

Cran-Raspberry Pie

Verona Koehlmoos, Pilger, Nebraska

Jewel-toned fruits team up to pack this lattice-topped pie with flavor. It's a lovely addition to holiday meals.

2	cups chopped fresh *or* frozen cranberries
5	cups fresh *or* frozen unsweetened raspberries, thawed
1/2	teaspoon almond extract
1	to 1-1/4 cups sugar
1/4	cup quick-cooking tapioca
1/4	teaspoon salt

Pastry for double-crust pie (9 inches)

In a large bowl, combine the cranberries, raspberries and almond extract. Combine the sugar, tapioca and salt. Add to the fruit mixture; toss gently to coat. Let stand for 15 minutes.

Line a 9-in. pie plate with bottom crust; trim to 1 in. beyond edge of plate. Add filling. Roll out remaining pastry; make a lattice crust. Trim, seal and flute edges. Cover edges loosely with foil.

Bake at 375° for 40-45 minutes or until crust is golden brown and filling is bubbly. Cool pie on a wire rack. **Yield:** 6-8 servings.

A Sparkling Crust To give some pizzazz to a pie crust, brush with a combination of one egg beaten with 1 tablespoon water. Then sprinkle with coarse sugar before baking.

Cranberry-Apple Mincemeat Pies

Lucinda Burton, Scarborough, Ontario

Traditional mincemeat is too heavy for me, but this fruity version hits the spot. Others agree—few folks who've tried it stop at just one slice!

- 4 cups fresh *or* frozen cranberries, thawed
- 4 cups chopped peeled tart apples
- 1-1/2 cups chopped dried apricots
- 1-1/2 cups golden raisins
- 1 medium unpeeled navel orange, finely chopped
- 1/4 cup *each* red and green candied cherries
- 2-3/4 cups sugar
- 1 cup apple juice
- 1/4 cup butter
- 1/4 cup orange marmalade
- 1 teaspoon ground ginger
- 3/4 teaspoon *each* ground allspice, cinnamon and nutmeg
- Pastry for double-crust pie (9 inches)

In a Dutch oven, combine the fruit, sugar, apple juice, butter, marmalade and spices. Bring to a boil over medium heat. Reduce heat; simmer, uncovered, for 50-60 minutes, stirring occasionally. Cool completely or refrigerate for up to 1 week.

Line two 9-in. pie plates with pastry; trim and flute edges. Divide filling between crusts. Cover edges loosely with foil. Bake at 400° for 20 minutes. Remove foil. Bake for 20-25 minutes or until crust is golden brown and filling is bubbly. Cool on wire racks. **Yield:** 2 pies (6-8 servings each).

Editor's Note: Mincemeat mixture may be frozen for up to 3 months. Thaw in the refrigerator.

Ruby Grape Pie

Fred Smeds, Reedley, California

Having a 75-acre vineyard, my wife and I use grapes in a lot of different recipes, from salads to desserts. This one calling for seedless red grapes is an unusual and tasty pie.

- 4 cups halved seedless red grapes (about 2 pounds)
- 2/3 cup sugar
- 1/2 teaspoon ground cinnamon
- 3 tablespoons cornstarch
- 2 tablespoons lemon juice
- 1 tablespoon grated lemon peel
- Pastry for double-crust pie (9 inches)
- 2 tablespoons butter

In a large saucepan, combine the grapes, sugar and cinnamon; toss to coat. Let stand for 15 minutes. Combine cornstarch, lemon juice and peel; stir into grape mixture. Bring to a boil; cook and stir for 2 minutes or until thickened.

Line a 9-in. pie plate with bottom crust. Pour grape mixture into crust. Dot with butter. Roll out remaining pastry to fit top of pie, Place over filling. Trim, seal and flute edges. Cut slits in top. Cover edges loosely with foil.

Bake at 425° for 20 minutes. Remove foil. Reduce heat to 350°; bake 30-35 minutes longer or until the crust is golden brown. Cool on a wire rack. Store in the refrigerator. **Yield:** 6-8 servings.

Poppy Seed Strawberry Pie

Kris Sackett, Eau Claire, Wisconsin

The combination of flavors in this pretty dessert won me over the first time I tasted it.

- 1-1/3 cups all-purpose flour
- 1 tablespoon poppy seeds
- 1/4 teaspoon salt
- 1/2 cup shortening
- 3 tablespoons cold water

FILLING:
- 2 pints strawberries, *divided*
- 2 cups whipped topping
- 2 tablespoons honey
- 1/4 cup slivered almonds, toasted, optional

In a small bowl, combine the flour, poppy seeds and salt; cut in shortening until crumbly. Gradually add water, tossing with a fork until dough forms a ball. Roll out pastry to fit a 9-in. pie plate.

Transfer pastry to plate; flute edges. Line unpricked pastry with a double thickness of heavy-duty foil. Bake at 450° for 8 minutes. Remove foil; bake 5 minutes longer. Cool on a wire rack.

Slice 1 pint of strawberries; fold into whipped topping. Spoon into pie shell. Cut remaining berries in half; arrange over top. Drizzle with honey. Sprinkle with almonds if desired. Refrigerate for at least 1 hour. **Yield:** 6-8 servings.

Candy Apple Pie

Cindy Kleweno, Burlington, Colorado

This is the only apple pie my husband will eat, but that's all right since he makes it as often as I do. Like a combination of apple and pecan pie, it's a sweet treat that usually tops off our holiday meals.

  6 cups thinly sliced peeled tart apples
  2 tablespoons lime juice
3/4 cup sugar
1/4 cup all-purpose flour
1/2 teaspoon ground cinnamon *or* nutmeg
1/4 teaspoon salt
Pastry for double-crust pie (9 inches)
  2 tablespoons butter
TOPPING:
1/4 cup butter
1/2 cup packed brown sugar
  2 tablespoons heavy whipping cream
1/2 cup chopped pecans

In a large bowl, toss apples with lime juice. Combine the sugar, flour, cinnamon and salt; add to the apples and toss lightly.

Line a 9-in. pie plate with bottom crust and trim even with edge; fill with apple mixture. Dot with butter. Roll out remaining pastry to fit top of pie. Place over filling. Trim, seal and flute edges high. Cut slits in pastry. Bake at 400° for 40-45 minutes or until golden brown and apples are tender.

Meanwhile, melt butter in a small saucepan. Stir in brown sugar and cream; bring to a boil, stirring constantly. Remove from the heat; and stir in pecans. Pour over top crust. Bake 3-4 minutes longer or until bubbly. Serve warm. **Yield:** 8 servings.

Raisin Custard Pie

Ruth Ann Stelfox, Raymond, Alberta

A comforting, old-fashioned dessert, this custard pie is one of my mom's best. The fluffy meringue makes it look so special, and the raisins are a nice surprise.

1/2 cup sugar
  3 tablespoons cornstarch
  2 cups milk
  3 egg yolks
1/2 cup raisins
  2 teaspoons lemon juice
  1 pastry shell (9 inches), baked
MERINGUE:
  3 egg whites
1/4 cup sugar

In a large saucepan, combine sugar and cornstarch. Stir in milk until smooth. Cook and stir over medium-high heat until thickened and bubbly. Reduce heat to low; cook and stir for 2 minutes longer. Remove from the heat. Stir a small amount of hot filling into egg yolks; return all to the pan, stirring constantly. Bring to a gentle boil; cook and stir for 2 minutes. Remove from the heat; gently stir in raisins and lemon juice. Pour hot filling into crust.

For meringue, in a small bowl, beat egg whites on medium speed until soft peaks form. Gradually beat in sugar, 1 tablespoon at a time, on high until stiff, glossy peaks form. Spread over hot filling, sealing edges to crust.

Bake at 350° for 10-15 minutes or until golden brown. Cool on a wire rack for 1 hour; refrigerate for 1-2 hours before serving. Store in the refrigerator. **Yield:** 8 servings.

Texas Lime Pie

Diane Bell, Manvel, Texas

With the perfect balance of sweet and tart, this velvety pie is a great way to beat the Texas heat. With this simple recipe, even a novice cook can make a really memorable dessert. The recipe yields two pies, so you'll have enough to go around.

  3 cups graham cracker crumbs
1/2 cup packed brown sugar
2/3 cup butter, melted
  3 cans (14 ounces *each*) sweetened condensed milk
  5 egg yolks
  2 cups lime juice
Whipped topping, lime slices and fresh mint, optional

In a large bowl, combine the cracker crumbs, brown sugar and butter until crumbly. Press onto the bottom and up the sides of two greased 9-in. pie plates.

In a large bowl, beat the milk, egg yolks and lime juice on low for 2 minutes or until smooth and slightly thickened.

Pour into prepared crusts. Bake at 350° for 18-22 minutes or until a knife inserted near the center comes out clean. Cool on wire racks for 1 hour. Chill for 6 hours. Garnish with whipped topping, lime and mint if desired. Store in the refrigerator. **Yield:** 2 pies (6-8 servings each).

Apple Cranberry Tart

Jo Ann Fisher, Huntington Beach, California

People practically inhale this dessert. I modified a standard recipe years ago to come up with a different way of using cranberries.

1-1/4   cups unsweetened apple juice *or* cider, *divided*
1-1/3   cups sugar
   3   medium tart apples, peeled and cubed
   1   package (12 ounces) fresh *or* frozen cranberries
1/2   cup all-purpose flour
Pastry for single-crust pie (10 inches)
TOPPING:
1/3   cup chopped pecans
1/3   cup all-purpose flour
   3   tablespoons butter, melted
1/4   cup packed brown sugar
 12   pecan halves

In a large saucepan over medium heat, bring 3/4 cup apple juice and sugar to a boil, stirring occasionally. Add apples and cranberries; return to a boil. Reduce heat; simmer, uncovered, for 5-8 minutes or until apples are tender and berries pop. Whisk flour and remaining juice until smooth; stir into cranberry mixture. Bring to a boil; cook and stir for 2 minutes or until thickened. Cool to room temperature.

Fit pastry into a 10-in. fluted tart pan with removable bottom or press into the bottom and 1 in. up the sides of a 10-in. springform pan. Line pastry with double thickness of heavy-duty foil. Bake at 450° for 5 minutes. Remove foil; bake 7-10 minutes or until pastry is nearly done. Cool.

Transfer cooled apple mixture to pastry. Combine first four topping ingredients; sprinkle over filling. Arrange pecan halves on top. Bake at 375° for 30-35 minutes or until golden brown. Store in the refrigerator. **Yield:** 12 servings.

Rhubarb Custard Pie

Dolly Piper, Racine, Wisconsin

My mother always made this creamy pie with the first rhubarb picked. It's one of my earliest memories of a favorite treat, so I feel lucky to have this recipe. Mother was famous for her gorgeous pies. Unfortunately, she didn't write down most of her recipes...just "a handful of this" and "a dab of that" until it feels "just right" guided her creations.

1-1/2   cups all-purpose flour
1/4   teaspoon salt
1/2   cup shortening
1/4   cup cold water
   3   to 4 cups diced fresh *or* frozen rhubarb, thawed and drained
1-1/2   cups sugar
   2   eggs
   2   tablespoons cornstarch
3/4   teaspoon ground nutmeg

In a large bowl, combine flour and salt. Cut in shortening until mixture resembles coarse crumbs. Sprinkle with water, 1 tablespoon at a time, and toss lightly with a fork until the dough forms a ball.

On a lightly floured surface, roll out dough to fit a 9-in. pie plate. Transfer pastry to pie plate. Trim pastry to 1/2 in. beyond edge of pie plate; flute edges. Spoon rhubarb into pie shell.

In a small bowl, beat the sugar, eggs, cornstarch and nutmeg. Pour over rhubarb. Bake at 375° for 45 minutes or until crust is golden brown and filling is bubbly. Cool on a wire rack. **Yield:** 6-8 servings.

Editor's Note: If using frozen rhubarb, measure rhubarb while it is still frozen, then thaw completely. Drain in a colander, but do not press liquid out.

Peach Blueberry Pie

Sue Thumma, Shepherd, Michigan

Boy, I never thought of putting these two fruits together. What a flavor! That's what I hear most often after folks try this pie I invented one day when I was short of peaches for a full crust.

    1   cup sugar
  1/3   cup all-purpose flour
  1/2   teaspoon ground cinnamon
  1/8   teaspoon ground allspice
    3   cups sliced peeled fresh peaches
    1   cup fresh *or* frozen unsweetened blueberries
    1   tablespoon butter
Pastry for double-crust pie (9 inches)
Milk
Cinnamon-sugar

In a large bowl, combine the sugar, flour, cinnamon and allspice. Add the peaches and blueberries; toss gently.

Line a 9-in. pie plate with bottom crust; trim pastry even with edge. Add the filling. Dot with butter. Roll out remaining pastry; make a lattice crust. Trim, seal and flute edges. Brush crust with milk; sprinkle with cinnamon-sugar.

Bake at 400° for 40-45 minutes or until crust is golden brown and filling is bubbly. Cool completely on a wire rack. **Yield:** 6-8 servings.

Editor's Note: If using frozen blueberries, do not thaw before adding to batter.

Lattice Crust with a Twist To obtain the look of the Peach Blueberry Pie below left, cut the top crust into strips using a fluted pastry wheel or waffle-edged cutter. Then lay some strips in a row, about 3/4 inch apart over the filling. For the top strips, twist the strips two or three times and lay crosswise over the bottom strips.

Old-Fashioned Chocolate Pie

Betsey Sue Halcott, Lebanon, Connecticut

Preparing this old-fashioned pie brings back memories. When I was a girl, we cranked homemade ice cream to serve alongside every slice.

  1/2   cup water
  1-1/2 squares (1-1/2 ounces) unsweetened baking chocolate
  1/4   cup butter, cubed
  2/3   cup sugar
  1-1/2 teaspoons vanilla extract
FILLING:
  1/4   cup shortening
  3/4   cup sugar
    1   egg
    1   cup all-purpose flour
    1   teaspoon baking powder
  1/2   teaspoon salt
  1/2   cup milk
    1   unbaked pastry shell (9 inches)
    2   tablespoons chopped nuts, optional

In a small saucepan, bring the water, chocolate and butter to a boil; boil for 1 minute. Remove from the heat; stir in sugar and vanilla until smooth. Set aside.

In a large bowl, cream shortening and sugar until light and fluffy. Beat in egg. Combine the flour, baking powder and salt; add to creamed mixture alternately with milk, beating well after each addition.

Pour filling into pastry shell. Carefully pour the reserved chocolate mixture over filling. Sprinkle with nuts if desired. Cover edges of pastry with foil. Bake at 350° for 55-60 minutes or until a toothpick inserted near the center comes out clean. Cool on a wire rack. Store in the refrigerator. **Yield:** 8 servings.

Baking Classics | Pies

Apple Meringue Pie

Virginia Kraus, Pocahontas, Illinois

I received this recipe from my mother-in-law, and it's one of my husband's favorites. It's a nice change of pace on traditional apple pie.

- 7 cups thinly sliced peeled tart apples
- 2 tablespoons lemon juice
- 2/3 cup sugar
- 2 tablespoons all-purpose flour
- 1/3 cup milk
- 2 egg yolks, beaten
- 1 teaspoon grated lemon peel

Pastry for single-crust pie (9 inches)

- 1 tablespoon butter

MERINGUE:

- 3 egg whites
- 1/4 teaspoon cream of tartar
- 6 tablespoons sugar

In a large bowl, toss apples with lemon juice. In a small bowl, whisk the sugar, flour, milk, egg yolks and lemon peel until smooth. Pour over apples and toss to coat.

Line a 9-in. pie plate with pastry; trim to 1/2 in. beyond edge of pie plate and flute edges. Pour filling into crust; dot with butter. Cover edges loosely with foil.

Bake at 400° for 20 minutes. Remove foil; bake for 25-30 minutes or until apples are tender. Reduce heat to 350°.

In a bowl, beat the egg whites and cream of tartar on medium speed until foamy. Gradually beat in sugar, 1 tablespoon at a time, on high just until stiff peaks form and sugar is dissolved.

Spread evenly over hot filling, sealing edges to crust. Bake for 15 minutes or until golden brown. Cool on a wire rack. Store in the refrigerator. **Yield:** 6-8 servings.

Deep-Dish Blackberry Pie

Dorothy Lilliquist, Brooklyn Center, Minnesota

I think back to 1942 whenever I make this dessert. We grew extra large and juicy blackberries that year, and Mother canned 400 quarts. For years, whenever we went home to visit, Mother brought up jars of blackberries from the cellar and treated us to the best cobblers, jam cakes or jams in the world.

> 3 cups fresh *or* frozen blackberries, thawed and drained
> 1/2 cup sugar
> 2 tablespoons cornstarch
> 1 teaspoon lemon juice
> 1/4 teaspoon ground cinnamon
> LATTICE CRUST:
> 3/4 cup all-purpose flour
> 3 teaspoons sugar, *divided*
> 1/4 teaspoon salt
> 3 tablespoons cold butter
> 1 tablespoon shortening
> 3 tablespoons cold water
> 1 egg white, beaten

Place the blackberries in a bowl. Combine the sugar and cornstarch; sprinkle over berries. Add the lemon juice and cinnamon; toss to coat. Spoon into a greased 1-qt. baking dish.

In a bowl, combine the flour, 1 teaspoon sugar and salt. Cut in butter and shortening until mixture resembles coarse crumbs. Add water; toss with a fork until a ball forms. Roll out pastry; cut into strips and make a lattice crust over filling. Crimp edges.

Brush with the egg white; sprinkle with remaining sugar. Bake at 375° for 40-45 minutes or until crust is golden brown and the filling is bubbly. Cool on a wire rack. Store in the refrigerator. **Yield:** 4 servings.

Editor's Note: Instead of a lattice crust, pastry can be rolled out to fit top of dish. Cut slits in pastry; place over berries. Trim, seal and flute edges.

Strawberry-Rhubarb Crumb Pie

Paula Phillips, East Winthrop, Maine

Everyone seems to have a rhubarb patch here in Maine. This pie won first prize at our church fair; I hope it's a winner at your house, too!

- 1 egg
- 1 cup sugar
- 2 tablespoons all-purpose flour
- 1 teaspoon vanilla extract
- 3/4 pound rhubarb, cut into 1/2-inch pieces *or* sliced frozen rhubarb, (about 3 cups)
- 1 pint fresh strawberries, halved
- 1 unbaked pastry shell (9 inches)

TOPPING:
- 3/4 cup all-purpose flour
- 1/2 cup packed brown sugar
- 1/2 cup quick-cooking *or* old-fashioned oats
- 1/2 cup cold butter, cubed

In a large bowl, beat egg. Beat in the sugar, flour and vanilla. Gently stir in rhubarb and strawberries. Pour into pastry shell.

For topping, in a small bowl, combine the flour, brown sugar and oats; cut in butter until crumbly. Sprinkle over fruit.

Bake at 400° for 10 minutes. Reduce heat to 350°; bake for 35 minutes longer or until crust is golden brown and filling is bubbly. Cool on a wire rack. **Yield:** 8 servings.

Editor's Note: If using frozen rhubarb, measure rhubarb while still frozen, then thaw completely. Drain in a colander, but do not press liquid out.

Raspberry Custard Pie

Karen Rempel Arthur, Wainfleet, Ontario

Whether my husband and I host a backyard barbecue or a formal dinner, we love treating guests to this raspberry pie.

- 1/3 cup plus 1/4 cup sugar, *divided*
- 3 tablespoons cornstarch
- 1-1/2 cups milk
- 4 eggs, *separated*
- 1 teaspoon butter
- 1/4 teaspoon almond extract
- 1 extra-servings-size graham cracker crust (9 ounces)
- 1-1/8 teaspoons unflavored gelatin
- 2 tablespoons plus 1/4 teaspoon cold water, *divided*
- 1 can (21 ounces) raspberry pie filling
- 3/4 teaspoon cream of tartar

In a saucepan, combine 1/3 cup sugar and cornstarch. Stir in milk until smooth. Cook and stir over medium heat until thickened and bubbly. Reduce heat; cook and stir 2 minutes longer. Remove from the heat. Stir in a small amount of mixture into egg yolks. Return all to the pan, stirring constantly. Bring to a gentle boil; cook and stir 2 minutes longer. Remove from the heat; stir in butter and extract. Pour hot filling into the crust.

Sprinkle gelatin over 2 tablespoons cold water; let stand for 2 minutes. In a saucepan, bring raspberry filling and gelatin mixture to a boil. Reduce heat; simmer, uncovered, for 5 minutes.

Meanwhile, in a large bowl, beat egg whites and cream of tartar on medium speed until soft peaks form. Beat in remaining water. Gradually beat in remaining sugar, 1 tablespoon at a time on high until stiff, glossy peaks form.

Pour hot raspberry filling over custard. Spread meringue evenly over hot filling, sealing edges to crust. Bake at 325° for 15-18 minutes or until meringue is golden brown. Cool on a wire rack for 1 hour. Chill for at least 3 hours before serving. Store in the refrigerator. **Yield:** 8-10 servings.

Macaroon Cherry Pie

Lori Daniels, Beverly, West Virginia

I use homegrown cherries in this pie with a unique crunchy coconut topping. But I've found that purchased tart cherries yield a dessert that's nearly as delicious. I always bake this pie around Presidents' Day or Valentine's Day, but it's popular with my family in any season.

Pastry for single-crust pie (9 inches)
3	cans (14-1/2 ounces *each*) pitted tart cherries
1	cup sugar
1/3	cup cornstarch
1/2	teaspoon ground cinnamon
1/4	teaspoon red food coloring, optional

TOPPING:
1	egg, lightly beaten
2	tablespoons milk
1	tablespoon butter
1/4	teaspoon almond extract
1/4	cup sugar
1/8	teaspoon salt
1	cup flaked coconut
1/2	cup sliced almonds

Line a 9-in. deep-dish pie plate with pastry. Trim to 1/2 in. beyond edge of plate; flute edges. Bake at 400° for 6 minutes; set aside.

Drain cherries, reserving 1 cup juice. Set the cherries aside. In a large saucepan, combine the sugar and cornstarch; gradually stir in the cherry juice until blended. Bring to a boil over medium heat; cook and stir for 2 minutes or until thickened.

Remove from the heat; stir in cinnamon and food coloring if desired. Gently fold in cherries. Pour into crust. Cover edges loosely with foil. Bake at 400° for 20 minutes.

Meanwhile, in a large bowl, combine the first six topping ingredients. Stir in coconut and almonds.

Remove foil from pie; spoon topping over pie. Bake at 350° for 20 minutes or until topping is lightly browned. Cool on a wire rack for 1 hour. Chill for 4 hours or overnight before cutting. **Yield:** 6-8 servings.

Grapefruit Meringue Pie

Barbara Soliday, Winter Haven, Florida

There's a grapefruit tree in our backyard, so I like to use fresh grapefruit juice when I make this pie. I just love the unique citrus flavor of this dessert.

1-1/3	cups sugar
1/3	cup cornstarch
2	cups pink grapefruit juice
3/4	cup water
3	egg yolks, lightly beaten
2	tablespoons butter, softened
1/2	teaspoon lemon extract
1	pastry shell (9 inches), baked

MERINGUE:
3	egg whites
1/4	teaspoon cream of tartar
6	tablespoons sugar

In a large saucepan, combine the sugar and cornstarch. Stir in grapefruit juice and water until smooth. Cook and stir over medium-high heat until thickened and bubbly. Reduce heat; cook and stir 2 minutes longer. Remove from the heat. Stir a 1/2 cup of hot filling into egg yolks; return all to pan, stirring constantly. Bring to a gentle boil; cook and stir 2 minutes longer. Remove from the heat. Gently stir in butter and extract. Pour hot filling into pastry shell.

In a large bowl, beat egg whites and cream of tartar on medium speed until soft peaks form. Gradually beat in sugar, 1 tablespoon at a time, on high until stiff, glossy peaks form and sugar is dissolved. Spread evenly over hot filling, sealing edges to crust.

Bake at 350° for 12-15 minutes or until the meringue is golden brown. Cool on a wire rack for 1 hour. Refrigerate for at least 3 hours before serving. Store leftovers in the refrigerator. **Yield:** 6-8 servings.

German Apple Pie

Mrs. Woodrow Taylor, Adams Center, New York

I tasted this pie many years ago when my children's babysitter made it. I asked for the recipe and have baked it many times since.

- 1-1/2 cups all-purpose flour
- 1/2 teaspoon salt
- 1/2 cup shortening
- 1 teaspoon vanilla extract
- 2 to 3 tablespoons ice water

FILLING:
- 1 cup sugar
- 1/4 cup all-purpose flour
- 2 teaspoons ground cinnamon
- 6 cups sliced peeled tart apples
- 1 cup heavy whipping cream

Whipped cream, optional

In a small bowl, combine flour and salt; cut in the shortening until crumbly. Add vanilla. Gradually add water, tossing with a fork until dough forms a ball. Roll out pastry to fit a 9-in. pie plate. Transfer pastry to pie plate. Trim pastry to 1/2 in. beyond edge of pie plate; flute edges.

For filling, combine the sugar, flour and cinnamon; sprinkle 3 tablespoons into crust. Layer with half of the apples; sprinkle with half of the remaining sugar mixture. Repeat layers. Pour cream over all.

Bake at 450° for 10 minutes. Reduce heat to 350°; bake 55-60 minutes longer or until apples are tender. Cool on a wire rack. Store in the refrigerator. Serve with whipped cream if desired. **Yield:** 8 servings.

Pick of the Apples Granny Smiths are a crisp, tart apple that would be suitable for this German Apple Pie. Other options would be Braeburn and Empire, which have a sweet-tart flavor. Cortland and Rome Beauty apples are mildly tart and would also be good choices.

Cranberry Cherry Pie

Marilyn Williams, Matthews, North Carolina

This sweet-tart pie is a snap to make and is so pretty.

- 3/4 cup sugar
- 2 tablespoons cornstarch
- 1 can (21 ounces) cherry pie filling
- 2 cups cranberries

Pastry for double-crust pie (9 inches)
Milk and additional sugar

In a bowl, combine sugar and cornstarch. Stir in pie filling and cranberries. Line a 9-in. pie plate with bottom pastry; trim to 1 in. beyond edge of plate. Pour filling into crust.

Roll out remaining pastry to fit top of pie. Cut slits in pastry or cut out stars with a star-shaped cookie cutter. Place pastry over filling; trim, seal and flute edges. Arrange star cutouts on pastry. Brush with milk and sprinkle with sugar.

Cover edges loosely with foil. Bake at 375° for 55-60 minutes or until crust is golden brown and filling is bubbly. Cool on a wire rack. Store in the refrigerator. **Yield:** 6-8 servings.

Molasses Pumpkin Pie

Lois Fetting, Nelson, Wisconsin

For more than 40 years, our Thanksgiving feast has included this pie. It's a special, old-fashioned treat. We love generous slices topped with whipped cream.

Pastry for single-crust pie (9 inches)
- 2 eggs
- 1/2 cup sugar
- 1 teaspoon ground cinnamon
- 1/2 teaspoon salt
- 1/2 teaspoon ground ginger
- 1/2 teaspoon ground nutmeg
- 1 can (15 ounces) solid-pack pumpkin
- 3 tablespoons molasses
- 3/4 cup evaporated milk

Whipped topping

Line a 9-in. pie plate with pastry. Trim to 1/2 in. beyond edge of plate; flute edges. Set aside.

In a large bowl, beat the eggs, sugar, cinnamon, salt, ginger and nutmeg. Beat in pumpkin and molasses; gradually add milk. Pour into crust. Cover edges loosely with foil.

Bake at 425° for 10 minutes. Remove foil. Reduce heat 350°; bake 28-32 minutes longer or until a knife inserted near the center comes out clean. Cool on a wire rack for 2 hours. Chill until ready to serve. Serve with whipped topping. Store in the refrigerator. **Yield:** 6-8 servings.

Cinnamon Chocolate Angel Pie

Donna Torres, Grand Rapids, Minnesota

Our Christmas dinner wouldn't be complete without a festive finale. I've served this satisfying pie for so many years that it's become a holiday tradition.

- 2 egg whites
- 1/2 teaspoon white vinegar
- 1/2 cup sugar
- 1/8 to 1/4 teaspoon ground cinnamon
- 1 pastry shell (9 inches), baked

FILLING:
- 2 egg yolks
- 1/4 cup water
- 1 cup (6 ounces) semisweet chocolate chips
- 1 cup heavy whipping cream
- 1/4 cup sugar
- 1/4 teaspoon ground cinnamon

In a bowl, beat egg whites and vinegar on medium speed until foamy. Combine sugar and cinnamon; gradually beat into egg whites, 1 tablespoon at a time, on high until stiff, glossy peaks form. Spread into the pastry shell. Bake at 325° for 20-25 minutes or until meringue is lightly browned. Cool.

For filling, whisk egg yolks and water in a saucepan. Add chocolate chips; cook and stir over low heat until a thermometer reads 160° and mixture is thickened (do not boil). Cool. Spread 3 tablespoons over meringue; set remainder aside.

In a bowl, beat the cream, sugar and cinnamon until stiff peaks form. Spread half over the chocolate layer. Fold reserved chocolate mixture into remaining whipped cream; spread over top. Chill for 6 hours or overnight. Store in the refrigerator. **Yield:** 8-10 servings.

Dixie Pie

Sandra Pichon, Slidell, Louisiana

When Mom baked this classic sugar pie, family members would clamor for second servings. We love the combination of cinnamon, coconut, nuts and raisins. She'd sometimes toss in a few chocolate chips for variety.

Pastry for two single-crust pies (9 inches)
- 1-1/2 cups raisins
- 1 cup butter, softened
- 1 cup sugar
- 1 cup packed brown sugar
- 6 eggs
- 2 teaspoons vanilla extract
- 2 to 4 teaspoons ground cinnamon
- 1 cup chopped nuts
- 1 cup flaked coconut

Whipped topping and additional chopped nuts, optional

Line two 9-in. pie plates with pastry. Trim pastry to 1/2 in. beyond edge of plate; flute edges. Line crusts with a double thickness of heavy-duty foil. Bake at 450° for 10 minutes. Discard foil. Cool on wire racks.

Place raisins in a saucepan and cover with water; bring to a boil. Remove from heat; set aside. In a large bowl, cream butter and sugars until light and fluffy. Beat in eggs, vanilla and cinnamon until smooth.

Drain raisins. Stir raisins, nuts and coconut into creamed mixture (mixture will appear curdled). Pour into the crusts. Bake at 350° for 30-35 minutes or until set. Cool on wire racks. Garnish with whipped topping and nuts if desired. Store in the refrigerator. **Yield:** 2 pies (6-8 servings each).

Miniature Almond Tarts

Karen Van Den Berge, Holland, Michigan

My family requests these adorable little tarts at the holidays. I always enjoy making them since the almond paste in the filling reflects our Dutch heritage, plus they're popular at special gatherings.

- 1 cup butter, softened
- 2 packages (3 ounces *each*) cream cheese, softened
- 2 cups all-purpose flour

FILLING:
- 6 ounces almond paste, crumbled
- 2 eggs, lightly beaten
- 1/2 cup sugar

FROSTING:
- 1-1/2 cups confectioners' sugar
- 3 tablespoons butter, softened
- 4 to 5 teaspoons milk

Maraschino cherry halves (about 48)

In a large bowl, cream the butter and cream cheese until smooth. Gradually add flour until well blended. Refrigerate for 1 hour.

Shape dough into 1-in. balls. Place in ungreased miniature muffin cups; press into the bottom and up the sides to form a shell.

For filling, in a small bowl, beat the almond paste, eggs and sugar until blended. Fill each shell with about 1-1/2 teaspoons filling.

Bake at 325° for 25-30 minutes or until edges are golden brown. Cool for 10 minutes before removing to wire racks to cool completely.

For frosting, combine confectioners' sugar, butter and enough milk to achieve desired consistency. Pipe or spread over tarts. Top each with a cherry half. **Yield:** about 4 dozen.

Ozark Mountain Berry Pie

Elaine Moody, Clever, Missouri

I taste the berries or filling before adding to the pie crust to make sure it's sweet enough. Slicing the berries will help them absorb more of the sugar or flavorings. It's absolutely delicious served warm.

- 1 cup sugar
- 1/4 cup cornstarch
- 1/2 teaspoon ground cinnamon, optional

Dash salt
- 1 cup blueberries
- 1 cup strawberries
- 3/4 cup blackberries
- 3/4 cup red raspberries
- 1/2 cup water
- 2 tablespoons lemon juice

Pastry for a double-crust pie (9 inches)
- 2 tablespoons butter

In a large saucepan, combine the sugar, cornstarch, cinnamon if desired and salt. Stir in the berries. Add water and lemon juice. Cook over medium heat until mixture just comes to a boil.

Line a 9-in. pie plate with bottom crust; trim pastry even with edge. Fill with berry filling and dot with butter. Roll out remaining pastry; make a lattice crust. Trim, seal and flute edges. Bake at 350° for 45-50 minutes or until the crust is golden brown. Cool on a wire rack. Store in the refrigerator. **Yield:** 8 servings.

Mom's Lemon Custard Pie

Jeannie Fritson, Kearney, Nebraska

My mother often made this pie back when we were growing up over 70 years ago. You might say it's stood the test of time, because today it's still my brother's favorite! The beaten egg whites give it a delicate texture and make this custard pie quite unique!

- 1 cup sugar
- 1 tablespoon butter, softened
- 3 tablespoons all-purpose flour
- 1/8 teaspoon salt
- 2 eggs, *separated*
- 1 cup milk
- 1/4 cup fresh lemon juice

Peel of 1 medium lemon
- 1 unbaked pastry shell (9 inches)

Whipped cream, optional

Using a wooden spoon, blend sugar and butter. Add the flour, salt and egg yolks. Stir in milk, lemon juice and peel until well blended. Set aside. In a small bowl, beat egg whites until stiff peaks form; gently fold into the lemon mixture.

Pour into pastry shell. Bake at 325° for 1 hour or until lightly browned and a knife inserted near the center comes out clean. Cool on a wire rack. Garnish with whipped cream if desired. Store in the refrigerator. **Yield:** 6-8 servings.

Double Peanut Pie

Vivian Cleeton, Richmond, Virginia

I created this recipe for a national pie contest and won second place for my state. Many peanuts are grown here, and I always look for delicious ways to use them.

- 2 eggs
- 1/3 cup creamy peanut butter
- 1/3 cup sugar
- 1/3 cup light corn syrup
- 1/3 cup dark corn syrup
- 1/3 cup butter, melted
- 1 teaspoon vanilla extract
- 1 cup salted peanuts
- 1 unbaked pastry shell (9 inches)

Whipped cream *or* ice cream, optional

In a large bowl, lightly beat the eggs. Gradually add the peanut butter, sugar, corn syrups, butter and vanilla until well blended. Fold in peanuts.

Pour into the crust. Bake at 375° for 30-35 minutes or until set. Cool. Serve with whipped cream or ice cream if desired. **Yield:** 6-8 servings.

Pistachio Pudding Tarts

Bettye Linster, Atlanta, Georgia

For St. Patrick's Day or any time you want a treat that's green, refreshing and delightful, try these tempting tarts.

　1　cup butter, softened
　1　package (8 ounces) cream cheese, softened
　2　cups all-purpose flour
1-3/4　cups cold milk
　1　package (3.4 ounces) instant pistachio pudding mix

In a large bowl, combine butter and cream cheese until smooth. Gradually add flour until blended.

Shape into 48 balls (1 in. each); press onto the bottom and up the sides of ungreased miniature muffin cups. Bake at 400° for 12-15 minutes or until lightly browned. Cool for 5 minutes; carefully remove from pans to a wire rack to cool completely.

For filling, in a small bowl, whisk milk and pudding for 2 minutes. Cover and refrigerate for 5 minutes. Spoon into tart shells. Store in the refrigerator. **Yield:** 4 dozen.

Golden Apricot Pie

Jo and Joe Martin, Patterson, California

This pie is pretty as a picture with the fruit's beautiful golden-orange color showing through its lattice top.

　2　packages (6 ounces *each*) dried apricots
2-3/4　cups water
Pastry for double-crust pie (9 inches)
　1　cup sugar
　3　tablespoons cornstarch
1/8　teaspoon ground nutmeg
　1　tablespoon butter

In a small saucepan, combine apricots and water; bring to a boil. Reduce heat and simmer for 20-22 minutes. Remove from the heat; cool.

Line a 9-in. pie plate with bottom crust; trim pastry even with edge. Drain apricots, reserving 3/4 cup liquid. Arrange apricots in pie shell. Combine the sugar, cornstarch, nutmeg and reserved apricot liquid.

Pour over apricots; dot with butter. Roll out remaining pastry; make a lattice crust. Trim, seal and flute edges. Bake at 400° for 50-55 minutes or until crust is golden brown and filling is bubbly. **Yield:** 8 servings.

Almond Pear Tartlets

Marie Rizzio, Traverse City, Michigan

Although they're quick to fix, these pretty pastries are worth savoring slowly. Delicately spiced pears are complemented by an almond sauce and a crispy crust. Be prepared to share the recipe.

　1　egg, lightly beaten
1/2　cup plus 6 tablespoons sugar, *divided*
3/4　cup heavy whipping cream
　2　tablespoons butter, melted
1/2　teaspoon almond extract
　1　package (10 ounces) frozen puff pastry shells, thawed
　2　small ripe pears, peeled and thinly sliced
1/2　teaspoon ground cinnamon
1/8　teaspoon ground ginger
1/2　cup slivered almonds, toasted, optional

In a small saucepan, combine the egg, 1/2 cup sugar, cream and butter. Cook and stir until the sauce is thickened and a thermometer reads 160°. Remove from the heat; stir in extract. Cover and refrigerate.

On an unfloured surface, roll each pastry into a 4-in. circle. Place in an ungreased 15-in. x 10-in. x 1-in. baking pan. Top each with pear slices. Combine the cinnamon, ginger and remaining sugar; sprinkle over pears.

Bake at 400° for 20 minutes or until pastry is golden brown. Sprinkle with almonds if desired. Serve warm with chilled cream sauce. **Yield:** 6 servings.

Walnut Applesauce Pie

Mrs. Verbrugge, Franklin Lakes, New Jersey

My mother baked this pie every autumn, and it's become a tradition at our house. My husband always asks for seconds.

1	cup packed dark brown sugar
1/3	cup sugar
1	tablespoon all-purpose flour
1	egg
1	egg white
1/2	cup unsweetened applesauce
2	tablespoons milk
1	teaspoon vanilla extract
1	cup chopped walnuts
1	unbaked pastry shell (9 inches)

Whipped cream, optional

In a large bowl, combine sugars and flour. Beat in the egg, egg white, applesauce, milk and vanilla until well blended. Stir in walnuts.

Pour into pastry shell. Bake at 375° for 40-45 minutes or until set. Cool completely on a wire rack. Serve with whipped cream if desired. Store in the refrigerator. **Yield: 6-8 servings.**

Protecting Pastry Edges The edges of a pie pastry often brown before the rest of the pie is thoroughly baked. To protect the edges, shield with a strip of aluminum foil.

115

Farm Apple Pan Pie

Dolores Skrout, Summerhill, Pennsylvania

You'll find this apple pie's very convenient for taking to a covered-dish supper, picnic, etc. But be prepared—people always ask for a copy of the recipe!

- 5 cups all-purpose flour
- 4 teaspoons sugar
- 1/2 teaspoon salt
- 1/2 teaspoon baking powder
- 1-1/2 cups shortening
- 2 egg yolks, lightly beaten
- 3/4 cup cold water

FILLING:
- 5 pounds tart apples, peeled and thinly sliced
- 4 teaspoons lemon juice
- 3/4 cup sugar
- 3/4 cup packed brown sugar
- 1 teaspoon ground cinnamon
- 1/2 teaspoon ground nutmeg
- 1/4 teaspoon salt

Milk

Additional sugar

In a large bowl, combine the flour, sugar, salt and baking powder; cut in shortening until the mixture resembles coarse crumbs. Combine yolks and cold water. Sprinkle over dry ingredients; toss with fork. If needed, add additional water, 1 tablespoon at a time, until mixture can be formed into a ball.

Divide dough in half. On a lightly floured surface, roll half of dough to fit a 15-in. x 10-in. x 1-in. baking pan.

Sprinkle apples with lemon juice; arrange half of them over dough. Combine the sugars, cinnamon, nutmeg and salt; sprinkle half over apples. Top with remaining apples; sprinkle with remaining sugar mixture.

Roll remaining pastry to fit pan; place on top of filling and seal edges. Brush with milk and sprinkle with sugar. Cut vents in top pastry. Bake at 400° for 50 minutes or until crust is golden brown and filling is bubbly. **Yield:** 18-24 servings.

Banana Split Brownie Pie

Tanna Walker, Salina, Kansas

I often use Neapolitan in place of three different ice cream flavors to make this luscious dessert. You can bake the brownie crust days ahead, top it with the ice cream and freeze until you need it.

4	ounces German sweet chocolate, chopped
1/2	cup butter, cubed
3	eggs
1	cup sugar
1/2	teaspoon vanilla extract
1/2	cup all-purpose flour
1-1/3	cups vanilla ice cream
1-2/3	cups chocolate ice cream
1-2/3	cups strawberry ice cream
2	medium firm bananas, sliced
1	cup fresh strawberries, sliced
1/2	to 3/4 cup hot fudge ice cream topping, warmed
1/2	to 3/4 cup strawberry ice cream topping
1/4	to 1/2 cup toffee bits *or* almond brickle chips

Whipping cream and sliced almonds

In a microwave, melt chocolate and butter; stir until smooth. Cool. In a small bowl, beat the eggs, sugar, vanilla and cooled chocolate mixture. Gradually add flour until well blended. Spread into a greased 9-in. springform pan.

Bake at 350° for 30-35 minutes or until a toothpick inserted near the center comes out clean. Cool on a wire rack. Cover and freeze until firm.

Using 1/3 cup for each scoop, place four scoops of vanilla ice cream, five scoops of chocolate ice cream and five scoops of strawberry ice cream on a waxed paper-lined baking sheet. Freeze until firm. Place vanilla scoops in center of brownie crust; alternate scoops of chocolate and strawberry around edge. Cover and freeze until firm.

Just before serving, remove sides of pan. Arrange bananas and strawberries over ice cream. Drizzle with hot fudge and strawberry toppings. Sprinkle with toffee bits. Garnish with whipped cream and almonds. Cut into wedges. **Yield:** 10 servings.

Orange Rhubarb Pie

Mrs. Kaufman, Haines City, Florida

This is one of my favorite ways to use our rhubarb crop. The rhubarb-orange combination gives this pie a nice flavor.

1-1/4	cups sugar, *divided*
1/4	cup all-purpose flour
1/4	teaspoon salt
3	tablespoons orange juice concentrate
1/4	cup butter, melted
3	eggs, *separated*
2-1/2	cups diced fresh *or* frozen rhubarb (cut into 1/2-inch pieces)
1	unbaked pastry shell (9 inches)
1/3	cup chopped walnuts

In a large bowl, combine 1 cup sugar, flour and salt. Stir in orange juice and butter. In a small bowl, lightly beat egg yolks; stir into the orange juice mixture until blended. Add the rhubarb.

In a large bowl, beat egg whites until soft peaks begin to form; gradually beat in remaining sugar, 1 tablespoon at a time, until stiff, glossy peaks form. Fold into the rhubarb mixture.

Pour into pastry shell. Top with nuts. Bake at 375° for 15 minutes. Reduce heat to 325°; bake for 40 minutes longer or until golden brown. Cover edges with foil during the last 15 minutes to prevent overbrowning if necessary. Cool on a wire rack. Store in the refrigerator. **Yield:** 6-8 servings.

Editor's Note: If using frozen rhubarb, measure rhubarb while it is still frozen, then thaw completely. Drain in a colander, but do not press liquid out.

Raspberry Meringue Pie

Mrs. Sohrwiede, McGraw, New York

We have raspberry bushes, so I'm always looking for recipes using this delicious fruit. This is a family favorite.

- 1 cup all-purpose flour
- 1/3 cup sugar
- 1 teaspoon baking powder
- 1/4 teaspoon salt
- 2 tablespoons cold butter
- 1 egg, lightly beaten
- 2 tablespoons milk

MERINGUE:

- 2 egg whites
- 1/2 cup sugar
- 2 cups fresh *or* frozen unsweetened raspberries

In a large bowl, combine the flour, sugar, baking powder and salt; cut in butter. Combine egg and milk; stir into flour mixture (dough will be sticky). Press into the bottom and up the sides of a greased 9-in. pie plate; set aside.

In a small bowl, beat egg whites on medium speed until soft peaks form. Gradually beat in sugar, 1 tablespoon at a time, until stiff, glossy peaks form. Fold in raspberries. Spoon into the crust.

Bake at 350° for 30-35 minutes or until the meringue is golden brown. Cool completely on a wire rack. Store in the refrigerator. **Yield:** 6-8 servings.

Editor's Note: If using frozen raspberries, do not thaw before adding to batter.

Pecan Macadamia Pie

Anne Simboli, Farmville, Virginia

It's bound to be a blue-ribbon Christmas when I serve this rich, nutty pie—it was a prize-winner at our county fair. My husband, who can take or leave sweets, can't resist it!

- 1 cup all-purpose flour
- 2 tablespoons sugar
- 1/2 teaspoon salt
- 1/4 cup shortening
- 3 to 4 tablespoons cold water

FILLING:

- 3 eggs
- 1/2 cup sugar
- 4-1/2 teaspoons all-purpose flour
- 1/4 teaspoon salt
- 1 cup light corn syrup
- 1 tablespoon butter, melted and cooled
- 1 teaspoon vanilla extract
- 1 cup coarsely chopped pecans
- 3/4 cup coarsely chopped macadamia nuts

In a large bowl, combine the flour, sugar and salt; cut in shortening until crumbly. Gradually add cold water, tossing with a fork until dough begins to cling together. Form into a ball.

On a lightly floured surface, roll dough to a 10-in. circle. Place in a 9-in. pie plate and set aside. For filling, beat eggs until blended but not frothy. Add the sugar, flour, salt and corn syrup until well blended. Add butter and vanilla just until blended. Stir in nuts.

Pour into crust. Bake at 325° for 55-60 minutes or until center is set. Cool on a wire rack. Store in the refrigerator. **Yield:** 8-10 servings.

County Fair Pie

Judy Acuff, Lathrop, Missouri

This quick and easy recipe is one my family asks for again and again. I've taken it to lots of potlucks and have been asked for the recipe many times.

- 1 cup butter, softened
- 1 cup sugar
- 1/2 cup all-purpose flour
- 2 eggs
- 1 teaspoon vanilla extract
- 1 cup coarsely chopped walnuts
- 1 cup (6 ounces) semisweet chocolate chips
- 1/2 cup butterscotch chips
- 1 unbaked pastry shell (9 inches)

In a bowl, beat the butter, sugar, flour, eggs, and vanilla until well blended. Stir in nuts and chips.

Pour into pastry shell. Bake at 325° for 1 hour or until golden brown. Cool on a wire rack. **Yield:** 6-8 servings.

Make a Rope Edge To make a rope edge, which is featured on the pie above, line the pie plate with the pastry and trim 1/2 inch beyond the edge of the pie plate. Turn the overhanging pastry under the pastry to form a rolled edge. Then make a fist with one hand and press your thumb at an angle in the pastry. Pinch some of the pastry between your thumb and index finger. Repeat at about 1/2-inch intervals around the crust. For a looser-looking rope, position your thumb at a wider angle and repeat at 1-inch intervals.

Triple Fruit Pie

Jeanne Freybler, Grand Rapids, Michigan

My goal is to create pies as good as my mother's. I came up with this recipe to use up fruit in my freezer. The first time I made it, my family begged for seconds. If I continue making pies this good, maybe someday our two daughters will be striving to imitate mine.

- 1-1/4 cups *each* fresh blueberries, raspberries and chopped rhubarb
- 1/2 teaspoon almond extract
- 1-1/4 cups sugar
- 1/4 cup quick-cooking tapioca
- 1/4 teaspoon ground nutmeg
- 1/4 teaspoon salt
- 1 tablespoon lemon juice
- Pastry for double-crust pie (9 inches)

In a large bowl, combine fruits and extract; toss to coat. In another bowl, combine sugar, tapioca, nutmeg and salt. Add to fruit; stir gently. Let stand for 15 minutes.

Line a 9-in. pie plate with bottom crust; trim pastry even with edge. Stir lemon juice into fruit mixture; spoon into the crust. Roll out remaining pastry; make a lattice crust. Seal and flute edges.

Bake at 400° for 20 minutes. Reduce heat to 350°; bake 30 minutes longer or until the crust is golden brown and the filling is bubbly. Cool on a wire rack. Store in the refrigerator. **Yield:** 6-8 servings.

Plum Pie

Shirley Smith, Noti, Oregon

My husband says this pie is his favorite. But he claims to like only two kinds of pies—warm and cold ones.

- 1/4 cup packed brown sugar
- 1/4 cup crushed saltines
- Pastry for double-crust pie (9 inches)
- 1-1/2 pounds fresh plums, pitted and quartered
- 1 cup sugar
- 1/4 cup all-purpose flour
- 1 teaspoon ground cinnamon
- 3 tablespoons cold butter
- 1 teaspoon cinnamon-sugar

In a small bowl, combine brown sugar and crumbs. Line a 9-in. pie pan with bottom crust; sprinkle with brown sugar mixture and pack gently. Cover with plums. Combine the sugar, flour and cinnamon; cut in butter until crumbly. Sprinkle over plums.

Roll out remaining pastry to fit top of pie. Place over filling. Trim, seal and flute edges. Cut slits in pastry. Sprinkle with cinnamon-sugar. Bake at 400° for 30 minutes. Reduce heat to 350°; bake 25 minutes longer or until golden brown. Cool on a wire rack. **Yield:** 6-8 servings.

Apple Blackberry Pie

Dorian Lucas, Corning, California

After a blackberry-picking trip, my husband and I decided to include a few in an apple pie we were making. It was the best we'd ever tasted! We live near the mountains with our two children. Ingredients for fruit pies grow all around us.

- 2 cups all-purpose flour
- 1 teaspoon sugar
- 1 teaspoon salt
- 1 teaspoon ground cinnamon
- 2/3 cup cold butter
- 4 to 6 tablespoons cold water

FILLING:
- 5 cups thinly sliced peeled tart apples (about 6 medium)
- 1 cup fresh blackberries
- 1/2 cup packed brown sugar
- 4-1/2 teaspoons cornstarch
- 1 teaspoon ground cinnamon
- 1 teaspoon ground nutmeg

In a large bowl, combine the flour, sugar, salt and cinnamon; cut in butter until crumbly. Gradually add water, tossing with a fork until dough forms a ball. Divide dough in half. Roll out one portion to fit a 9-in. pie plate; place pastry in plate and trim even with edge.

In a large bowl, combine apples and blackberries. Combine the brown sugar, cornstarch, cinnamon and nutmeg; add to fruit mixture and toss to coat. Pour into crust.

Roll out remaining pastry to fit top of pie; place over filling. Trim, seal and flute edges. Cut slits in pastry. Add decorative cutouts if desired. Cover edges loosely with foil.

Bake at 450° for 10 minutes. Reduce heat to 350°; remove foil. Bake 40-50 minutes longer or until lightly browned and filling is bubbly. Cool on a wire rack. Store in the refrigerator. **Yield:** 6-8 servings.

Golden Squash Pie

Patricia Hardin, Seymour, Tennessee

Whether you take this yummy pie to a party or potluck, be prepared to share the recipe. An alternative to pumpkin pie, it bakes up high and flavorful.

    4   eggs
    4   cups mashed cooked butternut squash
    1   cup buttermilk
  1/4   cup butter, melted
    2   teaspoons vanilla extract
    2   cups sugar
    2   tablespoons all-purpose flour
    1   teaspoon salt
  1/2   teaspoon baking soda
    2   unbaked pastry shell (9 inches)
Ground nutmeg, optional

In a bowl, combine the eggs, squash, buttermilk, butter and vanilla. Combine the sugar, flour, salt and baking soda; add to the squash mixture and mix until smooth. Pour into pastry shells. Cover edges loosely with foil.

Bake at 350° for 35 minutes. Remove foil. Bake 25 minutes longer or until a knife inserted near the center comes out clean. Cool on a wire rack. Sprinkle with nutmeg if desired. Store in the refrigerator. **Yield:** 2 pies (6-8 servings each).

Ambrosia Pecan Pie

Bernadine Stine, Roanoke, Indiana

Orange peel and coconut combine with pecans to make this truly special and rich-tasting dessert. It always wins compliments at Christmas dinner.

    3   eggs
  3/4   cup light corn syrup
  1/2   cup sugar
    3   tablespoons brown sugar
    3   tablespoons orange juice
    2   tablespoons butter, melted
    1   teaspoon grated orange peel
  1/8   teaspoon salt
1-1/2   cups chopped pecans
  2/3   cup flaked coconut
    1   unbaked pastry shell (9 inches)

In a large bowl, beat the eggs, corn syrup, sugars, orange juice, butter, orange peel and salt until well blended. Stir in pecans and coconut.

Pour filling into pastry shell. Bake at 350° for 50-60 minutes or until a knife inserted near the center comes out clean. Cover edges with foil during the last 15 minutes to prevent overbrowning if necessary. Cool on a wire rack. **Yield:** 8 servings.

Mom's Peach Pie

Sally Holbrook, Pasadena, California

A delightful summertime pie, this dessert is overflowing with fresh peach taste. Each sweet slice is packed with old-fashioned appeal. The streusel topping makes this pie a little different than the ordinary and adds homemade flair.

    1   egg white
    1   unbaked pastry shell (9 inches)
  3/4   cup all-purpose flour
  1/2   cup packed brown sugar
  1/3   cup sugar
  1/4   cup cold butter, cut into 6 pieces
    6   cups sliced peeled fresh peaches

Beat egg white until foamy; brush over the bottom and sides of the pastry shell. In a small bowl, combine flour and sugars; cut in butter until mixture resembles fine crumbs. Sprinkle two-thirds into the bottom of pastry; top with peaches. Sprinkle with remaining crumb mixture.

Bake at 375° for 40-45 minutes or until filling is bubbly and peaches are tender. Cool on a wire rack. **Yield:** 6-8 servings.

Cherry Berry Pie

Wanda Van Voorhis, Plain City, Ohio

Whenever I bake this dessert a neighbor shared with me, folks rave about it. I'm always looking for new treats to serve my family. This one's definitely a keeper.

1-1/2 cups sugar
1/4 cup plus 2 teaspoons quick-cooking tapioca
1/8 teaspoon salt
2-1/2 cups fresh *or* frozen pitted tart cherries, thawed
1-1/2 cups fresh *or* frozen unsweetened raspberries, thawed
1 teaspoon lemon juice
Pastry for double-crust pie (9 inches)
1 tablespoon butter

In a large bowl, combine the sugar, tapioca and salt. Add the cherries, raspberries and lemon juice; gently toss to coat. Let stand for 15 minutes.

Line a 9-in. pie plate with bottom crust. Trim to 1 in. beyond edge of pie plate. Pour filling into crust; dot with butter. Roll out remaining pastry; make a lattice crust. Trim, seal and flute high edges.

Cover edges loosely with foil. Bake at 400° for 30 minutes. Remove foil; bake 5-10 minutes longer or until crust is golden brown and filling is bubbly. Cool on a wire rack. **Yield:** 6-8 servings.

Perfect Rhubarb Pie

Ellen Benninger, Stoneboro, Pennsylvania

Nothing hides the tangy rhubarb in this lovely pie, which has just the right balance of sweet and tart. Serving this is a nice way to celebrate the end of winter!

    4   cups sliced fresh *or* frozen rhubarb
    4   cups boiling water
1-1/2   cups sugar
    3   tablespoons all-purpose flour
    1   teaspoon quick-cooking tapioca
    1   egg
    2   teaspoons cold water
Pastry for double-crust pie (9 inches)
    1   tablespoon butter

Place rhubarb in a colander; pour water over rhubarb and set aside. In a large bowl, combine the sugar, flour and tapioca. Add drained rhubarb; toss to coat. Let stand for 15 minutes. Beat egg and water; add to rhubarb mixture until well blended.

Line a 9-in. pie plate with bottom pastry. Add filling. Dot with butter. Roll out remaining pastry to fit top of pie. Place over filling. Trim, seal and flute edges. Cut slits in pastry. Bake at 400° for 15 minutes. Reduce heat to 350°; bake 40-50 minutes longer or until crust is golden brown and filling is bubbly. Cool on a wire rack. Store in the refrigerator. **Yield:** 8 servings.

Old-Fashioned Chess Pie

Christine Batts, Murray, Kentucky

This is the type of pie that your grandmother might have made. It's rich and delicious!

    1   cup butter, softened
    2   cups sugar
    6   egg yolks
    1   egg
  1/3   cup cornmeal
  1/4   cup all-purpose flour
  1/3   cup milk
    1   teaspoon vanilla extract
    1   unbaked deep-dish pastry shell (9 inches)
TOPPING:
    2   cups sugar, *divided*
  2/3   cup milk
  1/2   cup butter

In a bowl, cream butter and sugar until light and fluffy. Beat in egg yolks and egg. Add cornmeal and flour until well blended. Beat in milk and vanilla (do not over beat).

Pour into the pastry shell. Bake at 325° for 55-65 minutes or until the filling is almost set. Cool on a wire rack.

For topping, heat 1/2 cup sugar in a small heavy saucepan over low heat without stirring until partially melted, about 5 minutes. Cook and stir with a metal spoon until syrup is completely melted and golden, about 5 minutes. Stir in the milk, butter and remaining sugar (mixture will be lumpy). Cook over medium heat, stirring until a candy thermometer reads 234° (soft-ball stage).

Remove from the heat. Pour into a small bowl without stirring. Cool, without stirring, to 190°. Beat on high speed until mixture turns light brown and creamy and a candy thermometer reads 130°-137°, about 5 minutes. Immediately spread over pie. Store in the refrigerator. **Yield:** 8-10 servings.

Editor's Note: We recommend that you test your candy thermometer before each use by bringing water to a boil; the thermometer should read 212°. Adjust your recipe temperature up or down based on your test.

Easy Cranberry Pie

Marjorie Carey, Belfry, Montana

My mother made this pie with a lattice top. She'd sometimes place a marshmallow in the center of each lattice square. At Christmastime, she'd cut Christmas tree shapes from the pie dough and place them on top of the pie.

    2   cans (16 ounces *each*) whole-berry cranberry sauce
  1/4   cup packed brown sugar
    2   tablespoons butter, softened
Pastry for double-crust pie (9 inches)

In a large bowl, combine the cranberry sauce, brown sugar and butter. Line a 9-in. pie plate with bottom crust; trim pastry even with edge. Add filling. Roll out remaining pastry; make a lattice crust. Trim, seal and flute edges.

Bake at 350° for 50-60 minutes or until the crust is lightly browned. Store in the refrigerator. **Yield:** 6-8 servings.

Editor's Note: For festively decorated pie, use a cookie cutter to cut out Christmas tree shapes from the top pastry instead of using a lattice crust. Place the dough shapes on an ungreased baking sheet and bake at 350° for 10-15 minutes or until golden brown. Cool slightly; arrange on top of baked pie.

Rhubarb Crumb Tart

Rebecca Gairns, Prince George, British Columbia

My brother especially loves this tart. He says it's "the most awesome dessert" he's ever tasted!

- 1 cup all-purpose flour
- 1 teaspoon baking powder
- 3 tablespoons confectioners' sugar
- 1/3 cup butter
- 1 egg, beaten
- 4 teaspoons milk

FILLING:
- 3 cups diced fresh *or* frozen rhubarb
- 1 package (3 ounces) strawberry gelatin

TOPPING:
- 1/2 cup all-purpose flour
- 1 cup sugar
- 1/3 cup butter

For crust, in a small bowl, combine the flour, baking powder and confectioners' sugar. Cut in butter until mixture resembles coarse crumbs. Add egg and milk; stir until a ball forms. Pat into a greased 11-in. x 7-in. x 2-in. baking pan.

Spoon rhubarb into the crust. Sprinkle gelatin over rhubarb. In a small bowl, combine topping ingredients together until crumbly. Sprinkle over rhubarb mixture. Bake at 350° for 45-50 minutes. Cool completely on a wire rack until set. **Yield:** 12-15 servings.

Editor's Note: If using frozen rhubarb, measure rhubarb while still frozen, then thaw completely. Drain in a colander, but do not press liquid out.

German Chocolate Pie

Cheryl Jacobson, Chino Valley, Arizona

I'm known among family and friends for my fabulous desserts. This one is their very favorite. It's been a sweet standby of mine for over 20 years.

- 1 package (4 ounces) German sweet chocolate
- 1/4 cup butter, cubed
- 1 can (12 ounces) evaporated milk
- 1-1/2 cups sugar
- 3 tablespoons cornstarch
- 1/8 teaspoon salt
- 2 eggs, lightly beaten
- 1 teaspoon vanilla extract
- 1 unbaked deep-dish pastry shell (9 inches)
- 1/2 cup chopped pecans
- 1-1/3 cups flaked coconut

In a microwave, melt chocolate and butter; stir until smooth. Gradually add milk; set aside.

In a large bowl, combine the sugar, cornstarch and salt. Stir in eggs and vanilla. Gradually stir in chocolate mixture. Pour into pastry shell.

Combine pecans and coconut; sprinkle over filling. Bake at 375° for 45-50 minutes or until puffed and browned.

Cool for 4 hours. Chill until serving (filling will become firm as it cools). Store in the refrigerator. **Yield:** 6-8 servings.

Cherry Almond Pie

Ramona Pleva, Lincoln Park, New Jersey

I grew up in northern Michigan, where three generations of my family have been cherry producers. This traditional cherry pie is a mouthwatering dessert.

- 4 cups pitted canned *or* frozen tart red cherries
- 3/4 cup sugar
- 1 tablespoon butter

Dash salt
- 1/4 cup cornstarch
- 1/3 cup cold water
- 1/4 teaspoon almond extract
- 1/4 teaspoon red food coloring, optional

Pastry for double-crust pie (9 inches)

Drain cherries, reserving 2/3 cup juice in a saucepan; discard remaining juice. To the juice, add the cherries, sugar, butter and salt. In a small bowl, combine cornstarch and water until smooth; stir into cherry mixture. Bring to a boil over medium heat; cook and stir for 2 minutes or until thickened. Remove from the heat; stir in the almond extract and food coloring if desired. Cool.

Line a 9-in. pie plate with bottom crust; trim pastry even with edge. Add filling. Roll out remaining pastry; make a lattice crust. Trim, seal and flute edges. Bake at 375° for 45-50 minutes or until crust is golden and filling is bubbly. Cool on a wire rack. **Yield:** 6-8 servings.

Shamrock Pie

Gloria Warczak, Cedarburg, Wisconsin

Guests may wonder if the dessert has been touched by a leprechaun when they see the green layer in my lemon meringue pie. Then, after their first taste, they declare it to be absolutely delicious.

 1 cup sugar
 1/4 cup cornstarch
 1-1/2 cups water
 3 egg yolks, lightly beaten
 1/4 cup lemon juice
 1 tablespoon butter
 1-1/2 teaspoons grated lemon peel
 5 to 6 drops green food coloring
 1 pastry shell (9 inches), baked
MERINGUE:
 3 egg whites
 1/3 cup sugar

In a large saucepan, combine the sugar and cornstarch. Stir in water until smooth. Cook and stir over medium-high heat until thickened and bubbly. Reduce heat; cook and stir 2 minutes longer. Remove from the heat. Stir a small amount of hot filling into egg yolks; return all to pan, stirring constantly. Bring to a gentle boil; cook and stir 2 minutes longer. Remove from the heat. Gently stir in the lemon juice, butter, lemon peel and food coloring until smooth. Pour hot mixture into crust.

In a small bowl, beat egg whites until soft peaks form. Gradually beat in sugar, 1 tablespoon at a time, on high until stiff, glossy peaks form. Spread evenly over hot filling, sealing edges to crust.

Bake at 350° for 10-15 minutes or until the meringue is golden brown. Cool on a wire rack for 1 hour. Refrigerate for at least 3 hours before serving. Store in the refrigerator. **Yield:** 6-8 servings.

Vanilla Cream Fruit Tart

Susan Terzakis, Andover, Massachusetts

It's well worth the effort to prepare this spectacular tart, which is best made and served the same day. A friend gave me the recipe, and it is always well received at gatherings.

 3/4 cup butter, softened
 1/2 cup confectioners' sugar
 1-1/2 cups all-purpose flour
 1 package (10 to 12 ounces) vanilla *or* white chips, melted and cooled
 1/4 cup heavy whipping cream
 1 package (8 ounces) cream cheese, softened
 1 pint fresh strawberries, sliced
 1 cup fresh blueberries
 1 cup fresh raspberries
 1/2 cup pineapple juice
 1/4 cup sugar
 1 tablespoon cornstarch
 1/2 teaspoon lemon juice

In a large bowl, cream butter and confectioners' sugar until light and fluffy. Beat in flour (mixture will be crumbly). Pat into the bottom of a greased 12-in. pizza pan. Bake at 300° for 25-28 minutes or until lightly browned. Cool.

In another bowl, beat melted chips and cream until smooth. Beat in cream cheese until smooth. Spread over crust. Chill for 30 minutes. Arrange berries over filling.

In a small saucepan, combine the pineapple juice, sugar, cornstarch and lemon juice; bring to a boil over medium heat. Cook and stir for 2 minutes or until thickened. Cool; brush over fruit. Chill 1 hour before serving. Store in the refrigerator. **Yield:** 12-16 servings.

Banana Streusel Pie

Gayle Kuipers, Holland, Michigan

I obtained this recipe from my mom, who is a great cook. It's been in the family for years. We usually serve it at holiday meals—it's always a crowd-pleaser.

- 1 unbaked pastry shell (9 inches)
- 1/4 cup sugar
- 1/2 teaspoon ground cinnamon
- 1 teaspoon cornstarch
- 1/2 cup pineapple juice
- 2 tablespoons lemon juice
- 1-1/2 teaspoons grated lemon peel
- 4 cups sliced ripe bananas (5 to 6 medium)

STREUSEL:
- 1/2 cup all-purpose flour
- 1/2 cup packed brown sugar
- 1/3 cup chopped macadamia nuts *or* almonds
- 1 teaspoon ground cinnamon
- 1/4 cup cold butter

Line the unpricked pastry shell with a double thickness of foil. Bake at 450° for 10 minutes. Remove the foil and bake 2 minutes longer or until pastry is golden brown; set aside. Reduce heat to 375°.

In a small saucepan, combine the sugar, cinnamon and cornstarch. Stir in the pineapple juice, lemon juice and peel. Bring to a boil. Reduce heat; cook and stir for 2 minutes or until thickened. Remove from the heat. Fold in bananas; pour into crust.

For streusel, in a small bowl, combine flour, brown sugar, nuts and cinnamon; cut in butter until the mixture resembles coarse crumbs. Sprinkle over the filling.

Cover edges of pie with foil. Bake at 375° for 40 minutes or until topping is golden and filling is bubbly. Cool on a wire rack. **Yield:** 6-8 servings.

Baking Classics | Pies

Rhubarb Raspberry Pie

Lynda Bailey, Sandpoint, Idaho

My family loves rhubarb and raspberries, so I was happy to find this recipe several years ago. The pie always brings smiles to their faces whenever I set it on the dinner table.

    1   cup sugar
    1/4 cup quick-cooking tapioca
    4   cups chopped fresh *or* frozen rhubarb
    1   cup fresh *or* frozen unsweetened raspberries
    2   tablespoons lemon juice
Pastry for double-crust pie (9 inches)

In a large bowl, combine sugar and tapioca. Gently stir in the rhubarb, raspberries and lemon juice. Let stand for at least 15 minutes; stir gently several times.

Line a 9-in. pie plate with bottom crust; trim pastry even with edge. Pour filling into crust. Roll out remaining pastry; make a lattice crust. Trim, seal and flute edges. Bake at 375° for 45-55 minutes or until the crust is golden brown and filling is bubbly. Serve warm or at room temperature. Store in the refrigerator. **Yield:** 6-8 servings.

Editor's Note: If using frozen rhubarb, measure rhubarb while it is still frozen, then thaw completely. Drain in a colander, but do not press liquid out.

Maple Pecan Pie

Mildred Wescom, Belvidere, Vermont

Our Vermont maple syrup can't be beat, and I like to use it in a variety of recipes. This maple-flavored pie is easy to make and one of my favorites.

    3   eggs
    1/2 cup sugar
    1   cup maple syrup
    3   tablespoons butter, melted
    1/2 teaspoon vanilla extract
    1/4 teaspoon salt
    1   cup pecan halves
    1   unbaked pastry shell (9 inches)

In a bowl, whisk eggs and sugar until smooth. Add the maple syrup, butter, vanilla, salt and pecans. Pour into pastry shell.

Bake at 375° for 40-45 minutes or until a knife inserted near the center comes out clean. Cool on a wire rack for 1 hour. Store in the refrigerator. **Yield:** 8 servings.

Black Forest Pie

Trudy Black, Dedham, Massachusetts

With three active children, I don't usually bake fancy desserts. This one is simple but impressive—it's the one I make to show how much I care. The tempting combination of chocolate and tangy red cherries is guaranteed to make someone feel special.

    3/4 cup sugar
    1/3 cup baking cocoa
    2   tablespoons all-purpose flour
    1/3 cup milk
    1/4 cup butter, cubed
    2   eggs, lightly beaten
    1   can (21 ounces) cherry pie filling, *divided*
    1   unbaked pastry shell (9 inches)
Whipped topping, optional

In a small saucepan, combine the sugar, cocoa and flour. Stir in milk until smooth. Add butter. Cook and stir over medium-high heat until thickened and bubbly. Reduce heat; cook and stir 2 minutes longer. Remove from the heat. Stir a small amount of hot filling into eggs; return all to pan, stirring constantly. Fold in half of the pie filling.

Pour into pastry shell. Bake at 350° for 35-40 minutes or until filling is almost set. Cool completely on a wire rack. Just before serving, top with remaining pie filling and whipped topping if desired. Store in the refrigerator. **Yield:** 6-8 servings.

pg. 133

Cakes

pg. 175

pg. 143

pg. 140

Apricot Torte

Dorothy Pritchett, Wills Point, Texas

This elegant dessert is easy to make and so pretty. The chocolate buttercream really complements the apricot filling.

    6 eggs, *separated*
  1/2 cup plus 5 tablespoons sugar, *divided*
    1 cup all-purpose flour
CHOCOLATE BUTTERCREAM:
  1/4 cup sugar
    3 eggs plus 2 egg yolks
    1 teaspoon vanilla extract
    1 teaspoon instant coffee granules
    2 squares (1 ounce *each*) semisweet chocolate
    1 cup butter, softened
APRICOT FILLING:
    2 cans (17 ounces *each*) apricot halves, drained
    1 cup apricot preserves
Chocolate curls

In a large bowl, beat egg yolks and 1/2 cup sugar until thickened and pale yellow. In another large bowl and with clean beaters, beat egg whites until foamy. Gradually beat in remaining sugar, 1 tablespoon at a time, on high until stiff peaks form. Fold into egg yolk mixture. Gradually fold in flour.

Divide batter between three greased and floured 9-in. round baking pans. Bake at 350° for 15 minutes or until golden. Cool in pans for 5 minutes before removing to wire racks to cool completely.

For buttercream, in a saucepan, whisk the sugar, eggs, egg yolks, vanilla and coffee. Add chocolate; cook and stir over low heat until thickened (do not boil). Cool completely.

In a bowl, cream butter until light and fluffy. Gradually add chocolate mixture; set aside. Finely chop apricots; drain and place in a bowl. Stir in preserves; set aside.

Split each cake into two horizontal layers; place one on a serving plate. Spread with 2/3 cup buttercream. Top with a cake layer and 2/3 cup apricot filling. Repeat layers twice. Cover and refrigerate 3 hours before serving. Garnish with chocolate curls. **Yield:** 12 servings.

Cinnamon Nut Cake

Margaret Wilson, Hemet, California

Here's an easy-to-assemble moist bundt cake for brunch or dessert. Top with a dollop of whipped cream and you're ready to enjoy.

    1 package (18-1/4 ounces) yellow cake mix
    3 eggs
1-1/3 cups water
  1/4 cup canola oil
1-1/4 cups finely chopped walnuts
7-1/2 teaspoons sugar
4-1/2 teaspoons ground cinnamon

In a large bowl, combine the cake mix, eggs, water and oil. Beat on medium speed for 2 minutes. Combine the walnuts, sugar and cinnamon.

Sprinkle a third of the nut mixture into a greased 10-in. fluted tube pan. Top with half of the batter and another third of the nut mixture. Repeat layers.

Bake at 350° for 35-40 minutes or until a toothpick inserted near the center comes out clean. Cool for 10 minutes before removing from pan to a wire rack to cool completely. **Yield:** 12-14 servings.

Moist Chocolate Cake

Taste of Home Test Kitchen

Dark and richly chocolate, this cake is perfect for birthdays. The basic buttery frosting has an unmatchable homemade taste.

- 2 cups all-purpose flour
- 2 cups sugar
- 3/4 cup baking cocoa
- 2 teaspoons baking soda
- 1 teaspoon baking powder
- 1 teaspoon salt
- 1 cup canola oil
- 1 cup brewed coffee, room temperature
- 1 cup milk
- 2 eggs
- 1 teaspoon vanilla extract

BUTTERCREAM FROSTING:
- 1 cup butter, softened
- 8 cups confectioners' sugar
- 2 teaspoons vanilla extract
- 1/2 to 3/4 cup milk

In a large bowl, combine the flour, sugar, cocoa, baking soda, baking powder and salt. Add the oil, coffee and milk; beat at medium speed for 2 minutes. Add eggs and vanilla; beat 2 minutes longer.

Pour into two greased and floured 9-in. round baking pans. Bake at 325° for 25-30 minutes or until a toothpick inserted near the center comes out clean. Cool for 10 minutes before removing from pans to wire racks to cool completely.

For frosting, in a bowl, cream butter and confectioners' sugar until light and fluffy. Beat in vanilla. Add enough milk to achieve desired spreading consistency. Spread frosting between layers and over top and sides of cake. **Yield:** 12 servings.

Frosting Too Thick or Thin? If your frosting is not the right consistency for spreading, it's easily fixed. If it is too thick, add milk a teaspoon at a time until it's the right consistency. If it's too thin, let it stand for 10 to 20 minutes; it may thicken up by itself. If it's still too thin, beat in some sifted confectioners' sugar until it is spreadable.

133

Cinnamon-Apple Angel Food Cake

Marlys Benning, Wellsburg, Iowa

This heavenly dessert is as light as a feather and melts in your mouth. The cinnamon-apple glaze is delightful. The exquisite flavor and texture prove it's a true from-scratch dessert!

1-1/2   cups egg whites (about 12 eggs)
1-1/2   cups confectioners' sugar
   1   cup cake flour
1-1/2   teaspoons cream of tartar
   1   teaspoon vanilla extract
  1/2   teaspoon almond extract
  1/4   teaspoon salt
   1   cup sugar

GLAZE:
  1/3   cup butter, cubed
   2   cups confectioners' sugar
  1/2   teaspoon ground cinnamon
   3   to 4 tablespoons apple juice *or* cider

Place egg whites in a large bowl; let stand at room temperature for 30 minutes. Sift confectioners' sugar and flour together twice; set aside.

Add cream of tartar, vanilla, almond extract and salt to egg whites; beat on medium speed until soft peaks form. Gradually add sugar, about 2 tablespoons at a time, beating on high until stiff, glossy peaks form and sugar is dissolved. Gradually fold in flour mixture, about 1/2 cup at a time.

Gently spoon into an ungreased 10-in. tube pan. Cut through the batter with a knife to remove air pockets. Bake on the lowest oven rack at 375° for 35-40 minutes or until lightly browned and entire top appears dry. Immediately invert pan; cool completely, about 1 hour.

Run a knife around side and center tube of pan. Remove cake to a serving plate.

For glaze, melt butter in a small saucepan. Stir in the confectioners' sugar and cinnamon until blended. Add apple juice slowly until glaze is thin enough to achieve a drizzle consistency. Drizzle over cake. **Yield:** 12-16 servings.

Upside-Down Strawberry Shortcake

Debra Falkiner, St. Charles, Missouri

For a tasty twist at dessert time, this special spring shortcake has a heavenly berry layer on the bottom. The moist and tempting cake is a treat our family has savored for years.

- 1 cup miniature marshmallows
- 1 package (16 ounces) frozen sweetened sliced strawberries, thawed
- 1 package (3 ounces) strawberry gelatin
- 1/2 cup shortening
- 1-1/2 cups sugar
- 3 eggs
- 1 teaspoon vanilla extract
- 2-1/4 cups all-purpose flour
- 3 teaspoons baking powder
- 1/2 teaspoon salt
- 1 cup milk

Fresh strawberries and whipped cream

Sprinkle marshmallows evenly into a greased 13-in. x 9-in. x 2-in. baking dish; set aside. In a small bowl, combine strawberries and gelatin powder; set aside.

In a large bowl, cream shortening and sugar until light and fluffy. Add the eggs, one at a time, beating well after each addition. Beat in vanilla. Combine the flour, baking powder and salt; add to creamed mixture alternately with milk, beating well after each addition.

Pour batter over the marshmallows. Spoon strawberry mixture evenly over batter. Bake at 350° for 45-50 minutes or until a toothpick inserted near the center comes out clean. Cool on a wire rack. Cut into squares. Garnish with strawberries and whipped cream. Store in the refrigerator. **Yield:** 12-16 servings.

Walnut Apple Cake

Jacquelyn Remsberg, La Canada, California

I first tasted this delicious cake at a party and quickly asked for the recipe. It's not too sweet, and the butter sauce makes it a super ending to any meal.

- 2 cups sugar
- 1/2 cup canola oil
- 2 eggs
- 2 teaspoons vanilla extract
- 2 cups all-purpose flour
- 2 teaspoons baking soda
- 1 1/2 teaspoons ground cinnamon
- 1 teaspoon salt
- 1/4 teaspoon ground nutmeg
- 4 cups chopped peeled tart apple
- 1 cup chopped walnuts

BUTTER SAUCE:
- 3/4 cup sugar
- 3 tablespoons all-purpose flour
- 1 cup milk
- 2 tablespoons butter
- 1 teaspoon vanilla extract

Walnut halves, optional

In a large bowl, beat the sugar, oil, eggs and vanilla until well blended. In a large bowl, combine the flour, baking soda, cinnamon, salt and nutmeg; gradually add to the egg mixture until well blended (batter will be stiff). Stir in the apples and walnuts.

Spread into a greased 13-in. x 9-in. x 2-in. baking pan. Bake at 350° for 45-50 minutes or until a toothpick inserted near the center comes out clean. Cool on a wire rack.

For the sauce, in a small saucepan, combine sugar and flour. Gradually stir in milk until blended. Add butter. Bring to a boil over medium heat; cook and stir for 2 minutes. Remove from the heat; stir in vanilla. Cut cake into squares; serve with warm sauce. Garnish with walnut halves if desired. **Yield:** 12-15 servings.

In a heavy large saucepan, combine the frosting ingredients. With a portable mixer, beat on low speed for 1 minute. Continue beating over low heat until frosting reaches 160°, about 8-10 minutes.

Pour into a large bowl. Beat on high until stiff peaks form, about 7 minutes. Frost between layers and over top and sides of cake. **Yield:** 12-14 servings.

Editor's Note: A stand mixer is recommended for beating the frosting after it reaches 160°.

Mississippi Mud Cake

Tammi Simpson, Greensburg, Kentucky

Make this tempting cake and you'll satisfy kids of all ages! A fudgy brownie-like base is topped with marshmallow creme and a nutty frosting. Your family will be thrilled when you serve up big slices with glasses of cold milk or steaming mugs of coffee.

    1   cup butter, softened
    2   cups sugar
    4   eggs
1-1/2   cups self-rising flour
  1/2   cup baking cocoa
    1   cup chopped pecans
    1   jar (7 ounces) marshmallow creme
FROSTING:
  1/2   cup butter, softened
3-3/4   cups confectioners' sugar
    3   tablespoons baking cocoa
    1   tablespoon vanilla extract
    4   to 5 tablespoons milk
    1   cup chopped pecans

In a large bowl, cream butter and sugar until light and fluffy. Add eggs, one at a time, beating well after each addition. Combine flour and cocoa; gradually add to creamed mixture until blended. Fold in the pecans.

Transfer to a greased 13-in. x 9-in. x 2-in. baking pan. Bake at 350° for 35-40 minutes or until a toothpick inserted near the center comes out clean. Cool for 3 minutes (cake will fall in the center). Spoon the marshmallow creme over cake; carefully spread to cover top. Cool completely.

For frosting, in a small bowl, cream butter and confectioners' sugar until light and fluffy. Beat in the cocoa, vanilla and enough milk to achieve frosting consistency. Fold in pecans. Spread over marshmallow creme layer. Store in the refrigerator. **Yield:** 16-20 servings.

Editor's Note: As a substitute for 1-1/2 cups self-rising flour, place 2-1/4 teaspoons baking powder and 3/4 teaspoon salt in a measuring cup. Add all-purpose flour to measure 1 cup. Combine with an additional 1/2 cup all-purpose flour.

Maple Nut Cake

Emma Magielda, Amsterdam, New York

I like to use our locally made maple syrup in desserts because it lends such a distinct flavor.

  1/2   cup butter, softened
  1/2   cup sugar
    2   eggs
    1   cup maple syrup
2-1/4   cups cake flour
    3   teaspoons baking powder
    1   teaspoon salt
  1/2   cup milk
  1/2   cup chopped nuts
FROSTING:
    1   cup sugar
  1/2   cup maple syrup
    2   egg whites
    1   teaspoon corn syrup
  1/8   teaspoon salt
  1/4   teaspoon cream of tartar

In a large bowl, cream the butter and sugar until light and fluffy. Beat in the eggs until well blended. Beat in the syrup. Combine the flour, baking powder and salt; add to the creamed mixture alternately with milk, beating well after each addition. Fold in nuts.

Pour into two greased and floured 8-in. round baking pans. Bake at 350° for 20-25 minutes or until a toothpick inserted near the center comes out clean. Cool for 10 minutes before removing from pans to wire racks to cool completely.

Holiday Pound Cake

Ruby Williams, Bogalusa, Louisiana

We top off our Thanksgiving feast with this mellow, tender cake dressed up with a strawberry topping. Pound cake is a southern tradition, and I'm proud to say I've baked hundreds of them over the years.

- 1 cup butter, softened
- 1/2 cup shortening
- 1 package (3 ounces) cream cheese, softened
- 2-1/2 cups sugar
- 5 eggs
- 1 teaspoon lemon extract
- 1 teaspoon vanilla extract
- 3 cups cake flour
- 1 teaspoon baking powder
- 1/2 teaspoon salt
- 1 cup buttermilk
- Strawberry ice cream topping
- Sliced fresh strawberries, optional

In a large bowl, cream the butter, shortening, cream cheese and sugar until light and fluffy. Add eggs, one at a time, beating well after each addition. Beat in extracts. Combine the flour, baking powder and salt; add to creamed mixture alternately with the buttermilk, beating well after each addition.

Pour into a greased and floured 10-in. fluted tube pan. Bake at 325° for 1 hour and 20 minutes or until a toothpick inserted near the center comes out clean. Cool for 10 minutes before removing from pan to a wire rack to cool completely. Serve with strawberry topping and fresh strawberries if desired. **Yield:** 12-16 servings.

Double-Chocolate Yum-Yum Cake For a double-chocolate treat, melt about 1/4 cup semisweet chocolate chips and cool to room temperature. Stir into the confectioners' sugar with the vanilla. Add enough milk to achieve drizzling consistency.

Chocolate Yum-Yum Cake

Dorothy Colli, West Hartford, Connecticut

My grandmother first made this delicious cake, then my mother made it often when I was a little girl. You can frost it or just sprinkle it with a little powdered sugar.

- 1/2 cup butter, cubed
- 2 squares (1 ounce *each*) unsweetened baking chocolate, chopped
- 1 cup sugar
- 1/2 cup raisins
- 1-1/2 cups water
- 1/2 teaspoon ground cinnamon
- 1/4 teaspoon ground cloves
- Dash salt
- 1-1/2 teaspoons vanilla extract
- 1-3/4 cups all-purpose flour
- 1 teaspoon baking soda
- ICING:
- 1/2 cup confectioners' sugar
- 1/4 teaspoon vanilla extract
- 1 to 2 teaspoons milk

In a large saucepan, melt butter and chocolate over low heat, stirring constantly. Add the sugar, raisins, water, cinnamon and cloves; bring to a boil. Boil for 5 minutes, stirring occasionally.

Remove from the heat; pour into a large bowl and cool for 15 minutes. Stir in salt and vanilla. Combine flour and baking soda; add to chocolate mixture until well blended.

Pour into a greased and floured 10-in. fluted tube pan. Bake at 350° for 45-50 minutes or until a toothpick inserted near the center comes out clean. Cool for 10 minutes before removing from pan to a wire rack to cool completely.

In a small bowl, combine icing ingredients; drizzle over cooled cake. **Yield:** 8-10 servings.

Editor's Note: An 11-in. x 7-in. x 2-in. baking pan can be used. Bake for 25-30 minutes or until cake tests done.

Rice Pudding Cake

Nancy Horsburgh, Everett, Ontario

The secret ingredient in this delicious cake is rice. It tastes a lot like rice pudding, only in a different form.

- 5 eggs, *separated*
- 1 cup uncooked long grain rice
- Water
- 1/2 cup raisins
- Boiling water
- 4 cups milk
- 3/4 cup butter, softened
- 1 cup sugar
- 2 tablespoons grated orange peel
- 2 tablespoons graham cracker crumbs
- Confectioners' sugar

Place the egg whites in a large bowl; let stand at room temperature for 30 minutes.

In a large saucepan, cover rice with water; bring to a boil. Drain the liquid; add milk to rice. Bring to a boil. Reduce heat; cover and simmer for 15-20 minutes or until rice is tender; set aside. In a small bowl, cover raisins with boiling water. Let stand for 5 minutes; drain and set aside.

In a large bowl, cream butter and sugar until light and fluffy. Beat in egg yolks. Add the rice mixture, raisins and orange peel. Beat egg whites with clean beaters on medium speed until stiff; fold into batter. Spoon into a greased 10-in. tub pan. Sprinkle with crumbs.

Bake on the lowest oven rack at 350° for 55-60 minutes or until a toothpick inserted near the center comes out clean. Immediately invert pan; cool completely, about 1 hour.

Run a knife around side and center tube of pan. Remove cake to a serving plate. Dust with confectioners' sugar. Serve warm or chilled. **Yield:** 12-16 servings.

Strawberry Nut Roll

Judy Hayes, Peosta, Iowa

As the oldest of seven children, I did a lot of cooking and baking while I was growing up. Desserts like this refreshing rolled shortcake are my favorite. The nutty cake, creamy filling and fresh strawberries make pretty swirled slices.

- 6 eggs, *separated*
- 1/4 cup all-purpose flour
- 1/8 teaspoon salt
- 3/4 cup sugar, *divided*

1 cup ground walnuts, toasted
1/4 cup dry bread crumbs
Confectioners' sugar
FILLING:
1 pint fresh strawberries
1 cup heavy whipping cream
2 tablespoons sugar
1 teaspoon vanilla extract
Confectioners' sugar

Place the egg whites in large bowl; let stand at room temperature for 30 minutes. Line a greased 15-in. x 10-in. x 1-in. baking pan with waxed paper; grease the paper and set aside. Sift flour and salt together twice; set aside.

In a large bowl, beat yolks on high speed for 5 minutes or until thick and lemon-colored. Gradually beat in 1/2 cup sugar. Stir in walnuts and break crumbs. Gradually add flour mixture to yolk mixture and mix well (batter will be very thick).

In a large bowl and with clean beaters, beat egg whites on medium speed until soft peaks form. Gradually beat in remaining sugar, 1 tablespoon at a time, on high until stiff peaks form. Fold into batter.

Spread evenly into prepared pan. Bake at 375° for 15-17 minutes or until cake springs back when lightly touched. Cool for 5 minutes. Invert cake onto a kitchen towel dusted with confectioners' sugar. Gently peel off waxed paper. Roll up cake in the towel, jelly-roll style, starting with a short side. Cool completely on a wire rack.

Slice six large strawberries in half; set aside for garnish. Thinly slice the remaining berries; set aside. For the filling, in a chilled large bowl, beat the cream until soft peaks form. Gradually add the sugar and vanilla, beating until stiff peaks form.

Unroll cake; spread filling evenly over cake to within 1/2 in. of edges. Top with sliced berries. Roll up again. Place, seam side down, on serving platter. Cover and refrigerate for 1 hour. Dust with confectioners' sugar. Garnish with reserved strawberries. Store in the refrigerator. **Yield:** 12 servings.

Root Beer Float Cake

Kat Thompson, Prineville, Oregon

I add root beer to both the cake batter and fluffy frosting of this summery dessert to get that great root beer float taste. Serve this moist cake to a bunch of hungry kids and even adults...and watch it disappear.

1 package (18-1/4 ounces) white cake mix
1-3/4 cups cold root beer, *divided*
1/4 cup canola oil
2 eggs
1 envelope whipped topping mix

In a large bowl, combine the cake mix, 1-1/4 cups root beer, oil and eggs; beat on low speed for 30 minutes. Beat on medium for 2 minutes.

Pour into a greased 13-in. x 9-in. x 2-in. baking pan. Bake at 350° for 30-35 minutes or until a toothpick inserted near the center comes out clean. Cool completely on a wire rack.

In a small bowl, combine the whipped topping mix and remaining root beer. Beat until soft peaks form. Frost cake. Store in the refrigerator. **Yield:** 12-16 servings.

Ice Cream Cake Roll

Kathy Scott, Lingle, Wyoming

This cake roll can be made and filled in advance, then thawed once company comes. You can use whatever ice cream flavor you have on hand.

    4 eggs, *separated*
  3/4 cup sugar
    1 teaspoon vanilla extract
  3/4 cup cake flour
  1/4 cup baking cocoa
  3/4 teaspoon baking powder
  1/4 teaspoon salt
Confectioners' sugar
    3 cups ice cream, softened
CHOCOLATE SAUCE:
    2 squares (1 ounce *each*) unsweetened baking chocolate
  1/4 cup butter
  2/3 cup evaporated milk, heated to 160° to 170°
    1 cup sugar

Let eggs stand at room temperature for 30 minutes. Line a greased 15-in. x 10-in. x 1-in. baking pan with waxed paper; grease the paper and set aside.

In a large bowl, beat egg yolks on high for 3 minutes or until thick and lemon-colored. Gradually add sugar and vanilla, beating until thick and pale yellow. Combine flour, cocoa and baking powder; gradually add to yolk mixture Beat on low until well mixed (mixture will be thick).

In another large bowl and with clean beaters, beat the egg whites and salt on high speed until soft peaks form. Fold a fourth of egg whites into the batter, then fold in remaining whites.

Spread batter evenly in prepared pan. Bake at 350° for 15 minutes or until cake springs back when lightly touched. Turn cake onto a kitchen towel dusted with confectioners' sugar. Gently peel off waxed paper. Roll up cake in the towel jelly-roll style, starting with a short side. Cool completely on a wire rack.

Unroll the cake; spread with ice cream to within 1 in. of edges. Roll up again. Cover with plastic wrap and freeze until serving.

In a small heavy saucepan, melt chocolate and butter over low heat, stirring until smooth. Gradually add warm milk and sugar; stir constantly for 5 minutes or until sugar is completely dissolved. Serve with cake. **Yield:** 10 servings (1-1/2 cups sauce).

Lime Cream Torte

Theresa Tometich, Coralville, Iowa

This impressive-looking dessert is surprisingly simple to prepare. Light and refreshing, it's a super make-ahead treat...the flavor gets getter as it sits in the refrigerator. I've had many requests for the recipe.

- 1 package (18-1/4 ounces) butter recipe golden cake mix
- 3 eggs
- 1/2 cup butter, softened
- 7 tablespoons water
- 3 tablespoons lime juice

FILLING:
- 1 can (14 ounces) sweetened condensed milk
- 1/2 cup lime juice
- 2 cups heavy whipping cream, whipped

Lime slice, optional

In a large bowl, combine cake mix, eggs, butter, water and lime juice. Beat on medium speed for 4 minutes.

Pour into two greased and floured 9-in. round baking pans. Bake at 375° for 20-25 minutes or until a toothpick inserted near the center comes out clean. Cool for 10 minutes before removing from pans to wire racks. When cool, split each cake into two horizontal layers.

In a large bowl, combine milk and lime juice. Fold in the whipped cream. Spread about 1-1/4 cups between each layer and over top of cake. Refrigerate for at least 1 hour. Garnish with lime slices if desired. Store in the refrigerator. **Yield:** 10-14 servings.

Easy Red Velvet Cake

Priscilla Weaver, Hagerstown, Maryland

I've been making Red Velvet Cake for many years, trying slight changes in the recipe until coming up with one I consider tried and proven. Conveniently, it starts with a cake mix and turns out beautifully every time.

- 1 package (18-1/4 ounces) fudge marble cake mix
- 1 teaspoon baking soda
- 2 eggs
- 1-1/2 cups buttermilk
- 1 bottle (1 ounce) red food coloring
- 1 teaspoon vanilla extract

FROSTING:
- 5 tablespoons all-purpose flour
- 1 cup milk
- 1 cup butter, softened
- 1 cup sugar
- 2 teaspoons vanilla extract

In a large bowl, combine the contents of cake mix and baking soda. Add the eggs, buttermilk, food coloring and vanilla; beat on low speed just until moistened. Beat on high for 2 minutes. Pour into two greased and floured 9-in. round baking pans.

Bake at 350° for 30-35 minutes or until a toothpick inserted near the center comes out clean. Cool for 10 minutes before removing from pans to wire racks to cool completely.

For frosting, whisk flour and milk in a small saucepan until smooth. Bring to a boil; cook and stir for 2 minutes or until thickened. Cover and cool to room temperature.

In a small bowl, cream butter and sugar until light and fluffy. Beat in vanilla. Add milk mixture; beat for 10 minutes or until fluffy. Spread frosting between layers and over the top and sides of cake. **Yield:** 12 servings.

Crumb Cake

Kathy Lucas, Mechanicsburg, Pennsylvania

My favorite time to visit my grandmother was when she'd just taken her crumb cake out of the oven. A warm piece of that cake with a cold glass of milk was the best treat. I remember Grandma was able to simply look at the batter and know if it was right...and it was perfect every time.

- 1/2 cup shortening
-   1 cup sugar
-   2 cups all-purpose flour
-   1 teaspoon baking soda
- 1/2 teaspoon salt
-   1 cup buttermilk
- Confectioners' sugar

In a large bowl, cream shortening and sugar until light and fluffy. Combine the flour, baking soda and salt; add to creamed mixture alternately with buttermilk, beating well after each addition.

Pour into a greased 9-in. round baking pan. Bake at 375° for 35 minutes or until a toothpick inserted near the center comes out clean. Cool for 10 minutes before removing from pan to a wire rack to cool completely. Just before serving, dust with confectioners' sugar. **Yield:** 8 servings.

Eggnog Pound Cake

Theresa Koetter, Borden, Indiana

A flavorful blend of eggnog and nutmeg makes this cake a natural holiday staple. It uses a convenient boxed mix.

-   1 package (18-1/4 ounces) yellow cake mix
-   1 cup eggnog
-   3 eggs
- 1/2 cup butter, softened
- 1/2 to 1 teaspoon ground nutmeg
- CUSTARD SAUCE:
- 1/4 cup sugar
-   1 tablespoon cornstarch
- 1/4 teaspoon salt
-   1 cup milk
-   1 egg yolk, lightly beaten
-   1 teaspoon butter
-   1 teaspoon vanilla extract
- 1/2 cup heavy whipping cream, whipped

In a large bowl, combine the first five ingredients. Beat on low until moistened, scraping bowl occasionally. Beat on medium for 2 minutes.

Pour into a greased and floured 10-in. fluted tube pan. Bake at 350° for 40-45 minutes or until a toothpick inserted near the center comes out clean. Cool for 10 minutes before removing from pan to a wire rack to cool completely.

For sauce, in a small saucepan, combine the sugar, cornstarch and salt; gradually stir in milk. Bring to a boil over medium heat; boil for 1-2 minutes, stirring constantly. Stir a small amount of hot filling into egg yolk; return all to pan, stirring constantly. Bring to a gentle boil; cook and stir 2 minutes longer.

Remove from the heat; stir in butter and vanilla. Cool for 15 minutes. Fold in whipped cream. Store in the refrigerator. Serve with the cake. **Yield:** 16-20 servings.

Editor's Note: This recipe was tested with commercially prepared eggnog.

Layered Chocolate Cake

Dorothy Monroe, Pocatello, Idaho

It is hard to believe this fabulous dessert starts with a cake mix. Cream cheese in the icing provides the luscious finishing touch.

    1   package (18-1/4 ounces) German chocolate cake mix
1-1/3   cups water
    3   eggs
  1/3   cup canola oil
    1   package (3 ounces) cook-and-serve vanilla pudding mix
    1   teaspoon unflavored gelatin
    2   cups milk
    1   package (8 ounces) cream cheese, softened
  1/2   cup butter, softened
1-1/2   cups confectioners' sugar
    3   tablespoons baking cocoa
    1   teaspoon vanilla extract

In large bowl, combine the cake mix, water, eggs and oil until well combined. Pour into a greased 15-in. x 10-in. x 1-in. baking pan. Bake at 350° for 23-25 minutes or until a toothpick inserted near the center comes out clean. Cool on a wire rack.

In a large saucepan, combine the pudding mix, gelatin and milk; cook according to the package directions for pudding. Cool.

Cut cake into three 10-in. x 5-in. rectangles. Place one on a serving platter. Spread with half of the pudding mixture; repeat layers. Top with third layer.

In a large bowl, beat cream cheese and butter until fluffy. Beat in the sugar and cocoa and vanilla until smooth. Frost top and sides of cake. Store in the refrigerator. **Yield:** 10 servings.

Lemon Cake Roll

Dorothy Earl, Lancaster, South Carolina

This recipe dates back quite a few years. My mother made it for me when I was a child, and I'm now over 70!

- 3 eggs
- 1 cup sugar
- 3 tablespoons cold water
- 1 cup all-purpose flour
- 1 teaspoon baking powder
- 1/4 teaspoon salt
- Confectioners' sugar

FILLING:
- 1 cup sugar
- 3 tablespoons all-purpose flour
- 1 egg, lightly beaten
- 3/4 cup water
- 1/4 cup lemon juice

Line a greased 15-in. x 10-in. x 1-in. baking pan with waxed paper; grease the paper and set aside. In a large bowl, beat eggs for 3 minutes. Gradually add the sugar; beat for 2 minutes or until mixture becomes thick and lemon-colored. Stir in water. Combine the flour, baking powder and salt; fold into egg mixture. Spread batter evenly in prepared pan.

Bake at 375° for 12-14 minutes or until cake springs back when lightly touched. Cool cake in pan on a wire rack for 5 minutes. Invert onto a kitchen towel dusted with confectioners' sugar. Gently peel off waxed paper. Roll up cake in the towel jelly-roll style, starting with a short side. Cool completely on a wire rack.

For filling, in a small saucepan, combine the sugar, flour, egg, water and lemon juice. Cook and stir over medium heat until mixture comes to a boil. Cook and stir for 1 minute or until thickened. Remove from the heat; cool to room temperature.

Unroll cake; spread filling evenly over cake to within 1 in. of edges. Roll up again. Place seam side down on a serving platter. Frost top, sides and ends with remaining filling. Cover and refrigerate for 1-2 hours. Store in the refrigerator. **Yield:** 10-12 servings.

Marble Chiffon Cake

Sharon Evans, Rockwell, Iowa

This high cake won a blue ribbon for best chiffon cake at our country fair.

- 7 eggs, *separated*
- 1/3 cup baking cocoa
- 1/4 cup boiling water
- 3 tablespoons plus 1-1/2 cups sugar, *divided*
- 2 tablespoons plus 1/2 cup canola oil, *divided*
- 2-1/4 cups all-purpose flour
- 1 tablespoon baking powder
- 1 teaspoon salt
- 3/4 cup water
- 1/2 teaspoon cream of tartar
- 2 teaspoons grated orange peel

ORANGE GLAZE:
- 2 cups confectioners' sugar
- 1/3 cup butter, melted
- 3 to 4 tablespoons orange juice
- 1/2 teaspoon grated orange peel

Let eggs stand at room temperature for 30 minutes. In a bowl, whisk the cocoa, boiling water, 3 tablespoons sugar and 2 tablespoons oil until blended; cool and set aside.

In a large bowl, combine the flour, baking powder, salt and remaining sugar. In another bowl, whisk the egg yolks, water and remaining oil. Add to dry ingredients; beat until well blended. In another bowl and with clean beaters, beat egg whites and cream of tartar until stiff peaks form; fold into batter.

Remove 2 cups of batter; stir into cocoa mixture. To the remaining batter, add orange peel. Alternately spoon the batters into an ungreased 10-in. tube pan. Swirl with a knife. Bake on the lowest oven rack at 325° for 70-75 minutes or until cake springs back when lightly touched.

Immediately invert pan; cool completely, about 1 hour. Run a knife around side and center tube of pan. Remove cake to a serving plate.

For glaze, in a small bowl, combine the sugar, butter and enough orange juice to reach desired drizzling consistency. Add orange peel; Drizzle over cake. **Yield:** 12-14 servings.

Hawaiian Cake

JoAnn Fox, Johnson City, Tennessee

Pairing pineapple with coconut lent a tropical flavor to this cake. Shared by a former co-worker, this recipe has been in my file for 20 years and never fails to delight those who try a tender, sensational piece.

- 1 package (18-1/4 ounces) yellow cake mix
- 1-1/4 cups cold milk
- 1 package (3.4 ounces) instant vanilla pudding mix
- 1 can (20 ounces) crushed pineapple, drained
- 1 envelope whipped topping mix
- 1 package (3 ounces) cream cheese, softened
- 1/4 cup sugar
- 1/2 teaspoon vanilla extract
- 1/2 cup flaked coconut, toasted

Prepare and bake the cake according to package directions, using a greased 13-in. x 9-in. x 2-in. baking pan. Cool on a wire rack.

In a large bowl, whisk milk and pudding mix for 2 minutes. Let stand for 2 minutes or until soft-set. Stir in pineapple. Spread over cake. Prepare whipped topping mix according to package directions; set aside.

In a small bowl, beat the cream cheese, sugar and vanilla until smooth. Beat in 1 cup whipped topping. Fold in remaining topping. Spread over pudding. Sprinkle with coconut. Cover and refrigerate for 3 hours or overnight. **Yield:** 12-15 servings.

Praline Pumpkin Torte

Esther Sinn, Princeton, Illinois

This favorite harvest cake stays moist to the last bite. It's perfect for Thanksgiving or Christmas gatherings.

- 3/4   cup packed brown sugar
- 1/3   cup butter
- 3   tablespoons heavy whipping cream
- 3/4   cup chopped pecans

CAKE:
- 4   eggs
- 1-2/3   cups sugar
- 1   cup canola oil
- 2   cups canned pumpkin
- 1/4   teaspoon vanilla extract
- 2   cups all-purpose flour
- 2   teaspoons baking powder
- 2   teaspoons pumpkin pie spice
- 1   teaspoon baking soda
- 1   teaspoon salt

TOPPING:
- 1-3/4   cups heavy whipping cream
- 1/4   cup confectioners' sugar
- 1/4   teaspoon vanilla extract

Additional chopped pecans

In a heavy saucepan, combine the brown sugar, butter and cream. Cook and stir over low heat until sugar is dissolved. Pour into two well-greased 9-in. round baking pans. Sprinkle with pecans; cool.

For cake, in a large bowl, beat eggs, sugar and oil. Add pumpkin and vanilla. Combine the flour, baking powder, pie spice, baking soda and salt; add to pumpkin mixture and beat just until blended.

Carefully spoon batter over brown sugar mixture. Bake at 350° for 30-35 minutes or until a toothpick inserted near the center comes out clean. Cool for 5 minutes before removing from pans to wire racks to cool completely.

For topping, in a chilled small bowl, beat cream until it begins to thicken. Add confectioners' sugar and vanilla; beat until stiff peaks form.

Place one cake layer praline side up on a serving plate. Spread with two-thirds of the whipped cream mixture over cake. Top with second cake layer and remaining whipped cream. Sprinkle with additional pecans if desired. Store in the refrigerator. **Yield:** 14 servings.

Beet Cake

Vermadel Kirby, Milford, Delaware

I discovered this recipe handwritten in my grandmother's cookbook. I've made it many times, and my four grandchildren love it (they think it's just a tender chocolate cake).

- 4   squares (1 ounce *each*) semisweet chocolate
- 1   cup butter, softened, *divided*
- 1-1/2   cups packed dark brown sugar
- 3   eggs
- 2   cups pureed cooked beets
- 1   teaspoon vanilla extract
- 2   cups all-purpose flour
- 2   teaspoons baking soda
- 1/4   teaspoon salt

Confectioners' sugar

In a microwave, melt chocolate and 1/4 cup butter; stir until smooth. Cool slightly. Meanwhile, in a large bowl, cream the remaining butter and brown sugar until light and fluffy. Beat in eggs. In a small bowl, combine the chocolate mixture, beets and vanilla. Beat into creamed mixture (mixture will appear separated). Combine flour, baking soda and salt; gradually add to creamed mixture.

Pour into a greased and floured 10-in. fluted tube pan. Bake at 375° for 45-55 minutes or until a toothpick inserted near the center comes out clean. Cool for 10 minutes before removing from pan to a wire rack to cool completely. Before serving, dust with confectioners' sugar. **Yield:** 16-20 servings.

Cranberry-Orange Pound Cake

Sheree Swistun, Winnipeg, Manitoba

At the resort my husband and I operate, we prepare the meals for our guests. This recipe is a always well received.

1-1/2 cups butter, softened
2-3/4 cups sugar
    6 eggs
    1 teaspoon vanilla extract
2-1/2 teaspoons grated orange peel
    3 cups all-purpose flour
    1 teaspoon baking powder
  1/2 teaspoon salt
    1 cup (8 ounces) sour cream
1-1/2 cups chopped fresh *or* frozen cranberries
VANILLA BUTTER SAUCE:
    1 cup sugar
    1 tablespoon all-purpose flour
  1/2 cup half-and-half cream
  1/2 cup butter, softened
  1/2 teaspoon vanilla extract

In a large bowl, cream butter and sugar until light and fluffy. Add eggs, one at a time, beating well after each addition. Stir in vanilla and orange peel. Combine flour, baking powder and salt; add to creamed mixture alternately with sour cream. Fold in cranberries.

Pour into a greased and floured 10-in. fluted tube pan. Bake at 350° for 65-70 minutes or until a toothpick inserted near the center comes out clean. Cool for 10 minutes before removing from pan to a wire rack to cool completely.

In a small saucepan, combine sugar and flour. Stir in the cream until smooth. Add butter; bring to a boil over medium heat, stirring constantly. Boil and stir for 2 minutes. Remove from the heat and stir in vanilla. Serve warm over cake. **Yield:** 16 servings (1-1/2 cups sauce).

In a Pinch Cake Tester If you don't have a long wooden pick or metal cake tester to check for doneness for a cake baked in a tube or fluted tube pan, use a strand of uncooked, dry spaghetti. Insert it as you would a toothpick. Discard spaghetti after use.

Spoon into an ungreased 10-in. tube pan. Cut through batter with a knife to remove air pockets; smooth the top. Bake on the lowest oven rack at 325° for 50-55 minutes or until the cake springs back when lightly touched. Immediately invert pan; cool completely, about 1 hour.

In a large bowl, dissolve gelatin in boiling water. Add ice water and stir. Place bowl in ice water for about 5 minutes or until slightly thickened. Fold in strawberries and 1/2 cup whipped topping.

Run a knife around side and center tube of pan. Split cake into three horizontal layers; place bottom layer on a serving plate. Spread with half of gelatin mixture. Repeat. Top with remaining cake layer. Frost top and sides with remaining whipped topping. Garnish with strawberries. Store in the refrigerator. **Yield:** 12-16 servings.

Separating Eggs It's easiest to separate eggs when they are cold. Use an egg separator, which is available in the housewares section of stores. Place the separator over a custard cup. The yolk stays in the separator while the white drips into the custard cup.

Strawberry Sunshine Cake

Rosemary Binette, Les Cedres, Quebec

With fluffy whipped topping frosting and a fresh strawberry filling and garnish, this impressive three-layer sponge cake is a scrumptious summer dessert. For best results, be sure to slice it with a serrated knife.

- 1 cup egg whites (about 8)
- 5 egg yolks
- 1-1/2 cups sugar, *divided*
- 2 tablespoons water
- 1/2 teaspoon *each* almond, lemon and vanilla extracts
- 1 cup all-purpose flour
- 1/2 teaspoon cream of tartar
- 1/2 teaspoon salt

FILLING:
- 1 package (3 ounces) strawberry gelatin
- 1 cup boiling water
- 1/2 cup ice water
- 1 pint fresh strawberries, sliced
- 1 carton (8 ounces) frozen whipped topping, thawed, *divided*

Additional strawberries

Let egg whites stand for 30 minutes. In a large bowl, beat yolks on high speed for 5 minutes or until thick and lemon-colored. Gradually beat in 1/2 cup sugar. Stir in water and extracts. Sift flour twice; gradually add to yolk mixture and mix well (batter will be very thick).

In a large bowl with clean beaters, beat the egg whites, cream of tartar and salt until soft peaks form. Gradually add remaining sugar, 1 tablespoon at a time, beating until stiff peaks form; set aside. Fold into egg yolk mixture.

Sweet Potato Cake

Wanda Rolen, Sevierville, Tennessee

I bake a lot for church dinners and homecomings, and many people have told me how much they like this cake.

- 1 cup canola oil
- 2 cups sugar
- 4 eggs
- 1-1/2 cups finely shredded uncooked sweet potato (about 1 medium)
- 1/4 cup hot water
- 1 teaspoon vanilla extract
- 2-1/2 cups self-rising flour
- 1 teaspoon ground cinnamon
- 1 cup sliced almonds

FROSTING:
- 1/2 cup butter, cubed
- 1 cup packed brown sugar
- 1 cup evaporated milk
- 3 egg yolks, beaten
- 1-1/2 cups flaked coconut
- 1 cup sliced almonds
- 1 teaspoon vanilla extract

In a large bowl, beat oil and sugar. Beat in eggs. Beat in the sweet potato, water and vanilla. Combine flour and cinnamon; gradually add to potato mixture until well blended. Stir in almonds.

Pour into a greased 13-in. x 9-in. x 2-in. baking pan. Bake at 350° for 40-45 minutes or until a toothpick inserted near the center comes out clean.

For frosting, melt butter in a saucepan; whisk in sugar, milk and egg yolks until smooth. Bring to a boil over medium heat; boil gently for 2 minutes. Remove from the heat; stir in coconut, almonds and vanilla. Spread over warm cake. Cool on a wire rack. Store in the refrigerator. **Yield:** 12-15 servings.

Editor's Note: As a substitute for 2-1/2 cups self-rising flour, place 3-3/4 teaspoons baking powder and 1-1/4 teaspoons salt in a measuring cup. Add all-purpose flour to measure 1 cup. Combine with an additional 1-1/2 cups all-purpose flour.

Fast Fruit Cocktail Cake

Karen Naramore, Gillette, Wyoming

A convenient can of fruit cocktail is the key to this moist, down-home dessert. It's so comforting served warm with whipped cream or ice cream.

- 1 cup all-purpose flour
- 1 cup sugar
- 1 teaspoon baking soda
- 1 teaspoon salt
- 1 can (15-1/4 ounces) fruit cocktail, undrained
- 1 egg, lightly beaten
- 1/2 cup packed brown sugar
- 1/2 cup chopped walnuts

Whipped cream, optional

In a large bowl, combine the flour, sugar, baking soda, salt, fruit cocktail and egg; stir until smooth. Pour into a greased 9-in. square baking pan. Combine brown sugar and nuts; sprinkle over top.

Bake at 350° for 30-35 minutes or until a toothpick inserted near the center comes out clean. Serve with whipped cream if desired. **Yield:** 9 servings.

Raisin-Filled Torte

Jo Peapples, Brooksville, Florida

My mother used this recipe many times, and it was my favorite. She's gone now, but her memory lingers each time I bake this cake. The layers are different flavors, and combined they're deliciously unique. Every time I serve it, I have to send my guests home with the recipe!

- 1/2 cup shortening
- 1-1/4 cups sugar
- 2 eggs
- 2 cups cake flour
- 2 teaspoons baking powder
- 3/4 teaspoon salt
- 3/4 cup milk
- 1 teaspoon vanilla extract
- 1-1/2 teaspoons maple syrup
- 1/4 teaspoon ground cinnamon
- 1/8 teaspoon ground cloves
- 1/8 teaspoon ground nutmeg

FILLING:
- 1/3 cup sugar
- 1 tablespoon cornstarch
- 2/3 cup water
- 1-1/2 cups raisins
- 1 teaspoon lemon juice
- 1 teaspoon butter
- 1/4 teaspoon grated lemon peel

ICING:
- 1 cup confectioners' sugar
- 1 tablespoon butter, melted
- 1/4 teaspoon grated lemon peel
- 5 to 6 teaspoons milk

In a large bowl, cream shortening and sugar until light and fluffy. Add the eggs, one at a time, beating well after each. Combine the flour, baking powder and salt; add to creamed mixture alternately with the milk, beating well after each addition.

Pour half of the batter into another bowl. Add vanilla to one bowl; add the syrup, cinnamon, cloves and nutmeg to the second bowl. Pour each batter into a greased and floured 9-in. round baking pan.

Bake at 375° for 20-25 minutes or until a toothpick inserted near the center comes out clean. Cool for 10 minutes before removing from pans to wire racks to cool.

In a small saucepan, combine sugar and cornstarch; gradually stir in water until smooth. Add raisins. Bring to a boil; cook and stir for 2 minutes or until thickened. Remove from the heat; stir in lemon juice, butter and peel. Cool.

In a small bowl, whisk the sugar, butter and lemon peel. Add milk until icing reaches desired consistency. Place the spice cake layer on a serving platter; spread with filling. Top with vanilla cake layer; drizzle with icing. **Yield:** 12 servings.

Orange Blossom Cake

Mrs. Mueller, Mariposa, California

We maintained a grove of 250 orange trees for years, and this recipe became a family favorite. When I make this cake, I use oranges fresh off the tree. Our grown children say it brings back wonderful childhood memories.

- 1/2 cup butter, softened
- 1 cup sugar
- 2 eggs
- 1/2 cup applesauce
- 1 tablespoon grated orange peel
- 2-1/2 cups all-purpose flour
- 1 teaspoon baking powder
- 1 teaspoon baking soda
- 1/4 teaspoon salt
- 1 cup buttermilk
- 1 cup chopped dates
- 1 cup chopped nuts

GLAZE:
- 1 cup sugar
- 1/2 cup orange juice

In a large bowl, cream butter and sugar until light and fluffy. Beat in the eggs until blended. Beat in applesauce and orange peel. Combine the flour, baking powder, baking soda and salt. Add to creamed mixture alternately with the buttermilk, beating well after each addition. Fold in dates and nuts.

Pour into a greased 9-in. springform pan. Bake at 350° for 55-60 minutes or until a toothpick inserted near the center comes out clean.

Meanwhile, in a small saucepan, combine the glaze ingredients; bring to a boil. Pour over cake. Cool completely in pan on a wire rack. **Yield:** 10-12 servings.

Toothpick Doneness Test When a cake is not completely baked, the toothpick test will have crumbs clinging to the toothpick…the toothpick may even be wet. When the cake is completely baked, the toothpick test will produce a clean toothpick or one with a few dry crumbs on it.

Rhubarb Jelly-Roll Cake

Donna Stratton, Carson City, Nevada

This jelly-roll recipe came from my mom's cookbook, circa 1940. It's continued to be a family classic and is popular at church potlucks.

6	cups chopped fresh *or* frozen rhubarb
2-3/4	cups sugar, *divided*
2	teaspoons ground cinnamon
1/4	teaspoon ground allspice
1/8	teaspoon ground cloves
4	eggs
1	teaspoon lemon extract
3/4	cup all-purpose flour
1	teaspoon baking powder
1/2	teaspoon salt

Confectioners' sugar

In a large saucepan, combine the rhubarb, 2 cups sugar, cinnamon, allspice and cloves. Bring to a boil. Reduce heat; cook, uncovered, over medium heat until thickened, stirring occasionally. Cool completely.

Line a greased 15-in. x 10-in. x 1-in. baking pan with waxed paper; grease the paper and set aside. In a large bowl, beat eggs for 3 minutes. Gradually add remaining sugar; beat for 2 minutes or until mixture becomes thick and lemon-colored. Stir in extract. Combine the flour, baking powder and salt; fold into egg mixture. Spread batter evenly in prepared pan.

Bake at 375° for 15-17 minutes or until cake springs back when lightly touched. Cool for 5 minutes. Invert onto a kitchen towel dusted with confectioners' sugar. Gently peel off waxed paper. Roll up cake in the towel jelly-roll style, starting with a short side. Cool completely on a wire rack.

Unroll cake; spread filling evenly over cake to within 1/2 in. of edges. Roll up again. Place seam side down on a serving platter. Cover and refrigerate for 1 hour. Dust with confectioners' sugar just before serving. Store in the refrigerator. **Yield:** 10-12 servings.

Upside-Down Apple Gingerbread

Florence Palmer, Marshall, Illinois

Don't expect any leftovers when you serve this moist cake. People love it because it's a little different and has a wonderful flavor. Try it for your next gathering.

1/4	cup butter, melted
1/3	cup packed brown sugar
2	large apples, peeled and sliced

GINGERBREAD:

1/2	cup butter, melted
1/2	cup sugar
1/3	cup packed brown sugar
1/2	cup molasses
1	egg
2	cups all-purpose flour
1	teaspoon baking soda
1/2	teaspoon salt
1	teaspoon ground cinnamon
1	teaspoon ground ginger
1/2	teaspoon ground cloves
1/4	teaspoon ground nutmeg
3/4	cup hot tea

Pour butter into a 9-in. square baking pan; sprinkle with brown sugar. Arrange apples cut side up in a single layer over sugar; set aside.

For gingerbread, in a large bowl, beat butter, sugars, molasses and egg until blended. Combine the flour, baking soda, salt and spices; add to sugar mixture alternately with hot tea, beating well after each.

Pour over apples. Bake at 350° for 45 to 50 minutes or until a toothpick inserted near the center comes out clean. Cool for 10 minutes before inverting onto a serving plate. Serve warm. **Yield:** 9 servings.

Chocolate Zucchini Roll

Victoria Zmarzley-Hahn, Northhampton, Pennsylvania

I created this moist cake roll to use up my garden zucchini.

- 3 eggs
- 3/4 cup sugar
- 1 cup shredded peeled zucchini
- 1 teaspoon vanilla extract
- 1 cup all-purpose flour
- 1/2 cup baking cocoa
- 1 teaspoon baking soda
- 1 teaspoon ground cinnamon
- 1/4 teaspoon salt

FILLING:
- 1 package (8 ounces) cream cheese, softened
- 1/4 cup butter, softened
- 2 teaspoons vanilla extract
- 1 cup confectioners' sugar

Additional confectioners' sugar

Line a greased 15-in. x 10-in. x 1-in. baking pan with waxed paper; grease the paper and set aside. In a large bowl, beat eggs for 3 minutes. Gradually add sugar; beat for 2 minutes or until mixture becomes thick and lemon-colored. Stir in zucchini and vanilla. Combine the flour, cocoa, baking soda, cinnamon and salt; add to egg mixture until well blended. (Batter will be thick).

Spread batter evenly in prepared pan. Bake at 350° for 10-15 minutes or until cake springs back when lightly touched. Cool for 5 minutes. Invert onto a kitchen towel dusted with cocoa. Gently peel off waxed paper. Roll up cake in the towel jelly-roll style, starting with a short side. Cool completely on a wire rack.

For filling, in a bowl, beat cream cheese, butter and vanilla until fluffy. Beat in confectioners' sugar until smooth.

Unroll cake; spread filling evenly over cake to within 1/2 in. of edges. Roll up again. Place seam side down on a serving platter. Dust with confectioners' sugar. Cover and refrigerate for 1 hour before slicing. Store in the refrigerator. **Yield:** 10 servings.

Cream Cheese Sheet Cake

Gaye Mann, Rocky Mount, North Carolina

This buttery sheet cake with its fudgy chocolate glaze is a real crowd-pleaser. It's always popular at potlucks and parties. It's not uncommon to see folks going back for second and even third slices.

- 1 cup plus 2 tablespoons butter, softened
- 2 packages (3 ounces *each*) cream cheese, softened
- 2-1/4 cups sugar
- 6 eggs
- 3/4 teaspoon vanilla extract
- 2-1/4 cups cake flour

FROSTING:
- 1 cup sugar
- 1/3 cup evaporated milk
- 1/2 cup butter
- 1/2 cup semisweet chocolate chips

In a large bowl, cream the butter, cream cheese and sugar until light and fluffy. Add eggs, one at a time, beating well after each addition. Beat in vanilla. Add flour; stir until well blended.

Pour into a greased 15-in. x 10-in. x 1-in. baking pan. Bake at 325° for 30-35 minutes or until a toothpick inserted near the center comes out clean. Remove to a wire rack to cool completely.

For frosting, in a small saucepan, combine sugar and milk; bring to a boil over medium heat. Cover and cook for 3 minutes (do not stir). Stir in butter and chocolate chips until melted. Remove from the heat; cool slightly. Stir, then frost the top of the cake. **Yield:** 24-30 servings.

Sponge Cake with Blueberry Topping

Frances Colley, Coos Bay, Oregon

This recipe puts the blueberries grown in our area to good use. It's a great summertime treat.

   6 eggs, *separated*
1-1/2 cups sugar
  3/4 cup orange juice
1-1/2 cups all-purpose flour
1-1/2 teaspoons baking powder
  1/4 teaspoon cream of tartar
BLUEBERRY TOPPING:
  1/2 cup sugar
   2 teaspoons cornstarch
   1 tablespoon grated orange peel
  1/2 cup orange juice
   2 cups fresh *or* frozen blueberries
SOUR CREAM TOPPING:
   2 cups (16 ounces) sour cream
   1 tablespoon confectioners' sugar
   1 teaspoon vanilla extract
Grated orange peel, optional

Let eggs stand at room temperature for 30 minutes. Sift flour and baking powder; set aside.

In a large bowl, beat egg yolks until slightly thick and lemon-colored. Gradually add sugar, beating until thick and lemon-colored. Blend in orange juice. Add flour mixture to yolk mixture until well blended

In another bowl and with clean beaters, beat egg whites and cream of tartar on medium speed until soft peaks form. Fold a fourth of egg whites into the batter, then fold in remaining whites.

Gently spoon into an ungreased 10-in. tube pan. Cut through the batter with a knife to remove air pockets. Bake on the lowest oven rack at 325° for 50-55 minutes or until lightly browned and entire top appears dry. Immediately invert pan; cool completely, about 1 hour.

For blueberry topping, in a large saucepan, combine the sugar, cornstarch and orange peel. Stir in orange juice until smooth. Bring to a boil; cook and stir for 2 minutes or until thickened. Remove from the heat. Stir in blueberries.

For sour cream topping, in a large bowl, combine the sour cream, confectioners' sugar and vanilla.

Run a knife around side and center tube of pan. Remove cake to a plate; cut into slices. Serve with warm blueberry topping and the sour cream topping. Garnish with orange peel if desired. Store blueberry topping and sour cream topping in the refrigerator. **Yield:** 12-16 servings.

Orange Date Pound Cake

Ruth Bartz, Suring, Wisconsin

Loaded with chewy dates and crunchy pecans, this cake is a must at family gatherings. The sweet and zesty orange sauce tops it off just right. This cake slices nicely and looks so appetizing served on a pretty plate.

- 1 cup butter, softened
- 3 cups sugar, *divided*
- 4 eggs
- 1 tablespoon orange peel, *divided*
- 3 cups all-purpose flour
- 1 teaspoon baking soda
- 1-1/3 cups buttermilk
- 1 pound chopped dates
- 1 cup coarsely chopped pecans
- 1/2 cup orange juice

In a large bowl, cream butter and 2 cups sugar until light and fluffy. Add the eggs, one at a time, beating well after each addition. Beat in 2 teaspoons orange peel. Combine flour and baking soda; add to the creamed mixture alternately with buttermilk, beating well after each addition. Stir in dates and pecans.

Pour into a greased and floured 10-in. tube pan; spread evenly. Bake at 325° for 70-75 minutes or until a toothpick inserted near the center comes out clean. Cool for 10 minutes before removing from pan to a wire rack.

In a small bowl, combine the orange juice, remaining sugar and orange peel, until blended; drizzle over warm cake. **Yield:** 12-16 servings.

Sour Cream Chocolate Cake

Patsy Foster, Marion, Arkansas

For a special touch, top this classic with chocolate curls, raspberries and fresh mint sprigs.

    4   squares (1 ounce *each*) unsweetened chocolate, melted and cooled
    1   cup water
  3/4   cup sour cream
  1/4   cup shortening
    1   teaspoon vanilla extract
    2   eggs
    2   cups all-purpose flour
    2   cups sugar
1-1/4   teaspoons baking soda
    1   teaspoon salt
  1/2   teaspoon baking powder
FROSTING:
  1/2   cup butter, softened
    6   squares (1 ounce *each*) unsweetened chocolate, melted and cooled
    6   cups confectioners' sugar
  1/2   cup sour cream
    6   tablespoons milk
    2   teaspoons vanilla extract
  1/8   teaspoon salt

In a large bowl, combine the chocolate, water, sour cream, shortening, vanilla and eggs; mix well. Combine the flour, sugar, baking soda, salt and baking powder; gradually add to the chocolate mixture. Beat on low speed just until moistened. Beat on high for 3 minutes.

Pour into two greased and floured 9-in. round baking pans. Bake at 350° for 30 minutes or until a toothpick inserted near the center comes out clean. Cool for 10 minutes before removing from pans to wire racks to cool completely.

In a bowl, combine frosting ingredients. Beat until creamy. Spread between layers and over top and side of cake. Store in the refrigerator. **Yield:** 12-16 servings.

Cream Cake Dessert

Peggy Stott, Burlington, Iowa

Folks really go for this light cake with fluffy cream filling. My son first tried this treat while in high school and asked me to get the recipe. I've used it countless times since for all sorts of occasions. It's easy to transport to a potluck because the cream is on the inside.

    1   package (18-1/4 ounces) yellow cake mix
    1   package (3.4 ounces) instant vanilla pudding mix
  1/2   cup shortening
    1   cup water
    4   eggs
FILLING:
    5   tablespoons all-purpose flour
    1   cup milk
  1/2   cup butter, softened
  1/2   cup shortening
    1   cup sugar
    1   teaspoon vanilla extract
  1/2   teaspoon salt
Fresh raspberries, optional

In a large bowl, beat the cake mix, pudding mix and shortening on low speed until crumbly. Add the water and eggs; beat on medium for 2 minutes. Pour into a greased and floured 13-in. x 9-in. x 2-in. baking pan.

Bake at 350° for 30-35 minutes or until a toothpick inserted near the center comes out clean. Cool for 10 minutes; invert onto a wire rack to cool completely.

Meanwhile, in a small saucepan, combine flour and milk until smooth. Bring to a boil; cook and stir for 2 minutes or until thickened. Cool completely.

In a large bowl, cream butter, shortening and sugar, until light and fluffy. Beat in the milk mixture, vanilla and salt until smooth, about 5 minutes.

Split cake into two horizontal layers. Spread filling over the bottom layer; replace top layer. Garnish with raspberries if desired. **Yield:** 16-20 servings.

Coconut Poppy Seed Cake

Gail Cayce, Wautoma, Wisconsin

This tender coconut cake is definitely one of my most-requested desserts. Use different cake mixes and pudding flavors for variety.

 1 package (18-1/4 ounces) white cake mix
 1/4 cup poppy seeds
 1/4 teaspoon coconut extract, optional
 3-1/2 cups cold milk
 2 packages (3.4 ounces *each*) instant coconut cream pudding mix
 1 carton (8 ounces) frozen whipped topping, thawed
 1/3 cup flaked coconut, toasted, optional

Prepare cake batter according to package directions, adding poppy seeds and coconut extract if desired.

Pour into a greased 13-in. x 9-in. x 2-in. baking pan. Bake at 350° for 20-25 minutes or until a toothpick inserted near the center comes out clean. Cool completely.

In a large bowl, beat milk and pudding mix on low speed for 2 minutes. Spread over the cake. Spread with whipped topping. Sprinkle with coconut if desired. **Yield:** 20-24 servings.

Chocolate Creme Cakes

Faith Sommers, Beckwourth, California

Moist layers of chocolate cake sandwich a sweet and creamy filling in this irresistible recipe. The yummy treats are handy to keep in the freezer for lunches and after-school snacks.

 1 package (18-1/4 ounces) chocolate cake mix
 1 package (3.9 ounces) instant chocolate pudding mix
 3/4 cup canola oil
 3/4 cup water
 4 eggs

FILLING:
 3 tablespoons all-purpose flour
 1 cup milk
 1/2 cup butter, softened
 1/2 cup shortening
 1 cup sugar
 1 teaspoon vanilla extract

In a large bowl, beat the cake mix, pudding mix, oil, water and eggs. Pour into a greased and floured 13-in. x 9-in. x 2-in. baking pan.

Bake at 350° for 30-35 minutes or until a toothpick inserted near the center comes out clean. Cool for 10 minutes; invert onto a wire rack to cool completely.

In a small saucepan, combine flour and milk until smooth. Bring to a boil; cook and stir for 2 minutes or until thickened. Cool.

In a large bowl, cream the butter, shortening, sugar and vanilla until light and fluffy; beat in milk mixture until sugar is dissolved, about 5 minutes.

Split cake into two horizontal layers. Spread filling over the bottom layer; cover with top layer. Cut into serving-size pieces. Freeze in an airtight container for up to 1 month. Remove from freezer 1 hour before serving. **Yield:** 12-18 servings.

Sesame Pound Cake

Jane Finney, East Grand Forks, Minnesota

This sesame seed-studded cake has a pleasant crunch.
It's wonderful garnished with fresh fruit.

      1   cup butter, softened
      1   cup sugar
      4   eggs
    1/2   cup milk
      1   teaspoon vanilla extract
      1   teaspoon grated lemon peel
    1/3   cup sesame seeds, toasted, *divided*
      2   cups all-purpose flour
      1   teaspoon baking powder
    1/2   teaspoon salt
Fresh fruit, optional

In a large bowl, cream butter and sugar until light and fluffy. Beat in eggs, one at a time, beating well after each addition. Combine the milk, vanilla and lemon peel; set aside. Reserve 1 tablespoon sesame seeds. Combine remaining sesame seeds with the flour, baking powder and salt. Add flour mixture to creamed mixture alternately with milk mixture, beating well after each addition.

Pour into a greased and floured 9-in. x 5-in. x 3-in. loaf pan. Sprinkle with reserved sesame seeds. Bake at 325° for 60-70 minutes or until a toothpick inserted near the center comes out clean. Cool for 10 minutes before removing from pan to a wire rack to cool completely. Serve with fruit if desired. **Yield:** 8-10 servings.

For frosting, in a large bowl, beat butter and confectioners' sugar until smooth. Beat in the milk, orange juice and peel. Frost cooled cake. Garnish with candied peel if desired. **Yield:** 12 servings.

Give Nuts a Flavor Boost Toasting nuts before adding to a cake batter will enhance their flavor. To toast, spread nuts in a single layer in a 15-in. x 10-in. x 1-in. baking pan. Bake at 350° for 5 to 10 minutes or until lightly browned, stirring occasionally.

Nutmeg Pear Cake

Kim Rubner, Worthington, Iowa

I've been in love with baking since I was in seventh grade. I especially enjoy making this pear cake for my husband and our children. With its yummy apple cider sauce, it tastes like autumn.

- 3 cups all-purpose flour
- 1-1/2 teaspoons ground nutmeg
- 1 teaspoon baking soda
- 1 teaspoon ground cinnamon
- 3/4 teaspoon salt
- 1/2 teaspoon baking powder
- 2 cups sugar
- 1 cup canola oil
- 3 eggs, beaten
- 1/2 cup apple cider
- 3 teaspoons vanilla extract
- 1 can (29 ounces) pear halves, drained and mashed
- 1 cup chopped pecans

APPLE CIDER SAUCE:
- 3/4 cup butter
- 2/3 cup sugar
- 1/3 cup packed brown sugar
- 2 tablespoons cornstarch
- 2/3 cup apple cider
- 1/3 cup heavy whipping cream
- 1/3 cup lemon juice

In a large bowl, combine the flour, nutmeg, baking soda, cinnamon, salt and baking powder. In another bowl, whisk the sugar, oil, eggs, cider and vanilla. Add to the dry ingredients and stir well. Stir in pears and pecans.

Pour into a greased and floured 10-in. fluted tube pan. Bake at 350° for 65-70 minutes or until a toothpick inserted near the center comes out clean. Cool for 10 minutes before removing from pan to a wire rack.

For sauce, combine butter and sugars in saucepan. Cook over low heat for 2-3 minutes or until sugar is dissolved. Combine the cornstarch and cider until smooth; add to sugar mixture. Stir in the cream and lemon juice. Bring to a boil; cook and stir for 1-2 minutes or until thickened. Serve warm with cake. **Yield:** 12-15 servings.

Pumpkin Orange Cake

Shirley Glaab, Hattiesburg, Mississippi

This make-ahead spice cake with its flavorful orange frosting is popular at family gatherings. It's simple to prepare and it tastes so good, everyone asks for the recipe.

- 1/2 cup butter, softened
- 1-1/4 cups sugar
- 2 eggs
- 1 cup canned pumpkin
- 1/2 cup orange juice
- 1/4 cup milk
- 1 tablespoon grated orange peel
- 2 cups all-purpose flour
- 3 teaspoons baking powder
- 1 teaspoon ground cinnamon
- 1/2 teaspoon baking soda
- 1/2 teaspoon salt
- 1/2 teaspoon ground ginger
- 1/2 teaspoon ground allspice
- 1/2 cup chopped walnuts

ORANGE FROSTING:
- 1/3 cup butter, softened
- 3 cups confectioners' sugar
- 3 tablespoons milk
- 2 teaspoons orange juice
- 4-1/2 teaspoons grated orange peel

Candied orange peel, optional

In a large bowl, cream butter and sugar until light and fluffy. Add eggs, one at a time, beating well after each addition. In another bowl, beat pumpkin, orange juice, milk and orange peel. Combine the flour, baking powder, cinnamon, baking soda, salt, ginger and allspice; add to creamed mixture alternately with pumpkin mixture, beating well after each addition. Fold in walnuts.

Pour into a greased 13-in. x 9-in. x 2-in. baking pan. Bake at 350° for 30 minutes or until a toothpick inserted near the center comes out clean. Cool on a wire rack.

Carrot Layer Cake

Linda Van Holland, Innisfail, Alberta

My sister gave me this recipe for what she called "the ultimate carrot cake" and it really lives up to the name. People are bowled over with the moist, not-too-sweet cake that features an unexpected treat—a pecan filling.

FILLING:
- 1 cup sugar
- 2 tablespoons all-purpose flour
- 1/4 teaspoon salt
- 1 cup heavy whipping cream
- 1/2 cup butter
- 1 cup chopped pecans
- 1 teaspoon vanilla extract

CAKE:
- 1-1/4 cups canola oil
- 2 cups sugar
- 2 cups all-purpose flour
- 2 teaspoons ground cinnamon
- 2 teaspoons baking powder
- 1 teaspoon baking soda
- 1 teaspoon salt
- 4 eggs
- 4 cups finely shredded carrots
- 1 cup raisins
- 1 cup chopped pecans

FROSTING:
- 3/4 cup butter, softened
- 2 packages (3 ounces *each*) cream cheese, softened
- 1 teaspoon vanilla extract
- 3 cups confectioners' sugar

In a large heavy saucepan, combine the sugar, flour and salt. Stir in cream; add butter. Cook and stir over medium heat until the butter is melted; bring to a boil. Reduce heat. Simmer, uncovered, for 30 minutes, stirring occasionally. Remove from the heat. Stir in nuts and vanilla. Cool and set aside.

In a large bowl, beat oil and sugar until well blended. Combine the flour, cinnamon, baking powder, baking soda and salt; add to the sugar mixture alternately with eggs, beating well after each addition. Stir in the carrots, raisins and nuts.

Pour into three greased and floured 9-in. round baking pans. Bake at 350° for 35-40 minutes or until a toothpick inserted near the center comes out clean. Cool for 10 minutes before removing from pans to wire racks to cool completely.

For frosting, in a large bowl, beat the butter, cream cheese and vanilla until fluffy. Gradually beat in sugar until smooth. Spread filling between cake layers. Frost the sides and top of cake. Store in the refrigerator. **Yield:** 16-20 servings.

Sugar Plum Cake

Mark Brown, Birmingham, Alabama

I came by my love of preparing recipes as a boy in the South, where food is the center of every gathering. I worked with my grandmothers, who believed everyone should know how to cook. This cake recipe is a favorite. I bake several for Christmas each year to give as gifts.

- 2 cups sugar
- 2 jars (6 ounces *each*) strained plum baby food
- 3/4 cup canola oil
- 3 eggs, lightly beaten
- 2 cups self-rising flour
- 1 teaspoon ground cinnamon
- 1 teaspoon ground cloves
- 1 cup chopped pecans

GLAZE:
- 1 cup plus 2 tablespoons confectioners' sugar
- 1 jar (4 ounces) strained plum-apple baby food
- 2 tablespoons milk

In a large bowl, beat the sugar, baby food, oil and eggs until well blended. Combine the flour, cinnamon and cloves; gradually beat into plum mixture until blended. Stir in pecans.

Pour into a greased and floured 10-in. tube pan. Bake at 350° for 50-60 minutes or until a toothpick inserted near the center comes out clean. Cool for 10 minutes before removing from pan to a wire rack to cool completely.

In a small bowl, combine glaze ingredients until smooth. Drizzle over top and sides of cake. **Yield:** 16-20 servings.

Editor's Note: As a substitute for 2 cups self-rising flour, place 3 teaspoons baking powder and 1 teaspoon salt in a measuring cup. Add all-purpose flour to measure 1 cup. Combine with an additional 1 cup all-purpose flour.

Chocolate Raspberry Torte

Rosemary Ford Vinson, El Cajon, California

When our daughter requested this fancy layered cake for her birthday, I was afraid it would be difficult to make. But it's so easy! Everyone oohs and aahs at how pretty it is.

　1　package (18-1/4 ounces) chocolate cake mix
　1　package (3 ounces) cream cheese, softened
3/4　cup cold milk
　1　package (3.4 ounces) instant vanilla pudding mix
　1　carton (8 ounces) frozen whipped topping, thawed
　2　cups fresh raspberries
Confectioners' sugar
Fresh mint and additional raspberries, optional

Prepare the cake according to package directions. Pour into three greased and floured 9-in. round baking pans. Bake at 350° for 25-30 minutes or until a toothpick inserted near the center comes out clean. Cool for 10 minutes before removing from pans to wire racks to cool completely.

In a large bowl, beat cream cheese until fluffy. Combine milk and pudding mix; beat into cream cheese until smooth. Fold in whipped topping and raspberries.

Place one cake layer on a serving plate. Spread with half of the filling. Repeat layers. Top with remaining cake; dust with confectioners' sugar. Garnish with mint and raspberries if desired. Store in the refrigerator. **Yield:** 12 servings.

Golden Lemon Pound Cake

Douglas Jennings, Ottawa, Kansas

Years ago while pasturing a church in New Mexico, I worked in a nursing home. For a Christmas party, I baked this cake. Everyone raved over the treat my wife made. When I told them I'd made it myself, they were astonished.

- 2/3 cup butter-flavored shortening
- 1-1/4 cups sugar
- 3 eggs
- 2 tablespoons lemon juice
- 1 teaspoon lemon extract
- 2-1/4 cups cake flour
- 1-1/4 teaspoons salt
- 1 teaspoon baking powder
- 2/3 cup milk
- Confectioners' sugar

In a large bowl, cream shortening and sugar until light and fluffy, about 5 minutes. Add eggs, one at a time, beating well after each addition. Stir in lemon juice and extract. Combine the flour, salt and baking powder; add to the creamed mixture alternately with milk. Beat just until combined.

Pour into a greased and floured 9-in. x 5-in. x 3-in. loaf pan. Bake at 350° for 55-60 minutes or until a toothpick inserted near the center comes out clean.

Cool for 10 minutes before removing from pan to a wire rack to cool completely. Dust with confectioners' sugar. **Yield:** 1 loaf.

Eggnog Cake

Edith Disch, Fairview Park, Ohio

With its tender cake layers, creamy filling and chocolate frosting, this cake appeals to all palates!

- 2 eggs, *separated*
- 1/2 cup butter, softened
- 1 cup sugar, *divided*
- 3/4 cup orange juice
- 1-1/2 teaspoons grated orange peel
- 1 teaspoon vanilla extract
- 2 cups sifted cake flour
- 2 teaspoons baking powder
- 1/2 teaspoon ground nutmeg
- 1/4 teaspoon baking soda
- 1/4 teaspoon salt

EGGNOG FILLING:
- 5 tablespoons all-purpose flour
- 1-1/4 cups eggnog
- 1 cup butter, softened
- 3/4 cup sugar
- 1 teaspoon vanilla extract
- 1/4 teaspoon ground nutmeg

CHOCOLATE FROSTING:
- 2/3 cup confectioners' sugar
- 3 tablespoons butter, softened
- 2 tablespoons heavy whipping cream
- 2 ounces unsweetened chocolate, melted and cooled
- 1/4 teaspoon ground cinnamon
- 1/8 teaspoon ground nutmeg
- 2 to 3 tablespoons hot water

Let eggs stand at room temperature for 30 minutes. In a large bowl, cream butter and 3/4 cup sugar until light and fluffy. Add yolks, one at a time, beating well after each. Combine the orange juice, peel and vanilla. Combine the flour, baking powder, nutmeg, baking soda and salt; add to creamed mixture alternately with juice mixture, beating well after each addition.

In another bowl and with clean beaters, beat egg whites on medium speed until soft peaks form. Gradually beat in remaining sugar, 1 tablespoon at a time, on high until stiff peaks form. Fold into batter.

Line two greased 9-in. round baking pans with waxed paper; grease paper. Pour batter into pans. Bake at 350° for 20 minutes or until a toothpick inserted near the center comes out clean. Cool for 10 minutes before removing from pans to wire racks. Peel off paper; cool.

For filling, in a small saucepan, combine flour and a small amount of eggnog; stir until smooth. Stir in remaining eggnog. Bring to boil; cook, stir 2 minutes. Cool completely.

In a small bowl, cream butter and sugar until light and fluffy; beat in vanilla and nutmeg. Gradually beat in eggnog mixture until smooth; set aside.

For frosting, in another small bowl, beat confectioners' sugar and butter until light and fluffy. Beat in the cream, chocolate, cinnamon and nutmeg until smooth. Add water until frosting reaches spreading consistency.

Split cakes in half; spread filling on three layers. Stack with plain layer on top; frost the top. **Yield:** 14 servings.

Editor's Note: This recipe was tested with commercially prepared eggnog.

Caramel Apple Cake

Marilyn Paradis, Woodburn, Oregon

When I go to potlucks, family gatherings or on hunting and fishing trips with my husband and son, this cake is one of my favorite desserts to bring. The flavorful cake stays moist as long as it lasts, which isn't long!

- 1-1/2 cups canola oil
- 1-1/2 cups sugar
- 1/2 cup packed brown sugar
- 3 eggs
- 2 teaspoons vanilla extract
- 3 cups all-purpose flour
- 2 teaspoons ground cinnamon
- 1 teaspoon baking soda
- 1/2 teaspoon salt
- 1/2 teaspoon ground nutmeg
- 3-1/2 cups diced peeled apples
- 1 cup chopped walnuts
- CARAMEL ICING:
- 1/2 cup packed brown sugar
- 1/3 cup half-and-half cream
- 1/4 cup butter, cubed
- Dash salt
- 1 cup confectioners' sugar
- Chopped walnuts, optional

In a large bowl, combine oil and sugars until well blended. Add eggs, one at a time, beating well after each addition. Beat in vanilla. Combine the flour, cinnamon, baking soda, salt and nutmeg; gradually add to creamed mixture until blended. Fold in the apples and walnuts.

Pour into a greased and floured 10-in. tube pan. Bake at 325° for 1-1/2 hours or until a toothpick inserted near the center comes out clean. Cool for 10 minutes before removing from pan to a wire rack to cool completely.

In a small, saucepan, combine the brown sugar, cream, butter and salt until smooth. Cool to room temperature. Beat in confectioners' sugar until smooth; drizzle over cake. Sprinkle with nuts if desired. **Yield:** 12-16 servings.

Rich Butter Cake

Doris Schloeman, Chicago, Illinois

I've been bringing this cake to family get-togethers and church meetings since the 1950s. The scrumptious standby is topped with cream cheese and nuts.

- 1 package (16 ounces) pound cake mix
- 1/2 cup butter, melted
- 5 eggs
- 2 cups confectioners' sugar, *divided*
- 2 packages (one 8 ounces, one 3 ounces) cream cheese, softened
- 1/2 teaspoon vanilla extract
- 1 cup chopped walnuts

In a large bowl, combine the cake mix, butter and 3 eggs; beat until smooth. Spread into a greased 13-in. x 9-in. x 2-in. baking pan.

Set aside 2 tablespoons confectioners' sugar for topping. In a large bowl, beat the cream cheese, vanilla, remaining confectioners' sugar until smooth. Beat in remaining eggs. Pour over batter. Sprinkle with walnuts.

Bake at 350° for 35-40 minutes or until cake begins to pull away from sides of pan. Cool on a wire rack. Dust with reserved confectioners' sugar. Store in the refrigerator. **Yield:** 12-15 servings.

Traditional Sponge Cake

Arlene Murphy, Beverly Hills, Florida

My light sponge cake makes a fitting finale to any meal, especially when it's dressed up with a drizzle of chocolate sauce.

      6 eggs, *separated*
  1-1/2 cups all-purpose flour
    1/2 teaspoon salt
  1-1/2 cups sugar, *divided*
    1/2 cup warm water
      1 teaspoon vanilla extract
    1/2 teaspoon cream of tartar
    1/2 cup chocolate ice cream topping

Let eggs stand at room temperature for 30 minutes. Sift flour and salt; set aside.

In a large bowl, beat yolks until slightly thickened. Gradually add 1 cup sugar, beating until thick and lemon-colored. Blend in water and vanilla. Add flour mixture to yolk mixture; mix well.

In another bowl and with clean beaters, beat egg whites and cream of tartar on medium speed until soft peaks form. Gradually beat in remaining sugar, about 1 tablespoon at a time, on high until stiff, glossy peaks form and sugar is dissolved. Fold a fourth of egg whites into the batter, then fold in remaining whites.

Gently spoon into an ungreased 10-in. tube pan; smooth the top. Bake on the lowest rack at 325° for 55-60 minutes or cake springs back when lightly touched. Immediately invert the pan; cool completely, about 1 hour.

Run a knife around side and center tube of pan. Remove cake to a serving plate. Slice; drizzle with ice cream topping. **Yield:** 12 servings.

Old-Fashioned Carrot Cake

Muriel Doherty, Phoenix, Arizona

My family thinks this is the best carrot cake ever! We love the moist texture. The surprise is in the frosting. It's a pleasant departure from the usual cream cheese frosting that tops most carrot cakes. This cake doesn't last very long around our house!

4	eggs
2	cups sugar
3	cups finely shredded carrots
1	package (8 ounces) cream cheese, softened
1-1/2	cups canola oil
2	cups all-purpose flour
2	teaspoons baking soda
2	teaspoons ground cinnamon
1	teaspoon salt
1	can (8 ounces) crushed pineapple, drained
1	cup chopped walnuts

FLUFFY FROSTING:

1/4	cup all-purpose flour
3/4	cup milk
3/4	cup butter, softened
2	cups confectioners' sugar
3/4	cup sugar
1/2	teaspoon salt
1	teaspoon vanilla extract

Additional chopped walnuts

In a large bowl, beat eggs, sugar, carrots, cream cheese and oil until well blended. Combine the flour, baking soda, cinnamon and salt; gradually add to carrot mixture. Stir in pineapple and nuts.

Pour into a greased 13-in. x 9-in. x 2-in. baking pan. Bake at 350° for 55-60 minutes or until a toothpick inserted near the center comes out clean. Remove to a wire rack to cool.

In a heavy saucepan, cook and stir flour and milk over medium-low heat until a thick paste forms, about 10 minutes. Chill for 30 minutes. In a large mixer, cream the butter, sugars and salt until light and fluffy. Beat in the chilled flour mixture until smooth, about 5 minutes. Beat in vanilla. Frost cake. Sprinkle with nuts. Store in the refrigerator. **Yield:** 12-16 servings.

Beating Egg Whites To achieve the highest volume when beating egg whites, follow these tips. Allow whites to warm up by standing at room temperature for 30 minutes. Make sure there are no flecks of egg yolks in the whites. Beat the whites in a clean, dry metal or glass bowl with clean, dry beaters.

Marbled Peppermint Angel Cake

Kathy Kittell, Lenexa, Kansas

Although it doesn't puff up as much as other angel food cakes during baking, the refreshing minty flavor and festive red swirls raise this version above ordinary desserts!

1-1/2	cups egg whites (about 12)
3/4	cup all-purpose flour
1-1/2	cups sugar, *divided*
1-1/2	teaspoons cream of tartar
1-1/2	teaspoons vanilla extract
1	teaspoon peppermint extract
1/4	teaspoon salt
6	drops red food coloring, optional

GLAZE:

2	cups confectioners' sugar
1/4	cup milk
1/4	teaspoon peppermint extract
6	drops red food coloring, optional
1/4	cup crushed peppermint candies

Place the egg whites in a large bowl; let stand at room temperature for 30 minutes. Sift flour and 3/4 cup sugar together twice; set aside.

Add cream of tartar, extracts and salt to egg whites; beat on medium speed until soft peaks form. Gradually add remaining sugar, about 2 tablespoons at a time, beating on high until stiff, glossy peaks form and sugar is dissolved. Gradually fold in flour mixture, about 1/2 cup at a time. Divide batter in half; tint half with red food coloring.

Alternately spoon plain and pink batters into an ungreased 10-in. tube pan. Cut through the batter with a knife to remove air pockets. Bake on the lowest oven rack at 350° for 30-40 minutes or until lightly browned and entire top appears dry. Immediately invert pan; cool completely, about 1 hour.

Run a knife around side and center tube of pan. Remove cake to a serving plate.

For glaze, combine the confectioners' sugar, milk extract and food coloring if desired. Drizzle over cake. Sprinkle with crushed candies. **Yield:** 12-16 servings.

Blueberry Oat Cake

Linda Police, Dover, New Jersey

This is my favorite blueberry recipe. Everyone in my family likes it, so I make it rather frequently. It's tender and very easy to make.

- 2 eggs
- 2 cups buttermilk
- 1 cup packed brown sugar
- 1/2 cup canola oil
- 2 cups all-purpose flour
- 2 teaspoons baking powder
- 1 teaspoon baking soda
- 1 teaspoon ground cinnamon
- 1/2 teaspoon salt
- 2 cups quick-cooking oats
- 2 cups fresh *or* frozen blueberries
- 1 cup chopped walnuts, optional

Confectioners' sugar

In a large bowl, beat the eggs, buttermilk, brown sugar and oil. Combine the flour, baking powder, baking soda, cinnamon and salt; add to batter. Beat on low speed for 2 minutes. Fold in the oats, blueberries and walnuts if desired.

Transfer to a greased and floured 10-in. fluted tube pan. Bake at 375° for 45-50 minutes or until a toothpick inserted near the center comes out clean. Cool for 10 minutes before removing from pan to a wire rack to cool completely. Dust with confectioners' sugar. **Yield:** 12-16 servings.

Editor's Note: If using frozen blueberries, do not thaw before adding to batter.

Orange Cream Cake

Star Pooley, Paradise, California

Kids of all ages will enjoy the old-fashioned flavor of this cake topped with a soft light frosting. This dessert reminds me of the frozen Creamsicles I enjoyed as a child.

- 1 package (18-1/4 ounces) lemon cake mix
- 1 envelope unsweetened orange soft drink mix
- 3 eggs
- 1 cup water
- 1/3 cup canola oil
- 2 packages (3 ounces *each*) orange gelatin, *divided*
- 1 cup boiling water
- 1 cup cold water
- 1 cup cold milk
- 1 teaspoon vanilla extract
- 1 package (3.4 ounces) instant vanilla pudding mix
- 1 carton (8 ounces) frozen whipped topping, thawed

In a large bowl, combine cake and drink mixes, eggs, water and oil. Beat on medium speed for 2 minutes.

Pour into an ungreased 13-in. x 9-in. x 2-in. baking pan. Bake at 350° for 25-30 minutes or until a toothpick inserted near the center comes out clean. Using a meat fork, poke holes in cake. Cool on a wire rack for 30 minutes.

Meanwhile, in a large bowl, dissolve one package of gelatin in boiling water. Stir in cold water. Pour over cake. Cover and refrigerate for 2 hours.

In a large bowl, combine the milk, vanilla, pudding mix and remaining gelatin; whisk for 2 minutes. Let stand for 5 minutes; fold in whipped topping. Frost cake. Store in the refrigerator. **Yield:** 12-15 servings.

Chocolate Berry Pound Cake

Christi Ross, Guthrie, Texas

This moist cake topped with raspberry whipped cream is from a dear friend's vast recipe collection. It tastes like something Grandma would make and is pretty enough to serve for company.

- 1 jar (10 ounces) seedless blackberry *or* black raspberry spreadable fruit, *divided*
- 2/3 cup butter, softened
- 1-1/2 cups sugar
- 2 eggs
- 1 teaspoon vanilla extract
- 2 cups all-purpose flour
- 3/4 cup baking cocoa
- 1-1/2 teaspoons baking soda
- 1 teaspoon salt
- 2 cups (16 ounces) sour cream

Confectioners' sugar, optional

RASPBERRY CREAM:

- 1 package (10 ounces) frozen sweetened raspberries, thawed
- 1 carton (8 ounces) frozen whipped topping, thawed

Fresh raspberries and blackberries, optional

Place 3/4 cup spreadable fruit in a microwave-safe bowl. Cover and microwave on high for 30-50 seconds or until melted; stir until smooth and set aside.

In a large bowl, cream butter and sugar until light and fluffy. Beat in eggs and vanilla. Combine the flour, cocoa, baking soda and salt. Combine sour cream and melted fruit spread; add to creamed mixture alternately with dry ingredients, beating well after each addition.

Pour into a greased and floured 10-in. fluted tube pan. Bake at 350° for 50-55 minutes or until a toothpick inserted near the center comes out clean. Cool for 10 minutes before removing from pan to a wire rack.

Place remaining spreadable fruit in a microwave-safe bowl. Cover and microwave on high for 20-30 seconds or until melted; stir until smooth. Brush over warm cake. Cool. Dust with confectioners' sugar if desired.

For raspberry cream, place raspberries in a blender; cover and process for 2-3 minutes or until blended. Strain and discard seeds. Fold in whipped topping. Serve with the cake. Garnish with fresh berries if desired. **Yield:** 10-12 servings.

Special Rhubarb Cake

Biena Schlabach, Millersburg, Ohio

A rich vanilla sauce is served with this tender cake. The women at church made it for my birthday.

- 2 tablespoons butter, softened
- 1 cup sugar
- 1 egg
- 2 cups all-purpose flour
- 1 teaspoon baking powder
- 1/2 teaspoon baking soda
- 1/2 teaspoon salt
- 1 cup buttermilk
- 2 cups chopped fresh rhubarb *or* frozen rhubarb, thawed

STREUSEL TOPPING:

- 1/4 cup all-purpose flour
- 1/4 cup sugar
- 2 tablespoons butter, melted

VANILLA SAUCE:

- 1/2 cup butter
- 3/4 cup sugar
- 1/2 cup evaporated milk
- 1 teaspoon vanilla extract

In a large bowl, cream butter and sugar until light and fluffy. Beat in egg. Combine the flour, baking powder, baking soda and salt; add to creamed mixture alternately with buttermilk, beating just until moistened. Fold in the rhubarb. Pour into a greased 9-in. square baking dish.

Combine topping ingredients; sprinkle over batter. Bake at 350° for 40-45 minutes or until a toothpick inserted near the center comes out clean. Cool on a wire rack.

For sauce, melt butter in a saucepan. Add sugar and milk. Bring to a boil; cook and stir for 2-3 minutes or until thickened. Remove from the heat; stir in vanilla. Serve with cake. **Yield:** 9 servings (1-1/4 cups sauce).

Editor's Note: If using frozen rhubarb, measure rhubarb while still frozen, then thaw completely. Drain in a colander, but do not press liquid out.

Butter Pecan Ice Cream Roll

Elaine Hefner, Elida, Ohio

To keep things under control, I rely on recipes that keep entertaining simple. This cake roll can be chilling in the freezer long before guests arrive. Try varying the flavor of the ice cream to suit different tastes.

- 4 eggs
- 1 cup sugar
- 1/4 cup water
- 2 teaspoons vanilla extract
- 1 cup all-purpose flour
- 2 teaspoons baking powder
- 1/2 teaspoon salt
- 1-1/2 quarts butter pecan ice cream, softened

Confectioners' sugar

Pecan halves, optional

Line a greased 15-in. x 10-in. x 1-in. baking pan with waxed paper; grease the paper and set aside. In a large bowl, beat eggs for 3 minutes. Gradually add sugar; beat for 2 minutes or until mixture becomes thick and lemon-colored. Beat in water and vanilla. Combine the flour baking powder and salt; fold into egg mixture. Spread batter evenly in prepared pan.

Bake at 375° for 12-14 minutes or until cake is lightly browned. Cool for 5 minutes; turn onto a kitchen towel dusted with confectioners' sugar. Peel off waxed paper. Roll up cake in the towel jelly-roll style, starting with a short side. Cool on a wire rack.

Unroll cake; spread with ice cream to within 1 in. of edges. Roll up again; cover and freeze until firm. May be frozen for up to 2 months. Place seam side down on a serving platter. Dust with confectioners' sugar and decorate with pecans before serving if desired. **Yield:** 10 servings.

White Chocolate Pound Cake

Kimberley Thompson, Fayetteville, Georgia

I often bake this delicious bundt cake, drizzled with two types of chocolate glaze, for special occasions.

- 8 squares (1 ounce *each*) white baking chocolate
- 1 cup butter, softened
- 2 cups plus 2 tablespoons sugar, *divided*
- 5 eggs
- 2 teaspoons vanilla extract
- 1/2 teaspoon almond extract
- 3 cups all-purpose flour
- 1 teaspoon baking powder
- 1/2 teaspoon salt
- 1/2 teaspoon baking soda
- 1 cup (8 ounces) sour cream

GLAZE:
- 4 squares (1 ounce *each*) semisweet baking chocolate, melted
- 4 squares (1 ounce *each*) white baking chocolate, melted

Whole fresh strawberries, optional

Chop four squares of white chocolate and melt the other four; set both aside. In a bowl, cream butter and 2 cups sugar until light and fluffy. Add eggs, one at a time, beating well after each addition. Stir in extracts and the melted chocolate. Combine the flour, baking powder, salt and baking soda; add to the creamed mixture alternately with sour cream. Beat just until combined.

Grease a 10-in. fluted tube pan. Sprinkle with the remaining sugar. Pour a third of the batter into pan. Sprinkle with half of the chopped chocolate. Repeat. Pour remaining batter on top.

Bake at 350° for 55-60 minutes or until a toothpick inserted near the center comes out clean. Cool for 10 minutes before removing from pan to a wire rack to cool completely. Drizzle semisweet and white chocolate over cake. Garnish with strawberries if desired. **Yield:** 16 servings.

Strawberry Meringue Cake

Dorothy Anderson, Ottawa, Kansas

Guests say "Wow!" when I present this torte. Mashed berries add flavor to the cream filling.

- 4 eggs, *separated*
- 1 package (18-1/4 ounces) yellow cake mix
- 1-1/3 cups orange juice
- 1-1/2 teaspoons grated orange peel
- 1/4 teaspoon cream of tartar
- 1 cup plus 1/4 cup sugar, *divided*
- 2 cups heavy whipping cream
- 2 pints fresh strawberries, *divided*

Let eggs stand at room temperature for 30 minutes.

In a large bowl, combine the cake mix, orange juice, peel and egg yolks; beat on low speed for 30 seconds. Beat on medium for 2 minutes. Pour into two greased and floured 9-in. round baking pans; set aside.

In a large bowl with clean beaters, beat egg whites and cream of tartar on medium until soft peaks form. Gradually beat in 1 cup sugar, a tablespoon at a time, on high until stiff, glossy peaks form. Spread the meringue evenly over cake batter.

Bake at 350° for 35-40 minutes or until meringue is lightly browned. Cool in pans on wire racks (meringue will crack).

Meanwhile, in a chilled large bowl, beat cream until stiff peaks form. Mash 1/2 cup of strawberries with remaining sugar; fold into whipped cream.

Loosen edges of cakes from pans with a knife. Using two large spatulas, carefully remove one cake to a serving platter, meringue side up. Carefully spread with about two-thirds of the cream mixture. Slice the remaining berries; arrange half over cream mixture. Repeat layers. Store in the refrigerator. **Yield:** 12-16 servings.

Peanut Butter
Chocolate Cake

Dorcas Yoder, Weyers Cave, Virginia

In our chocolate-loving house, this cake disappears very quickly! Cream cheese and peanut butter make the frosting extra-creamy.

- 2 cups all-purpose flour
- 2 cups sugar
- 2/3 cup baking cocoa
- 2 teaspoons baking soda
- 1 teaspoon baking powder
- 1/2 teaspoon salt
- 2 eggs
- 1 cup milk
- 2/3 cup canola oil
- 1 teaspoon vanilla extract
- 1 cup brewed coffee, room temperature

PEANUT BUTTER FROSTING:
- 1 package (3 ounces) cream cheese, softened
- 1/4 cup creamy peanut butter
- 2 cups confectioners' sugar
- 2 tablespoons milk
- 1/2 teaspoon vanilla extract

Miniature semisweet chocolate chips, optional

In a bowl, combine the flour, sugar, cocoa, baking soda, baking powder and salt. Add the eggs, milk, oil and vanilla; beat for 2 minutes. Stir in the coffee (batter will be thin).

Pour into a greased 13-in. x 9-in. x 2-in. baking pan. Bake at 350° for 35-40 minutes or until a toothpick inserted near the center comes out clean. Cool completely on a wire rack.

For frosting, beat the cream cheese and peanut butter in a bowl until smooth. Beat in the sugar, milk and vanilla. Spread over cake. Sprinkle with chocolate chips if desired. Store in the refrigerator. **Yield:** 12-16 servings.

Cranberry Cake

Marion Lowery, Medford, Oregon

Always welcomed on holidays, this pudding-like dessert is my mother's recipe.

  3 tablespoons butter, softened
  1 cup sugar
  1 egg
  2 cups all-purpose flour
  2 teaspoons baking powder
  1 teaspoon ground nutmeg
  1 cup milk
  2 cups cranberries
  2 tablespoons grated orange *or* lemon peel
CREAM SAUCE:
1-1/3 cups sugar
  1 cup heavy whipping cream
 2/3 cup butter

In a large bowl, cream butter and sugar until light and fluffy. Beat in egg. Combine the flour, baking powder and nutmeg; add to the creamed mixture alternately with milk, beating well after each addition. Stir in cranberries and orange peel.

Pour into a greased 11-in. x 7-in. x 2-in. baking dish. Bake at 350° for 35-40 minutes or until a toothpick inserted near the center comes out clean.

Meanwhile, in a small saucepan, combine the sauce ingredients. Cook and stir over medium heat until heated through. Cut warm cake into squares; serve with cream sauce. **Yield:** 8-10 servings.

Stocking up on Cranberries When fresh cranberries are in season, buy extra bags so that you can make this delectable Cranberry Cake any time of year. All you need to do is toss the extra bags in the freezer. They can be frozen for up to a year.

About Poppy Seeds Poppy seeds add a nut-like flavor to baked goods. For best flavor, store poppy seeds in a cool, dry place away from the heat of a range and steam of a dishwasher. If you've had the container for several years, it's time to replace it with a new one.

Poppy Seed Bundt Cake

Kathy Schrecengost Oswego, New York

Who knew that you could get such old-fashioned flavor from a mix! A hint of coconut and the tender texture make it simply scrumptious. All you need to dress it up is a dusting of powdered sugar.

- 1 package (18-1/4 ounces) yellow cake mix
- 1 package (3.4 ounces) instant coconut cream pudding mix
- 1 cup water
- 1/2 cup canola oil
- 3 eggs
- 2 tablespoons poppy seeds

Confectioners' sugar

In a bowl, combine the cake mix, pudding mix, water, oil and eggs. Beat on low speed until moistened. Beat on medium for 2 minutes. Stir in the poppy seeds.

Pour into a greased and floured 10-in. fluted tube pan. Bake at 350° for 48-52 minutes or until a toothpick inserted near the center comes out clean. Cool for 10 minutes before removing from pan to a wire rack to cool completely. Dust with confectioners' sugar. **Yield:** 12-15 servings.

Spiced Apple Upside-Down Cake

Mavis Diment, Marcus, Iowa

I like unusual desserts like this one. From the condition of my recipe card, this must be very good—a messy, well-worn card shows I've made this cake countless times.

- 1 jar (14 ounces) spiced apple rings
- 6 tablespoons butter, softened
- 1/2 cup packed brown sugar
- 1/4 cup sliced almonds, toasted
- 1 egg
- 1/2 cup milk
- 1 teaspoon vanilla extract
- 1 cup all-purpose flour
- 1/2 cup sugar
- 1-1/2 teaspoons baking powder

Whipped cream, optional

Drain the apple rings, reserving 1 tablespoon syrup; set apple rings aside. In a small saucepan, melt 2 tablespoons butter; stir in brown sugar and reserved syrup until smooth. Spread evenly in a greased 9-in. round baking pan; sprinkle with almonds. Top with apple rings; set aside.

In a large bowl, beat the egg, milk, vanilla and remaining butter. Combine flour, sugar and baking powder; gradually add to egg mixture until well blended.

Spoon over apple rings. Bake at 350° for 35-40 minutes or until a toothpick inserted near the center comes out clean. Cool for 10 minutes before inverting onto a serving plate. Serve warm. Serve with whipped cream if desired. **Yield:** 6-8 servings.

Glazed Lemon Cake

Missy Andrews, Rice, Washington

My mother baked this light, moist treat when I was a child. I loved it as much then as my children do now.

- 1 package (18-1/4 ounces) white cake mix
- 1 package (3.4 ounces) instant lemon pudding mix
- 3/4 cup canola oil
- 3 eggs
- 1 cup lemon-lime soda
- 1 cup confectioners' sugar
- 2 tablespoons lemon juice

In a large bowl, combine the cake mix, pudding mix, oil and eggs; beat on medium speed for 1 minute. Gradually beat in soda just until blended.

Pour into a greased 13-in. x 9-in. x 2-in. baking dish. Bake at 350° for 40-45 minutes or until a toothpick inserted near the center comes out clean.

In a small bowl, combine the confectioners' sugar and lemon juice until smooth; carefully spread over warm cake. Cool on a wire rack. **Yield:** 12 servings.

Chocolate Angel Cake

Joyce Shiffler, Colorado Springs, Colorado

When I first got married, I could barely boil water. My dear mother-in-law taught me her specialty...the lightest angel food cakes ever. This chocolate version is an easy, impressive treat. For many years, it was our son's birthday cake.

- 1-1/2 cups egg whites (about 12)
- 1-1/2 cups confectioners' sugar
- 1 cup cake flour
- 1/4 cup baking cocoa

- 1-1/2 teaspoons cream of tartar
- 1/2 teaspoon salt
- 1 cup sugar

FROSTING:

- 1-1/2 cups heavy whipping cream
- 1/2 cup sugar
- 1/4 cup baking cocoa
- 1/2 teaspoon salt
- 1/2 teaspoon vanilla extract

Chocolate leaves, optional

Place egg whites in a large bowl; let stand at room temperature for 30 minutes. Sift confectioners' sugar, flour and cocoa three times; set aside.

Add cream of tartar and salt to egg whites; beat on medium speed until soft peaks form. Gradually add sugar, about 2 tablespoons at a time, beating on high until stiff, glossy peaks form and sugar is dissolved. Gradually fold in flour mixture, about 1/2 cup at a time.

Gently spoon into an ungreased 10-in. tube pan. Cut through the batter with a knife to remove air pockets. Bake on the lowest oven rack at 375° for 35-40 minutes or until lightly browned and entire top appears dry. Immediately invert pan; cool completely, about 1 hour.

Run a knife around side and center tube of pan. Remove cake to a serving plate.

In a bowl, combine the cream, sugar, cocoa, salt and vanilla; cover and refrigerate for 1 hour. Beat until stiff peaks form. Spread over the top and sides of cake. Store in the refrigerator. Garnish with chocolate leaves if desired. **Yield:** 12-16 servings.

Pumpkin Cake Roll

June Mullins, Livonia, Missouri

Roll out this well-rounded dessert and get set to harvest plenty of compliments. It earns me rave reviews whenever I serve it. My youngest daughter shared the recipe with me. It's a hit at her house, too.

     3   eggs
     1   cup sugar
   2/3   cup canned pumpkin
   3/4   cup biscuit/baking mix
     2   teaspoons ground cinnamon
     1   teaspoon pumpkin pie spice
   1/2   teaspoon ground nutmeg
     1   cup chopped walnuts
Confectioners' sugar
FILLING:
     2   packages (3 ounces *each*) cream cheese, softened
   1/4   cup butter, softened
     1   cup confectioners' sugar
     1   teaspoon vanilla extract

Line a greased 15-in. x 10-in. x 1-in. baking pan with waxed paper; grease the paper and set aside. In a large bowl, beat eggs for 3 minutes. Gradually add sugar; beat for 2 minutes or until mixture becomes thick and lemon-colored. Stir in pumpkin. Combine biscuit mix and spices; fold into pumpkin mixture. Spread batter evenly in prepared pan. Sprinkle with walnuts.

Bake at 350° for 13-15 minutes or until cake springs back when lightly touched. Cool for 5 minutes. Invert onto a kitchen towel dusted with confectioners' sugar. Gently peel off waxed paper. Roll up cake in the towel jelly-roll style, starting with a short side. Cool completely on a wire rack.

For filling, in a large bowl, beat the cream cheese, butter, confectioners' sugar and vanilla until smooth. Unroll cake. Spread filling over cake to within 1 in. of edges. Gently roll up; place seam side down on a platter. Store in the refrigerator. **Yield:** 10 servings.

Dinette Cake

Margaret Sanders, Indianapolis, Indiana

It only takes minutes to get this cake into the oven. It's one of my favorite desserts. I love serving this treat to guests, and it's also one my grandchildren frequently request I make for them.

- 1 cup sugar
- 2/3 cup milk
- 1/3 cup canola oil
- 1 egg
- 1 teaspoon vanilla extract
- 1-1/2 cups all-purpose flour
- 2 teaspoons baking powder
- 1/2 teaspoon salt

Fresh fruit *or* ice cream, optional

In a large bowl, beat the sugar, milk, oil, egg and vanilla until blended. Combine the flour, baking powder and salt; gradually add to sugar mixture until blended.

Pour into a greased 9-in. square baking pan. Bake at 350° for 30-35 minutes or until a toothpick inserted near the center comes out clean. Cool on a wire rack. Serve with fruit or ice cream if desired. **Yield:** 8-9 servings.

No-Fuss Frosting If you want to dress up the Dinette Cake, simply spread some whipped topping over the top of the cake and sprinkle with chocolate jimmies.

Mother's Walnut Cake

Helen Vail, Glenside, Pennsylvania

Even though Mother baked this tall, beautiful cake often when I was growing up, it was a real treat every time. I like the walnuts in the cake and the frosting.

- 1/2 cup butter, softened
- 1/2 cup shortening
- 2 cups sugar
- 4 eggs
- 3-1/2 cups all-purpose flour
- 2 teaspoons baking soda
- 1/2 teaspoon salt
- 1-1/2 cups buttermilk
- 2 teaspoons vanilla extract
- 1-1/2 cups ground walnuts

FROSTING:
- 2 packages (one 8 ounces, one 3 ounces) cream cheese, softened
- 3/4 cup butter, softened
- 5 to 5-1/2 cups confectioners' sugar
- 1-1/2 teaspoons vanilla extract
- 1/3 cup finely chopped walnuts

In a large bowl, cream the butter, shortening and sugar. Add eggs, one at a time, beating well after each addition. Combine the flour, baking soda and salt; gradually add to the creamed mixture alternately with the buttermilk and vanilla. Beat on low speed just until combined. Stir in the walnuts.

Pour into three greased and floured 9-in. round baking pans. Bake at 350° for 20-25 minutes or until a toothpick inserted near the center comes out clean. Cool for 5 minutes before removing from pans to wire racks to cool completely.

For frosting, beat cream cheese and butter in a large bowl. Add sugar; mix well. Beat in vanilla until smooth. Spread frosting between layers and over the top and sides of cake. Sprinkle with walnuts. Store in the refrigerator. **Yield:** 12-16 servings.

Sunny Sponge Cake

Candy Snyder, Salem, Oregon

This golden cake has a light texture and mild orange flavor that makes it a pleasant ending to most any meal. The spongy interior is flecked with bits of orange peel.

- 6 egg whites
- 3 egg yolks
- 1-1/2 cups all-purpose flour
- 1-1/4 teaspoons baking powder
- 1/4 teaspoon salt
- 1 cup sugar, *divided*
- 2 teaspoons hot water
- 1/2 cup orange juice, warmed
- 1-1/4 teaspoons vanilla extract
- 3/4 teaspoon grated orange peel
- 1/4 teaspoon grated lemon peel
- 3/4 cup reduced-fat whipped topping

Let egg whites and egg yolks stand at room temperature for 30 minutes. Sift together the flour, baking powder and salt; set aside.

In a large bowl, beat yolks for 5 minutes or until thick and lemon-colored. Gradually add 3/4 cup sugar and hot water, beating until thick and pale yellow. Blend in the orange juice, vanilla and orange and lemon peels. Beat in reserved flour mixture to egg yolk mixture.

In another bowl and with clean beaters, beat the egg whites on medium speed until soft peaks form. Gradually beat in remaining sugar, about 1 tablespoon at a time, on high until stiff, glossy peaks form and sugar is dissolved. Fold a fourth of egg whites into the batter, then fold in remaining whites.

Spoon batter into an ungreased 10-in. tube pan. Bake on the lowest rack at 350° for 25-30 minutes or until cake springs back when lightly touched. Immediately invert pan; cool completely, about 1 hour. Run a knife around sides and center tube of pan. Invert cake onto a serving plate. Serve with whipped topping. **Yield:** 12 servings.

Rhubarb Upside-Down Cake

Helen Breman, Marydale, New York

I've baked this cake every spring for many years, and my family loves it. At potluck dinners it disappears quickly, drawing compliments even from those who normally don't care for rhubarb. Use your own fresh rhubarb or find a neighbor who will trade stalks for the recipe!

TOPPING:
3   cups sliced fresh *or* frozen rhubarb
1   cup sugar
2   tablespoons all-purpose flour
1/4 teaspoon ground nutmeg
1/4 cup butter, melted

BATTER:
1/4 cup butter, melted
3/4 cup sugar
1   egg
1-1/2 cups all-purpose flour
2   teaspoons baking powder
1/2 teaspoon ground nutmeg
1/4 teaspoon salt
2/3 cup milk
Sweetened whipped cream, optional

Place rhubarb in a greased 10-in. heavy ovenproof skillet. Combine the sugar, flour and nutmeg; sprinkle over rhubarb. Drizzle with butter; set aside.

For batter, in a large bowl, beat the butter and sugar until blended. Beat in the egg. Combine the flour, baking powder, nutmeg and salt. Gradually add to egg mixture alternately with milk, beating well after each addition.

Spread over rhubarb mixture. Bake at 350° for 35-40 minutes or until a toothpick inserted near the center comes out clean. Loosen edges immediately and invert onto a serving dish. Serve warm. Serve with whipped cream if desired. Store in the refrigerator. **Yield:** 8-10 servings.

Peanut Crunch Cake

Sue Smith, Norwalk, Connecticut

Here's a recipe that dresses up a plain old box cake mix. Peanut butter and chocolate chips add fun, yummy flavor to this yellow cake.

1   package (18-1/4 ounces) yellow cake mix
1   cup peanut butter
1/2 cup packed brown sugar
1   cup water
3   eggs
1/4 cup canola oil
1/2 to 3/4 cup semisweet chocolate chips, *divided*
1/2 to 3/4 cup peanut butter chips, *divided*
1/2 cup chopped peanuts

In a large bowl, beat the cake mix, peanut butter and brown sugar on low speed until crumbly. Set aside 1/2 cup. Add water, eggs and oil to remaining crumb mixture; blend on low until moistened. Beat on high for 2 minutes. Stir in 1/4 cup each chocolate and peanut butter chips.

Pour into a greased 13-in. x 9-in. x 2-in. baking pan. Combine peanuts, reserved crumb mixture and the remaining chips; sprinkle over batter. Bake at 350° for 40-45 minutes or until a toothpick inserted near the center comes out clean. Cool completely on a wire rack. **Yield:** 12-16 servings.

Cream Cheese Pound Cake

Mrs. Michael Ewanek, Hastings, Pennsylvania

I received this recipe from a woman who came to my rummage sale. We got to talking about zucchini—she didn't know what the big squash could be used for. So I sent her some of my favorite zucchini recipes and, in return, she mailed me the recipe for this cake. It's absolutely delicious and I've made it often.

1-1/2 cups butter, softened
    1 package (8 ounces) cream cheese, softened
2-1/3 cups sugar
    6 eggs
    3 cups all-purpose flour
    1 teaspoon vanilla extract

In a large bowl, cream the butter, cream cheese and sugar until light and fluffy. Add eggs, one at a time, beating well after each addition. Stir in vanilla. Gradually add flour; beat just until blended.

Pour into a greased and floured 10-in. tube pan. Bake at 300° for 1-1/2 hours or until a toothpick inserted near the center comes out clean. Cool in pan 15 minutes before removing to a wire rack to cool completely. **Yield:** 12-16 servings.

Creaming Butter To get the best volume in your cakes, butter should be soft before creaming. If a table knife glides through the butter, it is perfect for creaming. If you softened it in the microwave and butter is partially melted, it will not cream properly and the cake will not rise as high as it should.

Pineapple Bundt Cake

Fayne Lutz, Taos, New Mexico

Fruity and firm-textured, this beautiful cake is sure to impress. Bits of pineapple are in every bite.

    1   cup butter, softened
1-1/2   cups sugar
    2   eggs, lightly beaten
    2   egg whites
    2   teaspoons lemon extract
2-2/3   cups all-purpose flour
    1   teaspoon baking powder
    1   can (8 ounces) crushed pineapple, undrained
GLAZE:
    1   cup confectioners' sugar
    1   to 2 tablespoons milk
  1/2   teaspoon lemon extract

In a large bowl, cream butter and sugar until light and fluffy. Beat in the eggs, egg whites and extract until well blended. Combine flour and baking powder; gradually add to creamed mixture, beating well after each addition. Stir in the pineapple.

Pour into a greased 10-in. fluted tube pan. Bake at 350° for 55-60 minutes. Cool for 10 minutes before removing from pan to a wire rack to cool completely. In a small bowl, combine glaze ingredients. Drizzle over cake. **Yield:** 12-16 servings.

Greasing a Fluted Tube Pan The easiest way to grease a fluted tube pan is to hold the pan over the kitchen sink and coat the inside of the pan with cooking spray. If you prefer to use shortening, take a dab of shortening on a paper towel and spread it over the interior of the pan, making sure to work the shortening into the grooves.

Baking Classics | Cakes

Caramel Pecan Pound Cake

Rosella Day, Waycross, Georgia

Pecans are plentiful in Georgia and are frequent additions to recipes in my area. The pecan flavor comes through nicely in this cake.

- 1 cup butter, softened
- 2-1/4 cups packed brown sugar
- 1 cup sugar
- 5 eggs
- 3 teaspoons vanilla extract
- 3 cups all-purpose flour
- 1/2 teaspoon baking powder
- 1/2 teaspoon salt
- 1 cup milk
- 1 cup finely chopped pecans

Confectioners' sugar

Fresh fruit, optional

In a large bowl, cream butter and sugars until light and fluffy. Add eggs, one at a time, beating well after each. Stir in vanilla. Combine the flour, baking powder and salt; add to the creamed mixture alternately with milk. Beat on low speed just until blended. Fold in pecans.

Pour into a greased and floured 10-in. tube pan. Bake at 325° for 1-1/2 hours or until a toothpick inserted near the center comes out clean. Cool for 10 minutes before removing from pan to a wire rack to cool completely. Dust with confectioners' sugar. Serve with fruit if desired. **Yield:** 16 servings.

Lazy Daisy Cake

Darlis Wilfer, West Bend, Wisconsin

We couldn't wait until Mom sliced this old-fashioned cake loaded with chewy coconut and topped with a caramel-like frosting. Even after one of Mom's delicious meals, one piece of this cake wasn't enough.

- 4 eggs
- 2 cups sugar
- 2 teaspoons vanilla extract
- 2 cups all-purpose flour
- 2 teaspoons baking powder
- 1/2 teaspoon salt
- 1 cup milk
- 1/4 cup butter

FROSTING:

- 1-1/2 cups packed brown sugar
- 3/4 cup butter, melted
- 1/2 cup half-and-half cream
- 2 cups flaked coconut

In a large bowl, beat the eggs, sugar and vanilla until thick and pale yellow, about 4 minutes. Combine the flour, baking powder and salt; add to egg mixture and beat just until combined. In a saucepan, bring milk and butter to a boil, stirring constantly. Add to batter and beat until combined.

Pour into a greased 13-in. x 9-in. x 2-in. baking pan. Bake at 350° for 30-35 minutes or until a toothpick inserted near the center comes out clean.

Combine frosting ingredients; spread over warm cake. Broil 4 in. from heat until lightly browned, about 3-4 minutes. **Yield:** 16-20 servings.

near the center comes out clean. Cool for 10 minutes before removing from pan to wire rack to cool completely.

For frosting, in a bowl, beat cream cheese, confectioners' sugar and vanilla until smooth. Frost cake; sprinkle with pecans. Store in the refrigerator. **Yield:** 12-16 servings.

Blueberry-Peach Pound Cake

Nancy Zimmerman, Cape May Court House, New Jersey

Blueberries and peaches give this pound cake a tasty twist.

- 1/2   cup butter, softened
- 1-1/4   cups sugar
- 3   eggs
- 1/4   cup milk
- 2-1/2   cups cake flour
- 2   teaspoons baking powder
- 1/4   teaspoon salt
- 2-1/4   cups chopped peeled fresh peaches (1/2-inch pieces)
- 2   cups fresh *or* frozen blueberries

Confectioners' sugar, optional

In a large bowl, cream butter and sugar until light and fluffy. Beat in eggs, one at a time, beating well after each addition. Beat in milk. Combine the flour, baking powder and salt; add to creamed mixture. Stir in peaches and blueberries.

Pour into a greased and floured 10-in. fluted tube pan. Bake at 350° for 60-70 minutes or until a toothpick inserted near the center comes out clean. Cool for 15 minutes before removing from pan to a wire rack to cool completely. Dust with confectioners' sugar if desired. **Yield:** 10-12 servings.

Editor's Note: If using frozen blueberries, do not thaw before adding to batter.

Pecan Carrot Bundt Cake

Joan Taylor, Adrian, Minnesota

The pecans and citrus flavor makes this dessert special. I use fresh carrots from my garden.

- 1   cup butter, softened
- 1   cup sugar
- 1   cup packed brown sugar
- 4   eggs
- 2   tablespoons grated lemon peel
- 2   tablespoons grated orange peel
- 3   cups all-purpose flour
- 2   teaspoons baking powder
- 1   teaspoon baking soda
- 1   teaspoon ground cinnamon
- 1/2   teaspoon salt
- 2   tablespoons orange juice
- 2   tablespoons lemon juice
- 1   pound carrots, grated
- 1   cup raisins
- 1   cup chopped pecans

FROSTING:
- 1   package (3 ounces) cream cheese, softened
- 1-1/2   to 2 cups confectioners' sugar
- 1   teaspoon vanilla extract
- 1/2   cup chopped pecans

In a large bowl, cream butter and sugars until light and fluffy. Add eggs, one at a time, beating well after each. Beat in lemon and orange peels. Combine the flour, baking powder, baking soda, cinnamon and salt; gradually add to creamed mixture alternately with juices. Stir in the carrots, raisins and pecans.

Pour into a greased and floured 10-in. fluted tube pan. Bake at 350° for 50-60 minutes or until a toothpick inserted

Midsummer Sponge Cake

Robin Fuhrman, Fond du Lac, Wisconsin

Guests at the bridal tea liked everything about this beautiful seasonal dessert—the tender cake layers, fluffy cream filling and glazed fresh fruit topping.

 4 eggs
1-1/4 cups sugar
1-1/4 cups all-purpose flour
 2 teaspoons baking powder
 1/2 cup water
1-1/2 cups cold milk
 1/2 teaspoon vanilla extract
 1 package (3.4 ounces) instant vanilla pudding mix
 2 cups whipped topping
 3 tablespoons lemon gelatin
 1/2 cup boiling water
 10 to 12 ribbons with small charms attached
Assorted fresh fruit

In a large bowl, beat eggs until light and fluffy. Gradually beat in sugar until light and lemon-colored. Combine flour and baking powder; add to egg mixture alternately with water, beating just until smooth. Pour into a greased and floured 10-in. springform pan.

Bake at 375° for 20-25 minutes or until cake springs back when lightly touched. Cool on a wire rack for 1 hour. Carefully run a knife around edge of pan; remove sides. Invert onto a wire rack. Remove bottom of pan; invert cake so top is up. Using a sharp knife, split cake into two horizontal layers; set aside.

For filling, in a large bowl, whisk the milk, vanilla and pudding mix for 2 minutes or until thickened; chill for 10 minutes. Fold in whipped topping.

For glaze, dissolve gelatin in boiling water. Add enough cold water to measure 1 cup. Chill for 15 minutes or until slightly thickened.

To assemble, place bottom cake layer on a cake plate. Spread filling over cake; top with second cake layer and fruit. Drizzle with glaze. Store in the refrigerator. **Yield:** 10-12 servings.

Old-Fashioned Raisin Cake

Norma Poole, Auburndale, Florida

This is a wonderful cake for the holidays. It fills the house with a heavenly aroma when it's baking.

- 1 large navel orange, cut into 8 wedges
- 1 cup raisins
- 1/2 cup pecans
- 1/2 cup butter, softened
- 1 cup sugar
- 2 eggs
- 1 teaspoon vanilla extract
- 2 cups all-purpose flour
- 1 teaspoon baking soda
- 1/2 teaspoon salt
- 2/3 cup buttermilk

GLAZE:
- 1/2 cup confectioners' sugar
- 2 tablespoons orange juice

In a food processor, combine the orange, raisins and pecans. Cover and process until mixture is finely chopped; set aside.

In a large bowl, cream butter and sugar until light and fluffy. Beat in eggs and vanilla until well blended. Combine the flour, baking soda and salt; add to creamed mixture alternately with buttermilk, beating well after each addition. Stir in orange mixture.

Pour into a greased and floured 10-in. floured tube pan. Bake at 325° for 45-55 minutes or until a toothpick inserted near the center comes out clean. Cool for 10 minutes before removing from pan to a wire rack to cool completely.

In a small bowl, combine glaze ingredients until smooth; drizzle over warm cake. **Yield:** 10-12 servings.

Praline Ice Cream Cake

Joan Hallford, North Richland Hills, Texas

Melted ice cream is a key ingredient in this delectable golden cake. It's been a family favorite for years—we just love the pecan praline flavor.

- 1 cup packed brown sugar
- 1/2 cup sour cream
- 2 tablespoons plus 1/2 cup butter, *divided*
- 2 teaspoons cornstarch
- 1 teaspoon vanilla extract, *divided*
- 2 cups vanilla ice cream, softened
- 2 eggs
- 1-1/2 cups all-purpose flour
- 1 cup graham cracker crumbs
- 2/3 cup sugar
- 2-1/2 teaspoons baking powder
- 1/2 teaspoon salt
- 1/2 cup chopped pecans, toasted

Whipped cream, optional

In a heavy saucepan, combine the brown sugar, sour cream, 2 tablespoons butter and cornstarch. Cook and stir over medium heat until mixture comes to a boil. Remove from the heat.

Stir in 1/2 teaspoon vanilla; set aside. Melt the remaining butter; place in a bowl. Add ice cream; stir to blend. Add eggs, one at a time, beating well after each addition; stir in the remaining vanilla. Combine the flour, cracker crumbs, sugar, baking powder and salt; gradually add to ice cream mixture until combined.

Pour into a greased 13-in. x 9-in. x 2-in. baking pan. Drizzle with half of the praline sauce. Bake at 350° for 25-30 minutes or until a toothpick inserted near the center comes out clean. Cool on a wire rack.

Add pecans to remaining sauce; spoon over warm cake (sauce will not cover the entire cake top). Cool in pan on a wire rack. Serve with whipped cream if desired. **Yield:** 15 servings.

Banana Upside-Down Cake

Ruth Andrewson, Leavenworth, Washington

For a fun and distinctive way to use bananas, I recommend this variation of an upside-down cake. Every time I serve this treat, someone requests the recipe.

- 1/2 cup packed brown sugar
- 2 tablespoons lemon juice, *divided*
- 1 tablespoon butter
- 1/2 cup pecan halves
- 2 medium firm bananas, sliced

CAKE:
- 1-1/2 cups all-purpose flour
- 1/2 cup sugar
- 1 teaspoon baking soda
- 1 teaspoon baking powder
- 1/4 teaspoon salt
- 1/4 cup cold butter, cubed
- 1 cup plain yogurt
- 2 eggs, lightly beaten
- 2 teaspoons grated lemon peel
- 1 teaspoon vanilla extract

Whipped cream, optional

In a small saucepan, combine the brown sugar, 1 tablespoon lemon juice and butter; bring to a boil. Reduce heat to medium; cook without stirring until the sugar is dissolved.

Pour into a greased 9-in. springform pan. Arrange pecans on top with flat side up. Pour remaining lemon juice into a small bowl; add bananas and stir carefully. Drain. Arrange bananas in a circular pattern over the pecans; set aside.

In a large bowl, combine the flour, sugar, baking soda, baking powder and salt. Cut in butter until mixture resembles coarse crumbs. In a small bowl, combine the yogurt, eggs, lemon peel and vanilla; stir into the dry ingredients just until moistened. Spoon over bananas.

Bake at 375° for 35-40 minutes or until a toothpick inserted near the center comes out clean. Cool for 10 minutes. Run a knife around edge of pan; invert cake onto a serving plate. Serve with whipped cream if desired. **Yield:** 6-8 servings.

Butterscotch Apple Cake

Beth Struble, Bryan, Ohio

My family often requests this easy old-fashioned cake for get-togethers—especially in the fall.

- 2 cups sugar
- 1-1/4 cups canola oil
- 3 eggs
- 1 teaspoon vanilla extract
- 2-1/2 cups all-purpose flour
- 2 teaspoons baking powder
- 1 teaspoon baking soda
- 1 teaspoon salt
- 1 teaspoon ground cinnamon
- 4 medium tart apples, peeled and chopped (4 cups)
- 1 cup chopped pecans
- 1 package (11 ounces) butterscotch chips

In a large bowl, beat the sugar, oil, eggs and vanilla until well blended. Combine the flour, baking powder, baking soda, salt and cinnamon; gradually add to egg mixture until blended. Stir in apples and pecans.

Pour into an ungreased 13-in. x 9-in. x 2-in. baking dish. Sprinkle with butterscotch chips. Bake at 325° for 40-45 minutes or until a toothpick inserted near the center comes out clean. Cool on a wire rack. **Yield:** 12-15 servings.

Peach Cake

Donna Britsch, Tega Cay, South Carolina

I first tasted this cake about 15 years ago when a dear aunt brought it to a family reunion.

- 3/4 cup cold butter
- 1 package (18-1/4 ounces) yellow cake mix
- 2 egg yolks
- 2 cups (16 ounces) sour cream
- 1 can (29 ounces) sliced peaches, drained
- 1/2 teaspoon ground cinnamon
- 1 carton (8 ounces) frozen whipped topping, thawed

In a large bowl, cut butter into dry cake mix until the mixture resembles coarse crumbs. Pat into a greased 13-in. x 9-in. x 2-in. baking pan.

In another bowl, beat yolks; add sour cream until smooth. Set aside 6-8 peach slices for garnish. Cut remaining peaches into 1-in. pieces; stir into the sour cream mixture. Spread over crust; sprinkle with cinnamon.

Bake at 350° for 25-30 minutes or until the edges begin to brown. Cool on a wire rack. Spread with whipped topping; top with reserved peaches. Store in the refrigerator. **Yield:** 12 servings.

Gingerbread with Brown Sugar Sauce

Toni Hamm, Vandergrift, Pennsylvania

The aroma of this gingerbread is what I remember most about my grandmother's kitchen. That was decades ago, but whenever I catch a whiff of ginger and cinnamon, I'm back with my grandmother.

6	tablespoons shortening
1/2	cup packed brown sugar
1/3	cup molasses
1	egg
1-1/2	cups all-purpose flour
1/2	teaspoon baking soda
1/2	teaspoon ground cinnamon
1/2	teaspoon ground ginger
1/8	teaspoon salt
1/2	cup buttermilk

BROWN SUGAR SAUCE:
1	cup packed brown sugar
4-1/2	teaspoons cornstarch
1/2	cup cold water
1-1/2	teaspoons white vinegar
1	tablespoon butter
1-1/2	teaspoons vanilla extract

In a large bowl, cream shortening and brown sugar until light and fluffy. Beat in molasses and egg until blended. Combine the flour, baking soda, cinnamon, ginger and salt; add to the molasses mixture alternately with buttermilk, beating well after each addition.

Pour into a greased 9-in. round baking pan. Bake at 350° for 25-30 minutes or until a toothpick inserted near the center comes out clean. Cool for 10 minutes before removing from pan to a wire rack.

For sauce, in a small saucepan, combine the brown sugar, cornstarch, water and vinegar; stir until smooth. Add butter. Bring to a boil; cook and stir for 2 minutes or until thickened. Remove from the heat and stir in vanilla. Serve with the gingerbread. **Yield:** 6-8 servings.

Chocolate Chip Pound Cake

Michele Strunks, Brookville, Ohio

My mom has been making this cake for over 30 years. Dotted with chips and topped with a chocolate glaze, it is absolutely divine.

- 1 cup butter, softened
- 2 cups sugar
- 4 eggs
- 1 teaspoon vanilla extract
- 4 cups all-purpose flour
- 4 teaspoons baking powder
- 1 teaspoon baking soda
- 2 cups (16 ounces) sour cream
- 2 cups (12 ounces) semisweet chocolate chips

GLAZE:
- 1/4 cup semisweet chocolate chips
- 2 tablespoons butter
- 1-1/4 cups confectioners' sugar
- 3 tablespoons milk
- 1/2 teaspoon vanilla extract

In a large bowl, cream butter and sugar until light and fluffy. Add the eggs, one at a time, beating well after each addition. Beat in vanilla. Combine the flour, baking powder and baking soda; add to creamed mixture alternately with sour cream, beating well after each addition. Fold in chocolate chips.

Pour into a greased and floured 10-in. fluted tube pan. Bake at 350° for 60-65 minutes or until a toothpick inserted near the center comes out clean. Cool for 10 minutes before removing from pan to a wire rack to cool completely.

For glaze, in a saucepan, melt chocolate chips and butter over low heat. Remove from the heat; whisk in the confectioners' sugar, milk and vanilla until smooth. Drizzle over cake. **Yield:** 12-14 servings.

Orange Dream Cake

Willa Govoro, St. Clair, Missouri

We try to save room for a big slice of this pretty cake. The flavor of orange and lemon really comes through. With a heavenly whipped cream frosting, this cake is a delightful end to a terrific meal.

- 2/3 cup butter, softened
- 1-1/3 cups sugar
- 2 eggs
- 2/3 cup orange juice
- 3 tablespoons lemon juice
- 1 teaspoon grated orange peel
- 1 teaspoon grated lemon peel
- 2 cups cake flour
- 2 teaspoons baking powder
- 1 teaspoon salt

FROSTING:
- 1 cup flaked coconut
- 1/4 cup sugar
- 2 tablespoons fresh orange juice
- 1 tablespoon fresh lemon juice
- 4 teaspoons grated orange peel, *divided*
- 1 cup heavy whipping cream, whipped

In a large bowl, cream butter and sugar until light and fluffy. Add eggs, one at a time, beating well after each addition. Beat in juices and peel until well blended (mixture may appear curdled). Combine flour, baking powder and salt. Gradually add to creamed mixture until well blended.

Pour into two greased and floured 9-inch baking pans. Bake at 375° for 25-30 minutes or until a toothpick inserted near the center comes out clean. Cool in pan for 10 minutes before removing to wire racks to cool completely.

For frosting, in a small bowl, combine the coconut, sugar, juices and 3 teaspoons peel. Let stand for 10 to 15 minutes or until sugar is dissolved. Fold in whipped cream. Spread between cake layers and over the top. Sprinkle with remaining orange peel. Chill for at least 1 hour. Store in the refrigerator. **Yield:** 10-12 servings.

White Chocolate Fudge Cake

Denise VonStein, Shiloh, Ohio

This sweet cake, with its thick frosting and rich chocolate layer, is a big hit at office potlucks. I have one co-worker who tells everyone it's awful so he can have it all to himself!

1	package (18-1/4 ounces) white cake mix
1-1/4	cups water
3	egg whites
1/3	cup canola oil
1	teaspoon vanilla extract
3	squares (1 ounce *each*) white baking chocolate, melted

FILLING:

3/4	cup semisweet chocolate chips
2	tablespoons butter

FROSTING:

1	can (16 ounces) vanilla frosting
3	squares (1 ounce *each*) white baking chocolate, melted
1	teaspoon vanilla extract
1	carton (8 ounces) frozen whipped topping, thawed

In a large bowl, combine the cake mix, water, egg whites, oil and vanilla. Beat on low for 30 seconds. Beat on medium for 2 minutes. Stir in white chocolate.

Pour into a greased 13-in. x 9-in. x 2-in. baking pan. Bake at 350° for 25-30 minutes or until a toothpick inserted near the center comes out clean. Cool for 5 minutes.

Meanwhile, in a microwave, melt chocolate chips and butter; stir until smooth. Carefully spread over warm cake. Cool completely.

In a small bowl, beat frosting until fluffy; beat in white chocolate and vanilla until smooth. Fold in whipped topping; frost cake. Store in the refrigerator. **Yield:** 16 servings.

Cranberry Sauce Cake

Marge Clark, West Lebanon, Indiana

This wonderful cake makes clean up a breeze because it's mixed in one bowl. Slice it at the table so everyone can see how beautiful it is.

1-1/2	cups sugar
1	cup mayonnaise
1/3	cup orange juice
1	tablespoon grated orange peel
1	teaspoon orange extract
3	cups all-purpose flour
1	teaspoon baking soda
1	teaspoon salt
1	can (16 ounces) whole-berry cranberry sauce
1	cup chopped walnuts

ICING:

1	cup confectioners' sugar
1	to 2 tablespoons orange juice

In a large bowl, combine sugar and mayonnaise until blended. Beat in orange juice, orange peel and extract. Combine the flour, baking soda and salt until blended. Stir in cranberry sauce and walnuts.

Cut waxed or parchment paper to fit the bottom of a 10-in. tube pan. Spray the pan and paper with cooking spray. Pour batter into paper-lined pan.

Bake at 350° for 60-70 minutes or until a toothpick inserted near the center comes out clean. Cool for 10 minutes before removing from pan to a wire rack. In a small bowl, combine icing ingredients; drizzle over warm cake. **Yield:** 12-16 servings.

Editor's Note: Reduced-fat or fat-free mayonnaise is not recommended for this recipe.

Prize-Winning Jelly Roll

Linda Anderson, Karlstad, Minnesota

Twice I've won first place at our county fair with this recipe. I enjoy trying new recipes and cooking for my family.

    6 eggs, *separated*
  1/4 cup water
1-1/2 cups sugar, *divided*
    1 teaspoon vanilla extract
    1 teaspoon lemon extract
1-1/4 cups cake flour
  1/2 teaspoon baking powder
  1/2 teaspoon salt
    1 teaspoon cream of tartar
Confectioners' sugar
    1 jar (12 ounces) strawberry, raspberry *or* currant jelly

Place egg whites in large bowl; let stand at room temperature for 30 minutes. Line a greased 15-in. x 10-in. x 1-in. baking pan with waxed paper; grease the paper and set aside.

In a large bowl, beat egg yolks and water on high speed for 5 minutes or until thick and lemon-colored. Gradually beat in 1 cup sugar. Stir in extracts. Sift flour, baking powder and salt together twice; gradually add to yolk mixture and mix well (batter will be very thick).

Beat egg whites and cream of tartar with clean beaters on medium speed until soft peaks form. Gradually beat in remaining sugar, 1 tablespoon at a time, on high until stiff peaks form. Gradually fold into batter. Spread evenly into prepared pan.

Bake at 350° for 15-18 minutes or until cake springs back when lightly touched. Cool for 5 minutes. Invert onto a kitchen towel dusted with confectioners' sugar. Gently peel off waxed paper. Roll up cake in the towel jelly-roll style, starting with a short side. Cool completely on a wire rack.

Unroll cake; spread evenly with jelly. Roll up; dust with confectioners' sugar. **Yield.** 8-10 servings.

Surprise Carrot Cake

Lisa Bowen, Little Britian, Ontario

A cousin gave me this recipe. It's a wonderful potluck pleaser with its "surprise" cream cheese center. My husband and our two young children love it, too! It's a great way to use up the overabundance of carrots from my garden.

- 3 cups shredded carrots
- 1-3/4 cups sugar
- 1 cup canola oil
- 3 eggs
- 2 cups all-purpose flour
- 2 teaspoons baking soda
- 2 teaspoons ground cinnamon
- 1 teaspoon salt
- 1/2 cup chopped pecans

FILLING:
- 1 package (8 ounces) cream cheese, softened
- 1/4 cup sugar
- 1 egg

FROSTING:
- 1 package (8 ounces) cream cheese, softened
- 1/4 cup butter, softened
- 2 teaspoons vanilla extract
- 4 cups confectioners' sugar

In a large bowl, beat the carrots, sugar, oil and eggs until well blended. In a large bowl, combine the flour, baking soda, cinnamon and salt; gradually beat into carrot mixture until blended. Stir in the pecans. Pour 3 cups batter into a greased and floured 10-in. fluted tube pan.

In a small bowl, beat cream cheese and sugar until smooth. Beat in egg. Spoon over batter. Top with remaining batter.

Bake at 350° for 55-60 minutes or until a toothpick inserted near the center comes out clean. Cool for 10 minutes before removing from pan to a wire rack to cool completely.

For frosting, in a small bowl, beat the cream cheese, butter and vanilla until fluffy. Gradually add confectioners' sugar until smooth. Frost cake. Store in the refrigerator. **Yield:** 12-16 servings.

Toffee-Mocha Cream Torte

Lynn Rogers, Richfield, North Carolina

When you really want to impress someone, this scrumptious torte is just the thing to make! Instant coffee granules give the moist chocolate cake a mild mocha flavor.

- 1 cup butter, softened
- 2 cups sugar
- 2 eggs
- 1-1/2 teaspoons vanilla extract
- 2-2/3 cups all-purpose flour
- 3/4 cup baking cocoa
- 2 teaspoons baking soda
- 1/4 teaspoon salt
- 1 cup buttermilk
- 2 teaspoons instant coffee granules
- 1 cup boiling water

TOPPING:
- 1/2 teaspoon instant coffee granules
- 1 teaspoon hot water
- 2 cups heavy whipping cream
- 3 tablespoons light brown sugar
- 6 Heath candy bars (1.4 ounces *each*), crushed, *divided*

In a large bowl, cream butter and sugar until light and fluffy. Beat in eggs, one at a time, beating well after each addition. Beat in vanilla. Combine the flour, cocoa, baking soda and salt; add to creamed mixture alternately with buttermilk, beating well after each addition. Dissolve coffee in water; add to batter. Beat for 2 minutes.

Pour into three greased and floured 9-in. round baking pans. Bake at 350° for 16-20 minutes or until a toothpick inserted near center comes out clean. Cool for 10 minutes before removing from pans to wire racks to cool completely.

For topping, in a large bowl dissolve coffee in water; cool. Add cream and brown sugar. Beat until stiff peaks form.

Place the bottom cake layer on a serving plate; top with 1-1/3 cups topping. Sprinkle with 1/2 cup crushed candy bars. Repeat layers twice. Store in the refrigerator. **Yield:** 12-14 servings.

Apricot Upside-Down Cake

Ruth Ann Stelfox, Raymond, Alberta

My Aunt Anne, who is a great cook, gave me a taste of this golden cake and I couldn't believe how delicious it was. Apricots give it an elegant twist from traditional pineapple versions.

- 2 cans (15 ounces *each*) apricot halves
- 1/4 cup butter, cubed
- 1/2 cup packed brown sugar
- 2 eggs, *separated*
- 2/3 cup sugar
- 2/3 cup cake flour
- 3/4 teaspoon baking powder
- 1/4 teaspoon salt

Drain apricots, reserving 3 tablespoons juice; set aside. Place butter in a greased 9-in. square baking pan; heat in a 350° oven for 3-4 minutes or until melted. Stir in the brown sugar. Arrange apricot halves cut side up in a single layer over sugar.

In a large bowl, beat yolks on high speed for 3 minutes or until thick and lemon-colored. Gradually add sugar, beating until thick and pale yellow. Stir in reserved apricot juice. Combine the flour, baking powder and salt; gradually add to egg yolk mixture. In another bowl and with clean beaters, beat egg whites until stiff. Fold into yolk mixture.

Carefully spread over apricots. Bake at 350° for 35-40 minutes or until a toothpick inserted near the center comes out clean. Cool for 10 minutes before inverting onto a serving plate. **Yield:** 9 servings.

Cupcakes

pg. 200

pg. 201

pg. 205

pg. 203

Kitty Cat Cupcakes

Doris Barb, El Dorado, Kansas

These fine feline treats are so simple to assemble. Kids will be clamoring to help decorate!

> 4 eggs, *separated*
> 2/3 cup shortening
> 1-3/4 cups sugar, *divided*
> 2-1/2 cups all-purpose flour
> 2-1/2 teaspoons baking powder
> 1/2 teaspoon salt
> 1 cup orange juice
> 1 cup flaked coconut
> FROSTING:
> 1-1/4 cups sugar
> 1/4 cup water
> 1/4 cup light corn syrup
> 1 egg white
> 1/8 teaspoon salt
> 1/2 cup miniature marshmallows (about 50)
> 1/2 teaspoons vanilla extract
> Assorted M&M's
> 1 piece red shoestring licorice, cut into 3/4-inch pieces
> Chocolate sprinkles
> About 9 vanilla wafers
> 2 cups flaked coconut, toasted

Let eggs stand at room temperature for 30 minutes. In a large bowl, cream shortening and 1-1/2 cups sugar until light and fluffy. Beat in egg yolks until well blended. Combine the flour, baking powder and salt; add to creamed mixture alternately with orange juice, beating well after each addition.

In a small bowl and with clean beaters, beat egg whites until soft peaks form. Gradually beat in the remaining sugar, 1 tablespoon at a time, on high until stiff, glossy peaks form. Gradually fold into batter with coconut.

Fill paper-lined muffin cups two-thirds full. Bake at 350° for 15 minutes or until a toothpick inserted near the center comes out clean. Cool for 10 minutes before removing from pans to wire racks to cool completely.

For frosting, in a heavy saucepan, combine the sugar, water, corn syrup, egg white and salt. With a portable mixer, beat on low speed for 1 minute. Continue beating on low over low heat until frosting reaches 160°, about 12-18 minutes. Pour into a large bowl; add marshmallows and vanilla. Beat on high until stiff peaks form, about 5 minutes. Frost cupcakes.

Arrange M&M's for eyes and nose, licorice for mouth and sprinkles for whiskers. For ears, cut wafers into quarters with a serrated knife; place two on each cupcake, rounded side down. Sprinkle with coconut. Refrigerate until serving. **Yield:** about 1-1/2 dozen.

Editor's Note: A stand mixer is recommended for beating the frosting after it reaches 160°.

Banana Nut Cupcakes

Vicki Abrahamson, Silverdale, Washington

These moist cupcakes taste like little loaves of banana bread. I keep ripe bananas in the freezer so I can whip up these cupcakes whenever I need them for a bake sale or party. I like to top them with cream cheese frosting.

> 1/3 cup butter-flavored shortening
> 2/3 cup sugar
> 2 eggs
> 1 cup mashed ripe bananas (about 2 medium)
> 2 tablespoons milk
> 1 tablespoon vanilla extract
> 1-1/3 cups all-purpose flour
> 2 teaspoons baking powder
> 1/2 teaspoon baking soda
> 1/4 teaspoon salt
> 1/4 cup chopped nuts

In a large bowl, cream shortening and sugar until light and fluffy. Beat in the eggs. Stir in the bananas, milk and vanilla. Combine the flour, baking powder, baking soda and salt; gradually add to creamed mixture and mix well. Stir in nuts.

Fill paper-lined muffin cups two-thirds full. Bake at 350° for 18-20 minutes or until a toothpick inserted near the center comes out clean. Cool for 10 minutes before removing from pans to wire racks. **Yield:** 15 cupcakes.

Pouring Batter Without a Mess Place the cupcake batter into a large resealable plastic bag. Press out air and seal the bag. Snip off one bottom corner with scissors, then squeeze out the batter into muffin cups.

Sugar-Topped Mocha Cupcakes

Jennifer Kraft, Hastings, Nebraska

I first made these cupcakes, adapted from an eggless cake recipe, for a school carnival. Light and tender, the cupcakes don't need frosting, thanks to the sparkly cinnamon-sugar topping.

2-1/2 cups all-purpose flour
1-1/2 cups plus 1/3 cup sugar, *divided*
  1/2 cup baking cocoa
    2 teaspoons baking soda
  1/2 teaspoon salt
  2/3 cup olive oil
    2 tablespoons white vinegar
    1 teaspoon vanilla extract
    2 cups cold brewed coffee
  1/2 teaspoon ground cinnamon

In a large bowl, combine the flour, 1-1/2 cups sugar, cocoa, baking soda and salt. Add the oil, vinegar and vanilla; beat on low speed until blended. Add coffee; beat on medium for 2 minutes.

Fill paper-lined muffin cups two-thirds full. Combine cinnamon and remaining sugar; sprinkle half of the mixture over batter. Bake at 350° for 20-25 minutes or until a toothpick inserted near the center comes out clean. Immediately sprinkle remaining cinnamon-sugar over cupcakes. Cool for 10 minutes before removing from pans to wire racks to cool completely. **Yield:** about 2-1/2 dozen.

Editor's Note: This recipe does not use eggs.

Cream-Filled Pumpkin Cupcakes

Ali Johnson, Petersburg, Pennsylvania

Here's a deliciously different use for pumpkin. Bursting with flavor and plenty of eye-catching appeal, these sweet and spicy filled cupcakes are certain to dazzle your family.

- 2 cups sugar
- 3/4 cup canola oil
- 1 can (15 ounces) solid-pack pumpkin
- 4 eggs
- 2 cups all-purpose flour
- 2 teaspoons baking soda
- 1 teaspoon salt
- 1 teaspoon baking powder
- 1 teaspoon ground cinnamon

FILLING:
- 1 tablespoon cornstarch
- 1 cup milk
- 1/2 cup shortening
- 1/4 cup butter, softened
- 2 cups confectioners' sugar
- 1/2 teaspoon vanilla extract, optional

In a large bowl, combine the sugar, oil, pumpkin and eggs. Combine flour, baking soda, salt, baking powder and cinnamon; add to pumpkin mixture and beat until well mixed.

Fill paper-lined muffin cups two-thirds full. Bake at 350° for 18-22 minutes or until a toothpick inserted near the center comes out clean. Cool for 10 minutes before removing from pans to wire racks to cool completely.

For filling, combine cornstarch and milk in a small saucepan until smooth. Bring to a boil; cook and stir for 2 minutes or until thickened. Remove from the heat; cool to room temperature.

In a large bowl, cream the shortening, butter and confectioners' sugar. Beat in vanilla if desired. Gradually add the cornstarch mixture, beating until light and fluffy.

Using a sharp knife, cut a 1-in. circle 1 in. deep in the top of each cupcake. Carefully remove tops and set aside. Spoon or pipe filling into cupcakes. Replace tops. **Yield:** about 1-3/4 dozen.

Mini Pineapple Upside-Down Cakes

Cindy Colley, Othello, Washington

These individual pineapple upside-down cakes are a pretty addition to my holiday dessert table. A cake mix makes them easy to bake anytime.

- 2/3 cup packed brown sugar
- 1/3 cup butter, melted
- 2 cans (20 ounces *each*) sliced pineapple
- 1 package (18-1/4 ounces) yellow cake mix
- 3 eggs
- 1/3 cup canola oil
- 12 maraschino cherries, halved

In a small bowl, combine the brown sugar and butter until blended. Spoon into 24 greased muffin cups. Drain pineapple, reserving the juice. Trim pineapple to fit the muffin cups; place one ring in each cup.

In a large bowl, combine the cake mix, eggs, oil and 1-1/4 cups reserved pineapple juice. Beat on low speed for 30 seconds. Beat on medium for 2 minutes. Spoon over pineapple, filling each cup two-thirds full.

Bake at 350° for 20-25 minutes or until a toothpick inserted near the center comes out clean. Immediately invert onto wire racks to cool. Place a cherry in the center of each pineapple ring. **Yield:** 2 dozen.

Buttermilk Chocolate Cupcakes

Ellen Moore, Springfield, New Hampshire

Good any time of the year, cupcakes make a great get-up-and-go treat.

- 1/2 cup butter, softened
- 1-1/2 cups sugar
- 2 eggs
- 1 teaspoon vanilla extract
- 1-1/2 cups all-purpose flour
- 1/2 cup baking cocoa
- 1 teaspoon baking soda
- 1/4 teaspoon salt
- 1/2 cup buttermilk
- 1/2 cup water

FROSTING:
- 1/2 cup butter, softened
- 3-3/4 cups confectioners' sugar
- 2 squares (1 ounce *each*) unsweetened chocolate, melted
- 2 tablespoons evaporated milk
- 1 teaspoon vanilla extract
- 1/4 teaspoon salt
- Chocolate sprinkles

In a bowl, cream butter and sugar until light and fluffy. Add eggs, one at a time, beating well after each addition. Beat in vanilla. Combine the flour, cocoa, baking soda and salt. Add flour mixture to creamed mixture alternately with buttermilk and water, beating well after each addition.

Fill paper-lined muffin cups two-thirds full. Bake at 375° for 15-20 minutes or until a toothpick inserted near the center comes out clean. Cool for 10 minutes before removing from pans to wire racks to cool completely.

For frosting, in a small bowl, beat butter and confectioners' sugar until smooth. Beat in the melted chocolate, milk, vanilla and salt. Frost cupcakes; garnish with chocolate sprinkles. **Yield:** 2 dozen.

St. Patrick's Day Cupcakes

Kathy Meyer, Almond, Wisconsin

These stir-and-bake cupcakes go together super-quick. Pistachio pudding mix gives them a mild flavor and a pretty pastel color that makes them perfect for St. Patrick's Day.

- 1-3/4 cups all-purpose flour
- 2/3 cup sugar
- 1 package (3.4 ounces) instant pistachio pudding mix
- 2 teaspoons baking powder
- 1/2 teaspoon salt
- 2 eggs
- 1-1/4 cups milk
- 1/2 cup canola oil
- 1 teaspoon vanilla extract
- Green food coloring, optional
- Cream cheese frosting

In a bowl, combine the flour, sugar, pudding mix, baking powder and salt. In another bowl, beat eggs, milk, oil and vanilla; add to flour mixture and mix until blended.

Fill paper-lined muffin cups three-fourths full. Bake at 375° for 18-22 minutes or until a toothpick inserted in the center comes out clean. Cool for 10 minutes before removing from pan to a wire rack to cool completely. Add food coloring to frosting if desired. Frost cupcakes. **Yield:** 1 dozen.

Cupcake Cones

Mina Dyck, Boissevain, Manitoba

Children love this treat. Since each one gets their own cupcake cone to eat, it's not as messy as a piece of cake.

    1/3 cup butter, softened
    1/2 cup creamy peanut butter
  1-1/2 cups packed brown sugar
      2 eggs
      1 teaspoon vanilla extract
      2 cups all-purpose flour
  2-1/2 teaspoons baking powder
    1/2 teaspoon salt
    3/4 cup milk
     24 ice cream cake cones (about 3 inches tall)
  Frosting of your choice
  Sprinkles *or* chopped peanuts, optional

In a large bowl, cream the butter, peanut butter and brown sugar until light and fluffy. Beat in eggs and vanilla. Combine the flour, baking powder and salt; add to creamed mixture alternately with milk, beating well after each addition. Place ice cream cones in muffin cups. Spoon about 3 tablespoons batter into each cone, filling to 3/4 in. from the top.

Bake at 350° for 25-30 minutes or until a toothpick inserted near the center comes out clean. Cool completely on wire racks. Frost and decorate as desired. **Yield:** about 2 dozen.

Editor's Note: Reduced-fat or generic brands of peanut butter are not recommended for this recipe.

German Chocolate Cupcakes

Lettice Charmasson, San Diego, California

These cupcakes disappear in a dash when I take them to the school where I teach. Pecans, coconut and brown sugar dress up the topping nicely.

      1 package (18-1/4 ounces) German chocolate cake mix
      1 cup water
      3 eggs
    1/2 cup canola oil
      3 tablespoons chopped pecans
      3 tablespoons flaked coconut
      3 tablespoons brown sugar

In a large bowl, combine cake mix, water, eggs and oil. Beat on low speed for 30 seconds. Beat on medium for 2 minutes.

Fill paper-lined muffin cups three-fourths full. Combine the pecans, coconut and brown sugar; sprinkle over batter. Bake at 400° for 15-20 minutes or until a toothpick inserted near the center comes out clean. Cool for 10 minutes before removing from pans to wire racks to cool completely. **Yield:** about 2 dozen.

Cream Cheese Cupcakes

Nancy Reichert, Thomasville, Georgia

It's hard to believe these cupcakes can taste so delicious, yet be so easy. Frost them if you wish, but my family likes them plain, which is great when I'm having an especially busy day.

      1 package (3 ounces) cream cheese, softened
      1 package (18-1/4 ounces) yellow cake mix
  1-1/4 cups water
    1/2 cup butter, melted
      3 eggs
  Chocolate frosting, optional

In a large bowl, beat cream cheese until smooth. Beat in the cake mix, water, butter and eggs.

Spoon batter by 1/4 cupfuls into paper-lined muffin cups. Bake at 350° for 25 minutes or until golden brown. Remove to a wire rack to cool completely. Frost if desired. Store in the refrigerator. **Yield:** 2 dozen.

Peanut Butter Brownie Cups

Karen Presbrey, Pascoag, Rhode Island

Two items are all you need to whip up these fudgy brownie cups with peanut butter centers. Your gang will request them time and again!

      1 package (21-1/2 ounces) fudge brownie mix
     15 to 18 miniature peanut butter cups

Mix brownie batter according to package directions. Fill paper-lined or foil-lined muffin cups two-thirds full.

Remove wrappers from peanut butter cups; set one in each muffin cup and press down until batter meets the top edge of the candy. Bake at 350° for 20-25 minutes. Cool for 10 minutes before removing from pans to wire racks to cool completely. **Yield:** about 1-1/2 dozen.

Chocolate Macaroon Cupcakes

Dolores Skrout, Summerhill, Pennsylvania

A delightful coconut and ricotta cheese filling is hidden inside these cupcakes.

- 2 egg whites
- 1 egg
- 1/3 cup unsweetened applesauce
- 1 teaspoon vanilla extract
- 1-1/4 cups all-purpose flour
- 1 cup sugar
- 1/3 cup baking cocoa
- 1/2 teaspoon baking soda
- 3/4 cup buttermilk

FILLING:

- 1 cup fat-free ricotta cheese
- 1/4 cup sugar
- 1 egg white
- 1/3 cup flaked coconut
- 1/2 teaspoon coconut *or* almond extract
- 2 teaspoons confectioners' sugar

Combine the first four ingredients. Combine flour, sugar, cocoa and baking soda; gradually add to egg white mixture alternately with buttermilk. Spoon half of the batter into 18 muffin cups coated with cooking spray.

In another bowl, beat the ricotta cheese, sugar and egg white until smooth. Stir in coconut and extract. Spoon 1 tablespoonful in the center of each muffin cup.

Fill muffin cups two-thirds full with remaining batter. Bake at 350° for 28-33 minutes or until a toothpick inserted in cupcake comes out clean. Cool for 10 minutes before removing from pans to wire racks; cool completely. Dust with confectioners' sugar. **Yield:** 1-1/2 dozen.

Chocolate Chip Cupcakes

Paula Zsiray, Logan, Utah

These crowd-pleasing cupcakes are quick and yummy!

- 1 package (18-1/4 ounces) yellow cake mix
- 1 package (3.4 ounces) instant vanilla pudding mix
- 1 cup water
- 1/2 cup canola oil
- 4 eggs
- 1 cup (6 ounces) miniature semisweet chocolate chips
- 1 can (16 ounces) chocolate *or* vanilla frosting

Additional miniature semisweet chocolate chips, optional

In a large bowl, combine the cake mix, pudding mix, water, oil and eggs; beat on low speed for 30 seconds. Beat on medium for 2 minutes. Stir in chocolate chips.

Fill paper-lined muffin cups two-thirds full. Bake at 375° for 18-22 minutes or until a toothpick inserted near the center comes out clean. Cool for 10 minutes before removing to wire racks to cool completely. Frost cupcakes. Sprinkle with additional chips if desired. **Yield:** 2-1/2 dozen.

Apple Spice Cupcakes

Taste of Home Test Kitchen

These adorable cupcakes are super sellers at bake sales. A spice cake mix makes the treats a snap to stir up and a fast frosting helps them stand out from an orchard of goodies.

- 1 package (18-1/4 ounces) spice cake mix
- 1-1/4 cups water
- 3 eggs
- 1/3 cup applesauce

FROSTING:

- 1 package (8 ounces) cream cheese, softened
- 1/4 cup butter, softened
- 1 teaspoon vanilla extract
- 4 cups confectioners' sugar

Red paste *or* liquid food coloring

- 24 pieces black licorice (3/4 inch)
- 12 green spice gumdrops

In a large bowl, beat the cake mix, water, eggs and applesauce on low speed for 30 seconds or just until moistened. Beat on medium for 2 minutes or until smooth.

Fill paper-lined muffin cups two-thirds full. Bake at 350° for 18-22 minutes or until a toothpick inserted near the center comes out clean. Cool for 10 minutes before removing from pans to wire racks to cool completely.

In a small bowl, beat the cream cheese, butter and vanilla until fluffy. Gradually add sugar, beating until smooth. Stir in food coloring.

Frost tops of cupcakes. Insert licorice into centers for apple stems. Cut gumdrops in half; flatten and pinch to form leaves. Place one leaf next to each stem. **Yield:** 2 dozen.

Lemon Tea Cakes

Charlene Crump, Montgomery, Alabama

Lemon and cream cheese make for a winning combination in these lovely, bite-size glazed cakes. They always get rave reviews, and I get requests for the recipe.

- 1-1/2 cups butter, softened
- 1 package (8 ounces) cream cheese, softened
- 2-1/4 cups sugar
- 6 eggs
- 3 tablespoons lemon juice
- 2 teaspoons lemon extract
- 1 teaspoon vanilla extract
- 1-1/2 teaspoons grated lemon peel
- 3 cups all-purpose flour

GLAZE:
- 5-1/4 cups confectioners' sugar
- 1/2 cup plus 3 tablespoons milk
- 3-1/2 teaspoons lemon extract

In a large bowl, cream the butter, cream cheese and sugar until light and fluffy. Add eggs, one at a time, beating well after each addition. Beat in the lemon juice, extracts and lemon peel. Add flour; beat just until moistened.

Fill greased miniature muffin cups two-thirds full. Bake at 325° for 10-15 minutes or until cakes pull away from sides of cups. Cool for 10 minutes before removing from pans to wire racks to cool completely.

In a small bowl, combine glaze ingredients. Dip tops of cakes into glaze; place on waxed paper to dry. Store in the refrigerator. **Yield:** 8-1/2 dozen.

Candy Corn Cupcakes

Renee Schwebach, Dumont, Minnesota

These tender white cupcakes are perfect for Halloween. But for fast yet fabulous results any time of year, simply choose candy decorations appropriate to the season.

- 1/2 cup shortening
- 1-1/2 cups sugar
- 1 teaspoon vanilla extract
- 2 cups all-purpose flour
- 3-1/2 teaspoons baking powder
- 1 teaspoon salt
- 1 cup milk
- 4 egg whites

Frosting of your choice

Candy corn *or* other decorations

In a large bowl, cream shortening and sugar until light and fluffy. Beat in vanilla. Combine the flour, baking powder and salt; add to the creamed mixture alternately with milk, beating well after each addition. Beat in the egg whites.

Fill paper-lined muffin cups half full. Bake at 350° for 18-22 minutes or until toothpick inserted near the center comes out clean. Cool for 10 minutes before removing from pans to wire racks to cool completely. Frost cooled cupcakes; decorate as desired. **Yield:** 2 dozen.

Carrot Cupcakes

Doreen Kelly, Rosyln, Pennsylvania

The carrots add wonderful texture to these cupcakes, which have a rich cream cheese frosting.

- 4 eggs
- 2 cups sugar
- 1 cup canola oil
- 2 cups all-purpose flour
- 2 teaspoons ground cinnamon
- 1 teaspoon baking soda
- 1 teaspoon baking powder
- 1 teaspoon ground allspice
- 1/2 teaspoon salt
- 3 cups grated carrots

CHUNKY FROSTING:
- 1 package (8 ounces) cream cheese, softened
- 1/4 cup butter, softened
- 2 cups confectioners' sugar
- 1/2 cup flaked coconut
- 1/2 cup chopped pecans
- 1/2 cup chopped raisins

In a large bowl, beat the eggs, sugar and oil. Combine the flour, cinnamon, baking soda, baking powder, allspice and salt; gradually add to egg mixture. Stir in carrots.

Fill greased or paper-lined muffin cups two-thirds full. Bake at 325° for 20-25 minutes or until a toothpick inserted near the center comes out clean. Cool for 10 minutes before removing from pans to wire racks.

For frosting, in a large bowl, beat cream cheese and butter until fluffy. Gradually beat in confectioners' sugar until smooth. Stir in the coconut, pecans and raisins. Frost cupcakes. Store in the refrigerator. **Yield:** 2 dozen.

Surprise Cupcakes

Edith Holliday, Flushing, Michigan

My mother taught me this simple way to fill cupcakes with fruit jelly. Take these tender treats to your next get-together and watch faces light up as they enjoy them.

- 1 cup shortening
- 2 cups sugar
- 2 eggs
- 2 teaspoons vanilla extract
- 3-1/2 cups all-purpose flour
- 5 teaspoons baking powder
- 1 teaspoon salt
- 1-1/2 cups milk
- 3/4 cup strawberry *or* grape jelly

Frosting of your choice
Colored sprinkles, optional

In a large bowl, cream shortening and sugar until light and fluffy. Add eggs, one at a time, beating well after each addition. Beat in vanilla. Combine the flour, baking powder and salt; add to creamed mixture alternately with milk, beating well after each addition.

Fill 36 paper-lined muffin cups half full. Spoon 1 teaspoon jelly in the center of each. Bake at 375° for 15-20 minutes or until a toothpick inserted 1 in. from the edge comes out clean. Cool for 10 minutes before removing from pans to wire racks to cool completely. Frost and decorate with sprinkles if desired. **Yield:** 3 dozen.

Raspberry Swirl Cupcakes

Christine Sohm, Newton, Ontario

These unique snacks taste fantastic. Garnish them with fresh raspberries and mint and they'll be pretty, too!

- 1 package (18-1/4 ounces) white cake mix
- 1/4 cup raspberry pie filling
- 1/2 cup shortening
- 1/3 cup milk
- 1 teaspoon vanilla extract
- 1/4 teaspoon salt
- 3 cups confectioners' sugar

Fresh raspberries and mint, optional

Prepare and bake the cake mix according to the package directions. Fill paper-lined muffin cups two-thirds full. Drop 1/2 teaspoon of the pie filling in the center of each; swirl with a knife.

Bake at 350° for 20-25 minutes or until a toothpick inserted near the center comes out clean. Cool for 10 minutes before removing from pans to wire racks to cool completely.

In a large bowl, beat shortening until fluffy. Add the milk, vanilla, salt and confectioners' sugar; beat until smooth. Frost cupcakes. Garnish with raspberries and mint if desired. **Yield:** about 1-1/2 dozen.

Cupcake Brownies

Nila Towler, Baird, Texas

Since there's no frosting on these cupcakes, they travel well. The pecans make them extra special.

- 1 cup butter, cubed
- 4 squares (1 ounce *each*) semisweet chocolate
- 4 eggs
- 1-3/4 cups sugar
- 1 teaspoon vanilla extract
- 1 cup all-purpose flour
- 1-1/2 cups chopped pecans

In a microwave, melt butter and chocolate; stir until smooth. Cool for 10 minutes.

In a large bowl, beat eggs and sugar until blended. Beat in vanilla and chocolate mixture; gradually stir in the flour and nuts.

Fill greased or paper-lined muffin cups two-thirds full. Bake at 350° for 18-20 minutes or until a toothpick inserted near the center comes out clean. Cool for 10 minutes before removing from pans to wire racks to cool completely. **Yield:** about 1-1/2 dozen.

Cream Cheese Chocolate Cupcakes

Shirley Dunbar, Mojave, California

Smooth cream cheese inside makes these cupcakes so rich. The classic combination of peanut butter and chocolate chips comes through in every yummy bite. You'll be asked to make them again and again.

- 1 package (8 ounces) cream cheese, softened
- 1/3 cup sugar
- 1 egg
- 1/8 teaspoon salt
- 1 cup semisweet chocolate chips
- 1 cup peanut butter chips

CUPCAKES:
- 1 cup sugar
- 1 cup water
- 1/3 cup canola oil
- 1 tablespoon white vinegar
- 1 teaspoon vanilla extract
- 1-1/2 cups all-purpose flour
- 1/4 cup baking cocoa
- 1 teaspoon baking soda
- 1/2 teaspoon salt

In a large bowl, beat cream cheese until fluffy. Beat the sugar, egg and salt until smooth. Fold in chocolate and peanut butter chips; set aside.

For cupcakes, in a large bowl, beat the sugar, water, oil, vinegar and vanilla until well blended. In a large bowl, combine the flour, cocoa, baking soda and salt; gradually beat into sugar mixture until blended.

Fill paper-lined muffin cups half full with batter. Top each with about 2 tablespoons of the cream cheese mixture. Bake at 350° for 25-30 minutes or until toothpick inserted into cupcake comes out clean. Cool for 10 minutes before removing from pans to wire racks to cool completely. **Yield:** 1-1/2 dozen.

Editor's Note: The filling will partially cover the tops of the cupcakes.

Chocolate-Coconut Angel Cupcakes

Bernice Janowski, Stevens Point, Wisconsin

These cupcakes don't taste light but they are. My guests are never satisfied with just one. The meringue-like tops make them different, but the chocolate and coconut make them memorable.

- 6 egg whites
- 1-1/3 cups sugar, *divided*
- 2/3 cup all-purpose flour
- 1/4 cup baking cocoa
- 1/2 teaspoon baking powder
- 1 teaspoon almond extract
- 1/2 teaspoon cream of tartar
- 1/4 teaspoon salt
- 1 cup flaked coconut

Place egg whites in a large bowl; let stand at room temperature for 30 minutes. Combine 1 cup sugar, flour, cocoa and baking powder. Sift together twice; set aside.

Add the almond extract, cream of tartar and salt to egg whites; beat on medium speed until soft peaks form. Gradually add the remaining sugar, about 2 tablespoons at a time, beating on high until stiff, glossy peaks form. Gradually fold in cocoa mixture, about 1/2 cup at a time. Gently fold in coconut.

Fill paper-lined muffin cups two-thirds full. Bake at 350° for 30-35 minutes or until golden brown and top appears dry. Cool for 10 minutes before removing from pans to wire racks. **Yield:** 1-1/2 dozen.

Chocolate Orange Cupcakes

Shirley Brazel, Coos Bay, Oregon

Chocolate and orange are perfect together in these fudgy morsels. To give them a moist, brownie-like texture, I add mayonnaise. The cupcakes taste even better when served with a scoop of homemade ice cream.

- 1-1/2 cups all-purpose flour
- 1/2 cup sugar
- 1/4 cup baking cocoa
- 1 teaspoon baking soda
- 1/4 teaspoon salt
- 1/2 cup mayonnaise
- 1 teaspoon grated orange peel
- 1 teaspoon vanilla extract
- 1/2 cup orange juice
- 1/2 cup semisweet chocolate chips
- Confectioners' sugar

In a bowl, combine the flour, sugar, cocoa, baking soda and salt. In another bowl, combine the mayonnaise, orange peel and vanilla; gradually add orange juice until blended. Stir into flour mixture just until combined. Stir in chocolate chips (batter will be thick).

Fill paper-lined muffin cups two-thirds full. Bake at 350° for 18-23 minutes or until a toothpick inserted near the center comes out clean. Cool for 10 minutes before removing from the pan to a wire rack to cool completely. Dust with confectioners' sugar. **Yield:** 9 cupcakes.

Editor's Note: Reduced-fat or fat-free mayonnaise is not recommended for this recipe.

Zucchini Cupcakes

Virginia Breitmeyer, Craftsbury, Vermont

I asked my grandmother for this recipe after trying these irresistible spice cupcakes at her home. I love their creamy caramel frosting. They're such a scrumptious dessert.

3	eggs
1-1/3	cups sugar
1/2	cup canola oil
1/2	cup orange juice
1	teaspoon almond extract
2-1/2	cups all-purpose flour
2	teaspoons ground cinnamon
2	teaspoons baking powder
1	teaspoon baking soda
1	teaspoon salt
1/2	teaspoon ground cloves
1-1/2	cups shredded zucchini

CARAMEL FROSTING:

1	cup packed brown sugar
1/2	cup butter
1/4	cup milk
1	teaspoon vanilla extract
1-1/2	to 2 cups confectioners' sugar

In a bowl, beat the eggs, sugar, oil, orange juice and extract. Combine the flour, cinnamon, baking powder, baking soda, salt and cloves; add to the egg mixture and mix well. Add zucchini and mix well.

Fill greased or paper-lined muffin cups two-thirds full. Bake at 350° for 20-25 minutes or until toothpick inserted near the center comes out clean. Cool for 10 minutes before removing to a wire rack.

For frosting, combine the brown sugar, butter and milk in a saucepan. Bring to a boil over medium heat; cook and stir for 2 minutes or until thickened. Remove from the heat; stir in the vanilla. Cool to lukewarm. Gradually beat in confectioners' sugar until frosting reaches spreading consistency. Frost cupcakes. **Yield:** 1-1/2 to 2 dozen.

Chocolate Cupcakes

Marlene Martin, Country Harbour Mines, Nova Scotia

If you are a fan of chocolate, you are going to love these scrumptious cupcakes. Chocolate shavings perfect the gorgeous gems. Enjoy with a tall glass of milk.

1/2	cup butter, softened
1	cup sugar
1	egg
1	teaspoon vanilla extract
1-1/2	cups all-purpose flour
1/2	cup baking cocoa
1	teaspoon baking soda
1/4	teaspoon salt
1/2	cup water
1/2	cup buttermilk

Frosting of your choice
Chocolate curls, optional

In a small bowl, cream butter and sugar until light and fluffy. Beat in egg and vanilla. Combine the flour, cocoa, baking soda and salt; add to creamed mixture alternately with water and buttermilk, beating well after each addition.

Fill paper-lined muffin cups two-thirds full. Bake at 375° for 12-15 minutes or until a toothpick inserted near the center comes out clean. Cool for 10 minutes before removing from the pan to a wire rack to cool completely. Frost and decorate with chocolate curls if desired. **Yield:** 1 dozen.

Shoofly Cupcakes

Beth Adams, Jacksonville, Florida

These moist, old-fashioned molasses cupcakes were my grandmother's specialty. To keep them from disappearing too quickly, she used to store them out of sight. Somehow, we always figured out her hiding places!

4	cups all-purpose flour
2	cups packed brown sugar
1/4	teaspoon salt
1	cup cold butter, cubed
2	teaspoons baking soda
2	cups boiling water
1	cup molasses

In a large bowl, combine the flour, brown sugar and salt. Cut in butter until crumbly. Set aside 1 cup for topping. Add baking soda to remaining crumb mixture. Stir in the water and molasses.

Fill paper-lined muffin cups two-thirds full. Sprinkle with reserved crumb mixture. Bake at 350° for 20-25 minutes or until a toothpick inserted near the center comes out clean. Cool for 10 minutes before removing from pans to wire racks to cool. **Yield:** 2 dozen.

Editor's Note: This recipe does not use eggs.

Coconut Cupcakes

Judy Wilson, Sun City West, Arizona

I took these yummy treats to a picnic for our computer club one year, and they went like hotcakes! I should have made a double batch. With their creamy frosting and sprinkling of coconut, they appeal to kids and adults alike.

1-1/2	cups butter, softened
2	cups sugar
5	eggs
1	to 1-1/2 teaspoons vanilla extract
1	to 1-1/2 teaspoons almond extract
3	cups all-purpose flour
1	teaspoon baking powder
1/2	teaspoon baking soda
1/2	teaspoon salt
1	cup buttermilk
1-1/4	cups flaked coconut

CREAM CHEESE FROSTING:

1	package (8 ounces) cream cheese, softened
3/4	cup butter, softened
1/2	teaspoon vanilla extract
1/2	teaspoon almond extract
2-3/4	cups confectioners' sugar

Additional flaked coconut, toasted

In a large bowl, cream butter and sugar until light and fluffy. Add eggs, one at a time, beating well after each addition. Beat in extracts. Combine the flour, baking powder, baking soda and salt; add to creamed mixture alternately with the buttermilk, beating well after each addition. Fold in coconut.

Fill paper-lined muffin cups two-thirds full. Bake at 350° for 18-20 minutes or until a toothpick inserted near the center comes out clean. Cool for 10 minutes before removing from pans to wire racks to cool completely.

For frosting, in a large bowl, beat cream cheese, butter and extracts until smooth. Gradually beat in confectioners' sugar. Frost the cupcakes; sprinkle with toasted coconut. **Yield:** 2-1/2 dozen.

Black Bottom Cupcakes

Julie Briceland, Windsor, Pennsylvania

This recipe's been in our family for years, but these cupcakes still go fast each time I make them. So I always double or triple the ingredients! You'll likely see what I mean if you make them at your place—I can't remember anyone who's tried them for the first time not asking for seconds.

FILLING:
- 1 package (8 ounces) cream cheese, softened
- 1/3 cup sugar
- 1 egg
- 1/8 teaspoon salt
- 1 cup semisweet chocolate chips

CUPCAKES:
- 1 cup sugar
- 1 cup water
- 1/3 cup canola oil
- 1 egg
- 1 tablespoon white vinegar
- 1 teaspoon vanilla extract
- 1-1/2 cups all-purpose flour
- 1/4 cup unsweetened cocoa
- 1 teaspoon baking soda
- 1/2 teaspoon salt

TOPPING:
Sugar

Chopped almonds, if desired

In a small bowl, beat the cream cheese, sugar, egg and salt until smooth. Stir in chips; set aside.

For cupcakes, in a large bowl, beat the sugar, water, oil, egg, vinegar and vanilla until well blended. Combine the flour, cocoa, baking soda and salt; gradually beat into egg mixture until blended.

Fill paper-lined muffin cups half full with chocolate batter. Drop a heaping teaspoon of cheese mixture in center of batter of each cupcake. Sprinkle with sugar and chopped almonds if desired.

Bake at 350° for 25 minutes or until a toothpick inserted near the center comes out clean. Cool in pans for 10 minutes before removing to racks to cool completely. Store in the refrigerator. **Yield:** 20-24 cupcakes.

Spice Cupcakes

Carla Hodenfield, New Town, North Dakota

Topped with a delightful caramel frosting, these moist cupcakes are a delicious treat.

- 2 cups water
- 1 cup raisins
- 1/2 cup shortening
- 1 cup sugar
- 1 egg
- 1-3/4 cups all-purpose flour
- 1 teaspoon baking soda

- 1/2 teaspoon salt
- 1/2 teaspoon *each* ground allspice, cloves, cinnamon and nutmeg
- 1/4 cup chopped walnuts

FROSTING:
- 1 cup packed brown sugar
- 1/3 cup half-and-half cream
- 1/4 teaspoon salt
- 3 tablespoons butter
- 1 teaspoon vanilla extract
- 1-1/4 cups confectioners' sugar

Coarsely chopped walnuts, optional

In a large saucepan, bring water and raisins to a boil. Reduce heat; simmer for 10 minutes. Remove from heat and set aside (do not drain).

Meanwhile, in a large bowl, cream shortening and sugar until light and fluffy. Beat in egg. Stir in raisins. Combine the flour, baking soda, salt and spices; add to creamed mixture until well blended. Stir in walnuts.

Fill paper-lined muffin cups with 1/3 cup batter each. Bake at 350° for 20-25 minutes or until a toothpick inserted near the center comes out clean. Cool for 10 minutes before removing from pans to wire racks to cool completely.

For frosting, in a large saucepan, combine the brown sugar, cream and salt. Bring to a boil over medium-low heat; cook and stir until smooth. Stir in butter and vanilla. Remove from the heat; cool slightly. Stir in confectioners' sugar until smooth. Frost cupcakes; top with the nuts if desired. **Yield:** 14 cupcakes.

Caramel Apple Cupcakes

Diane Halferty, Corpus Christi, Texas

Bring these extra-special cupcakes to your next bake sale and watch how quickly they disappear—if your family doesn't gobble them up first! Kids will go for the fun appearance and tasty toppings, while adults will appreciate the tasty spiced cake underneath.

- 1 package (18-1/4 ounces) spice cake mix *or* 1 package (18 ounces) carrot cake mix
- 2 cups chopped peeled tart apples
- 20 caramels
- 3 tablespoons milk
- 1 cup finely chopped pecans, toasted
- 12 Popsicle sticks

Prepare the cake batter according to package directions; fold in apples. Fill 12 greased or paper-lined jumbo muffin cups three-fourths full. Bake at 350° for 20 minutes or until a toothpick inserted near the center comes out clean. Cool for 10 minutes before removing from pans to wire racks to cool completely.

In a saucepan, heat the caramels and milk over low heat; stir until smooth. Spread over cupcakes. Sprinkle with pecans. Insert a wooden stick into the center of each cupcake. **Yield:** 1 dozen.

Easy Peel Cupcake Liners Spray cupcake liners with cooking spray before you fill them with batter. Then when the liners are peeled off, the cupcakes will be less likely to tear or crumble.

Pumpkin Pecan Bites

Carol Beyerl, East Wenatchee, Washington

I like sharing these bite-size treats at potlucks. To easily frost them, pipe the frosting on the top of the cupcakes.

- 1 package (18-1/4 ounces) spice cake mix
- 1 can (15 ounces) solid-pack pumpkin
- 3 eggs
- 1/2 cup canola oil
- 1 tablespoon ground cinnamon
- 1 teaspoon baking soda
- 1/4 teaspoon ground cloves
- 36 pecan halves, cut into halves

CREAM CHEESE FROSTING:
- 1/2 cup butter, softened
- 4 ounces cream cheese, softened
- 1 teaspoon vanilla extract
- 3-3/4 cups confectioners' sugar
- 2 to 3 tablespoons milk

Ground cinnamon

In a large bowl, combine the cake mix, pumpkin, eggs, oil, cinnamon, baking soda and cloves. Beat on low speed for 30 seconds. Beat on medium for 2 minutes.

Fill paper-lined miniature muffin cups two-thirds full. Press a pecan piece into each. Bake at 350° for 17-20 minutes or until a toothpick inserted near the center comes out clean. Cool for 10 minutes before removing from pans to wire racks to cool completely.

In a small bowl, cream the butter, cream cheese and vanilla until light and fluffy. Gradually add confectioners' sugar and mix well. Add enough milk to achieve spreading consistency. Frost cupcakes. Sprinkle with cinnamon. **Yield:** about 6 dozen.

Editor's Note: This recipe can be prepared in 2 dozen regular-size muffin cups. Bake for 22-26 minutes.

Berry Surprise Cupcakes

Susan Lucas, Brampton, Ontario

Strawberry is my favorite, but feel free to try other flavors of Fruit Roll-Ups in this recipe.

- 1 package (18-1/4 ounces) white cake mix
- 1-1/3 cups water
- 3 egg whites
- 2 tablespoons canola oil
- 3 strawberry Fruit Roll-Ups, unrolled
- 1 can (16 ounces) vanilla frosting
- 6 pouches strawberry Fruit Snacks

In a large bowl, combine the cake mix, water, eggs whites and canola oil. Beat on low speed for 30 seconds. Beat on medium for 2 minutes. Fill paper-lined muffin cups half full. Cut each fruit roll into eight pieces; place one piece over batter in each cup. Fill two-thirds full with remaining batter.

Bake at 350° for 15-20 minutes or until a toothpick inserted near the center comes out clean. Cool for 10 minutes; remove from pans to wire racks to cool completely. Frost with vanilla frosting; decorate with fruit snacks. **Yield:** 2 dozen.

Editor's Note: This recipe was tested with Betty Crocker Fruit Roll-Ups and Nabisco Fruit Snacks.

Cappuccino Cupcakes

Carol Forcum, Marion, Illinois

A dusting of cocoa powder deliciously tops off these pretty cupcakes. They're so scrumptious, no one ever guesses they're lighter.

- 2 cups all-purpose flour
- 1-1/2 cups sugar
- 1/2 cup baking cocoa
- 1 teaspoon baking soda
- 1/2 teaspoon salt
- 1/4 cup instant coffee granules
- 1/2 cup hot water
- 2 eggs
- 1/2 cup prune baby food
- 1/4 cup canola oil
- 2 teaspoons vanilla extract
- 1-1/2 cups reduced-fat whipped topping

Additional baking cocoa

In a bowl, combine the flour, sugar, cocoa, baking soda and salt. Dissolve coffee granules in hot water. In a large bowl, whisk the eggs, baby food, oil, vanilla and coffee mixture. Gradually stir into flour mixture just until moistened.

Fill paper-lined muffin cups two-thirds full. Bake at 350° for 18-20 minutes or until a toothpick inserted near the center comes out clean. Cool for 10 minutes before removing from pans to wire racks to cool completely.

Just before serving, frost cooled cupcakes with whipped topping and sprinkle with cocoa. **Yield:** 17 cupcakes.

Baking Classics | Cupcakes

Chocolate Caramel Cupcakes

Bev Spain, Belleville, Ohio

A few baking staples are all you need to throw together these chewy delights. A cake mix and a can of frosting make them fast, but caramel, walnuts and chocolate chips tucked inside make them memorable.

- 1 package (18-1/4 ounces) chocolate cake mix
- 24 caramels
- 3/4 cup semisweet chocolate chips
- 1 cup chopped walnuts

Chocolate frosting
Additional walnuts, optional

Prepare cake mix batter according to package directions. Fill 24 paper-lined muffin cups one-third full; set remaining batter aside. Bake at 350° for 7-8 minutes or until top of cupcake appears set.

Gently press a caramel into each cupcake; sprinkle with chocolate chips and walnuts. Top with remaining batter. Bake 15-20 minutes longer or until a toothpick inserted near the center comes out clean.

Cool for 10 minutes before removing from pans to wire racks to cool completely. Frost with chocolate frosting. Sprinkle with additional nuts if desired. **Yield:** 2 dozen.

Rosy Rhubarb Cupcakes

Sharon Nichols, Brookings, South Dakota

If you're in a big hurry, these cupcakes are wonderful even without frosting. The recipe works well with either fresh or frozen rhubarb, and a hint of nutmeg sparks the flavor.

- 1/2 cup shortening
- 1 cup packed brown sugar
- 1/2 cup sugar
- 1 egg
- 2 cups all-purpose flour
- 1 teaspoon baking soda
- 1/4 teaspoon ground nutmeg
- 1 cup buttermilk
- 1-1/2 cups finely chopped fresh *or* frozen rhubarb, thawed

Cream cheese frosting, optional

In a bowl, cream shortening and sugar until light and fluffy. Beat in egg. Combine the flour, baking soda and nutmeg; add to creamed mixture alternately with buttermilk, beating well after each addition. Fold in rhubarb.

Fill paper-lined muffin cups two-thirds full. Bake at 350° for 30-35 minutes or until a toothpick inserted near the center comes out clean. Frost if desired. **Yield:** about 1-1/2 dozen.

Editor's Note: If using frozen rhubarb, measure rhubarb while it is still frozen, then thaw completely. Drain in a colander, but do not press out liquid.

Peanut Butter Cupcakes

Ruth Hutson, Westfield, Indiana

Peanut butter lovers can double their pleasure with these tender treats. I use the popular ingredient in the cupcakes as well as their creamy homemade frosting.

- 1/3 cup butter, softened
- 1/2 cup peanut butter
- 1-1/4 cups packed brown sugar
- 1 egg
- 1 teaspoon vanilla extract
- 2 cups all-purpose flour
- 2 teaspoons baking powder
- 1/2 teaspoon salt
- 1/4 teaspoon ground cinnamon
- 3/4 cup milk

FROSTING:
- 1/3 cup peanut butter
- 2 cups confectioners' sugar
- 2 teaspoons honey
- 1 teaspoon vanilla extract
- 3 to 4 tablespoons milk

In a large bowl, cream the butter, peanut butter and brown sugar until light and fluffy. Beat in the egg and vanilla. Combine the flour, baking powder, salt and cinnamon; add to creamed mixture alternately with milk, beating well after each addition.

Fill paper-lined muffin cups two-thirds full. Bake at 350° for 26-30 minutes or until a toothpick inserted near the center comes out clean. Cool for 10 minutes before removing from pans to wire racks to cool completely.

For frosting, in a small bowl, cream peanut butter and sugar until light and fluffy. Beat in honey and vanilla. Beat in enough milk to achieve a spreading consistency. Frost cupcakes. **Yield:** about 1-1/2 dozen.

Editor's Note: Reduced-fat or generic brands of peanut butter are not recommended for this recipe.

Bananas for Baking When you have a too-ripe-to-eat banana, just toss it in a freezer bag (with the peel still on) and freeze. They can be frozen for up to 6 months and you'll have bananas at the ready when you want to whip up Chocolate Banana Split Cupcakes.

Chocolate Banana Split Cupcakes

Lorelie Miller, Benito, Manitoba

My mom often made these cute cupcakes when I was young. They go over just as well now when I bake them for our three children.

    1-1/4   cups all-purpose flour
      1/2   cup sugar
      1/4   teaspoon baking soda
      1/4   teaspoon salt
      1/2   cup mashed banana (about 1 medium)
      1/2   cup butter, melted
      1/4   cup buttermilk
        1   egg, lightly beaten
      1/2   teaspoon vanilla extract
      1/2   cup chopped walnuts
        2   milk chocolate bars (1.55 ounces *each*) broken into
              squares, *divided*
FROSTING:
    1-1/2   cups confectioners' sugar
        1   tablespoon butter, melted
      1/2   teaspoon vanilla extract
        1   to 2 tablespoons milk
       12   maraschino cherries with stems

In a bowl, combine the flour, sugar, baking soda and salt. In another bowl, combine the banana, butter, buttermilk, egg and vanilla. Add to the flour mixture; stir just until combined. Fold in nuts. Spoon 1 tablespoon of batter into each paper-lined muffin cup. Top each with one candy bar square. Fill remainder of each cup two-thirds full with batter.

Bake at 350° for 20-25 minutes or until a toothpick inserted in the cupcake comes out clean. Cool for 10 minutes before removing from pan to a wire rack to cool completely.

In a bowl, combine the confectioners' sugar, butter, vanilla and enough milk to achieve spreading consistency. Frost cupcakes. In a microwave, melt the remaining candy bar squares; drizzle over frosting. Top each with a cherry. **Yield: 1 dozen.**

Maple Carrot Cupcakes

Lisa Ann Panzino-DiNunzio, Vineland, New Jersey

I come from a family of cooks and was inspired to cook and bake ever since I was young. Mother and Grandmom were always in the kitchen cooking up something delicious. This recipe is handed down from Grandmom and is always requested at special gatherings.

        2   cups all-purpose flour
        1   cup sugar
        1   teaspoon baking powder
        1   teaspoon baking soda
        1   teaspoon ground cinnamon
      1/2   teaspoon salt
        4   eggs
        1   cup canola oil
      1/2   cup maple syrup
        3   cups grated carrots (about 6 medium)
FROSTING:
        1   package (8 ounces) cream cheese, softened
      1/4   cup butter, softened
      1/4   cup maple syrup
        1   teaspoon vanilla extract
Chopped walnuts, optional

In a large bowl, combine the flour, sugar, baking powder, baking soda, cinnamon and salt. In another bowl, beat the eggs, oil and syrup. Stir into flour mixture just until moistened. Fold in carrots.

Fill greased or paper-lined muffin cups two-thirds full. Bake at 350° for 20-25 minutes or until a toothpick inserted near the center comes out clean. Cool for 10 minutes before removing from pans to wire racks.

For frosting, combine the cream cheese, butter, syrup and vanilla in a bowl; beat until smooth. Frost cooled cupcakes. Sprinkle with nuts if desired. Store in the refrigerator. **Yield: 1-1/2 dozen.**

Mint Brownie Cupcakes

Carol Maertz, Spruce Grove, Alberta

Are they a brownie or are they a cupcake? There's no wrong answer to this question, I tell my first-grade students. I found the recipe when I began teaching years ago.

- 1 cup mint chocolate chips
- 1/2 cup butter
- 1/2 cup sugar
- 2 eggs
- 1/2 cup all-purpose flour
- 1 teaspoon baking powder

TOPPING:
- 4 cups miniature marshmallows
- 3/4 cup milk
- 1-1/2 teaspoons peppermint extract
- Green *or* red food coloring, optional
- 1-1/2 cups heavy whipping cream, whipped
- Additional chocolate chips, optional

In a heavy saucepan, melt chips and butter; stir until smooth. Remove from the heat. Cool slightly.

Stir in sugar and eggs. Combine flour and baking powder; gradually stir into chocolate mixture until smooth.

Fill paper-lined muffin cups half full. Bake at 350° for 15-20 minutes or until a toothpick inserted near the center comes out clean (cupcakes will fall in center). Cool for 10 minutes before removing from pans to wire racks to cool completely.

In a large saucepan, cook and stir marshmallows and milk over low heat until smooth. Remove from the heat; stir in extract and food coloring if desired.

Cover and refrigerate for about 15 minutes or until cool. Fold in whipped cream. Spread over cupcakes or top each with a dollop of topping. Refrigerate for at least 1 hour. Sprinkle with chocolate chips if desired. Store in the refrigerator. **Yield:** 16 cupcakes.

Secret Kiss Cupcakes

Carol Hillebrenner, Fowler, Illinois

I earned a merit badge by dreaming up these cupcakes for a Cub Scouts meeting. You should have seen the grins when the kids bit into the chocolate kisses in the middle. My grandkids say I don't make them often enough.

- 3-1/3 cups all-purpose flour
- 2 cups sugar
- 1 cup baking cocoa
- 2 teaspoons baking soda
- 1 teaspoon salt
- 2 cups buttermilk
- 1 cup butter, melted
- 2 eggs, lightly beaten
- 2 teaspoons vanilla extract
- 30 milk chocolate kisses
- 1 can (16 ounces) fudge frosting

In a large bowl, combine the flour, sugar, cocoa, baking soda and salt. Combine the buttermilk, butter, eggs and vanilla. Add to the flour mixture just until blended.

Fill paper-lined muffin cups two-thirds full. Press a chocolate kiss into the center of each cupcake until batter completely covers candy.

Bake at 375° for 20-25 minutes or until a toothpick inserted into the cakes comes out clean. Cool for 10 minutes before removing from pans to wire racks to cool completely. Frost cupcakes. **Yield:** about 2-1/2 dozen.

Keep Your Fingers Clean When making Secret Kiss Cupcakes, fill all the cupcake cups with batter. Then place all the chocolate kisses on top and use a wooden skewer to push the chocolate kisses into the batter.

Bunny Cupcakes

Taste of Home Test Kitchen

Celebrate spring with these cute critters created from a cake mix, frosting and marshmallows. Cookies form the ears while candy gives the rapid rabbits their funny faces.

- 1 package (18-1/4 ounces) yellow cake mix
- 1 can (16 ounces) cream cheese frosting, *divided*
- 8 drops green food coloring
- 12 large marshmallows
- 3/4 cup flaked coconut, chopped
- 24 miniature pink jelly beans
- 12 miniature red jelly beans
- 24 miniature white jelly beans
- Red shoestring licorice
- 1 to 2 drops red food coloring
- 48 small oval sugar cookies

Prepare and bake cupcakes according to package directions. Cool for 10 minutes before removing from pans to wire racks to cool completely.

In a bowl, combine 1 cup frosting and green food coloring; frost the cupcakes. Set remaining frosting aside. Cut the marshmallows in half; immediately dip cut ends into coconut. Place coconut side up on cupcakes to form heads.

Cut pink and red jelly beans in half widthwise. Cut white jelly beans in half lengthwise. With a toothpick, dab reserved frosting onto cut sides of pink jelly bean halves; attach to marshmallows for eyes. Attach red jelly beans for noses and white jelly beans for teeth.

For whiskers, cut licorice into 1-in. pieces; attach four pieces to each cupcake. Tint remaining frosting pink. Cut a small hole in corner of a resealable plastic bag; add pink frosting. For ears, pipe an oval outline toward center of each cookie; insert two ears into each cupcake. **Yield:** 2 dozen.

Blueberry Angel Cupcakes

Kathy Kittell, Lenexa, Kansas

Like angel food cake, these yummy cupcakes don't last long. They're so light and airy that they melt in your mouth.

- 11 egg whites
- 1 cup plus 2 tablespoons cake flour
- 1-1/2 cups sugar, *divided*
- 1-1/4 teaspoons cream of tartar
- 1 teaspoon vanilla extract
- 1/2 teaspoon salt
- 1-1/2 cups fresh *or* frozen blueberries
- 1 teaspoon grated lemon peel

GLAZE:
- 1 cup confectioners' sugar
- 3 tablespoons lemon juice

Place the egg whites in a large bowl; let stand at room temperature for 30 minutes. Sift together flour and 1/2 cup sugar three times; set aside.

Add cream of tartar, vanilla and salt to egg whites; beat on medium speed until soft peaks form. Gradually add remaining sugar, about 2 tablespoons at a time, beating on high until stiff, glossy peaks form and sugar is dissolved. Gradually fold in flour mixture, about 1/2 cup at a time. Fold in blueberries and lemon peel.

Fill paper-lined muffin cups three-fourths full. Bake at 375° for 14-17 minutes or until cupcakes spring back when lightly touched. Immediately remove from pans to wire racks to cool completely.

In a small bowl, whisk confectioners' sugar and lemon juice until smooth. Brush over cupcakes. Let stand until set. **Yield:** 2-1/2 dozen.

Editor's Note: If using frozen blueberries, do not thaw before adding to batter.

Spiced Cocoa Cupcakes

Shirley Glaab, Hattiesburg, Mississippi

To me, a good cup of hot spiced cocoa is heavenly, and that's what these remind me of. These are a great snack or the perfect finish to any meal.

- 1-1/2 cups all-purpose flour
- 3/4 cup sugar
- 1/4 cup baking cocoa
- 3/4 teaspoon baking soda
- 1/4 teaspoon salt
- 1/4 teaspoon ground cinnamon
- 1/4 teaspoon ground nutmeg
- 1 egg
- 3/4 cup applesauce
- 1/4 cup butter, melted
- 1/2 cup dried cranberries
- 1 cup confectioners' sugar
- 4-1/2 teaspoons milk

In a bowl, combine the flour, sugar, cocoa, baking soda, salt, cinnamon and nutmeg. In another bowl, whisk the egg, applesauce and butter; stir into flour mixture just until combined. Fold in the cranberries.

Fill greased or paper lined muffin cups two-thirds full. Bake at 350° for 18-20 minutes or until a toothpick inserted near the center comes out clean. Cool for 10 minutes before removing from pan to a wire rack to cool completely.

In a small bowl, combine the confectioners' sugar and milk until smooth. Drizzle over cupcakes. **Yield:** 1 dozen.

Lemon Sparkle Cupcakes

Janice Porter, Platte, South Dakota

Bursting with lemony zing, these cupcakes don't require frosting. In fact, my family prefers the crunchy sugar-and-spice topping. A dear friend shared the recipe with me, and it has long been in demand at our house.

- 2/3 cup shortening
- 1 cup sugar
- 3 eggs
- 1-2/3 cups all-purpose flour
- 2-1/2 teaspoons baking powder
- 1/2 teaspoon salt
- 2/3 cup milk
- 1 tablespoon grated lemon peel

TOPPING:
- 1/4 cup sugar
- 1 tablespoon grated lemon peel
- 1/8 teaspoon ground nutmeg

In a large bowl, cream shortening and sugar until light and fluffy. Add eggs, one at a time, beating well after each addition. Combine the flour, baking powder and salt; add to the creamed mixture alternately with milk, beating well after each addition. Stir in lemon peel.

Fill paper-lined muffin cups two-thirds full. Combine the topping ingredients; sprinkle a rounded 1/2 teaspoonful over each cupcake. Bake at 350° for 20-24 minutes or until a toothpick inserted near the center comes out clean. Cool for 10 minutes before removing from pans to wire racks to cool completely. **Yield:** about 1-1/4 dozen.

Desserts

pg. 240

pg. 257

pg. 232

217

Chocolate Peanut Delight

Karen Kutruff, New Berlin, Pennsylvania

Peanut lovers will appreciate this yummy dessert I dreamed up. A brownie-like crust is packed with nuts, topped with a fluffy peanut butter layer and covered with whipped topping and more nuts. It was so well received that I made it for a local restaurant where I used to work.

     1   package (18-1/4 ounces) chocolate cake mix
    1/2 cup butter, melted
    1/4 cup milk
     1   egg
     1   cup chopped peanuts, *divided*
     1   package (8 ounces) cream cheese, softened
     1   cup peanut butter
     1   cup confectioners' sugar
     1   can (14 ounces) sweetened condensed milk
    1-1/2 teaspoons vanilla extract
     1   carton (16 ounces) frozen whipped topping, thawed, *divided*
    1/2 cup semisweet chocolate chips
    4-1/2 teaspoons butter
    1/2 teaspoon vanilla extract

In a large bowl, combine the cake mix, butter, milk and egg. Add 3/4 cup of peanuts. Spread into a greased 13-in. x 9-in. x 2-in. baking pan. Bake at 350° for 30 minutes or until a toothpick inserted near the center comes out clean. Cool on a wire rack.

In a large bowl, beat the cream cheese, peanut butter, sugar, condensed milk and vanilla until smooth. Fold in 3 cups whipped topping. Spread over the crust; top with the remaining whipped topping and peanuts.

In a microwave, melt chocolate chips and butter; stir until smooth. Stir in vanilla until smooth; drizzle over the dessert. Refrigerate for 2-3 hours before serving. **Yield:** 12-15 servings.

About Phyllo Dough Phyllo (pronounced FEE-lo) is a tissue-thin dough, generally sold in the freezer section of supermarkets. Thaw phyllo dough according to package directions. It dries out quickly, so always have all the other ingredients assembled and ready to go before unwrapping the dough. Phyllo is fragile and tears easily…work on a smooth, dry surface. Unopened packages of phyllo dough can be refrigerated for up to 3 weeks or frozen for up to 3 months. Opened dough that is well wrapped can be refrigerated for up to 3 days.

Honey Chocolate Pastries

Germaine Stank, Pound, Wisconsin

These pretty pastries are worth the effort to make, especially for special occasions.

    1-1/2 cups chopped pecans
    1-1/2 cups semisweet chocolate chips, *divided*
    1-1/4 cups sugar, *divided*
    1-1/2 teaspoons ground cinnamon
    1-1/4 cups butter, melted, *divided*
     34 sheets phyllo dough (14 inches x 9 inches)
    3/4 cup orange juice
    1/2 cup honey
     2   tablespoons lemon juice
     2   tablespoons water

Combine pecans, 1 cup chocolate chips, 3/4 cup sugar and cinnamon; set aside. Brush the bottom of a 15-in. x 10-in. x 1-in. baking pan with some of the melted butter. Unroll phyllo dough; cut stack into a 10-1/2-in. x 9-in. rectangle. Repeat with remaining phyllo. Discard scraps. (Keep dough covered with plastic wrap and a damp towel until ready to use to prevent it from drying out.)

Line bottom of prepared pan with two sheets of phyllo dough (sheets will overlap slightly). Brush with butter. Repeat layers 7 times, brushing each with butter. Sprinkle with half of the nut mixture.

Top with another five layers of phyllo dough, and brush with butter. Sprinkle remaining nut mixture on top.

Layer with remaining phyllo dough, each brushed with butter, in pan. Drizzle remaining butter on top. Cut all the way through pastry into 48 diamond or square shapes. Bake at 325° for 1 hour.

Meanwhile, combine the orange juice, honey, lemon juice and remaining sugar in a saucepan; bring to a boil. Reduce heat and simmer for 20 minutes. Pour over pastry as soon as it's removed from the oven. Cool.

In a small saucepan, combine water and remaining chocolate chips; stir over low heat until smooth. Drizzle over pastry. **Yield:** 4 dozen.

Pumpkin Cheesecake

Evonne Wurmnest, Normal, Illinois

When I was young, I lived on my family's farm, and we produced several ingredients for this longtime favorite.

CRUST:
- 1 cup graham cracker crumbs
- 1 tablespoon sugar
- 1/4 cup butter, melted

FILLING:
- 2 packages (8 ounces *each*) cream cheese, softened
- 3/4 cup sugar
- 2 eggs
- 1 can (15 ounces) solid-pack pumpkin
- 1-1/4 teaspoons ground cinnamon
- 1/2 teaspoon ground ginger
- 1/2 teaspoon ground nutmeg
- 1/4 teaspoon salt

TOPPING:
- 2 cups (16 ounces) sour cream
- 2 tablespoons sugar
- 1 teaspoon vanilla extract
- 12 to 16 pecan halves

In a small bowl, combine the graham cracker crumbs and sugar; stir in butter. Press into the bottom of a 9-in. springform pan; chill.

For filling, in a large bowl, beat cream cheese and sugar until smooth. Add eggs; beat on low speed just until combined. Stir in the pumpkin, spices and salt.

Pour into crust. Place pan on a baking sheet. Bake at 350° for 50 minutes.

Meanwhile, for topping, combine the sour cream, sugar and vanilla until smooth. Spread over filling; return to the oven for 5 minutes. Cool on rack for 10 minutes. Carefully run a knife around edge of pan to loosen; cool 1 hour longer.

Refrigerate overnight. Remove sides of pan. Garnish each slice with a pecan half. Store in the refrigerator. **Yield:** 12-16 servings.

Strawberry Cheesecake Minis

Lori Lewis, St. Johns, Michigan

My daughter and I trimmed down a recipe from a cooking show, and these little cheesecakes were the result. No one suspects they're on the light side.

   2 packages (8 ounces *each*) reduced-fat cream cheese
Sugar substitute equivalent to 1/2 cup sugar
1/2 cup sugar
   1 teaspoon vanilla extract
   1 egg, lightly beaten
1/4 cup egg substitute
 12 reduced-fat vanilla wafers
   1 can (12 ounces) strawberry cake and pastry filling

In a small bowl, beat cream cheese until smooth. Gradually beat in sugar substitute and sugar. Beat in vanilla. Add egg and egg substitute; beat until blended.

Place each vanilla wafer flat side down in a foil-lined muffin cup. Fill with cream cheese mixture. Bake at 350° for 15-20 minutes or until puffed and set. Cool on a wire rack for 1 hour (centers will sink slightly).

Spoon strawberry filling into the center of each cheesecake. Store in the refrigerator. **Yield:** 1 dozen.

Editor's Note: This recipe was tested with Splenda No Calorie Sweetener and Solo brand cake and pastry filling.

Picture Perfect To keep the cheesecake minis looking their best when you take them to potlucks, try this. Place the unfilled minis back in the muffin pan and transport them to the event. Once you've arrived, remove the cheesecakes from the pan and top with the pastry filling. Then arrange on a plate and serve.

Chocolate Cheesecake Squares

Helen Longmire, Austin, Texas

These bite-size bars are very rich, so small servings are satisfying. They're perfect for parties because they don't require a fork and plate to eat.

- 1 cup all-purpose flour
- 1/2 cup sugar
- 3 tablespoons baking cocoa
- 1 teaspoon baking powder
- 1/4 teaspoon salt
- 1/2 cup cold butter
- 1 egg yolk
- 1 teaspoon vanilla extract
- 1/2 cup finely chopped walnuts

FILLING:
- 1 package (8 ounces) cream cheese, softened
- 1/3 cup sugar
- 1/2 cup sour cream
- 1 tablespoon all-purpose flour
- 2 teaspoons grated orange peel
- 1/4 teaspoon salt
- 1 egg
- 1 egg white
- 1/2 teaspoon vanilla extract

Chocolate sprinkles, optional

Line a 9-in. square baking pan with foil; grease the foil and set aside. In a large bowl, combine the flour, sugar, cocoa, baking powder and salt. Cut in butter until fine crumbs form. Stir in the egg yolk, vanilla and walnuts. Press onto the bottom of prepared pan. Bake at 325° for 15 minutes.

In a small bowl, beat cream cheese and sugar until smooth. Beat in the sour cream, flour, orange peel and salt. Beat in the egg, egg white and vanilla on low speed just until combined.

Pour over warm crust. Bake for 20-25 minutes or until center is almost set. Cool on a wire rack for 1 hour.

Garnish top with chocolate sprinkles if desired. Refrigerate overnight. Lift out of the pan; remove foil. Cut into 1-in. squares. **Yield:** 25 servings.

Blueberry Raspberry Crunch

Harriett Catlin, Nanticoke, Maryland

This quick-to-fix dessert comes in handy when I need to make something sweet in a hurry. I often have the ingredients in my pantry.

- 1 can (21 ounces) blueberry pie filling
- 1 can (21 ounces) raspberry pie filling
- 1 package (18-1/4 ounces) white cake mix
- 1/2 cup chopped walnuts
- 1/2 cup butter, melted

Combine pie fillings in a greased 13-in. x 9-in. x 2-in. baking dish. In a bowl, combine cake mix, walnuts and butter until crumbly; sprinkle over filling.

Bake at 375° for 25-30 minutes or until filling is bubbly and topping is golden brown. Serve warm. **Yield:** 12 servings.

Mocha Meringue Cups

Helen Davis, Waterbury, Vermont

Folks can't resist a rich mocha filling sitting on top of a crisp, chewy meringue cup. My clan expects me to make these treats for many special occasions throughout the year.

- 3 egg whites
- 1/4 teaspoon cream of tartar

Dash salt
- 1 cup sugar

CHOCOLATE FILLING:
- 2 cups milk chocolate chips
- 1 cup heavy whipping cream
- 1 teaspoon instant coffee granules
- 1 teaspoon vanilla extract

Place egg whites in a small bowl; let stand at room temperature for 30 minutes. Add the cream of tartar and salt; beat on medium speed until soft peaks form. Gradually beat in sugar, 1 tablespoon at a time, on high until stiff, glossy peaks form and sugar is dissolved.

Spoon meringue into eight mounds on parchment-lined baking sheets. Shape into 3-in. cups with the back of a spoon. Bake at 275° for 45-50 minutes. Turn oven off; leave meringues in oven for 1 hour. Remove from the oven and cool on baking sheets. When completely cooled, remove meringues from the paper and store in an airtight container at room temperature.

For filling, in a microwave, melt the chocolate chips, cream and coffee granules; stir until smooth. Stir in vanilla. Transfer to a small bowl; refrigerate until chilled. Beat until stiff peaks form. Immediately spoon into a pastry bag or plastic bag with a #20 star tip. Pipe filling into meringue cups. Store in the refrigerator. **Yield:** 8 servings.

Meringue Ice Cream Torte

Alice Christmas, Statesboro, Georgia

*This recipe looks a little long, but it really isn't complicated.
The sweet result is certainly worth the effort.*

      3 egg whites
    1/2 teaspoon cream of tartar
      1 cup sugar
RASPBERRY SAUCE:
      1 package (12 ounces) frozen unsweetened raspberries,
         thawed
      2 tablespoons sugar
      2 tablespoons cornstarch
    1/3 cup maple syrup
ICE CREAM LAYERS:
      1 quart coffee ice cream, softened
  1-1/3 cups sliced almonds, toasted
      1 quart chocolate chip ice cream, softened
      2 cups heavy whipping cream
      2 tablespoons sugar
    1/2 teaspoon almond extract
Fresh raspberries

Place egg whites in a small bowl. Let stand at room
temperature for 30 minutes. Line two large baking sheets
with parchment paper; draw three 8-1/2-in. circles on paper.

Beat egg whites and cream of tartar on medium speed until
soft peaks form. Gradually add sugar, 1 tablespoon at a
time, beating on high until stiff, glossy peaks form and
sugar is dissolved. Drop meringue in mounds onto circles;
spread to cover.

Bake at 250° for 1-1/4 hours or until set. Turn oven off;
leave meringues in oven for 1 hour. Remove from the oven
and cool on baking sheets. When completely cooled,
remove meringues from paper.

Drain raspberries, reserving juice. Set berries aside. Add
enough water to juice to measure 1/2 cup. In a small
saucepan, combine sugar and cornstarch. Stir in maple

syrup and juice mixture until smooth. Bring to a boil over
medium heat; cook and stir for 1-2 minutes or until
thickened. Remove from the heat; gently stir in the reserved
berries. Cool.

To assemble, place one meringue in a 10-in. springform
pan. Spread with coffee ice cream; sprinkle with a third of
the almonds. Top with a second meringue. Spread with the
chocolate chip ice cream; sprinkle with a third of the
almonds. Top with the remaining meringue. Cover and
freeze overnight.

In a large bowl, beat cream until it begins to thicken. Add
sugar and almond extract; beat until stiff peaks form.
Remove torte from freezer; carefully run a knife around
edge of pan to loosen. Remove side of pan. Frost with
whipped cream.

Garnish with fresh raspberries and remaining almonds.
Cover and freeze for at least 2 hours. Remove from the
freezer 20 minutes before serving. Serve with raspberry
sauce. **Yield:** 14-16 servings.

Lemon Crackle

Ruth Tiedeman, Bartlesville, Oklahoma

*I think this dessert is a cross between lemon pie and fruit
crisp. It's refreshingly tart.*

    1/4 cup butter, softened
      1 cup packed brown sugar
      1 cup all-purpose flour
    1/2 teaspoon baking soda
      1 cup flaked coconut
    1/3 cup finely crushed saltines
FILLING:
      1 cup sugar
      2 tablespoons cornstarch
      1 cup water
      2 egg yolks, lightly beaten
    1/2 cup butter, cubed
      6 tablespoons lemon juice
    1/4 teaspoon salt
Whipped topping, optional

In a large bowl, cream butter and brown sugar until light
and fluffy. Combine flour and baking soda; add to creamed
mixture with coconut and cracker crumbs until crumbly.
Press half into a greased 11-in. x 7-in. x 2-in. baking dish.

For filling, in a large saucepan, combine sugar and
cornstarch. Stir in water until smooth. Cook and stir over
medium-high heat until thickened and bubbly. Reduce
heat to low; cook and stir 2 minutes longer. Remove from
the heat. Stir a small amount of hot filling into egg yolks;
return all to the pan, stirring constantly. Bring to a gentle
boil; cook and stir for 2 minutes. Remove from the heat;
gently stir in the butter, lemon juice and salt.

Pour over crust. Top with reserved crumb mixture. Bake at
325° for 20 minutes. Cool. Spoon into dessert dishes. Serve
with whipped topping if desired. Store in the refrigerator.
Yield: 12-16 servings.

Sugared Raisin Pear Diamonds

Jeanne Allen, Rye, Colorado

With their tender golden crust and tempting pear and raisin filling, these fabulous bars stand out on any buffet table. For equally yummy results, substitute apples for the pears!

2-1/2 cups plus 4-1/2 teaspoons all-purpose flour, *divided*
 1/4 cup plus 6 tablespoons sugar, *divided*
 1/2 teaspoon salt
 3/4 cup cold butter, cubed
 1/2 teaspoon grated lemon peel
 1/2 cup half-and-half cream
   6 cups diced peeled ripe pears (about 7)
   6 tablespoons golden raisins
 1/4 cup lemon juice
 1/8 to 1/4 teaspoon ground cinnamon
   1 egg, lightly beaten
Additional sugar

In a large bowl, combine 2-1/2 cups flour, 1/4 cup sugar and salt. Cut in butter and lemon peel until the mixture resembles coarse crumbs. Gradually add cream, tossing with a fork until dough forms a ball.

Divide in half. On a large piece of lightly floured waxed paper, roll out one portion of dough into a 16-in. x 11-1/2-in. rectangle. Transfer to an ungreased 15-in. x 10-in. x 1-in. baking pan.

Bake at 350° for 10-15 minutes or until lightly browned. Cool on a wire rack. Increase oven temperature to 400°.

In a large bowl, combine the pears, raisins, lemon juice, cinnamon and remaining flour and sugar. Spread over crust. Roll out remaining dough into a 16-in. x 12-in. rectangle; place over filling. Trim and seal edges. Brush top with egg; sprinkle with additional sugar.

Bake for 30-34 minutes or until golden brown. Cool on a wire rack. Cut into diamond-shaped bars. **Yield:** about 2 dozen.

Cherry Nut Crisp

Melissa Radulovich, Byers, Colorado

This unusual crisp has a pie pastry bottom and a crunchy pecan-oat topping.

   2 cans (14-1/2 ounces *each*) pitted tart cherries
   1 cup sugar
 1/4 cup quick-cooking tapioca
   1 teaspoon almond extract
 1/8 teaspoon salt
   4 to 5 drops red food coloring, optional
CRUST:
   1 cup all-purpose flour
 1/3 cup sugar
 1/4 teaspoon salt
 1/8 teaspoon baking powder
   6 tablespoons butter, melted
TOPPING:
 1/2 cup all-purpose flour
 1/2 cup packed brown sugar
 l/2 cup chopped pecans
 1/3 cup quick-cooking oats
   6 tablespoons cold butter, cubed

Drain cherries, reserving 3/4 cup juice. In a large bowl, combine the cherries, sugar, tapioca, extract, salt, food coloring if desired and reserved juice; let stand for 15 minutes, stirring occasionally.

In a small bowl, combine the crust ingredients. Press onto the bottom and 1 in. up the sides of a greased 9-in. square baking pan; set aside.

For topping, in another small bowl, combine the flour, brown sugar, pecans and oats. Cut in butter until mixture resembles coarse crumbs. Stir cherry mixture; pour into crust. Sprinkle with topping. Bake at 400° for 10 minutes. Reduce heat to 375°; bake 30-35 minutes longer or until filling is bubbly and topping is golden brown. **Yield:** 9 servings.

Berry Apple Crumble

Ginger Isham, Williston, Vermont

You can serve this crumble as a snack, and it's also a great contribution to a breakfast meeting or church supper. It is just as good on the second day.

- 8 to 10 tart apples, peeled and sliced
- 2 tablespoons cornstarch
- 1 can (12 ounces) frozen apple juice concentrate, thawed
- 2 tablespoons butter
- 1 teaspoon ground cinnamon
- 1 teaspoon lemon juice
- 1 cup fresh *or* frozen raspberries

TOPPING:
- 2 cups quick-cooking oats
- 1/2 cup all-purpose flour
- 1/2 cup chopped walnuts
- 1/3 cup canola oil
- 1/3 cup maple syrup

Place the apples in a greased 13-in. x 9-in. x 2-in. baking dish; set aside. In a small saucepan, combine cornstarch and apple juice until smooth. Bring to a boil; cook and stir for 2 minutes or until thickened. Add the butter, cinnamon and lemon juice.

Pour over the apples. Sprinkle with berries. In a small bowl, combine the oats, flour and walnuts; add oil and syrup. Sprinkle over berries.

Bake at 350° for 40-45 minutes or until filling is bubbly and topping is golden brown. **Yield:** 10-12 servings.

A Tasty Treat If you like pears as much as apples, then substitute 8 to 10 peeled and sliced pears for the apples in Berry Apple Crumble. The apple juice concentrate and raspberries will be a nice complement to the fresh pears.

Raspberry Crisp

Donna Craik, Vancouver Island, British Columbia

This is a delicious crisp that's sure to be a family pleaser.

- 4 cups fresh raspberries, *divided*
- 3/4 cup sugar
- 2 tablespoons cornstarch
- 1-3/4 cups quick-cooking oats
- 1 cup all-purpose flour
- 1 cup packed brown sugar
- 1/2 teaspoon baking soda
- 1/2 cup cold butter

Whipped cream

Crush 1 cup raspberries; add enough water to measure 1 cup. In a saucepan, combine sugar and cornstarch; stir in raspberry mixture until well blended. Bring to a boil; cook and stir for 2 minutes or until thickened. Remove from the heat; stir in remaining raspberries. Cool.

In a large bowl, combine oats, flour, brown sugar and baking soda. Cut in butter until mixture resembles coarse crumbs. Press half of the crumbs into a greased 9-in. square baking pan. Spread with cooled berry mixture. Sprinkle with remaining crumbs. Bake at 350° for 25-30 minutes or until top is lightly browned. Serve warm with whipped cream. **Yield:** 8 servings.

Go Anywhere Rhubarb Squares

Pat Habiger, Spearville, Kansas

This recipe combines rhubarb filling with a cookie crust. Everyone loves these squares, which travel well to picnics and potlucks.

- 1 cup all-purpose flour
- 1/3 cup confectioners' sugar
- 1/3 cup cold butter

FILLING:
- 1 cup sugar
- 1/4 cup all-purpose flour
- 2 eggs, lightly beaten
- 1 teaspoon vanilla extract
- 3 cups finely chopped fresh *or* frozen rhubarb

In a small bowl, combine flour and confectioners' sugar; cut in butter until mixture resembles coarse crumbs. Press into the bottom of a greased 11-in. x 7-in. x 2-in. baking pan. Bake at 350° for 12 minutes.

For filling, in a large bowl, combine the sugar, flour, eggs and vanilla. Stir in rhubarb; pour over warm crust.

Bake at 350° for 35-40 minutes or until toothpick inserted near the center comes out clean. Cool on wire rack. Serve warm if desired. Store in the refrigerator. **Yield:** 16 servings.

Editor's Note: If using frozen rhubarb, measure rhubarb while still frozen, then thaw completely. Drain in a colander, but do not press liquid out.

Baked Lemon Pudding

Aida Von Babbel, Coquitlam, British Columbia

Looking for a lemony, delicate delight of a dessert? Try this old-fashioned family favorite. It is cake-like on top with a custard texture on the bottom.

     2/3 cup sugar, *divided*
       5 tablespoons all-purpose flour
     1/4 teaspoon baking powder
     1/8 teaspoon salt
       2 eggs, *separated*
       1 cup milk
       3 tablespoons lemon juice
       2 tablespoons butter, melted
    1-1/2 teaspoons grated lemon peel
Confectioners' sugar, optional

In a large bowl, combine 1/3 cup sugar, flour, baking powder and salt. In another bowl, beat egg yolks; add milk, lemon juice, butter and lemon peel. Gradually add to the flour mixture and mix well.

Beat egg whites until soft peaks form; gradually add remaining sugar, beating until stiff peaks form. Fold into lemon mixture.

Pour into a lightly greased 1-1/2-qt. baking dish. Place in a large baking pan. Add 1 in. of hot water to larger pan. Bake, uncovered, at 350° for 45-50 minutes or until lightly browned. Serve warm or chilled. Dust with confectioners' sugar if desired. **Yield:** 4 servings.

Coconut Crunch Delight

Debby Chiorino, Oxnard, California

I tasted this light dessert years ago at a gathering and got the recipe from my mom's dear friend. I've made it dozens of times since for my family and friends, who go wild over it. This is a terrific way to end a heavy meal.

     1/2 cup butter, melted
       1 cup all-purpose flour
    1-1/4 cups flaked coconut
     1/4 cup packed brown sugar
       1 cup slivered almonds
    2-2/3 cups cold milk
       1 package (3.4 ounces) instant vanilla pudding mix
       1 package (3.4 ounces) instant coconut cream pudding
          mix
       2 cups whipped topping
Fresh strawberries, optional

In a bowl, combine the butter, flour, coconut, brown sugar and almonds; press lightly into a greased 13-in. x 9-in. x 2-in. baking pan. Bake at 350° for 25-30 minutes or until golden brown, stirring every 10 minutes to form coarse crumbs. Cool.

Divide crumb mixture in half; press half into the same baking pan. In a large bowl, whisk milk and pudding mixes for 2 minutes. Fold in whipped topping; spoon over the crust. Top with remaining crumb mixture. Cover and refrigerate overnight. Garnish with fresh strawberries if desired. **Yield:** 12-16 servings.

Fruit 'n' Nut Turnovers

Aneta Kish, La Crosse, Wisconsin

These flaky Danish nicely round out a holiday or other special occasion brunch.

- 1-1/2 cups cold butter, cut into 1/2-inch slices
- 5 cups all-purpose flour, *divided*
- 1 package (1/4 ounce) active dry yeast
- 1-1/4 cups half-and-half cream
- 1/4 cup sugar
- 1/4 teaspoon salt
- 1 egg

FILLING:
- 1 cup chopped dried apricots *or* cherries
- 1-1/2 cups water
- 1 cup chopped walnuts
- 1/2 cup packed brown sugar
- 2 tablespoons all-purpose flour
- 1/8 teaspoon ground cinnamon

ICING:
- 1 cup confectioners' sugar
- 1/4 teaspoon vanilla extract
- 2 to 3 tablespoons apricot nectar *or* maraschino cherry juice

In a bowl, toss butter with 3 cups flour until well coated; refrigerate for 1 hour or until well chilled. In a large bowl, combine yeast and 1-1/2 cups flour. In a saucepan, heat the cream, sugar and salt to 120°-130°. Add to yeast mixture with the egg. Beat on medium for 3 minutes. Stir in the chilled butter mixture just until combined (butter will remain in large pieces).

Turn onto a well-floured surface; gently knead 6-8 times. Coat rolling pin with the remaining flour. Roll dough into a 21-in. x 12-in. rectangle. Starting with a short side, fold dough in thirds, forming a 12-in. x 7-in. rectangle. Cover and refrigerate for 1 to 1-1/2 hours or until firm but not stiff.

Turn dough onto a well-floured surface; roll into a 21-in. x 12-in. rectangle. Starting with a short side, fold dough in thirds, forming a 12-in. x 7-in. rectangle. Give dough a quarter turn; roll into a 21-in. x 12-in. rectangle. Fold into thirds, starting with a short side. Repeat, flouring surface as needed. (Do not chill dough between each rolling and folding.) Cover and refrigerate for 4 to 24 hours or until dough is firm.

For filling, in a small saucepan, bring fruit and water to a boil. Remove from the heat. Cover and let stand for 5 minutes; drain. Stir in the walnuts, brown sugar, flour and cinnamon; set aside.

Cut dough in half lengthwise. Roll each portion into a 12-in. square; cut each square into nine 4-in. squares. Spoon about a rounded tablespoonful of filling onto the center of each square. Brush edges of dough with water; fold dough diagonally in half, forming a triangle. Press edges to seal. Place 4 in. apart on greased baking sheets. Cover and let rise in a warm place until doubled, about 1 hour.

Bake at 375° for 16-18 minutes or until golden brown. Remove to wire racks. Combine icing ingredients; drizzle over warm turnovers. **Yield:** 1-1/2 dozen.

Caramel Apricot Grunt

Shari Dore, Brantford, Ontario

This recipe is one we enjoyed at my grandmother's house for years. It's perfect for dessert or church socials.

- 2 cans (15-1/4 ounces *each*) apricot halves, undrained
- 2 teaspoons quick-cooking tapioca
- 1/3 cup packed brown sugar
- 1 tablespoon butter
- 1 tablespoon lemon juice

DUMPLINGS:
- 1-1/2 cups all-purpose flour
- 1/2 cup sugar
- 2 teaspoons baking powder
- 2 tablespoons cold butter
- 1/2 cup milk

TOPPING:
- 1/4 cup packed brown sugar
- 2 tablespoons water

Half-and-half cream, optional

In a large saucepan, combine apricots and tapioca; let stand for 15 minutes. Add the brown sugar, butter and lemon juice. Cook and stir until mixture comes to a full boil. Reduce heat to low; keep warm.

For dumplings, in a large bowl, combine the flour, sugar and baking powder; cut in butter until crumbly. Add milk; mix just until combined. Pour warm fruit mixture into an ungreased 2-qt. baking dish (mixture will be very thick). Drop the batter into six mounds onto fruit mixture.

Cover and bake at 425° for 15 minutes or until a toothpick inserted into a dumpling comes out clean (do not lift the cover while baking).

In a small saucepan, bring brown sugar and water to a boil; cook until sugar is dissolved. Spoon over dumplings; bake, uncovered, 5 minutes longer. Serve with cream if desired. **Yield:** 6 servings.

Fabulous Fudge Cheesecake

Scott Fox, Fergus Falls, Minnesota

This fudgy cheesecake is particularly popular with my two children. It's also a favorite with guests at a cheesecake party my wife and I host every year.

  1   cup crushed vanilla wafers (about 30 wafers)
1/2   cup confectioners' sugar
1/3   cup baking cocoa
1/3   cup butter, melted
FILLING:
  3   packages (8 ounces *each*) cream cheese, softened
  1   can (14 ounces) sweetened condensed milk
  2   teaspoons vanilla extract
  2   cups (12 ounces) semisweet chocolate chips
  4   eggs

In a small bowl, combine the wafer crumbs, sugar and cocoa; stir in butter. Press onto the bottom of a greased 9-in. springform pan; set aside. In a large bowl, beat the cream cheese, milk and vanilla until smooth. Add chocolate. Add eggs; beat on low speed just until combined. Pour over crust. Place pan on a baking sheet.

Bake at 325° for 40-45 minutes or until center is almost set. Cool on a wire rack for 10 minutes. Carefully run a knife around edge of the pan to loosen; cool 1 hour longer. Refrigerate overnight. Remove sides of pan. Store in the refrigerator. **Yield:** 10-12 servings.

Check the Seal on a Springform Pan For best results, a springform pan should not be warped and should seal tightly. If in doubt about the tightness of the seal, securely wrap heavy-duty foil around the outside of the pan to prevent the butter in the crust from leaking out.

Almond Fruit Squares

Iola Egle, Bella Vista, Arkansas

These sweet squares are a breeze to fix, thanks to the refrigerated crescent roll dough that serves as the crust. With a layer of cream cheese, berries, grapes and kiwifruit, they can be served for breakfast or even as a refreshing summer dessert.

- 2 tubes (8 ounces *each*) refrigerated crescent rolls
- 3 tablespoons sugar, *divided*
- 1 package (8 ounces) cream cheese, softened
- 1/3 cup almond paste
- 1/2 teaspoon almond extract
- 2 cups halved fresh strawberries
- 1 can (11 ounces) mandarin oranges, drained
- 1 cup fresh raspberries
- 1 cup halved green grapes
- 2 kiwifruit, peeled, quartered and sliced
- 1/2 cup apricot preserves, warmed
- 1/2 cup slivered almonds, toasted

Unroll crescent dough and separate into eight rectangles. Place in an ungreased 15-in. x 10-in. x 1-in. baking pan. Press onto bottom and up sides; seal seams and perforations. Sprinkle with 1 tablespoon sugar.

Bake at 375° for 14-16 minutes or until golden brown. Cool. In a large bowl, beat the cream cheese, almond paste, extract and remaining sugar until smooth. Spread over crust. Top with fruit. Brush with preserves; sprinkle with almonds. **Yield:** 16 servings.

Baking Classics | Desserts

Chocolate Macadamia Cheesecake

Bob Weaver, University Place, Washington

When one of my co-workers turned 50, I created this recipe for her birthday. There wasn't a crumb left on the platter when I left for that day!

1-1/4   cups chocolate wafer crumbs (about 25 wafers)
1/4   cup ground macadamia nuts
2   tablespoons sugar
3   tablespoons butter, melted
1/8   teaspoon almond extract
FILLING:
8   squares (1 ounce *each*) white baking chocolate
4   packages (8 ounces *each*) cream cheese, softened
3/4   cup sugar
3   tablespoons all-purpose flour
1   teaspoon vanilla extract
5   eggs
1/3   cup milk chocolate chips
TOPPING:
8   squares (1 ounce *each*) semisweet chocolate
7   tablespoons heavy whipping cream
White chocolate shavings and chopped macadamia nuts

In a bowl, combine the wafer crumbs, nuts and sugar; stir in butter and almond extract. Press onto the bottom of a greased 10-in. springform pan. Place pan on a baking sheet. Bake at 350° for 10 minutes. Cool on a wire rack. Reduce heat to 325°.

In a saucepan over low heat, melt white chocolate, stirring frequently until smooth. Cool. In a large bowl, beat the cream cheese, sugar, flour and vanilla until well blended. Add eggs; beat on low speed just until combined.

Remove 1 cup and set aside. Stir melted white chocolate into remaining cream cheese mixture; beat just until combined. Pour over crust.

In a microwave, melt milk chocolate chips; stir until smooth. Cool slightly. Stir in reserved cream cheese mixture; drop by spoonfuls over filling. Cut through filling with a knife to swirl chocolate mixture.

Return pan to baking sheet. Bake at 325° for 55-60 minutes or until center is almost set. Cool on a wire rack for 10 minutes. Carefully run a knife around edge of pan to loosen. Cool 1 hour longer.

In a saucepan over low heat, melt semisweet chocolate with cream; stir until smooth. Cool slightly. Spread over cheesecake. Cool on a wire rack for 10 minutes. Refrigerate for 4 hours or overnight.

Remove sides of the pan. Store in the refrigerator. Garnish with the chocolate shavings and macadamia nuts. **Yield:** 12 servings.

Applescotch Crisp

Elaine Nicholl, Nottingham, Pennsylvania

Just as soon as the first crop of apples is off the trees, I fix this crisp. Thanks to the butterscotch pudding, it's moist and sweet. It's popular at potlucks, and it's a nice snack. In fact, I'm reluctant to make it in the evening—I'm afraid someone will sneak down to the refrigerator at midnight and claim it!

4   cups sliced peeled tart apples
1/2   cup packed brown sugar
1   tablespoon plus 2/3 cup all-purpose flour, *divided*
1/2   cup water
1/4   cup milk
1/2   cup quick-cooking oats
1   package (3-1/2 ounces) cook-and-serve butterscotch pudding mix
1/4   cup sugar
1   teaspoon ground cinnamon
1/2   teaspoon salt
1/2   cup butter, cubed
Ice cream, optional

Place the apples in an ungreased 11-in. x 7-in. x 2-in. baking dish. In a large bowl, whisk the brown sugar, 1 tablespoon flour, water and milk. Pour over apples.

In another bowl, combine the oats, pudding mix, sugar, cinnamon, salt and the remaining flour. Cut in butter until mixture resembles coarse crumbs. Sprinkle over apples.

Bake at 350° for 45-50 minutes or until topping is golden brown and fruit is tender. Serve with ice cream if desired. **Yield:** 8 servings.

Peanut Butter Cup Cheesecake

Dawn Lowenstein, Hatboro, Pennsylvania

I said I'd bring dessert to a holiday party and tried this recipe. I'm sure you'll agree it tastes as luscious as it looks!

1-1/4 cups graham cracker crumbs
1/4 cup crushed cream-filled chocolate sandwich cookies
1/4 cup sugar
6 tablespoons butter, melted
3/4 cup creamy peanut butter

FILLING:
3 packages (8 ounces *each*) cream cheese, softened
1 cup sugar
1 cup (8 ounces) sour cream
3 eggs, lightly beaten
1-1/2 teaspoons vanilla extract
1 cup hot fudge ice cream topping, *divided*
6 peanut butter cups, cut into small wedges

In a bowl, combine cracker crumbs, cookie crumbs, sugar and butter. Press onto the bottom and 1 in. up the sides of a greased 9-in. springform pan. Place on a baking sheet.

Bake at 350° for 7-9 minutes or until set. Cool on a wire rack. In a microwave-safe bowl, heat peanut butter on high for 30 seconds or until softened. Spread over crust to within 1 in. of edges.

In a large bowl, beat the cream cheese, sugar and sour cream until smooth. Add eggs; beat on low speed just until combined. Stir in vanilla. Pour 1 cup into a bowl; set aside. Pour remaining filling over peanut butter layer.

In a microwave-safe bowl, heat 1/4 cup fudge topping on high for 30 seconds or until thin; fold into reserved cream cheese mixture. Carefully pour over filling; cut through with a knife to swirl.

Return pan to baking sheet. Bake at 350° for 55-65 minutes or until center is almost set. Cool on a wire rack for 10 minutes. Carefully run a knife around edge of pan to loosen; cool 1 hour longer.

Microwave remaining fudge topping for 30 seconds or until warmed; spread over cheesecake. Garnish with peanut butter cups. Refrigerate overnight. Remove sides of pan. Store in the refrigerator. **Yield:** 12-14 servings.

Editor's Note: Reduced-fat or generic brands of peanut butter are not recommended for this recipe.

Two-Stage Cooling for Cheesecakes It's important to cool a cheesecake for 10 minutes and then carefully run a metal spatula or knife between the cheesecake and pan to loosen it from the pan side. If it's not loosened at this point, part of the cheesecake may stick to the pan side, causing the cheesecake to crack as it cools further.

Eclair Torte

Kathy Shepard, Shepherd, Michigan

The pastry part of this torte bakes into one big crust, which eliminates filling individual eclairs. The filling is a snap to blend together using convenient instant pudding and cream cheese. My friends and family really enjoy this fun dessert.

1 cup water
1/2 cup butter
1/4 teaspoon salt
1 cup all-purpose flour
4 eggs
1 package (8 ounces) cream cheese, softened
3 cups cold milk
2 packages (3.4 ounces *each*) instant vanilla pudding mix
1 carton (12 ounces) frozen whipped topping, thawed
2 to 3 tablespoons chocolate syrup

In a small saucepan, bring the water, butter and salt to a boil over medium heat. Add flour all at once and stir until a smooth ball forms. Remove from the heat; let stand for 5 minutes. Add eggs, one at a time, beating well after each addition. Continue beating until mixture is smooth and shiny.

Spread into a greased 13-in. x 9-in. x 2-in. baking pan. Bake at 400° for 30-35 minutes or until puffed and golden brown. Cool completely on a wire rack. If desired, remove puff from pan and place on a serving platter.

In a large bowl, beat cream cheese until light. Add milk and pudding mix; beat until smooth. Spread over puff; refrigerate for 20 minutes. Spread with whipped topping; refrigerate. Drizzle with chocolate syrup just before serving. Store in the refrigerator. **Yield:** 12 servings.

Cheesecake Praline Squares

Barbara McCalley, Allison Park, Pennsylvania

A smooth cheesecake layer, a nutty crust and a praline-like topping make this dessert. I fix these squares often for friends and when my big family gets together.

2-1/2 cups all-purpose flour
1 cup butter, melted
2/3 cup finely chopped pecans
2 tablespoons confectioners' sugar
FILLING:
3 packages (8 ounces *each*) cream cheese, softened
2/3 cup sugar
1 can (14 ounces) sweetened condensed milk
2 teaspoons vanilla extract
1/2 teaspoon grated lemon peel
4 eggs, lightly beaten
TOPPING:
1 cup packed brown sugar
1 cup heavy whipping cream
1 cup chopped pecans
1-1/2 teaspoons vanilla extract

In a large bowl, combine the flour, butter, pecans and confectioners' sugar. Press into an ungreased 13-in. x 9-in. x 2-in. baking dish. Bake at 350° for 20-24 minutes or until lightly browned. Cool on a wire rack.

In a large bowl, beat cream cheese and sugar until smooth. Add the milk, vanilla and lemon peel. Add eggs; beat on low speed just until combined. Pour over crust.

Bake at 350° for 35-40 minutes or until edges are lightly browned. Cool on a wire rack.

In a saucepan, combine brown sugar and cream. Cook and stir over medium heat until mixture comes to a boil. Reduce heat; simmer, uncovered, for 10 minutes. Remove from the heat; stir in pecans and vanilla. Pour over cheesecake. Refrigerate for 4 hours or overnight. Cut into squares. **Yield:** 15 servings.

Spice it Up If you would like the Pecan Pumpkin Dessert to taste more like a pumpkin pie, add some spices to the pumpkin layer. Try adding 1 teaspoon ground cinnamon, 3/4 teaspoon ground ginger and 1/4 teaspoon ground cloves.

Pecan Pumpkin Dessert

Sue Williams, Mt. Holly, North Carolina

I always bake this recipe for Thanksgiving. It was given to me by a friend, and I've shared it with many others.

2 cans (15 ounces *each*) solid-pack pumpkin
1 can (12 ounces) evaporated milk
1 cup sugar
3 eggs
1 teaspoon vanilla extract
1 package (18-1/4 ounces) yellow cake mix
1 cup butter, melted
1-1/2 cups chopped pecans
FROSTING:
1 package (8 ounces) cream cheese, softened
1-1/2 cups confectioners' sugar
1 teaspoon vanilla extract
1 carton (12 ounces) frozen whipped topping, thawed

Line a 13-in. x 9-in. x 2-in. baking pan with waxed paper and coat the paper with cooking spray; set aside.

In a large bowl, combine the pumpkin, milk and sugar. Beat in eggs and vanilla. Pour into prepared pan. Sprinkle with cake mix and drizzle with butter. Sprinkle with pecans.

Bake at 350° for 1 hour or until golden brown. Cool completely in pan on a wire rack. Invert onto a large serving platter; carefully remove waxed paper.

In a large bowl, beat the cream cheese, confectioners' sugar and vanilla until smooth. Fold in whipped topping. Frost dessert. Store in the refrigerator. **Yield:** 16 servings.

Raisin-Apple Bread Pudding

Cora Uden, Juniata, Nebraska

The original recipe for this dessert came from a farming magazine. I changed several ingredients in it to cut down on calories, but it's still homey and satisfying. In fact, we like this version as well as the original.

- 1 medium tart apple, peeled, cored and cut into thin rings
- 1 tablespoon lemon juice
- 1 tablespoon butter
- 1-1/2 teaspoons plus 1/2 cup sugar, *divided*
- 1/8 teaspoon ground cinnamon
- 1/8 teaspoon ground nutmeg
- 3 slices day-old raisin bread, cubed
- 2 tablespoons raisins
- 2 eggs
- 1 cup milk

Dash salt
- 1/4 teaspoon vanilla extract
- 1/4 teaspoon lemon extract *or* additional vanilla extract

Half-and-half cream, optional

In a small bowl, toss apple rings with lemon juice. In a small skillet, saute apple in butter for 3 minutes or just until tender. Remove from the heat. Combine 1-1/2 teaspoons sugar, cinnamon and nutmeg; sprinkle over apple. Toss to coat evenly; set aside.

Place bread cubes in a greased 8-in. x 4-in. x 2-in. loaf pan. Top with raisins and apple mixture. In a bowl, whisk the eggs and remaining sugar. In a small saucepan, combine milk and salt; cook just until the mixture begins to bubble around sides of pan. Gradually whisk into egg mixture. Stir in extracts. Pour over apple and raisins.

Place dish in an ungreased 11-in. x 7-in. x 2-in. baking dish; add 1 in. of hot water to larger pan. Bake, uncovered, at 350° for 40-50 minutes or until a knife inserted near the center comes out clean. Serve warm with cream if desired. **Yield:** 2-3 servings.

Chocolate Eclairs

Jessica Campbell, Viola, Wisconsin

With creamy filling and fudgy frosting, these eclairs add a festive touch to any meal.

- 1 cup water
- 1/2 cup butter, cubed
- 1/4 teaspoon salt
- 1 cup all-purpose flour
- 4 eggs

FILLING:
- 2-1/2 cups cold milk
- 1 package (5.1 ounces) instant vanilla pudding mix
- 1 cup heavy whipping cream
- 1/4 cup confectioners' sugar
- 1 teaspoon vanilla extract

FROSTING:
- 2 squares (1 ounce *each*) semisweet chocolate
- 2 tablespoons butter
- 1-1/4 cups confectioners' sugar
- 2 to 3 tablespoons hot water

In a large saucepan, bring water, butter and salt to a boil. Add flour all at once and stir until a smooth ball forms. Remove from the heat; let stand for 5 minutes. Add eggs, one at a time, beating well after each addition. Continue beating until mixture is smooth and shiny.

Using a tablespoon or a pastry tube with a No. 10 or large tip, form dough into 4-in. x 1-1/2-in. strips on a greased baking sheet. Bake at 400° for 35-40 minutes or until puffed and golden. Remove to a wire rack. Immediately split eclairs open; remove tops and set aside. Discard soft dough from inside. Cool eclairs.

In a large bowl, whisk milk and pudding mix for 2 minutes. In another bowl, whip cream until soft peaks form. Beat in sugar and vanilla; fold into pudding. Split eclair; remove soft dough from inside. Fill eclairs (chill any remaining filling for another use).

For frosting, in a microwave, melt chocolate and butter; stir until smooth. Stir in sugar and enough hot water to achieve a smooth consistency. Cool slightly. Frost eclairs. Store in refrigerator. **Yield:** 9 servings.

Baking Eclairs and Cream Puffs Both eclairs and cream puffs use the same dough. The dough puffs up and expands during baking. So for best results, don't overcrowd the baking sheet. Leave about 3 inches of space around each. They are done when they're golden brown and have a dry, crisp exterior.

Blueberry Swirl Cheesecake

Cathy Medley, Clyde, Ohio

This is my all-time favorite blueberry recipe, which I often make for family get-togethers.

1-1/2 cups fresh blueberries
1/4 cup sugar
1 tablespoon lemon juice
2 teaspoons cornstarch
1 tablespoon cold water

CRUST:
1 cup graham cracker crumbs (about 16 squares)
2 tablespoons sugar
2 tablespoons butter, melted

FILLING:
3 packages (8 ounces *each*) cream cheese, softened
1 cup sugar
2 tablespoons all-purpose flour
4 eggs, beaten
1 cup (8 ounces) sour cream
2 teaspoons vanilla extract

In a small saucepan, combine the blueberries, sugar and lemon juice. Cook and stir over medium heat for 5 minutes or until the berries are softened. Combine cornstarch and water until smooth; stir into the blueberry mixture. Bring to a boil; cook and stir for 2 minutes or until thickened. Remove from the heat; cool to room temperature. Transfer to a blender; cover and process until smooth. Set aside.

For crust, in a small bowl, combine the crumbs and sugar; stir in the butter. Press onto the bottom of a greased 9-in. springform pan. Place pan on a baking sheet. Bake at 350° for 10 minutes. Cool on a wire rack.

In a large bowl, beat the cream cheese, sugar and flour until smooth. Add eggs; beat on low speed just until combined. Stir in sour cream and vanilla. Pour into crust. Drizzle with blueberry mixture; cut through batter with a knife to swirl. Place pan on a baking sheet.

Bake at 350° for 1 hour or until center is almost set. Cool on a wire rack for 10 minutes. Carefully run a knife around the edge of pan to loosen; cool 1 hour longer. Refrigerate overnight. Remove sides of pan. Store in the refrigerator. **Yield:** 12 servings.

White Chocolate Bread Pudding

Wendy Sleicher, Quakertown, Pennsylvania

This delectable dessert features vanilla chips, apples and a sweet caramel sauce. It's a hit with our boys.

2 cups milk
2 cups heavy whipping cream
1 cup sugar
1 cup vanilla *or* white chips
8 eggs
1 tablespoon vanilla extract
1 loaf (1 pound) egg bread, crust removed, cut into 1-inch cubes
2 medium tart apples, peeled and chopped

CARAMEL SAUCE:
1-1/4 cups sugar
1/2 cup water
1/4 cup light corn syrup
1 tablespoon lemon juice
1-1/4 cups heavy whipping cream
1 cup chopped pecans, toasted
2 teaspoons vanilla extract

In a large saucepan, combine the milk, cream and sugar. Cook over medium heat until mixture comes to a boil. Remove from the heat; stir in chips until melted. In a large bowl, whisk eggs and vanilla. Gradually whisk in cream mixture. Add bread. Let stand for 15 minutes, stirring occasionally.

Stir in the apples. Pour into a greased 13-in. x 9-in. x 2-in. baking dish. Cover and bake at 350° for 45 minutes. Uncover; bake 30 minutes longer or until a knife comes out clean.

Meanwhile, for sauce, in a large saucepan combine the sugar, water, corn syrup and lemon juice. Cook and stir over medium heat until sugar is dissolved. Bring to a boil over medium-high heat; boil, without stirring, until a candy thermometer reads 295° and mixture turns a deep amber color.

Remove from the heat; stir in cream. Cook and stir over low heat until mixture is smooth. Bring to a boil over medium heat; cook and stir for 4 minutes. Stir in nuts and vanilla. Stir before serving. Serve warm with warm bread pudding. **Yield:** 12-15 servings.

Editor's Note: We recommend that you test your candy thermometer before each use by bringing water to a boil; the thermometer should read 212°. Adjust your recipe temperature up or down based on your test.

Giant Ice Cream Sandwich

Charlene Turnbull, Wainwright, Alberta

I was an inexperienced cook when I married. A good friend, who was a cooking inspiration to me, shared many of her recipes, including this scrumptious dessert. It's handy to pull out of the freezer for unexpected guests.

- 2 packages fudge brownie mix (8-inch square pan size)
- 1 cup (6 ounces) semisweet chocolate chips
- 4 cups vanilla ice cream, softened
- 1/2 cup English toffee bits *or* almond brickle chips

CHOCOLATE SAUCE:
- 1/3 cup evaporated milk
- 1/4 cup butter
- 1/3 cup semisweet chocolate chips
- 2 cups confectioners' sugar
- 1/2 teaspoon vanilla extract

Prepare the brownie mixes according to package directions, adding chocolate chips to batter. Pour into two greased 9-in. springform pans or two 9-in. round baking pans.

Bake at 350° for 25-30 minutes or until a toothpick inserted near the center comes out clean. Cool for 10 minutes before removing from pans to wire racks to cool completely. Freeze for 2 hours or until easy to handle.

Spoon ice cream on top of one brownie layer; top with toffee bits and second brownie layer. Wrap in plastic wrap; freeze until set. May be frozen for up to 2 months. Remove from freezer 10-15 minutes before serving.

For chocolate sauce, in a small saucepan, combine the milk, butter and chocolate chips. Cook and stir until chips are melted; stir until smooth. Stir in confectioners' sugar and vanilla. Cut the ice cream sandwich into wedges; serve with chocolate sauce. **Yield:** 10-12 servings.

Almond Rhubarb Cobbler

Pat Habiger, Spearville, Kansas

In spring, I frequently make this tangy biscuit-topped treat.

- 1 cup sugar, *divided*
- 1/2 cup water
- 6 cups chopped fresh *or* frozen rhubarb
- 2 tablespoons all-purpose flour
- 2 tablespoons butter
- 1/2 cup slivered almonds, toasted

TOPPING:
- 1 cup all-purpose flour
- 2 tablespoons sugar
- 1-1/2 teaspoons baking powder
- 1/4 teaspoon salt
- 1/4 cup cold butter
- 1 egg
- 1/4 cup milk

In a large saucepan, bring 1/2 cup sugar and water to a boil. Add the rhubarb. Reduce heat; cover and simmer until tender, about 5 minutes. Combine flour and remaining sugar; stir into rhubarb mixture. Return to a boil; cook and stir for 2 minutes or until thickened and bubbly. Stir in butter and almonds. Reduce heat to low; cook until butter is melted, stirring occasionally.

In a large bowl, combine the flour, sugar, baking powder and salt; cut in butter until crumbly. Whisk egg and milk; stir into crumb mixture just until moistened. Pour hot rhubarb mixture into a 2-qt. shallow baking dish. Drop topping into six mounds over the rhubarb mixture.

Bake, uncovered, at 400° for 20-25 minutes or until golden brown. Serve warm. **Yield:** 6 servings.

Almond Puff Pastries

Barbara Harrison, Monte Sereno, California

My husband comes from a family of almond growers, so I use almonds often in my baking. These puff pastries have a crisp topping and creamy filling.

- 1 package (17.3 ounces) frozen puff pastry, thawed
- 1 egg, *separated*
- 1 tablespoon water
- 1 cup sliced almonds
- 1 cup sugar
- 2 cups heavy whipping cream, whipped

Confectioners' sugar

Unfold pastry sheets onto a lightly floured surface. Cut each sheet into nine 3-in. squares. Place 1 in. apart on greased baking sheets; set aside. In a small bowl, beat egg yolk and water; brush over pastry squares. In another bowl, beat egg white; add almonds and sugar. Spread over each square.

Bake at 375° for 20-25 minutes or until well puffed and browned. Cool completely on wire racks.

Split pastries in half horizontally. Fill with whipped cream; replace tops. Sprinkle with confectioners' sugar. Serve immediately. **Yield:** 18 servings.

Berry Whirligig

Pearl Stanford, Medford, Oregon

I was a crew cook at a lake resort for many years, and the folks ate up this dessert to the very last berry!

- 1/2 cup sugar
- 2 tablespoons cornstarch
- 1/2 teaspoon salt
- 1/4 teaspoon ground cinnamon
- 1 cup water
- 3 cups fresh *or* frozen blackberries *or* a mixture of berries

WHIRLIGIGS:

- 1 cup all-purpose flour
- 2 teaspoons baking powder
- 1/2 teaspoon salt
- 2 tablespoons shortening
- 1 egg, lightly beaten
- 2 tablespoons milk
- 1/4 cup butter, softened
- 1/2 cup sugar
- 1 teaspoon grated lemon peel
- 1/4 teaspoon ground cinnamon

In a large saucepan, combine the sugar, cornstarch, salt and cinnamon. Stir in water until smooth. Cook until mixture boils and thickens. Stir in berries; cook over low heat for 5 minutes.

Pour into a greased 8-in. square baking dish; set aside. In a large bowl, combine the flour, baking powder and salt. Cut in shortening until coarse crumbs form.

In a small bowl, mix egg and milk. Add to flour mixture; stir until mixture forms a soft ball. Knead several minutes. Roll into a 12-in. x 8-in. rectangle. Spread with butter. Combine the sugar, peel and cinnamon; sprinkle over the dough.

Starting at a long end, roll up; seal edges. Cut into 9 slices. Place slices over berry mixture. Bake at 400° for 22-25 minutes or until golden brown. **Yield:** 9 servings.

Testing Bread Puddings for Doneness Always test bread puddings to make sure they are thoroughly cooked. The best way to test them for doneness is to insert a stainless steel flatware knife about an inch from the center. When you pull it out, the blade should be clean. If it is wet, continue baking the dessert.

Warm Banana Pudding

Dawn Harvey, Danville, Pennsylvania

I've lighted up my mother's recipe for banana pudding. With its meringue-like top and soft vanilla wafer layers, it's a Southern dessert at its finest.

Sugar substitute equivalent to 1/2 cup sugar
- 1/2 cup sugar, *divided*
- 3 tablespoons cornstarch
- 2 cups fat-free milk
- 2 eggs, *separated*
- 2 tablespoons butter
- 1 teaspoon vanilla extract
- 2 large ripe bananas, sliced
- 1 teaspoon lemon juice
- 12 reduced-fat vanilla wafers

In a large saucepan, combine the sugar substitute, 1/4 cup sugar and cornstarch. Gradually stir in milk until smooth. Bring to a boil, stirring constantly. Cook and stir until thickened. Remove from the heat. Stir a small amount of hot filling into egg yolks; return all to the pan, stirring constantly. Bring to a gentle boil; cook and stir for 2 minutes. Remove from the heat; stir in butter and vanilla.

Pour half of the pudding into an ungreased 1-qt. baking dish. Toss bananas with lemon juice; layer over pudding. Arrange vanilla wafers in a single layer over bananas. Pour remaining pudding over wafers.

In a large bowl, beat egg whites on medium speed until soft peaks form. Beat in remaining sugar, 1 tablespoon at a time, on high until stiff, glossy peaks form and sugar is dissolved. Spread the meringue evenly over pudding. Bake, uncovered, at 350° for 12-15 minutes or until golden brown. Store in the refrigerator. **Yield:** 6 servings.

Editor's Note: This recipe was tested with Splenda No Calorie Sweetener.

Strawberry-Lemon Cream Puffs

Janice Mitchell, Aurora, Colorado

A tangy lemon filling chock-full of berry slices is tucked inside these tender puffs. My husband is impressed with their great taste and appearance. I like how easy the puffs are to make.

- 1 cup water
- 1/4 cup butter, cubed
- 1 cup all-purpose flour
- 4 eggs

FILLING:
- 1/4 cup sugar
- 1-1/2 tablespoons cornstarch
- 1 can (5 ounces) evaporated milk
- 1 cup (8 ounces) vanilla yogurt
- 1-1/2 teaspoons lemon extract
- 1/4 teaspoon butter flavoring
- 1 cup sliced fresh strawberries
- 1/2 teaspoon confectioners' sugar

In a large saucepan, bring water and butter to a boil. Add flour all at once and stir until a smooth ball forms. Remove from the heat; let stand for 5 minutes. Add eggs, one at a time, beating well after each addition. Continue beating until mixture is smooth and shiny.

Drop by 1/4 cupfuls 3 in. apart onto greased baking sheets. Bake at 400° for 30 minutes or until golden brown. Remove to wire racks. Immediately split puffs open and remove tops; discard soft dough from inside. Cool puffs.

For filling, combine sugar and cornstarch in a saucepan. Stir in milk and yogurt until smooth. Bring to a boil; cook and stir for 2 minutes or until thickened. Remove from the heat. Stir in lemon extract and butter flavoring. Cool. Fold in strawberries. Chill.

Fill the cream puffs just before serving. Dust with confectioners' sugar. Store in the refrigerator. **Yield:** 10 servings.

Grandma Buelah's Apple Dumplings

Jenny Hughson, Mitchell, Nebraska

My grandma settled in Sioux County, Nebraska in the early 1900's. She had a reputation for being a talented musician, avid card player and a marvelous cook! I always make a double batch of her dumplings for my husband and our children.

Pastry for double-crust pie
- 6 small cooking apples, peeled and cored
- 1/3 cup sugar
- 2 tablespoons half-and-half cream
- 3/4 cup maple *or* maple-flavored syrup, warmed

On a floured surface, roll out pastry to an 18-in. x 12-in. rectangle. Cut into six 6-in. squares. Place an apple on each square. Combine sugar and cream and spoon into apple

center. Moisten edges of pastry; fold up the corners to center and pinch to seal.

Place on an ungreased 13-in. x 9-in. x 2-in. baking pan. Bake at 450° for 15 minutes. Reduce heat to 350°; bake 30 minutes longer or until golden brown, basting twice with syrup. Serve warm. **Yield:** 6 servings.

Brownie Pizza

Loretta Wohlenhaus, Cumberland, Iowa

Kids of all ages will find this a delightfully different way to serve brownies. Use whatever toppings you like to suit your family's tastes.

- 3/4 cup butter, softened
- 1 cup sugar
- 1 egg
- 1 teaspoon vanilla extract
- 1-1/2 cups all-purpose flour
- 1/4 cup baking cocoa
- 1/2 teaspoon baking powder
- 1/4 teaspoon salt
- 3/4 cup milk chocolate M&M's, *divided*
- 1/2 cup chopped walnuts, *divided*
- 1/4 cup miniature marshmallows
- 1/4 cup flaked coconut

In a large bowl, cream butter and sugar until light and fluffy. Beat in egg and vanilla. Combine the flour, cocoa, baking powder and salt; gradually add to creamed mixture until well blended. Stir in 1/2 cup M&M's and 1/4 cup walnuts.

Spread onto a greased 14-in. pizza pan to within 1/2 in. of edges. Sprinkle with remaining M&M's and walnuts. Top with marshmallows and coconut. Bake at 350° for 15-20 minutes or until a toothpick inserted near the center comes out clean. Cool on a wire rack. Cut into wedges. **Yield:** 10-12 servings.

Key Lime Cheesecake

Darlene Kohler, Flower Mound, Texas

I modified this old family recipe to use healthier ingredients. The texture is so smooth and light. It is a favorite treat that is enjoyed by all.

- 3/4 cup reduced-fat graham crackers crumbs (about 4 whole crackers)
- Sugar substitute equivalent to 2 tablespoons sugar
- 2 tablespoons butter, melted
- FILLING:
- 2 packages (8 ounces *each*) reduced-fat cream cheese, cubed
- 1 package (8 ounces) fat-free cream cheese, cubed
- Sugar substitute equivalent to 2/3 cup sugar
- 1/3 cup sugar
- 3 tablespoons all-purpose flour
- 3 eggs, lightly beaten
- 1 cup (8 ounces) reduced-fat sour cream
- 1/3 cup key lime *or* lime juice
- 2 teaspoons grated lime peel
- 2 teaspoons vanilla extract
- 2 drops green food coloring, optional

Place a greased 9-in. springform pan on a double thickness of heavy-duty foil (about 18 in. square). Securely wrap foil around pan.

In a large bowl, combine graham cracker crumbs and sugar substitute; stir in butter. Press onto the bottom of prepared pan. Place pan on a baking sheet. Bake at 350° for 10 minutes. Cool on a wire rack.

In a large bowl, beat cream cheese until smooth. Combine the sugar substitute, sugar and flour; gradually beat into cream cheese. Add eggs; beat on low speed just until combined. Stir in the sour cream, lime juice, peel, vanilla and food coloring if desired.

Pour into crust. Place springform pan in a large baking pan; add 1 in. of hot water to larger pan. Bake at 350° for

40-45 minutes or until center is just set and top appears dull. Remove springform pan from water bath. Cool on a wire rack for 10 minutes. Remove foil from pan. Carefully run a knife around edge of pan to loosen; cool for 1 hour.

Chill overnight. Remove sides of pan. Store in the refrigerator. **Yield:** 14 servings.

Editor's Note: This recipe was tested with Splenda No Calorie Sweetener.

Old-Fashioned Rice Custard

Shirley Leister, West Chester, Pennsylvania

I don't remember where or how I found this rice custard recipe. When I took it to a family reunion many years ago, a great-uncle was sure I'd used my great-grandmother's recipe! I like to have it warm for dinner. Then, the next morning, I enjoy the cold leftovers for my breakfast.

- 1/2 cup uncooked long-grain rice
- 4 cups milk, *divided*
- 1/4 cup butter, cubed
- 3/4 cup sugar
- 3 eggs
- 1 teaspoon vanilla extract
- 1/4 teaspoon salt
- 1/2 teaspoon ground nutmeg

In a large saucepan, bring rice and 2 cups milk to a boil. Reduce heat; cover and simmer for 15-18 minutes or until liquid is absorbed and rice is tender. Stir in the butter. Cool slightly.

In a large bowl, beat the sugar, eggs, vanilla, salt and remaining milk; stir into the rice mixture.

Pour into a lightly greased 2-qt. casserole; sprinkle with nutmeg. Bake at 350° for 50 minutes or until knife inserted near the center comes out clean. **Yield:** 6-8 servings.

Cinnamon Cream Cheese Squares

Gay Snyder, Deerfield, Ohio

I like to make these cream cheese squares for a quick breakfast treat or simple dessert. It's so easy, even my daughter helps out.

- 2 tubes (8 ounces *each*) refrigerated crescent rolls
- 2 packages (8 ounces *each*) cream cheese, softened
- 1-1/2 cups sugar, *divided*
- 1 teaspoon vanilla extract
- 1/4 cup butter, melted
- 1 teaspoon ground cinnamon

Unroll one tube of dough and place in a lightly greased 13-in. x 9-in. x 2-in. baking pan. Seal seams and perforations; set aside. In a large bowl, beat the cream cheese, 1 cup of sugar and vanilla until smooth. Spread over dough.

Unroll remaining tube of dough and place over cream cheese mixture, stretching to fit. Brush butter evenly over top; sprinkle with cinnamon and remaining sugar. Bake at 350° for 30 minutes or until golden brown. Cool; cut into squares. **Yield:** about 3 dozen.

Blueberry Cream Dessert

Mildred Sherrer, Fort Worth, Texas

This layered treat consists of a no-fuss crust that's spread with sweetened cream cheese. After baking, it's topped with convenient pie filling and whipped topping.

- 1-1/2 cups graham cracker crumbs
- 3/4 cup sugar, *divided*
- 1/2 cup butter, melted
- 1 package (8 ounces) cream cheese, softened
- 2 eggs
- 1 teaspoon vanilla extract
- 1/2 teaspoon ground cinnamon
- 1 can (21 ounces) blueberry pie filling
- 1 carton (8 ounces) frozen whipped topping, thawed

In a large bowl, combine the cracker crumbs, 1/4 cup sugar and butter. Press into a greased 13-in. x 9-in. x 2-in. baking dish. In another bowl, beat cream cheese and remaining sugar until smooth; stir in eggs and vanilla. Pour over crust.

Bake at 350° for 15-20 minutes or until set. Sprinkle with cinnamon. Cool on a wire rack. Spread with pie filling and whipped topping. Chill until serving. Store in the refrigerator. **Yield:** 12-16 servings.

Chocolate Cherry Heart

Jackie Hannahs, Fountain, Michigan

My family enjoys this so much that I make it throughout the year by simply using the pie pastry circles. Packaged products make it a snap to prepare.

- 1 package (15 ounces) refrigerated pie pastry
- 2 teaspoons all-purpose flour
- 1 egg white, lightly beaten
- 1/4 cup ground almonds
- 2 tablespoons sugar
- 1 package (8 ounces) cream cheese, softened
- 1 cup confectioners' sugar
- 1/4 to 1/2 teaspoon almond extract
- 1/2 cup heavy whipping cream
- 1 jar (16 ounces) hot fudge ice cream topping
- 2 cans (21 ounces *each*) cherry pie filling

Let pastry stand at room temperature for 15-20 minutes. Unfold pastry and place each circle on an ungreased baking sheet. Sprinkle each with 1 teaspoon flour; turn over. Using a 9-in. paper heart pattern, cut out a heart from each circle. Prick pastries all over with a fork.

Brush with egg white. Combine almonds and sugar; sprinkle over pastries. Bake at 450° for 7-9 minutes or until lightly browned. Carefully slide crusts onto wire racks to cool completely.

In a large bowl, combine the cream cheese, confectioners' sugar and almond extract; beat until smooth. Add cream; beat until thickened.

Place one crust on a serving plate; spread with half of the fudge topping. Carefully spread with half of the cream cheese mixture; top with half of the cherry pie filling. Top with remaining crust, fudge topping and cream cheese mixture. Spoon the remaining cherry pie filling to within 1 in. of edges. Chill until set. Store in the refrigerator. **Yield:** 6-8 servings.

Apple Crisp Pizza

Nancy Preussner, Delhi, Iowa

While visiting a Wisconsin apple orchard bakery, I tried this tempting treat. At home, I put together this recipe. My family thinks it tastes better than the one used by the bakery. As it bakes, the enticing aroma fills my kitchen, and friends and family linger waiting for a sample.

Pastry for a single-crust pie
- 2/3 cup sugar
- 3 tablespoons all-purpose flour
- 1 teaspoon ground cinnamon
- 4 medium baking apples, peeled and cut into 1/2-inch slices

TOPPING:
- 1/2 cup all-purpose flour
- 1/3 cup packed brown sugar
- 1/3 cup old-fashioned oats
- 1 teaspoon ground cinnamon
- 1/4 cup butter, softened
- 1/4 to 1/2 cup caramel ice cream topping *or* caramel apple dip

Vanilla ice cream, optional

Roll out pastry to fit a 12-in. pizza pan; fold under or flute the edges. Combine sugar, flour and cinnamon in a bowl. Add apples and toss. Arrange the apples in a single layer in a circular pattern to completely cover pastry. For topping, combine the flour, brown sugar, oats, cinnamon and butter; sprinkle over apples.

Bake at 350° for 35-40 minutes or until apples are tender. Remove from the oven and immediately drizzle with caramel topping or dip. Serve warm with ice cream if desired. **Yield:** 12 servings.

Blueberry Cheese Danish

Taste of Home Test Kitchen

A layer of blueberries is the sweet surprise hidden inside this pretty pastry.

- 3/4 cup 1% cottage cheese
- 1/3 cup sugar
- 1/3 cup 1% milk
- 1/4 cup canola oil
- 1 teaspoon vanilla extract
- 2 cups all-purpose flour
- 2 teaspoons baking powder
- 1/2 teaspoon salt

FILLING:
- 4 ounces reduced-fat cream cheese
- 1/4 cup sugar
- 1 egg, *separated*
- 1 teaspoon grated lemon peel
- 1 teaspoon vanilla extract
- 1 cup fresh *or* frozen blueberries
- 1 tablespoon water

GLAZE:
- 1/2 cup confectioners' sugar
- 2 teaspoons lemon juice

In a blender, cover and process cottage cheese until smooth. Add the sugar, milk, oil and vanilla; process until smooth. Combine the flour, baking powder and salt; add to cheese mixture. Process just until dough forms a ball (dough will be sticky). Turn onto a floured surface; knead 4-5 times. Place in a large bowl; cover and refrigerate for 30 minutes.

In another large bowl, beat cream cheese and sugar until smooth. Beat in the egg yolk, lemon peel and vanilla. Turn dough onto a 17-in. x 13-in. piece of parchment paper. Roll into a 16-in. x 12-in. rectangle. Transfer with paper to a baking sheet. Spread cream cheese mixture lengthwise in a 3-1/2-in.-wide strip down center of dough; sprinkle with blueberries. On each long side, cut 1-in.-wide strips about 3-3/4 in. into center. Fold alternating strips at an angle across berries. Pinch ends to seal and tuck under. Beat egg white and water; brush over dough.

Bake at 400° for 20-22 minutes or until golden brown. Remove to a wire rack. Combine the glaze ingredients; drizzle over the warm pastry. Store in the refrigerator. **Yield:** 10 servings.

Editor's Note: If using frozen blueberries, do not thaw before using.

Lemon Cheesecake Squares

Peggy Reddick, Cumming, Georgia

Whether I'm hosting friends or sending a plate to work with my husband, these creamy elegant cheesecake squares are always a hit. It's a wonderful make-ahead dessert that easily serves a large group.

- 3/4 cup shortening
- 1/3 cup packed brown sugar
- 1-1/4 cups all-purpose flour
- 1 cup old-fashioned oats
- 1/4 teaspoon salt
- 1/2 cup seedless raspberry jam

FILLING:
- 4 packages (8 ounces *each*) cream cheese, softened
- 1-1/2 cups sugar
- 1/4 cup all-purpose flour
- 4 eggs
- 1/3 cup lemon juice
- 4 teaspoons grated lemon peel

In a large bowl, cream shortening and brown sugar until light and fluffy. Combine the flour, oats and salt; gradually add to creamed mixture.

Press dough into a greased 13-in. x 9-in. x 2-in. baking dish. Bake at 350° for 15-18 minutes or until golden brown. Spread with jam.

For filling, in a large bowl, beat the cream cheese, sugar and flour until smooth. Beat in the eggs, lemon juice and peel just until blended. Carefully spoon over jam.

Bake at 350° for 30-35 minutes or until center is almost set. Cool on a wire rack. Cover and store in the refrigerator. **Yield:** 20 servings.

Strawberry Shortcake

Shirley Joan Helfenbein, Lapeer, Michigan

When I think back to my childhood, I can still taste the sweet juicy berries piled over warm biscuits and topped with a huge dollop of fresh whipped cream. My father added even more indulgence to this strawberry dessert by first buttering the biscuits.

- 2 cups all-purpose flour
- 2 tablespoons sugar
- 1 tablespoon baking powder
- 1/2 teaspoon salt
- 1/2 cup cold butter
- 1 egg, beaten
- 2/3 cup half-and-half cream
- 1 cup heavy whipping cream
- 2 tablespoons confectioners' sugar
- 1/8 teaspoon vanilla extract

Additional butter

- 1-1/2 quarts fresh strawberries, sliced

In a bowl, combine the flour, sugar, baking powder and salt. Cut in butter until mixture resembles coarse crumbs. In a small bowl, whisk egg and half-and-half cream; add all at once to the crumb mixture and stir just until moistened.

Spread batter into a greased 8-in. round baking pan, slightly building up around the edges. Bake at 450° for 16-18 minutes or until golden brown. Remove from pan and cool on a wire rack.

In a chilled small bowl, beat whipping cream until it begins to thicken. Add confectioners' sugar and vanilla; beat until stiff peaks form. Split cake widthwise in half; butter bottom layer. Spoon half of the strawberries over bottom layer. Spread with some of the whipped cream. Cover with top cake layer. Top with remaining berries and whipped cream. Cut into wedges. **Yield:** 6-8 servings.

Dairy Kugel

Dawn Lowenstein, Hatboro, Pennsylvania

Kugel is served often in this area of the country and can be served as a side or dessert. I use this noodle dish as a dessert since it's really rich and tastes like cheesecake.

- 4 cups uncooked egg noodles
- 1/4 cup butter, melted
- 5 eggs
- 2 cups (16 ounces) 4% cottage cheese
- 2 cups (16 ounces) sour cream
- 2 cups milk
- 1 package (8 ounces) cream cheese, softened
- 1-1/4 cups sugar, *divided*
- 1 teaspoon vanilla extract
- 1/8 teaspoon salt
- 1 tablespoon ground cinnamon

Cook noodles according to package directions; drain. Toss with butter; set aside. In a large bowl, beat the eggs for 3-4 minutes or until thickened and lemon-colored. Beat in the cottage cheese, sour cream, milk, cream cheese, 1 cup sugar, vanilla and salt until blended. Stir in noodles.

Transfer to a greased 13-in. x 9-in. x 2-in. baking dish. Combine the cinnamon and remaining sugar; sprinkle over noodle mixture. Bake, uncovered, at 350° for 55-60 minutes or until a knife inserted near the center comes out clean. Let stand for 10 minutes before serving. **Yield:** 15-20 servings.

Raspberry Custard Meringue

Bette Berry, Alamogordo, New Mexico

Whenever I serve this meringue at a dinner, I can count on one thing—hearing a few husbands asking their wives to make sure to get the recipe!

MERINGUE:

- 4 egg whites
- 1 teaspoon vanilla extract
- 1/2 teaspoon salt
- 1/4 teaspoon cream of tartar
- 1 cup sugar
- 1 cup finely chopped walnuts

CUSTARD:

- 3/4 cup sugar
- 1/4 cup flour
- 2 cups milk
- 3 to 4 egg yolks
- 1/4 cup butter, cubed
- 1-1/2 teaspoons vanilla extract
- 1/8 teaspoon salt

TOPPING:

- 1 cup heavy whipping cream
- 1/3 cup semisweet chocolate chips
- 3 tablespoons butter
- 1 quart fresh raspberries

For meringue, place egg whites in a large bowl; let stand at room temperature for 30 minutes. Line a baking sheet with parchment paper.

Beat the egg whites, vanilla, salt and cream of tartar until soft peaks form. Add sugar, 1 tablespoon at a time, beating until stiff, glossy peaks form and sugar is dissolved. Fold in the nuts.

To form crust, place meringue mixture on parchment paper; spread in a 14-in. diameter circle (or in several smaller circles for individual servings). Bake at 275° for 1 hour; turn oven off; leave meringue in oven for 1 hour.

Remove from the oven and cool on baking sheets. When cooled completely, remove meringue from paper.

For custard, in a large saucepan, combine sugar and flour. Stir in milk until smooth. Cook and stir over medium-high heat until thickened and bubbly. Reduce heat to low; cook and stir for 2 minutes longer. Remove from the heat. Stir a small amount of hot filling into egg yolks; return all to the pan, stirring constantly. Bring to a gentle boil; cook and stir for 2 minutes. Remove from the heat; gently stir in the butter, vanilla and salt.

Pour into bowl; cover with plastic wrap and cool completely. (Can be made a day in advance.)

Just before serving, beat cream and sweeten to taste. In a microwave, melt chocolate chips and butter; stir until smooth. Spoon custard mixture on meringue; top with whipped cream and fresh berries. Drizzle with chocolate mixture. **Yield:** 10 servings.

Flaky Apricot Pastries

Ed Patterson, Greenville, Texas

These tender fruit-filled pastries can be made ahead and frozen. If apricot is not your favorite filling, try blueberry, cherry, strawberry or raspberry preserves.

- 3 packages (3 ounces *each*) cream cheese, softened
- 1 cup butter, softened
- 2 cups all-purpose flour
- 1/4 cup sugar
- 1 teaspoon ground cinnamon
- 1/2 cup apricot preserves
- 4 teaspoons ground pecans

GLAZE:

- 1 cup confectioners' sugar
- 2 tablespoons butter, softened
- 1 to 2 tablespoons milk

In a large bowl, beat cream cheese and butter until smooth. Gradually add flour and mix well. Divide dough into four pieces. Cover and refrigerate for 2 hours.

On a floured surface, roll each portion of dough into a 12-in. x 8-in. rectangle. Combine sugar and cinnamon; sprinkle over dough. Spread with preserves; sprinkle with pecans. Roll up tightly, starting with a short side; pinch ends. Place seam side down on a greased baking sheet. Using a sharp knife, make three slashes across the top of each roll.

Bake at 350° for 28-32 minutes or until golden brown. Remove to wire racks to cool. Combine glaze ingredients until smooth; drizzle over pastries. **Yield:** 4 pastries.

Brownie Cheesecake

Dorothy Olivares, El Paso, Texas

Crumbled brownies are stirred into the batter before baking, which makes this chocolate cheesecake a delectable treat.

- 1-1/2 cups crushed vanilla wafers (about 45 wafers)
- 6 tablespoons confectioners' sugar
- 6 tablespoons baking cocoa
- 6 tablespoons butter, melted

FILLING:
- 3 packages (8 ounces *each*) cream cheese, softened
- 1/4 cup butter, melted
- 1 can (14 ounces) sweetened condensed milk
- 3 teaspoons vanilla extract
- 1/2 cup baking cocoa
- 4 eggs, lightly beaten
- 1-1/2 cups crumbled brownies

Whipped topping and pecan halves, optional

In a small bowl, combine the wafer crumbs, confectioners' sugar and cocoa; stir in the butter. Press onto the bottom of a greased 9-in. springform pan; set aside.

In a large bowl, beat the cream cheese and butter until smooth. Beat in milk and vanilla. Beat in cocoa until well blended. Add eggs; beat on low just until combined. Fold in brownies. Spoon into crust. Place pan on a baking sheet.

Bake at 350° for 50-55 minutes or until center is almost set. Cool on a wire rack for 10 minutes. Carefully run a knife around the edge of pan to loosen. Cool 1 hour longer. Refrigerate overnight.

Remove sides of pan. Garnish with whipped topping and pecans if desired. Store in the refrigerator. **Yield:** 10-12 servings.

Giant Pineapple Turnover

Carolyn Kyzer, Alexander, Arkansas

Fresh apple, canned pineapple and plump raisins make this comforting turnover a surefire hit. Made from refrigerated pie pastry, the crust is as easy as it is tasty.

- 1 sheet refrigerated pie pastry
- 1 medium tart apple, peeled and coarsely chopped
- 1 can (8 ounces) crushed pineapple, well drained
- 3/4 cup sugar
- 1/3 cup finely chopped celery
- 1/3 cup raisins
- 1/3 cup chopped walnuts
- 1/4 cup all-purpose flour

Ice cream, optional

Unfold pastry and place on a baking sheet. In a bowl, combine the apple, pineapple, sugar, celery, raisins, walnuts and flour; toss gently. Spoon filling onto half of crust, leaving 1 in. around edge. Fold pastry over filling and seal edge well. Cut slit in top.

Bake at 400° for 30-35 minutes or until crust is golden brown and filling is bubbly. Cool on a wire rack. Cut into wedges. Serve with ice cream if desired. **Yield:** 4 servings.

Chocolate Souffle

Linda Blaska, Atlanta, Georgia

I serve this rich chocolate dessert when entertaining. The sumptuous souffle has a light, airy texture, yet its center is moist and almost fudge-like.

- 1/2 cup sugar
- 2 tablespoons cornstarch
- 1/4 teaspoon salt
- 3/4 cup milk
- 2 squares (1 ounce *each*) unsweetened chocolate
- 3 tablespoons butter
- 4 eggs, *separated*
- 1 teaspoon vanilla extract
- 1/4 teaspoon cream of tartar

Confectioners' sugar, optional

In a large saucepan, combine the sugar, cornstarch and salt. Add milk. Bring to a boil; cook and stir for 2 minutes or until thickened. Add the chocolate and butter; cook until chocolate and butter are melted. Stir until smooth. Remove from the heat. Add 1/3 cup chocolate mixture to the egg yolks; return all to the pan, stirring constantly. Stir in vanilla; cool slightly.

In a large bowl, beat egg whites until foamy. Add the cream of tartar; beat until stiff peaks form. Fold the whites into the chocolate mixture.

Pour into a greased 2-qt. souffle dish. Bake at 350° for 45-50 minutes or until a knife inserted near the center comes out clean. Dust with confectioners' sugar if desired. Serve immediately. **Yield:** 8-10 servings.

Blackberry Cobbler

Tina Hankins, Laconia, New Hampshire

In summer, blackberries abound in fields and along country roads around here. It's fun to pick them, especially when we know this dessert will be the result.

- 1/4 cup butter, softened
- 1/2 cup sugar
- 1 cup all-purpose flour
- 2 teaspoons baking powder
- 1/2 cup milk
- 2 cups fresh *or* frozen blackberries
- 3/4 cup raspberry *or* apple juice

Ice cream *or* whipped cream, optional

In a small bowl, cream butter and sugar until light and fluffy. Combine flour and baking powder; add to creamed mixture alternately with milk just until moistened.

Pour into a greased 1-1/2-qt. baking pan. Sprinkle with blackberries. Pour juice over all. Bake at 350° for 45-50 minutes or until golden brown. Serve warm; top with ice cream or cream if desired. **Yield:** 6-8 servings.

What's in a Name? Cobbler or crisp...what do they mean? A cobbler has a biscuit-like topping over a fruit base. The topping can be either a single layer or dropped over the fruit to give it a cobblestone effect. Crisps have a crumb topping of flour, sugar and butter that is sprinkled over the fruit base. A crisp topping may also include oats, nuts and spices.

Caramelized Pear Strudel

Leah Beatty, Cobourg, Ontario

This easy, stylish dessert is sure to please everyone. Best served warm, it's delicious with a scoop of light vanilla ice cream or reduced-fat whipped topping.

- 1/2 cup sugar
- 1 tablespoon cornstarch
- 3 large pears, peeled and finely chopped
- 1/2 cup fresh *or* frozen cranberries, thawed
- 2 tablespoons butter
- 1/2 cup dried cranberries
- 1 teaspoon ground ginger
- 1 teaspoon grated orange peel
- 1/2 teaspoon ground cinnamon
- 6 sheets phyllo dough (14 inches x 9 inches)
- 1 teaspoon confectioners' sugar

In a large bowl, combine sugar and cornstarch. Add pears and cranberries; toss gently to coat. In a large nonstick skillet, melt butter over medium-high heat. Add fruit mixture; cook and stir for 7-8 minutes or until cranberries pop. Stir in the dried cranberries, ginger, orange peel and cinnamon. Cool.

Line a baking sheet with foil and coat the foil with cooking spray; set aside. Place one sheet of phyllo dough on a work surface; coat with cooking spray. (Until ready to use, keep phyllo covered with plastic wrap and a damp towel to prevent drying out.) Repeat five times with remaining phyllo. Spread cranberry mixture over dough to within 1 in. of edges. Fold in sides. Roll up, starting at a long side. Place seam side down on prepared baking sheet.

Bake at 400° for 20-23 minutes or until golden brown. Remove from pan to a wire rack to cool. Dust with confectioners' sugar before serving. **Yield:** 10 servings.

Pear Melba Dumplings

Doreen Kelly, Hatboro, Pennsylvania

Special meals call for elegant desserts like this. A whole pear is packaged inside a pretty pastry pocket.

- 2 cups all-purpose flour
- 1-1/4 teaspoons salt
- 1/2 teaspoon cornstarch
- 2/3 cup butter-flavored shortening
- 4 to 5 tablespoons cold water
- 6 small ripe pears, peeled and cored
- 6 tablespoons packed brown sugar
- 1/4 teaspoon ground cinnamon
- 2 tablespoons milk
- 1 tablespoon sugar

RASPBERRY SAUCE:

- 1 tablespoon sugar
- 1 tablespoon cornstarch

- 2 tablespoons water
- 1 package (10 ounces) frozen raspberries, thawed
- 1/4 teaspoon almond extract

Ice cream, optional

In a large bowl, combine flour, salt and cornstarch. Cut in shortening until mixture resembles coarse crumbs. Gradually add the water, tossing with a fork until pastry forms a ball. On a floured surface, roll into a 21-in. x 14-in. rectangle. Cut into six squares.

Place one pear in center of each square. Pack pear centers with brown sugar; sprinkle with cinnamon. Brush the edges of squares with milk; fold up corners to center and pinch to seal.

Place in a greased 15-in. x 10-in. x 1-in. baking pan. Brush with milk; sprinkle with sugar. Bake, uncovered, at 375° for 35-40 minutes or until golden brown.

For sauce, in a small saucepan, combine the sugar, cornstarch and water until smooth. Add raspberries. Bring to a boil; cook and stir for 2 minutes or until thickened. Remove from the heat; stir in extract. Serve warm over dumplings with ice cream if desired. **Yield:** 6 servings.

Other Uses for Melba Sauce The raspberry sauce in Pear Melba Dumplings is a variation of the classic raspberry-based Melba Sauce, which is named for the opera singer Nellie Melba. Besides being delectable on these dumplings, you can use it to dress up ice cream, pound cake and fresh fruit.

George Washington Cherry Cobbler

Juanita Sherwood, Charleston, Illinois

Since Dad loved fruit, my mother prepared this dessert often in many different ways. You can try it with blackberries or blueberries, too.

- 1/2 cup sugar
- 2 tablespoons cornstarch
- 1/4 teaspoon ground cinnamon
- 3/4 cup water
- 1 package (12 ounces) frozen pitted dark sweet cherries, thawed
- 1 tablespoon butter

TOPPING:
- 1 cup all-purpose flour
- 4 tablespoon sugar, *divided*
- 2 teaspoons baking powder
- 1/2 teaspoon salt
- 3 tablespoons shortening
- 1/2 cup milk

Ice cream, optional

In a large saucepan, combine the sugar, cornstarch and cinnamon. Stir in water until smooth. Add the cherries and butter. Bring to a boil over medium heat; cook and stir for 2 minutes or until thickened. Pour into an 8-in. square baking dish; set aside.

For topping, in a large bowl, combine the flour, 2 tablespoons sugar, baking powder and salt. Cut in shortening until mixture resembles coarse crumbs. Stir in milk just until moistened.

Drop by spoonfuls over the cherries; sprinkle with remaining sugar. Bake at 400° for 30-35 minutes or until golden brown. Serve warm with ice cream if desired. **Yield:** 8 servings.

Brown Sugar Pudding Cake

Violet Koecke, Bagley, Wisconsin

This is a wonderful old recipe that's been handed down through our family from my grandmother.

SAUCE:
- 1 cup packed brown sugar
- 1 tablespoon all-purpose flour
- 2 tablespoons butter, melted
- 1/4 teaspoon salt
- 2 cups boiling water

PUDDING:
- 2 tablespoons butter, melted
- 1/2 cup packed brown sugar
- 1 cup all-purpose flour
- 1 teaspoon baking powder
- 1/2 teaspoon salt
- 1/2 cup chopped nuts
- 1/2 cup milk

In a small bowl, combine all the sauce ingredients. Pour into a 1-1/2-qt. baking dish; set aside.

For pudding, in a large bowl, beat butter and sugar until blended. Combine the flour, baking powder, salt and nuts; gradually add to butter mixture alternately with milk. Spoon into baking dish. Bake at 350° for 40-45 minutes until a knife inserted near the center comes out clean. **Yield:** 6-8 servings.

Cinnamon Peach Cobbler

Victoria Lowe, Lititz, Pennsylvania

Prepared biscuit mix makes this comforting cobbler a quick favorite. My husband loves the warm peaches, cinnamony sauce and golden crumb topping.

- 4 cups sliced peeled fresh *or* frozen unsweetened peaches, thawed
- 1/2 cup sugar
- 1 tablespoon plus 2/3 cup biscuit/baking mix, *divided*
- 1/2 teaspoon ground cinnamon
- 2 to 3 tablespoons brown sugar
- 1/4 cup cold butter, cubed
- 3 tablespoons milk

In a large bowl, combine the peaches, sugar, 1 tablespoon biscuit mix and cinnamon. Transfer to a greased shallow 1-1/2-qt. baking dish.

In another bowl, combine brown sugar and remaining biscuit mix. Cut in butter until crumbly. Stir in milk just until blended.

Drop by rounded tablespoonfuls onto peach mixture. Bake at 400° for 20-25 minutes or until top is golden brown and filling is bubbly. **Yield:** 6-8 servings.

Butterscotch Delight

Barbara Edgemon, Belleview, Florida

This creamy layered dessert is popular whenever I serve it.

- 1/2 cup cold butter
- 1 cup all-purpose flour
- 1 cup finely chopped walnuts
- 1 package (8 ounces) cream cheese, softened
- 1 cup confectioners' sugar
- 1 carton (8 ounces) frozen whipped topping, thawed, *divided*
- 3-1/2 cups cold milk
- 2 packages (3.5 ounces *each*) instant butterscotch pudding mix
- 1/2 cup coarsely chopped walnuts

In a bowl, cut butter into flour; stir in the finely chopped walnuts. Press into a greased 13-in. x 9-in. x 2-in. baking pan. Bake at 350° for 20 minutes or until golden brown. Cool on a wire rack.

In a large bowl, beat cream cheese and confectioners' sugar until smooth. Fold in 1 cup whipped topping. Spread over crust. In another bowl, whisk milk and pudding mix for 2 minutes or until thickened. Spread over cream cheese layer. Spread with the remaining whipped topping; sprinkle with coarsely chopped walnuts. Chill until set. Store in the refrigerator. **Yield:** 12-15 servings.

Saucy Cherry Enchiladas

Helen Craft, Robstown, Texas

Enchiladas for dessert? When they're filled with fruit and covered with a sweet syrup, why not? Apple or blueberry pie filling is good inside the tortillas too.

- 2 cups sugar
- 1-1/2 cups water
- 1 cup butter, cubed
- 2 tablespoons lemon juice
- 1 can (21 ounces) cherry, apple *or* blueberry pie filling
- 16 flour tortillas (6 inches)
- 1 cup chopped pecans
- 1 teaspoon ground cinnamon

Vanilla ice cream

In a large saucepan, bring the sugar, water, butter and lemon juice to a boil over medium heat. Reduce heat; simmer, uncovered, for 30 minutes or until mixture has the consistency of syrup. Remove from the heat; set aside.

Spoon about 3 tablespoons of the pie filling off-center on each tortilla; fold sides and ends over filling and roll up. Place in a greased 13-in. x 9-in. x 2-in. baking dish. Pour the sugar syrup over tortillas; let stand at room temperature for 30 minutes.

Bake, uncovered, at 350° for 30 minutes. Sprinkle with pecans and cinnamon. Bake 15 minutes longer or until golden brown and sauce bubbles around the edges. Serve warm with ice cream. **Yield:** 16 servings.

Black 'n' White Cheesecake Bars

Bertille Cooper, California, Maryland

Whenever it's my turn to make dessert for an event, I get requests for these scrumptious bars.

- 2 cups (12 ounces) semisweet chocolate chips
- 1/2 cup butter
- 2 cups graham cracker crumbs
- 1 package (8 ounces) cream cheese, softened
- 1 egg
- 1 can (14 ounces) sweetened condensed milk
- 1 teaspoon vanilla extract

In a microwave, melt chocolate chips and butter; stir until smooth. Stir in graham cracker crumbs. Set aside 1/4 cup for topping. Press the remaining crumbs into an ungreased 13-in. x 9-in. x 2-in. baking pan.

In a large bowl, beat cream cheese until smooth. Add the egg and condensed milk; beat on low speed just until combined. Stir in vanilla. Sprinkle with reserved crumbs. Pour into crust. Place pan on a baking sheet.

Bake at 325° for 25-30 minutes or until lightly browned. Cool. Refrigerate 3 hours or until completely chilled. Cut into bars. Store in the refrigerator. **Yield:** 4 dozen.

Clean Cut Bars A bench knife can be used to quickly cut desserts and pan cookies into bars. Press the bench knife down into the dessert or cookie to cut, then pull straight up; don't drag it through. If crumbs stick to the knife, wipe it off with a damp paper towel and dry between each cut.

Chocolate-Dipped Phyllo Sticks

Taste of Home Test Kitchen

For something a little special to bake for holidays, try these elegant, festive sweets.

- 4 sheets phyllo dough (14 inches x 9 inches)
- 2 tablespoons butter, melted
- 1 tablespoon sugar
- 1/4 teaspoon ground cinnamon
- 2 squares (1 ounce *each*) semisweet chocolate, finely chopped
- 1/2 teaspoon shortening
- 1/2 ounce white baking chocolate, melted

Place one sheet of phyllo dough on a work surface; brush with butter. Cover with a second sheet of phyllo; brush with butter. (Keep remaining phyllo dough covered with plastic wrap and a damp towel to prevent it from drying out.) Cut phyllo in half lengthwise. Cut each half into five 4-1/2-in. x 2-3/4-in. rectangles. Tightly roll each rectangle from one long side, forming a 4-1/2-in.-long stick. Combine sugar and cinnamon. Coat sticks with cooking spray; sprinkle with cinnamon-sugar.

Place on an ungreased baking sheet. Bake at 425° for 3-5 minutes or until lightly browned. Remove to a wire rack to cool. Repeat with the remaining phyllo dough, butter and cinnamon-sugar.

In a microwave, melt semisweet chocolate and shortening; stir until smooth. Dip top half of phyllo sticks in chocolate; allow extra to drip off. Place on waxed paper; let stand until set. Drizzle with white chocolate. **Yield:** 20 sticks.

Pear Crisp

Joanne Korevaar, Burgessville, Ontario

Since he's a livestock truck driver, my husband often starts work around 2 or 3 a.m. A serving of this crisp will keep him going till breakfast.

- 8 medium ripe pears, peeled and thinly sliced
- 1/4 cup orange juice
- 1/2 cup sugar
- 1 teaspoon ground cinnamon
- 1/4 teaspoon ground allspice
- 1/4 teaspoon ground ginger

TOPPING:

- 1 cup all-purpose flour
- 1 cup old-fashioned oats
- 1/2 cup packed brown sugar
- 1/2 teaspoon baking powder
- 1/2 cup cold butter, cubed

Fresh mint and additional pear slices, optional

Toss pears with orange juice; place in a greased 13-in. x 9-in. x 2-in. baking dish. Combine the sugar, cinnamon, allspice and ginger; sprinkle over pears.

In a large bowl, combine the flour, oats, brown sugar and baking powder; cut in butter until crumbly. Sprinkle over the pears.

Bake at 350° for 35-40 minutes or until topping is golden brown and fruit is tender. Serve warm. Garnish with mint and additional pears if desired. **Yield:** 12 servings.

Rich Chocolate Cheesecake

Mary Walker, Berlin, Maryland

With seven children and 15 grandchildren, I'm always looking for desserts that serve a bunch. Here's a special treat that will easily satisfy the chocolate cravings of up to 16 hungry people.

1-1/2　cups chocolate wafer crumbs (about 24 wafers)
　1/4　cup butter, melted
　　2　tablespoons sugar
　1/4　cup finely chopped almonds
FILLING:
　　3　packages (8 ounces *each*) cream cheese, softened
　3/4　cup sugar
　　3　eggs
　1/3　cup strong brewed coffee
　　1　teaspoon vanilla extract
　3/4　cup baking cocoa
　　1　cup (6 ounces) semisweet chocolate chips
TOPPING:
　　1　cup (8 ounces) sour cream
　　2　tablespoons brown sugar
　　1　teaspoon vanilla extract
　1/2　cup sliced almonds

In a bowl, combine the wafer crumbs, butter, sugar and almonds. Press onto the bottom and 1 in. up the sides of a 9-in. springform pan; set aside. In a large bowl, beat cream cheese and sugar until smooth. Add eggs; beat on low speed just until combined. Stir in coffee and vanilla. Beat in cocoa just until blended. Stir in chocolate chips.

Pour into prepared crust. Place pan on a baking sheet. Bake at 375° for 30-35 minutes or until center is almost set.

Remove from the oven; increase temperature to 425°. Combine the sour cream, brown sugar and vanilla until smooth. Spread over warm cheesecake; sprinkle with almonds. Bake for 10 minutes or until lightly browned.

Cool on a wire rack for 10 minutes. Carefully run a knife around the edge of pan to loosen; cool for 1 hour longer. Refrigerate overnight. Remove sides of pan. Store in the refrigerator. **Yield:** 16 servings.

Triple Chocolate Bundles

Taste of Home Test Kitchen

No one will be able to resist three kinds of chocolate wrapped up in a fuss-free flaky dough. Instead of sprinkling the bundles with sugar, try drizzling with melted chocolate.

　3　tablespoons semisweet chocolate chips
　3　tablespoons vanilla *or* white chips
　3　tablespoons milk chocolate chips
　1　tube (8 ounces) refrigerated crescent rolls
Confectioners' sugar, optional

In a small bowl, combine all the chips. Separate crescent dough into eight triangles. Place triangles on a work surface with the short edge toward you.

For each bundle, place 1 tablespoon of chips in the center of each triangle. Bring top point over chips and tuck underneath dough. Fold side points over top; press to seal.

Place on an ungreased baking sheet. Bake at 375° for 10-12 minutes or until golden brown. Cool on a wire rack until serving. Sprinkle with sugar if desired. **Yield:** 8 bundles.

Strawberry Brownie Bombe

Joanne Watts, Kitchener, Ontario

A friend and I dreamed up this recipe. We use it to entertain and for special family dinners. For an extra touch, you can dip the strawberries in chocolate.

    1   package fudge brownie mix (13-inch x 9-inch pan size)
  1/2   cup chopped walnuts
  1/2   cup strawberry preserves
    1   quart strawberry ice cream, softened
    2   cups heavy whipping cream
    3   drops red food coloring, optional
  1/4   cup confectioners' sugar
Fresh strawberries and mint, optional

Prepare brownie mix according to package directions for cake-like brownies. Stir in walnuts. Pour the batter into two greased and waxed paper-lined 8-in. round baking pans. Bake at 350° for 30 minutes or until a toothpick inserted near the center comes out clean. Cool completely in pans.

Line a 1-1/2-qt. metal bowl with foil. Cut and fit one brownie layer to evenly line the inside of a bowl (brownie may crack). Spread preserves over brownie layer. Freeze for 15 minutes. Fill brownie-lined bowl with ice cream; smooth top. Cover and freeze for 3 hours or until ice cream is firm.

Place remaining brownie layer on a serving plate. Remove bowl from freezer; uncover. Invert onto brownie layer; remove bowl and foil. Return to freezer.

In a chilled large bowl, beat cream and food coloring until soft peaks form. Add sugar and beat until stiff peaks form; set aside 1-1/2 cups. Spread remaining whipped cream over top and sides of bombe.

Cut a small hole in the corner of a pastry or plastic bag and insert star tip. Fill with reserved whipped cream; pipe border at base of bombe. Holding the bag straight up and down, form stars on top. Garnish with strawberries and mint if desired. **Yield:** 16 servings.

Mini Apple Turnovers

Merrill Powers, Spearville, Kansas

These cute little pastries are so yummy. I'm tempted to hoard them for myself when I make a batch, but I always end up sharing.

    1   package (8 ounces) cream cheese, softened
  3/4   cup butter, softened
    1   egg, *separated*
    3   tablespoons cold water, *divided*
    2   cups all-purpose flour
    7   cups thinly sliced peeled tart apples (about 6 medium)
  3/4   cup sugar
1-1/2   teaspoons ground cinnamon
Additional sugar, optional
Vanilla ice cream, optional

In a large bowl, beat cream cheese and butter until smooth. Refrigerate the egg white. Beat egg yolk and 2 tablespoons water into cream cheese mixture. Gradually add flour until well blended. Shape pastry into a ball. Cover and refrigerate for 1 hour.

Meanwhile, in a large skillet, combine the apples, sugar and cinnamon. Cover and cook over low heat for 8-10 minutes or until apples are tender. Remove from the heat.

Turn the pastry onto a lightly floured surface. Roll to 1/8-in. thickness; cut into 4-in. circles. Top each circle with apple mixture. Brush edges of pastry with water; fold pastry over filling and seal edges well.

In a small bowl, whisk egg white and remaining water; brush over pastry. Sprinkle with additional sugar if desired.

Place on greased baking sheets. Bake at 375° for 18-22 minutes or until golden brown. Remove to wire racks to cool. Serve with ice cream if desired. **Yield:** 2 dozen.

Cherry Kolaches

Evelyn Nesiba, Ravenna, Nebraska

I am of Czechoslovakian descent, and baking kolaches is my specialty. They are also popular in other Slavic nations, which sometimes use the spellings kolacky or kolachke. The Cherry Kolaches recipe I'm sharing reflects my filling preference. But I also make apricot, apple, pineapple, prune and poppy seed kolaches.

- 2 packages (1/4 ounce *each*) active dry yeast
- 1/2 cup warm water (110° to 115°)
- 2-1/2 cups warm milk (110° to 115°)
- 3/4 cup sugar
- 3/4 cup butter, softened
- 2 teaspoons salt
- 4 eggs
- 11 to 11-1/2 cups all-purpose flour

FILLING:
- 2 cans (21 ounces *each*) cherry pie filling
- 1/2 cup sugar
- 2 tablespoons cornstarch
- 2 tablespoons cold water

TOPPING:
- 1 package (8 ounces) cream cheese, softened
- 2/3 cup sugar
- 1 egg yolk

Melted butter

In a large bowl, dissolve yeast in warm water. Add the milk, sugar, butter, salt, eggs and 5 cups flour; beat until smooth. Stir in enough remaining flour to form a very soft dough. Do not knead. Cover and let rise in a warm place until doubled, about 75 minutes.

Turn onto a well-floured surface. Shape into 1-1/2-in. balls. Place 2 in. apart on greased baking sheets. Cover and let rise until doubled, about 45 minutes.

Meanwhile, in a small saucepan, combine pie filling and sugar. Combine cornstarch and cold water until smooth; gradually stir into filling. Bring to a boil over medium heat. Cook and stir for 1 minute or until thickened; set aside.

In a large bowl, beat the cream cheese, sugar and egg yolk until smooth. Using the end of a wooden spoon handle, make an indentation in the center of each dough ball; fill with 2 rounded teaspoons of filling. Make a small indentation in center of filling; add 1 teaspoon topping.

Bake at 400° for 10-15 minutes or until lightly browned. Brush melted butter over rolls. Remove from pans to wire racks to cool. Store in the refrigerator. **Yield:** about 6 dozen.

Peach-Filled Pastries

Taste of Home Test Kitchen

When your family has a taste for pie but time is ticking away, make this fast and fruity dessert. For a tasty twist, use cherry pie filling instead of the peach.

- 1 sheet frozen puff pastry, thawed
- 1 egg white
- 1 tablespoon water
- 1-1/2 teaspoons sugar
- 1 can (21 ounces) peach *or* cherry pie filling
- 1/4 teaspoon almond extract
- 2 cups whipped topping

On a lightly floured surface, unfold pastry and roll to 3/8-in. thickness. Cut along fold seams into three pieces. Cut each piece in half widthwise; place on an ungreased baking sheet.

Beat egg white and water; brush over pastry. Sprinkle with sugar. Bake at 400° for 9-11 minutes or until golden brown. Cool on a wire rack.

Split each pastry in half horizontally. Combine pie filling and extract; spoon over bottom halves of pastries. Top with whipped topping and pastry tops. **Yield:** 6 servings.

Crustless New York Cheesecake

Mrs. George Parsell, Flushing, New York

This rich and flavorful cheesecake uses an abundance of dairy products. Even though the cake doesn't have a crust, I guarantee everyone will love it.

- 2 packages (8 ounces *each*) cream cheese, softened
- 3 cups (24 ounces) ricotta cheese
- 1-1/2 cups sugar
- 1/2 cup butter, softened
- 4 eggs, lightly beaten
- 2 cups (16 ounces) sour cream
- 3 tablespoons all-purpose flour
- 3 tablespoons cornstarch
- 2 tablespoons lemon juice
- 1 teaspoon vanilla extract

Assorted fresh fruit

In a large bowl, beat the cream cheese, ricotta, sugar and butter until smooth. Add eggs; beat on low speed just until combined. Stir in the sour cream, flour, cornstarch, lemon juice and vanilla. Pour into a greased 9-in. springform pan. Place pan on a baking sheet.

Bake at 325° for 70-75 minutes or until edges are lightly browned and top is dry to the touch (center 5 inches of cheesecake will not be set). Cool on a wire rack for 10 minutes. Carefully run a knife around the edge of pan to loosen; cool 1 hour longer. Refrigerate overnight. Remove sides of pan. Garnish with fruit. Store in the refrigerator. **Yield:** 12-16 servings.

Softening Cream Cheese If the cream cheese is not softened before it's beaten for a cheesecake, you may end up with cream cheese lumps in the baked product. The simplest way to soften cream cheese is to let it stand at room temperature for 30 minutes before using. It can also be softened in the microwave...make sure to remove the foil packaging before warming in the microwave.

Chocolate Almond Stacks

Leah Lyon, Ada, Oklahoma

A yummy blend of almonds, whipped cream and chocolate sauce goes into this showpiece dessert. I lightly toast the almonds for extra flavor.

- 1 square (1 ounce) bittersweet chocolate
- 3/4 cup heavy whipping cream, *divided*
- 1 egg
- 3 tablespoons sugar
- 1 teaspoon vanilla extract
- 2 tablespoons all-purpose flour
- 1/3 cup semisweet chocolate chips
- 1/2 cup sliced almonds
- 1/8 teaspoon almond extract

In a small saucepan, melt chocolate with 1 tablespoon cream; stir until smooth. In a small bowl, beat the egg, sugar and vanilla on high speed for 5 minutes or until thick and pale yellow. Fold in flour and melted chocolate. Pour into two 5-in. x 3-in. x 2-in. loaf pans coated with cooking spray.

Bake at 350° for 8-10 minutes or until cake springs back when lightly touched. Cool for 5 minutes before removing from pans to wire racks. Cut cakes in half widthwise.

In a small saucepan, melt chocolate chips with 3 tablespoons cream, stirring constantly. Spread over top of cakes; sprinkle with almonds. Refrigerate for 15 minutes.

In a chilled small bowl, beat almond extract with remaining cream until stiff peaks form. Spread half of the whipped cream on top of two cake squares; top each with a remaining cake square and remaining whipped cream. **Yield:** 2 servings.

Strawberry Meringue Desserts

Susan Maraffin, Canfield, Ohio

When time is short, use thawed whipped topping instead of making sweetened whipped cream.

- 4 egg whites
- 1-1/2 teaspoons vanilla extract, *divided*
- 1/4 teaspoon cream of tartar
- 1/8 teaspoon salt
- 1 cup sugar
- 1 cup (6 ounces) semisweet chocolate chips
- 4 teaspoons shortening
- 2 cups heavy whipping cream
- 2 tablespoons confectioners' sugar
- 5 cups fresh strawberries
- Chocolate syrup

Place egg whites in a large bowl; let stand at room temperature for 30 minutes. Line baking sheets with parchment paper. Draw twenty-four 4-in. x 2-1/2-in. rectangles on the paper; set aside.

Add 1 teaspoon vanilla, cream of tartar and salt to egg whites; beat on medium speed until soft peaks form. Gradually beat in sugar, 1 tablespoon at a time, on high until stiff, glossy peaks form and sugar is dissolved.

Insert a #12 round pastry tip in a pastry bag or heavy-duty plastic bag. Fill bag with meringue. Pipe meringue in long rows on rectangles until each is completely filled. Bake at 250° for 1 hour or until set and dry. Turn oven off; leave meringues in oven for 1 hour.

Remove from the oven and cool on baking sheets. When cooled completely, remove meringues from paper and store in an airtight container at room temperature.

In a microwave, melt chocolate chips and shortening; stir until smooth. Spread 1 tablespoon over each meringue. Let stand until chocolate is set.

In a chilled large bowl, beat cream until soft peaks form. Gradually add confectioners' sugar and remaining vanilla, beating on high until stiff peaks form.

Set aside 12 strawberries; cut remaining strawberries into 1/4-in. slices. Place 12 meringues on a flat serving platter. Spread each with 2 tablespoons whipped cream; top with sliced strawberries. Spread each with 2 tablespoons whipped cream. Top with remaining meringues and whipped cream. Loosely cover; refrigerate for up to 2 hours.

Just before serving, drizzle with chocolate syrup. Cut reserved strawberries in half. Arrange cut side down over whipped cream. Store in the refrigerator. **Yield:** 12 servings.

Sugared Twists

Shelley Blythe, Indianapolis, Indiana

Folks like these tender twists because they aren't rich or overly sweet. I usually double the recipe to feed our five eager eaters and to fill holiday gift plates for friends.

3-1/2 cups all-purpose flour
2 tablespoons plus 1 cup sugar, *divided*
1 teaspoon salt
1/2 cup cold butter, cubed
1/2 cup shortening
1 package (1/4 ounce) active dry yeast
1/4 cup warm water (110° to 115°)
2 eggs, lightly beaten
1/2 cup sour cream
2-1/2 teaspoons vanilla extract, *divided*
Red and green *or* multicolored nonpareils

In a large bowl, combine the flour, 2 tablespoons sugar and salt. Cut in butter and shortening until mixture resembles coarse crumbs.

In a small bowl, dissolve yeast in warm water; set aside. Add the eggs, sour cream and 1 teaspoon vanilla. Stir into flour mixture; beat until smooth. Cover and refrigerate overnight.

Punch dough down; divide in half. Combine remaining sugar and vanilla; sprinkle some over work surface. Roll each portion of dough into a 15-in. x 5-in. rectangle. Fold in thirds; sprinkle with additional sugar mixture. Repeat rolling and folding twice.

Cut into 5-in. x 1-in. strips. Sprinkle with nonpareils; press down lightly. Twist and place on greased baking sheets. Bake at 350° for 18-20 minutes or until golden brown. Remove from pans to wire racks to cool. **Yield:** 2-1/2 dozen.

Strawberry Almond Pastries

Connie Moore, Medway, Ohio

I try hard to avoid sugar, but I don't want to give up sweet treats altogether. Fruit spread provides wonderful flavor in desserts like these pastries. Made with convenient phyllo dough, they are light and crisp—flaky on the outside and chewy inside.

12 sheets phyllo dough (14 inches x 9 inches)
1 jar (10 ounces) strawberry all-fruit spread
1/4 cup slivered almonds

Place one sheet of phyllo dough on a work surface with a long side facing you; spray dough with cooking spray. Layer with two more sheets, spraying in between. (Keep remaining phyllo dough covered with plastic wrap and a damp towel to prevent it from drying out.) Spread half of the fruit spread over dough to within 1/2 in. of edges. Sprinkle with half of the almonds.

Roll up, jelly-roll style, starting with a long side; moisten edges with water and press to seal. Cut into three pieces. Repeat three more times with remaining ingredients.

Place pieces, cut side down, 1 in. apart on a baking sheet coated with cooking spray. Lightly spray tops with cooking spray. Bake at 375° for 12-15 minutes or until golden brown. Remove to wire racks to cool. **Yield:** 1 dozen.

Lemon Meringue Desserts

Taste of Home Test Kitchen

These pretty individual dessert cups are cute as can be—and yummy, too. A sweet and fluffy golden meringue tops the pudding that's rich with lemony flavor.

2 egg whites
2/3 cup sugar plus 2 tablespoons sugar, *divided*
2 tablespoons cornstarch
1 cup cold water
1 egg, lightly beaten
1/2 cup lemon juice
1 tablespoon butter
1 teaspoon grated lemon peel
1/8 teaspoon cream of tartar

Let egg whites stand at room temperature for 30 minutes. In a small saucepan, combine 2/3 cup sugar and cornstarch. Stir in water until smooth. Cook and stir over medium-high heat until thickened and bubbly. Reduce heat; cook and stir 2 minutes longer.

Remove from the heat. Stir a small amount of hot filling into egg; return all to pan, stirring constantly. Bring to a gentle boil; cook and stir 2 minutes longer. Remove from the heat. Gently stir in the lemon juice, butter and peel. Pour into four 6-oz. custard cups; set aside.

In a bowl, beat egg whites and cream of tartar on medium speed until soft peaks form. Gradually beat in remaining sugar, 1 tablespoon at a time, on high until stiff, glossy peaks form and sugar is dissolved. Spread meringue over lemon mixture, sealing edges to sides of cups. Bake at 375° for 5-7 minutes or until golden brown. **Yield:** 4 servings.

Apricot Strudel Sticks

Caroline Anderson, Toledo, Ohio

When I share this recipe, folks often do a double take when they see ice cream in the pastry! The recipe makes 6 dozen, so you have plenty to both keep and share.

- 4 cups all-purpose flour
- 1/4 teaspoon salt
- 2 cups cold butter, cubed
- 2 cups French vanilla ice cream, softened

Confectioners' sugar

- 1 can (12 ounces) apricot cake and pastry filling
- 1/2 cup golden raisins
- 1/2 cup chopped pecans

Cinnamon-sugar

In a large bowl, combine the flour and salt; cut in butter until crumbly. Add ice cream, tossing with a fork until a ball forms. Refrigerate overnight.

Shape dough into six balls. Lightly sprinkle work surface with confectioners' sugar; roll out each ball into a 13-in. x 8-in. rectangle. Spread apricot filling evenly over dough to within 1/2 in. of edges. Top with raisins and pecans; sprinkle with cinnamon-sugar. Roll up jelly-roll style into a tight roll, starting with a long side; pinch seam to seal.

Carefully place on three greased baking sheets. Bake at 350° for 25-30 minutes or until lightly browned. Remove to wire racks to cool completely. Cut each roll into 12 slices; sprinkle cut sides with confectioners' sugar. **Yield:** 6 dozen.

Editor's Note: This recipe was tested with Solo brand cake and pastry filling. Look for it in the baking aisle.

Vanilla Custard Cups

Billie Bohannan, Imperial, California

When I was living with my mother, she loved custard, so I'd make this comforting dessert each week. Without leftovers, there's no chance of getting tired of this treat!

- 1 egg
- 1 cup milk
- 3 tablespoons brown sugar
- 3/4 teaspoon vanilla extract
- 1/8 teaspoon salt, optional
- 1/8 teaspoon ground nutmeg

In a small bowl, beat the egg, milk, brown sugar, vanilla and salt if desired until blended. Pour into two ungreased 6-oz. custard cups. Sprinkle with nutmeg.

Place cups in a 9-in. square baking pan. Fill pan with hot water to a depth of 1 in. Bake, uncovered, at 350° for 30-35 minutes or until a knife inserted near the center comes out clean. **Yield:** 2 servings.

Layered Brownie Dessert

Muriel Ledeboer, Oostburg, Wisconsin

A tasty brownie is the base for cream cheese and chocolate pudding layers in this make-ahead dessert.

- 1 cup butter, softened
- 2 cups sugar
- 2 eggs
- 1 teaspoon vanilla extract
- 2 cups all-purpose flour
- 1/2 cup baking cocoa
- 1/2 teaspoon salt
- 1/2 teaspoon baking powder
- 1 cup chopped walnuts

FILLLING:

- 2 packages (one 8 ounces, one 3 ounces) cream cheese, softened
- 2 cups confectioners' sugar
- 2 cups whipped topping

TOPPING:

- 2 cups cold milk
- 1 package (3.9 ounces) instant chocolate pudding mix

Whipped topping and chopped walnuts

In a large bowl, cream butter and sugar. Add eggs, one at a time, beating well after each addition. Add vanilla. Combine the flour, cocoa, salt and baking powder; add to creamed mixture just until moistened. Stir in nuts.

Transfer to a greased 13-in. x 9-in. x 2-in. baking pan. Bake at 350° for 20-25 minutes or until a toothpick inserted near the center comes out clean. Cool completely on a wire rack.

In a small bowl, beat cream cheese and confectioners' sugar until smooth. Fold in whipped topping; spread over brownies. In a bowl, whisk milk and pudding mix for 2 minutes. Let stand for 2 minutes or until soft-set. Spread over filling. Refrigerate for 1 hour or until serving. Cut into squares; garnish with whipped topping and nuts. Store in the refrigerator. **Yield:** 12-15 servings.

Great Flavor Combinations The chocolate brownie with the chocolate topping combination in Layered Brownie Dessert will definitely be a hit. However, you don't have to limit yourself to that flavor combo. When you feel like experimenting, try vanilla, French vanilla, white chocolate or even butterscotch pudding for the topping.

Burnt Custard

Heidi Main, Anchorage, Alaska

The recipe for this smooth-as-silk custard came from a local restaurant years ago. With its broiled topping, it looks pretty in individual cups.

    4   egg yolks
    1/2 cup plus 6 teaspoons sugar, *divided*
    2   cups heavy whipping cream
    3   teaspoons vanilla extract

In a small bowl, whisk egg yolks and sugar. In a small saucepan, heat cream over medium heat until bubbles form around sides of pan. Remove from the heat; stir a small amount of hot cream into egg yolk mixture. Return all to the pan, stirring constantly. Stir in vanilla.

Transfer to six 6-oz. ramekins or custard cups. Place cups in a baking pan; add 1 in. of boiling water to pan. Bake, uncovered, at 350° for 40-45 minutes or until centers are just set (mixture will jiggle). Remove ramekins from water bath; cool for 10 minutes. Cover and refrigerate for at least 4 hours.

Before serving, let stand at room temperature for 15 minutes. Sprinkle top with remaining sugar. Broil 8 in. from the heat for 2-4 minutes or until the sugar is caramelized. **Yield:** 6 servings.

Luscious Lemon Cheesecake

Kaaren Jurack, North Riverside, Illinois

I'm always greeted with oohs and aahs when I bring out this exquisite dessert. It has a wonderful lemony flavor, creamy texture and rich sour cream topping.

CRUST:
- 1-1/4 cups graham cracker crumbs (about 20 squares)
- 3/4 cup finely chopped nuts
- 1/4 cup sugar
- 1/3 cup butter, melted

FILLING:
- 4 packages (8 ounces *each*) cream cheese, softened
- 1-1/4 cups sugar
- 4 eggs
- 1 tablespoon lemon juice
- 2 teaspoons grated lemon peel
- 1 teaspoon vanilla extract

TOPPING:
- 2 cups (16 ounces) sour cream
- 1/4 cup sugar
- 1 teaspoon grated lemon peel
- 1 teaspoon vanilla extract

In a bowl, combine the crumbs, nuts and sugar; stir in butter. Press onto the bottom of a greased 10-in. springform pan; set aside. In a large bowl, beat cream cheese and sugar until smooth. Add eggs, beating on low speed just until combined. Stir in the lemon juice, peel and vanilla; beat just until blended. Pour into crust. Place on a baking sheet.

Bake at 350° for 55 minutes or until center is almost set. Remove from the oven; let stand for 5 minutes. Combine topping ingredients; spread over filling. Return to the oven for 5 minutes.

Cool on a wire rack for 10 minutes. Carefully run a knife around edge of pan to loosen; cool 1 hour longer. Refrigerate overnight. Remove sides of pan. Let stand at room temperature for 30 minutes before slicing. **Yield:** 12-14 servings.

Berries in a Nest

Iola Egle, Bella Vista, Arkansas

This medley of fresh berries with sugar, pepper and balsamic vinegar makes a fun summer salad when served on lettuce. Or for an impressive dinner finale, serve this the refreshing treat in phyllo cups.

- 4 cups halved fresh strawberries
- 1 cup fresh blackberries
- 1 cup fresh raspberries
- 1/3 cup sugar
- 3 tablespoons balsamic vinegar
- 1/4 to 1/2 teaspoon coarsely ground pepper

PHYLLO NESTS:
- 8 sheets phyllo dough (14 inches x 9 inches)
- 2 teaspoons sugar
- 1/4 teaspoon ground cinnamon

In a large bowl, combine the strawberries, blackberries and raspberries. Sprinkle with sugar; gently toss to coat. Let stand for 20 minutes. Pour vinegar over berries; sprinkle with pepper. Gently toss to coat. Cover and refrigerate for 2 hours.

For phyllo nests, coat giant nonstick muffin cups with a cooking spray; set aside. Unroll phyllo dough sheets; remove one sheet. (While assembling, keep remaining dough covered with plastic wrap and a damp cloth.)

For each nest, cut one sheet in half lengthwise and cut in thirds widthwise. Stack three sections and place in a prepared cup; spray with cooking spray. Stack remaining three sections and place in cup, alternating points. Spray with cooking spray. Combine the sugar and cinnamon; sprinkle about 1/4 teaspoon cinnamon-sugar over dough. Repeat with remaining sheets of dough.

Bake at 375° for 7-8 minutes or until golden brown. Cool for 5 minutes before carefully removing from pan to a wire rack to cool completely.

Using a slotted spoon, fill each nest with about 3/4 cup berry mixture. Drizzle with a small amount of juice. Serve immediately. **Yield:** 8 servings.

Cookies

pg. 309

pg. 287

pg. 322

pg. 332

Macaroon Kisses

Angie Lansman, Perry, Iowa

One bite and I think you'll agree this is the best coconut cookie you've ever tasted. These eye-catching cookies are always the first to disappear from my cookie tray.

- 1/3 cup butter, softened
- 1 package (3 ounces) cream cheese, softened
- 3/4 cup sugar
- 1 egg yolk
- 2 teaspoons orange juice
- 2 teaspoons almond extract
- 1-1/4 cups all-purpose flour
- 2 teaspoons baking powder
- 1/4 teaspoon salt
- 1 package (14 ounces) flaked coconut, *divided*
- 1 package (13 ounces) milk chocolate kisses

In a large bowl, cream the butter, cream cheese and sugar until light and fluffy. Beat in the egg yolk, orange juice and extract. Combine the flour, baking powder and salt; gradually add to the creamed mixture and mix well. Stir in 3-2/3 cups coconut. Cover and refrigerate for 30 minutes or until easy to handle.

Roll into 1-in. balls, then roll in remaining coconut. Place 1 in. apart on ungreased baking sheets. Bake at 350° for 12-15 minutes or until the edges are lightly browned.

Immediately press a chocolate kiss into the center of each cookie. Cool for 1 minute before removing to wire racks. **Yield:** about 4-1/2 dozen.

Pistachio Orange Drops

Susan Zarzycki, Saratoga, California

These shaped sugar cookies are topped with melted chocolate and chopped pistachios, making them a pretty treat for special occasions.

- 1 cup butter, softened
- 1 cup confectioners' sugar
- 2 cups all-purpose flour
- 1 cup finely chopped pistachios
- 1 teaspoon grated orange peel
- 1 cup (6 ounces) semisweet chocolate chips
- 2 tablespoons shortening

In a large bowl, cream butter and sugar until light and fluffy. Gradually add flour and mix well. Set aside 3 tablespoons pistachios for topping; stir remaining pistachios and orange peel into dough.

Roll into 1-in. balls. Place 1-1/2 in. apart on ungreased baking sheets. Bake at 375° for 8-10 minutes or until lightly browned. Remove to wire racks to cool.

In a microwave, melt chocolate chips and shortening; stir until smooth. Dip each cookie halfway, allowing excess to drip off. Dip in reserved pistachios. Place on waxed paper; let stand until set. **Yield:** about 4-1/2 dozen.

Cappuccino Flats

Jacqueline Cline, Drummond, Wisconsin

These coffee-flavored cookies are so delectable most people can't believe they're made in my own kitchen instead of a gourmet bakery!

- 1/2 cup butter, softened
- 1/2 cup shortening
- 1/2 cup sugar
- 1/2 cup packed brown sugar
- 1 tablespoon instant coffee granules
- 1 teaspoon warm water
- 1 egg
- 2 squares (1 ounce *each*) unsweetened chocolate, melted and cooled
- 2 cups all-purpose flour
- 1 teaspoon ground cinnamon
- 1/4 teaspoon salt
- 1-1/2 cups semisweet chocolate chips
- 3 tablespoons shortening

In a large bowl, cream butter, shortening and sugars until light and fluffy. Dissolve coffee in water; add to creamed mixture with egg and melted chocolate until blended. Combine the flour, cinnamon and salt; gradually add to creamed mixture and mix well (dough will be sticky). Shape into two 6-1/2-in. rolls; wrap each in plastic wrap. Refrigerate for 4 hours or until firm.

Unwrap and cut into 1/4-in. slices. Place 2 in. apart on ungreased baking sheets. Bake at 350° for 10-12 minutes or until firm. Remove to wire racks to cool.

In a microwave, melt chocolate chips and shortening; stir until smooth. Dip each cookie halfway in chocolate; allow excess to drip off. Place on waxed paper; let stand until set. **Yield:** 4-1/2 dozen.

Raspberry Coconut Cookies

Lesley Mansfield, Monroe, North Carolina

My mother gave me the recipe for these rich, buttery cookies. Raspberry preserves and a cream filling make them doubly delicious.

- 3/4 cup butter, softened
- 1/2 cup sugar
- 1 egg
- 1 teaspoon vanilla extract
- 2 cups all-purpose flour
- 1/2 cup flaked coconut
- 1-1/2 teaspoons baking powder
- 1/4 teaspoon salt

FILLING:
- 1/4 cup butter, softened
- 3/4 cup confectioners' sugar
- 2 teaspoons milk
- 1/2 teaspoon vanilla extract
- 1/2 cup raspberry preserves

In a large bowl, cream butter and sugar until light and fluffy. Beat in egg and vanilla. Combine the flour, coconut, baking powder and salt; gradually add to the creamed mixture and mix well.

Shape into 1-in. balls. Place 1-1/2 in. apart on ungreased baking sheets; flatten with a glass dipped in flour. Bake at 350° for 12-14 minutes or until edges begin to brown. Cool on wire racks.

In a small bowl, beat the butter, confectioners' sugar, milk and vanilla until smooth. Place 1/2 teaspoon preserves and a scant teaspoon of filling on the bottom of half of the cookies; top with remaining cookies. **Yield:** 2-1/2 dozen.

Chocolate-Filled Poppy Seed Cookies

Karen Mead, Granville, New York

While these cookies have been around for years, they remain enjoyable to this day. A co-worker prepared them for a cookie exchange a while back...they were the biggest hit of the party.

1 cup butter, softened
1/2 cup sugar
2 egg yolks
1 teaspoon vanilla extract
2 cups all-purpose flour
3 tablespoons poppy seeds
1/4 teaspoon salt
1 cup (6 ounces) semisweet chocolate chips, melted

In a small mixing bowl, cream butter and sugar until light and fluffy. Beat in egg yolks and vanilla. Combine the flour, poppy seeds and salt; gradually add to the creamed mixture and mix well.

Roll into 1-in. balls. Place 2 in. apart on ungreased baking sheets. Using the end of a wooden spoon handle, make an indentation in the center of each.

Bake at 375° for 10-12 minutes or until lightly browned. Immediately make an indentation in the center again. Remove to wire racks to cool slightly; fill with melted chocolate. **Yield:** 6-1/2 dozen.

Chocolate Macadamia Meltaways

Barbara Sepcich, Galt, California

I came up with this recipe by accident one day when I wanted to make some cookies. Rather than go to the store, I decided to use ingredients already in my cupboard, and these were the delicious result.

- 1/2 cup butter, softened
- 1/4 cup confectioners' sugar
- 1/2 teaspoon vanilla extract
- 1-1/4 cups all-purpose flour
- 1 jar (3-1/2 ounces) macadamia nuts, finely chopped

FILLING:
- 1 cup (6 ounces) semisweet chocolate chips
- 1/2 cup coarsely chopped macadamia nuts

Additional confectioners' sugar

In a small bowl, cream butter and sugar until light and fluffy. Beat in vanilla. Gradually add flour and mix well. Stir in nuts (dough will be stiff); set aside.

For filling, in a microwave, melt chocolate chips; stir until smooth. Stir in nuts; cool slightly. Drop by 1/2 teaspoonfuls onto a waxed paper-lined baking sheet; cover and refrigerate for 30 minutes.

Shape teaspoonfuls of the dough around each piece of chocolate-nut mixture so it is completely covered. Place 2 in. apart on ungreased baking sheets. Bake at 375° for 12-14 minutes or until lightly browned. Gently roll warm cookies in confectioners' sugar; cool on wire racks. **Yield:** 2-1/2 dozen.

Michigan Cherry Drops

Carol Blue, Barnesville, Pennsylvania

I usually double this recipe so that I have plenty to share during the holidays. Pretty pink cookies, such as these, are a wonderful treat.

- 1 cup butter, softened
- 1 cup sugar
- 1/2 cup packed brown sugar
- 4 eggs
- 1-1/2 teaspoons vanilla extract
- 4 cups all-purpose flour
- 1 teaspoon salt
- 1 teaspoon ground cinnamon
- 1/2 teaspoon ground nutmeg
- 3-1/2 cups chopped walnuts
- 3 cups chopped maraschino cherries
- 2-2/3 cups raisins

In a large bowl, cream the butter and sugars until light and fluffy. Add eggs, one at a time, beating well after each addition. Beat in vanilla. Combine the flour, salt, cinnamon and nutmeg; gradually add to the creamed mixture and mix well. Transfer to a large bowl if necessary. Stir in the walnuts, cherries and raisins.

Drop by tablespoonfuls 2 in. apart onto ungreased baking sheets. Bake at 350° for 16-18 minutes or until lightly browned. Remove to wire racks to cool. Store in an airtight container. **Yield:** about 14 dozen.

Peanut Butter Treats

Judy Stanton, Thonotosassa, Florida

You can't miss with these no-fuss cookies. People are surprised to see the short list of ingredients. The goodies are fragile, so store them carefully when completely cooled.

- 2 cups peanut butter
- 1-1/4 cups sugar
- 2 eggs
- 52 milk chocolate stars *or* kisses

In a large bowl, cream peanut butter and sugar until light and fluffy. Add eggs, one at a time, beating well after each addition (dough will be sticky).

With floured hands, roll tablespoonfuls into 1-1/4-in. balls. Place 2 in. apart on ungreased baking sheets. Bake at 350° for 14-16 minutes or until tops are cracked. Remove to wire racks. Immediately press a chocolate star in the center of each. Cool. **Yield:** 4-1/2 dozen.

Editor's Note: Reduced-fat or generic brands of peanut butter are not recommended for this recipe.

Orange Sugar Rollouts

Margaret Hancock, Camp Verde, Arizona

When my children were young, we would bake and decorate these cookies every Christmas. Now I carry on this family tradition with my grandchildren.

- 2/3 cup shortening
- 3/4 cup sugar
- 1 egg
- 4 teaspoons milk
- 1/2 to 1 teaspoon grated orange peel
- 1/2 teaspoon vanilla extract
- 2 cups all-purpose flour
- 1-1/2 teaspoons baking powder
- 1/4 teaspoon salt

FROSTING:
- 1/2 cup butter, softened
- 4 cups confectioners' sugar
- 1 teaspoon vanilla extract
- 1/2 teaspoon grated orange peel
- 2 to 4 tablespoons orange juice
- Yellow food coloring, optional

In a large bowl, cream shortening and sugar until light and fluffy. Beat in the egg, milk, orange peel and vanilla. Combine the flour, baking powder and salt; gradually add to the creamed mixture and mix well.

On a lightly floured surface, roll out to 1/4-in. thickness. Cut with a floured 2-1/2-in. cookie cutter dipped in flour. Place 1 in. apart on greased baking sheets. Bake at 375° for 6-8 minutes or until lightly browned. Remove to wire racks to cool.

In a large bowl, beat the butter, confectioners' sugar, vanilla, orange peel and enough orange juice to achieve spreading consistency. Add food coloring if desired. Frost cooled cookies. **Yield:** about 3-1/2 dozen.

Special Oatmeal Chip Cookies

Carol Poskie, Pittsburgh, Pennsylvania

My son dubbed these "the cookie" after just one taste, and they've become my signature cookie since then. I haven't shared my secret recipe until now.

- 1 cup butter, softened
- 1 cup peanut butter
- 1 cup sugar
- 1 cup packed brown sugar
- 2 eggs
- 1 teaspoon vanilla extract
- 3 cups old-fashioned oats
- 1 cup all-purpose flour
- 2 teaspoons ground cinnamon
- 1 teaspoon baking soda
- 1/4 teaspoon ground nutmeg
- 1-1/2 cups semisweet chocolate chips

DRIZZLE:
- 1 cup white chocolate candy coating, melted
- 1 cup dark chocolate candy coating, melted

In a large bowl, cream the butter, peanut butter and sugars until light and fluffy. Add eggs, one at a time, beating well after each addition. Beat in vanilla. Combine the oats, flour, cinnamon, baking soda and nutmeg; gradually add to the creamed mixture and mix well. Stir in the chocolate chips.

Roll into 1-in. balls. Place 2 in. apart on greased baking sheets; flatten to 1/2-in. thickness. Bake at 350° for 10-12 minutes or until golden brown. Remove to wire racks to cool completely.

Drizzle with white coating in one direction, then with dark coating in the opposite direction to form a crisscross pattern. **Yield:** about 5-1/2 dozen.

Editor's Note: Reduced-fat or generic brands of peanut butter are not recommended for this recipe.

Chocolate Jubilees

LaVera Fenton, Colorado Springs, Colorado

Rich and fudgy, these cookies make many appearances in care packages I send out. I combined several recipes and added maraschino cherries for this fabulous recipe.

- 1 cup butter, softened
- 1 cup shortening
- 2 cups packed brown sugar
- 1 cup sugar
- 4 eggs
- 2 to 3 teaspoons almond extract
- 4 cups all-purpose flour
- 1 cup quick-cooking oats
- 1 cup baking cocoa
- 2 teaspoons baking soda
- 2 teaspoons salt
- 3 cups (18 ounces) semisweet chocolate chips
- 1 jar (16 ounces) maraschino cherries, drained and chopped
- 1 cup sliced almonds, optional

In a large bowl, cream butter, shortening and sugars until light and fluffy. Add eggs, one at a time, beating well after each addition. Beat in extract. Combine the flour, oats, cocoa, baking soda and salt; gradually add to the creamed mixture and mix well. Transfer to a larger bowl if necessary. Stir in chocolate chips, cherries and almonds if desired.

Roll into 1-1/2-in. balls. Place 3 in. apart on ungreased baking sheets. Bake at 375° for 12-14 minutes or until the edges are firm. Remove to wire racks to cool. **Yield:** about 5-1/2 dozen.

Buttery Lace Cookies

Lillie Duhon, Port Neches, Texas

I worked with a group of engineers for over 30 years, and these cookies were a favorite of theirs. They go so well with a steaming cup of coffee or tea.

- 2 cups quick-cooking oats
- 2 cups sugar
- 3 tablespoons all-purpose flour
- 1/2 teaspoon baking powder
- 2 eggs
- 1 teaspoon vanilla extract
- 1 teaspoon lemon extract
- 1/4 teaspoon almond extract
- 1 cup butter, melted
- 1 cup chopped pecans

In a bowl, combine the oats, sugar, flour and baking powder. Add eggs, one at a time, beating well after each addition. Beat in extracts. Stir in butter and pecans.

Drop by teaspoonfuls 3 in. apart onto lightly greased foil-lined baking sheets. Bake at 350° for 10-12 minutes or until lacy and golden brown. Cool completely on pans before carefully removing to wire racks. **Yield:** about 9 dozen.

Hint O' Mint Cookies

Janet Hartmann, Gibbon, Minnesota

After I experimented in the kitchen mixing and matching ingredients to come up with a new and different cookie recipe, my husband proclaimed these the winner! With a little peppermint extract, these fabulous cake-like cookies bring a nice close to any meal.

1/2	cup butter, softened
1	cup sugar
1	egg
1/2	teaspoon vanilla extract
1/4	teaspoon peppermint extract
2	cups all-purpose flour
1/2	teaspoon baking soda
1/4	teaspoon cream of tartar
1/2	cup buttermilk

FROSTING:

3	tablespoons butter, softened
2	cups confectioners' sugar
1/3	cup baking cocoa
1/8	teaspoon salt
1	teaspoon vanilla extract
2	to 4 tablespoons milk

In a large bowl, cream butter and sugar until light and fluffy. Beat in egg and extracts. Combine the flour, baking soda and cream of tartar; add to the creamed mixture alternately with buttermilk, beating well after each addition.

Drop by heaping teaspoonfuls 2 in. apart onto ungreased baking sheets. Flatten with a glass dipped in sugar. Bake at 350° for 6 to 8 minutes or until set. Remove to wire racks to cool completely.

In a small bowl, cream butter, confectioners' sugar, cocoa and salt until light and fluffy. Beat in vanilla and enough milk to achieve spreading consistency. Frost cooled cookies. **Yield:** 4 dozen.

Pecan Fingers

Irene Risbry, Colorado Springs, Colorado

You can't go wrong with the combination of butter and pecans in these cookies. I never serve them without receiving requests for the recipe.

1	cup butter, softened
1/2	cup confectioners' sugar
2	cups all-purpose flour
1/2	teaspoon salt
1	cup finely chopped pecans

Additional confectioners' sugar

In a large bowl, cream butter and sugar until light and fluffy. Combine flour and salt; gradually add to creamed mixture and mix well. Stir in pecans.

Shape tablespoonfuls into 2-in. fingers. Place 2 in. apart on ungreased baking sheets. Bake at 350° for 15-18 minutes or until lightly browned. Roll warm cookies in confectioners' sugar; cool on wire racks. **Yield:** about 4 dozen.

Lemon Poppy Seed Slices

Pauline Piraino, Bay Shore, New York

My mom taught me to bake, and I use lots of recipes from her abundant collection, including this one.

3/4	cup butter, softened
1	cup sugar
1	egg
1	tablespoon milk
2	teaspoons finely grated lemon peel
1/2	teaspoon vanilla extract
1/2	teaspoon lemon extract, optional
2-1/2	cups all-purpose flour
1/4	cup poppy seeds

In a large bowl, cream butter and sugar until light and fluffy. Beat in the egg, milk, lemon peel and extracts. Gradually add flour and mix well. Stir in poppy seeds. Shape into two 8-in. rolls; wrap each in plastic wrap. Refrigerate for 3 hours or until firm.

Unwrap and cut into 1/4-in. slices. Place 2 in. apart on ungreased baking sheets. Bake at 350° for 10-12 minutes or until edges are golden. Cool for 2 minutes before removing to wire racks to cool completely. **Yield:** 5-1/2 dozen.

German Spice Cookies

Joan Tyson, Bowling Green, Ohio

These chewy spice cookies are great with coffee and taste even better the next day. The recipe has been a family favorite for a long time.

- 3 eggs
- 2 cups packed brown sugar
- 1 teaspoon ground cloves
- 1 teaspoon ground cinnamon
- 1/2 teaspoon pepper
- 2 cups all-purpose flour
- 1/2 teaspoon baking soda
- 1/2 teaspoon salt
- 1 cup raisins
- 1 cup chopped walnuts

In a large bowl, beat eggs. Add the brown sugar, cloves, cinnamon and pepper. Combine the flour, baking soda and salt; gradually add to the egg mixture. Stir in raisins and walnuts.

Drop by tablespoonfuls 2 in. apart onto lightly greased baking sheets. Bake at 400° for 8-10 minutes or until the surface cracks. Remove to wire racks to cool. **Yield:** 3-1/2 dozen.

Nutty Orange Spritz Strips

Jeannie Mayfield, Santa Rosa, California

I participated in an annual cookie exchange with my co-workers, and the other women raved about these. The recipe now holds a treasured place in our family cookbook.

- 3/4 cup butter, softened
- 1 cup sugar
- 1 egg
- 4 teaspoons grated orange peel
- 2-3/4 cups all-purpose flour
- 1 teaspoon baking powder
- 1/4 teaspoon salt
- 2 tablespoons orange juice
- 1 cup (6 ounces) semisweet chocolate chips
- 1 tablespoon shortening
- 1 cup ground walnuts

In a large bowl, cream butter and sugar until light and fluffy. Beat in egg and orange peel. Combine the flour, baking powder and salt; add to creamed mixture alternately with orange juice, beating well after each addition.

Using a cookie press fitted with a bar disk, form dough into long strips on ungreased baking sheets. Cut each strip into 3-in. pieces (there is no need to separate the pieces).

Bake at 350° for 12-14 minutes or until edges are golden. Cut into pieces if necessary. Remove to wire racks to cool.

In microwave, melt chocolate and shortening; stir until smooth. Dip each end of cookies in chocolate mixture; allow excess to drip off. Roll in walnuts. Place on waxed paper; let stand until set. **Yield:** about 4-1/2 dozen.

Caramel Creams

Barbara Yongers, Kingman, Kansas

These cookies are delicious plain, but I like to make them into sandwich cookies with the brown butter filling. In a pinch, use a can of frosting instead of making your own.

- 1 cup butter, softened
- 2/3 cup packed brown sugar
- 2 egg yolks
- 1/2 teaspoon vanilla extract
- 2-1/2 cups all-purpose flour
- 1/3 cup finely chopped pecans
- 1/4 teaspoon salt

FILLING:
- 2 tablespoons plus 1-1/2 teaspoons butter
- 1-1/2 cups confectioners' sugar
- 1/2 teaspoon vanilla extract
- 2 to 3 tablespoons heavy whipping cream

In a large bowl, cream butter and brown sugar until light and fluffy. Beat in egg yolks and vanilla. Combine the flour, pecans and salt; gradually add to the creamed mixture and beat well. Shape into two 10-in. rolls; wrap each in plastic wrap. Refrigerate for 1-2 hours.

Unwrap and cut into 1/4-in. slices. Place 2 in. apart on ungreased baking sheets. Bake at 350° for 11-13 minutes or until golden brown. Remove to wire racks to cool.

For filling, in a small saucepan, cook butter over medium heat until golden brown. Pour into a large bowl, beat in the confectioners' sugar, vanilla and enough cream to achieve spreading consistency. Spread on the bottom of half of the cookies; top with remaining cookies. **Yield:** about 3 dozen.

Lollipop Cookies

Jean Edwards, Indianapolis, Indiana

You can use your imagination with this recipe to create designs for any season—the possibilities are endless! Cookie "lollipops" are always a hit with the kids.

    1   cup butter, softened
1-1/2   cups confectioners' sugar
    1   egg
    1   teaspoon vanilla extract
    1/4 to 1/2 teaspoon almond extract
2-1/2   cups all-purpose flour
    1   teaspoon baking soda
    1   teaspoon cream of tartar
    2   squares (1 ounce *each*) semisweet chocolate, melted
FROSTING:
    1   cup confectioners' sugar
    1/4 to 1/2 teaspoon almond extract
    1/4   teaspoon salt
    1   to 2 teaspoons milk
Red-hot candies and red sprinkles

In a large bowl, cream butter and confectioners' sugar until light and fluffy. Beat in egg and extracts. Combine the flour, baking soda and cream of tartar; gradually add to the creamed mixture and mix well. Divide dough in half; stir chocolate into one half. Refrigerate for 2 hours or until easy to handle.

On a lightly floured surface, roll out each portion to 1/8-in. thickness. Cut with a 2-1/2-in. cookie cutter. Place 1 in. apart on lightly greased baking sheets.

Bake at 375° for 7-8 minutes or until lightly browned. Remove to wire racks to cool.

For frosting, combine the confectioners' sugar, extract, salt and enough milk to achieve spreading consistency. Frost chocolate cookies. Place a wooden stick on each cookie, leaving 3 in. for handle. Top each with a plain cookie. Frost tops; sprinkle with candies. **Yield:** 3 dozen.

Maple Sugar Cookies

Anna Glaus, Greensburg, Pennsylvania

This recipe is requested by friends and family every time I'm asked to bring cookies for an event. Folks enjoy the subtle maple flavor in this crisp cookie.

    1   cup butter-flavored shortening
1-1/4 cups sugar
    2   eggs
 1/4 cup maple syrup
    3   teaspoons vanilla extract
    3   cups all-purpose flour
 3/4 teaspoon baking powder

 1/2 teaspoon baking soda
 1/2 teaspoon salt

In a large bowl, cream shortening and sugar until light and fluffy. Add eggs, one at a time, beating well after each addition. Beat in syrup and vanilla. Combine the remaining ingredients; gradually add to the creamed mixture and mix well. Cover and refrigerate for 2 hours or until easy to handle.

On a lightly floured surface, roll out to 1/8-in. thickness. Cut with floured 2-1/2-in. cookie cutters. Place 1 in. apart on ungreased baking sheets.

Bake at 350° for 9-12 minutes or until golden brown. Remove to wire racks to cool. **Yield:** 4 dozen.

Five-Chip Cookies

Sharon Hedstrom, Minnetonka, Minnesota

With peanut butter, oats and five kinds of chips, these cookies make a hearty snack that appeals to kids of all ages. I sometimes double the recipe to share with friends and neighbors.

- 1 cup butter, softened
- 1 cup peanut butter
- 1 cup sugar
- 2/3 cup packed brown sugar
- 2 eggs
- 1 teaspoon vanilla extract
- 2 cups all-purpose flour
- 1 cup old-fashioned oats
- 2 teaspoons baking soda
- 1/2 teaspoon salt
- 2/3 cup *each* milk chocolate chips, semisweet chocolate chips, peanut butter chips, vanilla chips and butterscotch chips

In a large bowl, cream the butter, peanut butter and sugars until light and fluffy. Add eggs, one at a time, beating well after each addition. Beat in vanilla. Combine the flour, oats, baking soda and salt; gradually add to the creamed mixture and mix well. Stir in chips.

Drop by rounded tablespoonfuls 2 in. apart onto ungreased baking sheets. Bake at 350° for 10-12 minutes or until lightly browned. Cool for 1 minute before removing to wire racks. **Yield:** 4-1/2 dozen.

Editor's Note: Reduced-fat or generic brands of peanut butter are not recommended for this recipe.

Oatmeal Crispies

Karen Henson, St. Louis, Missouri

My husband, who normally isn't fond of oatmeal, thinks these old-fashioned cookies are great. With a hint of nutmeg, their aroma is wonderful as they bake...and they taste even better!

- 1 cup shortening
- 1 cup sugar
- 1 cup packed brown sugar
- 2 eggs
- 1 teaspoon vanilla extract
- 3 cups quick-cooking oats
- 1-1/2 cups all-purpose flour
- 1 teaspoon baking soda
- 1 teaspoon salt
- 1/4 teaspoon ground nutmeg
- 1/4 teaspoon ground cinnamon

In a large bowl, cream shortening and sugars until light and fluffy. Add eggs, one at a time, beating well after each addition. Beat in vanilla. Combine the oats, flour, baking soda, salt, nutmeg and cinnamon and mix well; gradually add to creamed mixture.

Drop by tablespoonfuls 2 in. apart onto ungreased baking sheets. Flatten with a fork. Bake at 350° for 10-12 minutes or until lightly browned. Remove to wire racks to cool. **Yield:** 5-1/2 dozen.

Mixing It Up Drop cookie dough is usually so thick that it can be dropped from a spoon and requires no shaping. If while you're mixing the dough the mixer begins to strain, use a wooden spoon to stir in the last of the flour or all of the nuts, chips and dried fruit.

Apricot Almond Blondies

Amy Forkner, Cheyenne, Wyoming

My mom shared this recipe with me after sampling these cookies at a bed-and-breakfast. For a little variation, I sometimes substitute cranberries and pecans for the apricots and almonds.

- 3/4 cup butter, softened
- 1 cup packed brown sugar
- 1 egg
- 1 teaspoon vanilla extract
- 1-2/3 cups all-purpose flour
- 1/2 teaspoon baking soda
- 1/4 teaspoon salt
- 1 package (10 to 12 ounces) vanilla *or* white chips
- 3/4 cup chopped almonds
- 3/4 cup chopped dried apricots

In a large bowl, cream butter and brown sugar until light and fluffy. Beat in egg and vanilla. Combine the flour, baking soda and salt; gradually add to the creamed mixture and mix well. Stir in the vanilla chips, almonds and apricots.

Drop by heaping tablespoonfuls 2 in. apart onto ungreased baking sheets. Bake at 350° for 7-9 minutes or until lightly browned. Remove to wire racks to cool. **Yield:** 6 dozen.

Sponge Cake Cookies

Terry Carpenter, Vineland, New Jersey

My heart's warmed by these cookies because the recipe comes from my grandmother. No wedding, shower or holiday gathering went by without our caring matriarch or her pretty little treats.

- 1 cup butter, softened
- 1-1/2 cups sugar
- 8 eggs
- 2 tablespoons lemon extract
- 4 cups all-purpose flour
- 1/4 cup baking powder

FROSTING:
- 1/2 cup butter, softened
- 3-3/4 cups confectioners' sugar
- 1 teaspoon lemon extract
- 1/8 teaspoon salt
- 3 to 4 tablespoons milk

Food coloring, optional
- 4 cups flaked coconut, optional

In a large bowl, cream butter and sugar until light and fluffy. Add eggs, one at a time, beating well after each addition. Beat in extract. Combine the flour and baking powder; gradually add to the creamed mixture and mix well.

Drop by teaspoonfuls 3 in. apart onto ungreased baking sheets. Bake at 400° for 6-8 minutes or until the edges are lightly browned. Remove to wire racks to cool.

In a small bowl, beat the butter, sugar, extract and salt until smooth. Add enough milk to achieve spreading consistency. Tint with food coloring if desired. Frost cooled cookies. Sprinkle with coconut if desired. **Yield:** 11 dozen.

Peanut Butter Jumbos

Deborah Huffer, Staunton, Virginia

Oats, peanut butter and chocolate make these soft, chewy cookies hearty. My whole family agrees this recipe is great.

- 1-1/2 cups peanut butter
- 1/2 cup butter, softened
- 1 cup sugar
- 1 cup packed brown sugar
- 3 eggs
- 1 teaspoon vanilla extract
- 4-1/2 cups quick-cooking oats
- 2 teaspoons baking soda
- 1 cup miniature semisweet chocolate chips
- 1 cup M&M's miniature baking bits

In a large bowl, cream the peanut butter, butter and sugars until light and fluffy. Add eggs, one at a time, beating well after each addition. Beat in vanilla. Combine oats and baking soda; gradually add to creamed mixture and mix well. Stir in chocolate chips and baking bits.

Drop by heaping tablespoonfuls 2 in. apart onto ungreased baking sheets. Bake at 350° for 12-14 minutes or until edges are browned. Remove to wire racks. **Yield:** 9 dozen.

Editor's Note: Reduced-fat or generic brands of peanut butter are not recommended for this recipe.

Butter Mint Cookies

Anita Epitropou, Zion, Illinois

These delicate cookies with a touch of mint were a big hit when I made them for a party at work.

    1   cup butter, softened
  1/2   cup confectioners' sugar
1-1/2   teaspoons peppermint extract
1-3/4   cups all-purpose flour
Green colored sugar

In a large bowl, cream butter and confectioners' sugar until light and fluffy. Beat in extract. Gradually add flour and mix well.

Roll tablespoonfuls of dough into balls. Place 1 in. apart on ungreased baking sheets; flatten with a glass dipped in colored sugar. Bake at 350° for 12-14 minutes or until firm. Remove to wire racks to cool. **Yield:** 3 dozen.

Surprise Cookies

Charmaine Martin, McAllen, Texas

Cottage cheese is the secret ingredient in these tender, flaky cookies. I'm not sure where the recipe came from, but my grandmother was a baker, so I like to believe it was one of hers.

- 1 cup butter, softened
- 3/4 cup 4% cottage cheese
- 2 cups all-purpose flour
- 1 egg, beaten
- 1 cup finely chopped walnuts
- 1/2 cup sugar
- 1/8 teaspoon ground cinnamon

In a large bowl, beat butter and cottage cheese until blended; gradually add flour and mix well. Cover and refrigerate for 2 hours or until easy to handle.

On a lightly floured surface, roll out to 1/8-in. thickness. Cut with a floured 2-in. round cookie cutter. Place 1 in. apart on ungreased baking sheets.

Brush tops with egg. Combine the walnuts, sugar and cinnamon; sprinkle over tops. Bake at 350° for 15-20 minutes or until golden brown. Remove to wire racks to cool. **Yield:** 6 dozen.

Crispy Scotchies

Joanne Kramer, Manchester, Iowa

I first tasted these cookies as a newlywed in 1959. Over the years, I've made a few modifications, and now they turn out perfectly every time.

- 6 tablespoons butter, softened
- 6 tablespoons butter-flavored shortening
- 1 cup sugar
- 1 cup packed brown sugar
- 2 eggs
- 1 teaspoon vanilla extract
- 4 cups crisp rice cereal, *divided*
- 1-1/2 cups all-purpose flour
- 1 teaspoon baking soda
- 1/2 teaspoon baking powder
- 1 cup butterscotch chips

TOPPING:
- 1/2 cup sugar
- 1/2 cup packed brown sugar

In a large bowl, cream the butter, shortening and sugars until light and fluffy. Add eggs, one at a time, beating well after each addition. Beat in vanilla. Crush 2 cups of cereal; add the flour, baking soda and baking powder. Gradually add to the creamed mixture and mix well. Stir in the butterscotch chips and remaining cereal. Combine topping ingredients in a small bowl.

Roll dough into 1-1/4-in. balls, then roll in topping. Place 2 in. apart on ungreased baking sheets; flatten slightly with a glass.

Bake at 350° for 10-12 minutes or until golden brown. Cool for 1 minute before removing to wire racks. **Yield:** about 5-1/2 dozen.

Marbled Chocolate Peanut Cookies

Shirley De Lange, Byron Center, Michigan

This recipe came about by accident when I was making both my husband's favorite peanut butter cookies and my favorite chocolate cookies. I had two small portions of dough left over and decided to combine them into one cookie.

PEANUT BUTTER DOUGH:
- 1 cup butter, softened
- 1 cup peanut butter
- 1-1/4 cups sugar
- 1-1/4 cups packed brown sugar
- 3 eggs
- 2 teaspoons vanilla extract
- 2-1/2 cups all-purpose flour
- 1/2 teaspoon baking soda
- 1/2 teaspoon salt
- 1 cup chopped peanuts

CHOCOLATE DOUGH:
- 1 cup butter, softened
- 1 cup packed brown sugar
- 3/4 cup sugar
- 3 eggs
- 2 teaspoons vanilla extract
- 2-1/2 cups all-purpose flour
- 1/2 cup baking cocoa
- 1/2 teaspoon baking soda
- 1/2 teaspoon salt
- 2 cups (12 ounces) semisweet chocolate chips

In a large bowl, cream the butter, peanut butter and sugars until light and fluffy. Add eggs one at a time, beating well after each addition. Beat in vanilla. Combine the flour, baking soda and salt; gradually add to the creamed mixture and mix well. Stir in peanuts; set aside.

For chocolate dough, in another bowl, cream butter and sugars until light and fluffy. Add eggs, one at a time, beating well after each addition. Beat in vanilla. Combine the flour, cocoa, baking soda and salt; gradually add to the creamed mixture and mix well. Stir in chocolate chips. Gently fold in peanut butter dough until slightly marbled.

Drop by heaping tablespoonfuls 3 in. apart onto greased baking sheets. Bake at 350° for 14-16 minutes or until lightly browned and firm. Remove to wire racks to cool completely. **Yield:** 9-1/2 dozen.

Spread the bottom half of the cookies with raspberry preserves; top with remaining cookies.

For icing, combine the confectioners' sugar, lemon juice, food coloring if desired and enough milk to achieve a drizzling consistency. Drizzle over cookies. **Yield:** about 4-1/2 dozen.

Flourless Peanut Butter Cookies

Margaret Forger, Norwalk, Connecticut

Next time your family begs you for a homemade treat, don't fret! With only three ingredients, you can have a batch of these cookies baking in mere minutes.

- 4 egg whites
- 2 cups peanut butter
- 1-2/3 cups sugar

In a large bowl, beat egg whites until stiff peaks form. In another bowl, combine peanut butter and sugar; fold in egg whites.

Drop by heaping teaspoonfuls 2 in. apart onto lightly greased baking sheets. Flatten slightly with a fork. Bake at 325° for 15-20 minutes or until set. Remove to wire racks to cool. **Yield:** about 6-1/2 dozen.

Editor's Note: This recipe does not use flour. Reduced-fat or generic brands of peanut butter are not recommended for this cookie.

Maple Sandwich Cookies

Barbara Scacchi, Limestone, New York

Mom loves maple flavoring, so I created this recipe just for her. But the whole family loves these tasty cookies.

- 1 cup butter, softened
- 3/4 cup packed brown sugar
- 1 egg yolk
- 2 cups all-purpose flour
Sugar
FILLING:
- 1-1/4 cups confectioners' sugar
- 2 tablespoons milk
- 2 tablespoons butter, softened
- 1/2 teaspoon maple flavoring

In a large bowl, cream butter and brown sugar until light and fluffy. Beat in egg yolk. Gradually add flour and mix well.

Shape into 1-in. balls. Dip the tops in sugar. Place sugar side up 2 in. apart on ungreased baking sheets. Flatten with a fork. Bake at 325° for 10-12 minutes or until golden brown. Remove to wire racks to cool.

In a small bowl, beat the filling ingredients until smooth. Spread on the bottoms of half of the cookies; top with remaining cookies. **Yield:** about 3 dozen.

Raspberry Dreams

Lori Brown, Sioux Falls, South Dakota

I made variations to my friend's recipe to come up with this version. Family and friends look forward to me baking these each Christmas.

- 2 cups butter, softened
- 1 cup sugar
- 4 egg yolks
- 2 teaspoons vanilla extract
- 1 drop lemon juice
- 5-1/3 cups all-purpose flour
- 1/4 teaspoon salt
FILLING:
- 1 jar (12 ounces) raspberry preserves
ICING:
- 1 cup confectioners' sugar
- 1 drop lemon juice
- 1 drop red food coloring, optional
- 1 to 2 tablespoons milk

In a large bowl, cream butter and sugar until light and fluffy. Add egg yolks, one at a time, beating well after each addition. Beat in vanilla and lemon juice. Combine flour and salt; gradually add to the creamed mixture and mix well. Refrigerate for 1 hour or until easy to handle.

Divide dough into three portions. On a lightly floured surface, roll out each portion to 1/4-in. thickness. Cut with a 2-in. round cookie cutter. Place 1 in. apart on ungreased baking sheets. Bake at 350° for 8-10 minutes or until edges are very lightly browned. Remove to wire racks to cool.

Lemon Leaves

Karen Minthorne, Rancho Cucamonga, California

Sugar, chopped pistachios and lemon peel sprinkled on top of these cookies make them extra special. Feel free to use whatever cookie cutters you have on hand.

1/2	cup butter, softened
1-1/3	cups sugar, *divided*
1	egg
1	tablespoon half-and-half cream
1	teaspoon lemon extract
2-1/4	cups all-purpose flour
3	teaspoons baking powder
1/2	teaspoon salt
2	egg yolks
1	teaspoon water
1/4	cup finely chopped pistachios
1-1/2	teaspoons grated lemon peel

In a large bowl, cream butter and 1 cup of sugar until light and fluffy. Beat in egg, cream and extract. Combine the flour, baking powder and salt; gradually add to the creamed mixture and mix well. Cover and refrigerate for 2 hours or until easy to handle.

In a small bowl, beat egg yolks and water. In another bowl, combine pistachios, lemon peel and remaining sugar.

On a lightly floured surface, roll out dough to 1/8-in. thickness. Cut with a floured 2-1/2-in. leaf-shaped cookie cutter. Place 1 in. apart on ungreased baking sheets. Brush with egg yolk mixture; sprinkle with pistachio mixture.

Bake at 350° for 6-8 minutes or until edges are set (do not brown). Remove to wire racks to cool completely. **Yield:** about 4-1/2 dozen.

Cocoa Surprise Cookies

Debra Himes, Cedar Rapids, Iowa

These rich cookies are truly a chocolate-lover's delight. Miniature marshmallows are the delectable surprise in every bite.

- 1 cup butter, softened
- 1 cup sugar
- 1 cup packed brown sugar
- 2 eggs
- 2 teaspoons vanilla extract
- 3 cups all-purpose flour
- 2/3 cup baking cocoa
- 1/2 teaspoon baking soda
- 2 cups (12 ounces) semisweet chocolate chips
- 2 cups miniature marshmallows, frozen

In a large bowl, cream butter and sugars until light and fluffy. Add eggs, one at a time, beating well after each addition. Beat in vanilla. Combine the flour, cocoa and baking soda; gradually add to the creamed mixture and mix well. Stir in chocolate chips.

Roll the dough into 1-1/2-in. balls. Press two to three frozen marshmallows into each; reshape balls.

Place 2 in. apart on ungreased baking sheets. Bake at 400° for 8-10 minutes or until set. Cool for 5 minutes before removing to wire racks to cool completely. **Yield:** 5 dozen.

Yummy Pecan Bites

Alice Marie Puckett, Spokane, Washington

After experimenting with different recipes and ingredients, I came up with this simply delicious cookie that's reminiscent of the ever-popular Snickerdoodle.

    1   cup shortening
 1-1/2 cups sugar
    2   eggs
 2-3/4 cups all-purpose flour
    2   teaspoons cream of tartar
    1   teaspoon baking soda
  1/4   teaspoon salt
    1   cup finely chopped pecans
TOPPING:
    3   tablespoons sugar
 1-1/2 teaspoons ground cinnamon

In a large bowl, cream shortening and sugar until light and fluffy. Add eggs, one at a time, beating well after each addition. Combine the flour, cream of tartar, baking soda and salt; gradually add to creamed mixture and mix well. Stir in pecans. Combine topping ingredients.

Roll dough into 1-in. balls, then roll in topping. Place 2 in. apart on ungreased baking sheets; flatten slightly. Bake at 400° for 10-12 minutes or until surface cracks. Remove to wire racks to cool. **Yield:** 5 dozen.

Butterscotch Banana Drops

Sonja Oberkramer, Pacific, Missouri

Most folks are surprised to learn that banana is the secret ingredient in these soft cookies. My grandmother shared the recipe with me many years ago, and I've relied on it since.

  3/4   cup butter, softened
    1   cup sugar
    1   egg
 1-1/2 cups all-purpose flour
  1/2   teaspoon salt
  1/2   teaspoon baking soda
  1/2   teaspoon ground nutmeg
    1   cup mashed ripe bananas (about 2 medium)
 1-1/2 cups quick-cooking oats
 1-1/2 cups chopped pecans
    1   cup butterscotch chips
    1   cup chopped dates

In a large bowl, cream butter and sugar until light and fluffy. Beat in egg. Combine the flour, salt, baking soda and nutmeg; gradually add to the creamed mixture and mix well. Beat in bananas. Stir in the oats, pecans, butterscotch chips and dates.

Drop by rounded teaspoonfuls 2 in. apart onto lightly greased baking sheets. Bake at 350° for 12-14 minutes or until lightly browned. Remove to wire racks to cool. **Yield:** 11 dozen.

Soft Orange Molasses Drops

Beverly Steiner, Mt. Cory, Ohio

Orange juice and peel add a slight citrus twist to ordinary molasses cookies. I've also stirred in some chopped nuts, raisins, prunes and apricots.

  1/2   cup butter, softened
  1/2   cup sugar
    1   egg
 2-1/2 cups all-purpose flour
    1   teaspoon baking soda
    1   teaspoon ground ginger
  1/2   teaspoon *each* ground cinnamon, cloves and nutmeg
  1/2   cup molasses
  1/4   cup orange juice
    2   teaspoons grated orange peel
GLAZE:
    1   cup confectioners' sugar
    1   to 2 tablespoons orange juice

In a large bowl, cream butter and sugar until light and fluffy. Beat in egg. Combine the flour, baking soda and spices; set aside. Combine the molasses, orange juice and peel. Add flour mixture to the creamed mixture alternately with the molasses mixture, beating well after each addition.

Drop by tablespoonfuls 2 in. apart onto greased baking sheets. Bake at 375° for 10-12 minutes or until edges are set. Remove to wire racks to cool.

For glaze, combine confectioners' sugar and enough orange juice to achieve desired consistency. Spread over cooled cookies. **Yield:** 5 dozen.

Rainbow Swirls

Gail Russler, Lander, Wyoming

The students in my home economics class enjoy choosing and mixing in the food coloring for these cookies.

　1/2　cup butter, softened
　1/2　cup shortening
　　1　cup sugar
　　1　egg
　　1　teaspoon vanilla extract
　　2　cups all-purpose flour
　1/2　teaspoon baking powder
Green and red liquid food coloring

In a large bowl, cream the butter, shortening and sugar until light and fluffy. Beat in egg and vanilla. Combine flour and baking powder; gradually add to creamed mixture and mix well.

Divide dough into three portions. Tint one portion pink and one green. Leave one portion plain. Refrigerate for 30 minutes or until easy to handle.

Shape each portion into a 15-in. roll. Place all three rolls on a large piece of plastic wrap. Wrap tightly; roll gently until rolls form one log. Refrigerate overnight.

Unwrap and cut into 1/4-in. slices. Place 2 in. apart on ungreased baking sheets. Bake at 375° for 10-12 minutes or until the edges are lightly browned. Remove to wire racks to cool. **Yield:** about 4 dozen.

Candied Cherry Hermits

Joy Townsend, Ponte Vedra Beach, Florida

Candied cherries give traditional spice hermit cookies a new taste twist. They're so moist and chewy, it's hard to eat just one.

　1/2　cup butter
　　1　cup packed brown sugar
　　2　eggs
1-1/2　cups all-purpose flour
　　1　to 2 teaspoons ground cinnamon
　1/2　teaspoon baking soda
　　1　cup chopped pecans
　3/4　cup raisins, chopped
　3/4　cup candied cherries, chopped

In a large bowl, cream butter and brown sugar until light and fluffy. Add eggs, one at a time, beating well after each addition. Combine the flour, cinnamon and baking soda; gradually add to the creamed mixture. Stir in the pecans, raisins and cherries.

Drop by rounded tablespoonfuls 2 in. apart onto ungreased baking sheets. Bake at 375° for 10-12 minutes or until golden brown. Remove to wire racks to cool. **Yield:** about 3-1/2 dozen.

White Chocolate Macadamia Cookies

Mrs. Eddie Lennon, Newport, Tennessee

Vanilla chips and macadamia nuts are a delightful duo in these rich, buttery morsels. They are a nice change from chocolate chip cookies.

　1/2　cup butter, softened
　2/3　cup sugar
　　1　egg
　　1　teaspoon vanilla extract
　　1　cup plus 2 tablespoons all-purpose flour
　1/2　teaspoon baking soda
　　1　jar (3-1/2 ounces) macadamia nuts, chopped
　　1　cup vanilla *or* white chips

In a large bowl, cream butter and sugar until light and fluffy. Beat in egg and vanilla. Combine flour and baking soda; gradually add to creamed mixture and mix well. Stir in nuts and vanilla chips.

Drop by heaping teaspoonfuls 2 in. apart onto ungreased baking sheets. Bake at 350° for 10-12 minutes or until golden brown. Cool for 1 minute before removing to wire racks to cool completely. **Yield:** about 4-1/2 dozen.

Coconut Lemon Crisps

Segarie Moodley, Longwood, Florida

We had these cookies at our wedding reception, where they brought smiles and compliments. They've become one of our anniversary dinner trademarks.

- 7 tablespoons butter, softened
- 1/4 cup sugar
- 1/2 teaspoon vanilla extract
- 1 cup all-purpose flour
- 1 egg white, beaten
- 1/2 cup flaked coconut

FILLING:

- 1/3 cup sugar
- 4-1/2 teaspoons cornstarch
- 3/4 cup water
- 1 egg yolk, beaten
- 3 tablespoons butter, softened
- 2 tablespoons lemon juice

In a bowl, cream butter, sugar and vanilla until light and fluffy. Gradually add flour and mix well. On a lightly floured surface, roll out half of the dough to 1/8-in. thickness. Cut with a 2-in. round cookie cutter. Repeat with remaining dough, using a 2-in. doughnut cutter so the center is cut out of each cookie.

Place 1 in. apart on lightly greased baking sheets. Brush egg white over cookies with cutout centers; sprinkle with coconut. Bake at 350° for 8-10 minutes. Remove to wire racks to cool.

For filling, in a large saucepan, combine sugar and cornstarch. Stir in water until smooth. Cook and stir over medium-high heat until thickened and bubbly. Reduce heat to low; cook and stir for 2 minutes longer. Remove from the heat. Stir a small amount of hot filling into egg yolk; return all to the pan, stirring constantly. Bring to a gentle boil; cook and stir for 2 minutes. Remove from the heat; gently stir in butter and lemon juice. Cool to room temperature without stirring.

Spread a teaspoonful of filling on the bottom of each solid cookie; place coconut topped cookie over lemon filling. Store in the refrigerator. **Yield:** 1-1/2 dozen.

Cinnamon Stars

Jean Jones, Peachtree City, Georgia

While they are baking, these cookies fill your home with an irresistible aroma. My grandmother made them every Christmas when I was a child. I have fond memories of helping her in the kitchen.

  1 cup butter, softened
  2 cups sugar
  2 eggs
2-3/4 cups all-purpose flour
  1/3 cup ground cinnamon

In a large bowl, cream butter and sugar until light and fluffy. Add eggs, one at a time, beating well after each addition. Combine flour and cinnamon; gradually add to creamed mixture and mix well. Cover and refrigerate for 1 hour or until easy to handle.

On a lightly floured surface, roll out to 1/4-in. thickness. Cut with a floured 2-1/2-in. star-shaped cookie cutter. Place 1 in. apart on ungreased baking sheets.

Bake at 350° for 15-18 minutes or until edges are firm and bottom of cookies are lightly browned. Remove to wire racks to cool. **Yield:** 5 dozen.

Double Nut Crunchies

Pia Harrison, Green Valley, Arizona

Chopped cashews lend to the delectable crunch of these cookies, while peanut butter gives them even more great nutty flavor.

- 1 cup butter-flavored shortening
- 1 cup chunky peanut butter
- 1 cup sugar
- 1 cup packed brown sugar
- 2 eggs
- 1 teaspoon vanilla extract
- 2 cups all-purpose flour
- 1/2 cup baking cocoa
- 2 teaspoons baking soda

Dash salt
- 1 cup coarsely chopped salted cashews

In a large bowl, cream the shortening, peanut butter and sugars until light and fluffy. Add the eggs, one at a time, beating well after each addition. Beat in vanilla. Combine the flour, cocoa, baking soda and salt; gradually add to the creamed mixture and mix well. Stir in cashews.

Roll into 1-in. balls. Place 2 in. apart on ungreased baking sheets. Flatten with a fork dipped in sugar. Bake at 350° for 8-10 minutes or until lightly browned. Remove to wire racks to cool. **Yield:** about 5 dozen.

Golden Harvest Cookies

Florence Pope, Denver, Colorado

Folks may be skeptical when you tell them the ingredients in these slightly sweet cookies.

- 2/3 cup butter, softened
- 1/3 cup packed brown sugar
- 1 egg
- 1 teaspoon vanilla extract
- 3/4 cup self-rising flour
- 1 teaspoon ground cinnamon
- 1/8 teaspoon ground cloves
- 1-1/2 cups quick-cooking oats
- 1 cup shredded carrots
- 1 cup (4 ounces) shredded cheddar cheese
- 1 cup chopped pecans
- 1/2 cup raisins

In a large bowl, cream butter and brown sugar until light and fluffy. Beat in egg and vanilla. Combine the flour, cinnamon and cloves; gradually add to the creamed mixture and mix well. Stir in remaining ingredients.

Drop by heaping tablespoonfuls 2 in. apart onto ungreased baking sheets. Bake at 375° for 12-14 minutes or until golden brown. Remove to wire racks to cool completely. Store in the refrigerator. **Yield:** 3-1/2 dozen.

Editor's Note: As a substitute for self-rising flour, place 1 teaspoon baking powder and 1/4 teaspoon salt in a measuring cup. Add all-purpose flour to measure 3/4 cup.

Quick Chocolate Sandwich Cookies

Mary Rempel, Altona, Manitoba

These treats freeze well, so it's easy to keep some on hand for last-minute munching. In summer, I often make them larger to use for ice cream sandwiches.

- 2 packages (18-1/4 ounces *each*) devil's food cake mix
- 1 cup canola oil
- 4 eggs

FILLING:
- 1 package (8 ounces) cream cheese, softened
- 1/4 cup butter, softened
- 2-1/2 cups confectioners' sugar
- 1 teaspoon vanilla extract

In a large bowl, combine the cake mixes, oil and eggs until well blended. Roll into 1-in. balls. Place 2 in. apart on ungreased baking sheets. Do not flatten.

Bake at 350° for 8-10 minutes or until set. Cool for 5 minutes before removing to wire racks (cookies will flatten as they cool).

In a small bowl, beat cream cheese and butter until fluffy. Beat in sugar and vanilla until smooth. Spread on the bottom of half of the cookies; top with remaining cookies. Store in the refrigerator. **Yield:** about 6 dozen.

Double Chocolate Sprinkle Cookies

Barb Meinholz, South Milwaukee, Wisconsin

Chock-full of chocolate chips and sprinkles, these chewy cookies never last long around our house.

 2 cups butter, softened
 2 cups sugar
 2 cups packed brown sugar
 4 eggs
 2 teaspoons vanilla extract
 5 cups old-fashioned oats
 4 cups all-purpose flour
 2 teaspoons baking soda
 2 teaspoons baking powder
 1 teaspoon salt
 4 cups (24 ounces) semisweet chocolate chips
 3 cups chopped walnuts
 2 cups chocolate sprinkles

In a large bowl, cream the butter and sugar. Add eggs, one at a time, beating well after each addition. Beat in vanilla.

Place the oats in a blender or food processor; cover and process until finely ground. Combine the ground oats, flour, baking soda, baking powder and salt; gradually add to creamed mixture. Transfer to a larger bowl if necessary. Stir in chocolate chips, walnuts and sprinkles.

Roll into 1-1/2-in. balls. Place 2 in. apart on ungreased baking sheets. Flatten with a glass. Bake at 350° for 12-14 minutes or until golden brown. Remove to wire racks to cool. **Yield:** about 9 dozen.

Gingered Molasses Cookies

Mrs. Donald Mitchell, Fredericksburg, Texas

A nice blend of spices and grated orange peel makes these a little different than your basic molasses cookies. My son loved these when he was growing up.

 1/2 cup butter, softened
 1/4 cup shortening
 1-1/4 cups sugar, *divided*
 1 egg
 1/4 cup molasses
 1/2 teaspoon grated orange peel
 2 cups all-purpose flour
 2 teaspoons baking soda
 1/2 teaspoon salt
 1/2 teaspoon ground ginger
 1/2 teaspoon ground cinnamon
 1/4 teaspoon ground cloves

In a large bowl, cream the butter, shortening and 1 cup sugar until light and fluffy. Beat in egg, molasses and orange peel. Combine the flour, baking soda, salt, ginger, cinnamon and cloves; gradually add to creamed mixture and mix well.

Roll into 1-1/4-in. balls, then in remaining sugar. Place 2 in. apart on ungreased baking sheets. Bake at 350° for 10-12 minutes or until edges are firm and surface cracks. Remove to wire racks to cool. **Yield:** 5-1/2 dozen.

Buttermilk Spice Crisps

Marla Mason, Cedar Rapids, Iowa

These cookies were a Christmas tradition for one of the families in my childhood church. I looked forward to caroling at their house because we were always rewarded with one of these tasty morsels!

 1 cup butter, softened
 2 cups sugar
 1 egg
 1/3 cup buttermilk
 4-2/3 cups all-purpose flour
 2 teaspoons baking soda
 2 teaspoons ground cinnamon
 1 teaspoon *each* ground allspice, ground cloves and ground nutmeg

In a large bowl, cream butter and sugar until light and fluffy. Beat in egg and buttermilk. Combine the flour, baking soda, cinnamon, allspice, cloves and nutmeg; gradually add to the creamed mixture and mix well. Shape into two 9-in. rolls; wrap each in plastic wrap. Refrigerate for 4 hours or until firm.

Unwrap and cut into 1/4-in. slices. Place 2 in. apart on ungreased baking sheets. Bake at 350° for 10-12 minutes or until golden brown. Remove to wire racks to cool. **Yield:** 6 dozen.

Vanilla Butter Rollouts

Colleen Sickman, Charles City, Iowa

Even cooks who normally shy away from rolled cookies can make these with confidence. The dough is so easy to work with after a mere 30 minutes of chilling.

1-1/2 cups butter, softened
1-1/2 cups sugar
   2 eggs
   3 teaspoons vanilla extract
   4 cups all-purpose flour
   1 teaspoon baking soda
   1 teaspoon cream of tartar
   1 teaspoon salt
FROSTING:
   6 tablespoons butter, softened
   3 cups confectioners' sugar
1/4 cup milk
   3 teaspoons vanilla extract
Colored frosting and sugar, optional

In a large bowl, cream butter and sugar until light and fluffy. Add eggs, one at a time, beating well after each addition. Beat in vanilla. Combine the flour, baking soda, cream of tartar and salt; gradually add to the creamed mixture and mix well. Cover and refrigerate for 30 minutes or until easy to handle.

On a lightly floured surface, roll out to 1/4-in. thickness. Cut with floured 2-1/2-in. cookie cutters. Place 2 in. apart on ungreased baking sheets. Bake at 350° for 8-10 minutes or until lightly browned.

For frosting, in a large bowl, beat the butter, confectioners' sugar, milk and vanilla until smooth. Spread or drizzle over cookies. Decorate with colored frosting and sugar if desired. **Yield:** about 7 dozen.

Spread Too Thin If cookie dough spreads too thin when it's baked, make sure the baking sheet is completely cooled before placing the next batch of dough on it. Also, try chilling the dough before baking it.

291

Date Nut Icebox Cookies

Gladys Maurer, Laramie, Wyoming

A dear friend shared this recipe with me many years ago. The snacks have become a much-requested treat at my house, so it's a good thing the recipe yields a lot.

- 1 cup butter, softened
- 1 cup shortening
- 2-1/2 cups sugar
- 2 eggs
- 1-1/2 teaspoons vanilla extract
- 1 tablespoon light corn syrup
- 5 cups all-purpose flour
- 1 teaspoon salt
- 1 teaspoon baking soda
- 1 cup finely chopped walnuts
- 1 cup finely chopped dates

In a large bowl, cream the butter, shortening and sugar until light and fluffy. Add eggs, one at a time, beating well after each addition. Beat in vanilla and corn syrup. Combine the flour, salt and baking soda; gradually add to the creamed mixture and mix well. Stir in the walnuts and dates. Shape into four 6-in. rolls; wrap each in plastic wrap. Refrigerate overnight.

Unwrap and cut into 1/4-in. slices. Place 2-1/2 in. apart on ungreased baking sheets. Bake at 375° for 10-12 minutes or until lightly browned. Cool for 2-3 minutes before removing to wire racks to cool completely. **Yield:** about 8 dozen.

Cream Cheese Bells

Charlene Grimminger, Paris, Ohio

Since I was raised on a dairy farm, the ingredients in this recipe suit me fine! These delicious cookies freeze well, although most of them get gobbled up before I have a chance to get them in the freezer.

- 7 tablespoons butter, softened
- 1 package (8 ounces) cream cheese, softened
- 2 egg yolks
- 2-1/2 cups all-purpose flour
- FILLING:
- 2-1/2 cups ground pecans *or* walnuts
- 1/2 cup sugar
- 1/4 cup butter, melted
- 1 egg white
- Confectioners' sugar

In a large bowl, cream butter and cream cheese until light and fluffy. Beat in egg yolks. Gradually add the flour and mix well. Cover and refrigerate overnight. Remove from refrigerator about 1 hour before rolling.

For filling, in a small bowl, combine the nuts, sugar, butter and egg white; set aside. Divide dough into fourths. On a floured surface, roll out each portion to 1/8-in. thickness. Cut with a 2-3/4-in. round cookie cutter.

Place 1 in. apart on ungreased baking sheets. Place 1 teaspoon filling in center of each circle. Shape into a cone by folding edges of dough to meet over filling. Moisten edges with water and pinch edges together.

Bake at 350° for 12-15 minutes or until lightly browned. Cool on wire racks. Sprinkle the cooled cookies with confectioners' sugar. **Yield:** about 4 dozen.

Snow-Topped Chocolate Mint Cookies

Arlene Hurst, Ephrata, Pennsylvania

Our local newspaper had a cookie contest a while back. This was one of the recipes featured, and it caught my eye because I love mint flavor. My family really likes these change-of-pace treats.

- 1 package (10 ounces) mint semisweet chocolate chips, *divided*
- 6 tablespoons butter, softened
- 1 cup sugar
- 2 eggs
- 1-1/2 teaspoons vanilla extract
- 1-1/2 cups all-purpose flour
- 1-1/2 teaspoons baking powder
- 1/4 teaspoon salt
- Confectioners' sugar

In a microwave, melt 1 cup of the chocolate chips; stir until smooth and set aside to cool.

In a large bowl, cream butter and sugar until light and fluffy. Add eggs, one at a time, beating well after each addition. Beat in the melted chocolate chips and vanilla. Combine the flour, baking powder and salt; gradually add to the creamed mixture and mix well. Stir in the remaining chocolate chips. Cover and refrigerate for 2 hours or until easy to handle.

Roll into 1-in. balls, then roll in confectioners' sugar. Place 2 in. apart on ungreased baking sheets. Bake at 350° for 10-12 minutes or until edges are set and centers are almost set. Cool for 10 minutes before removing to wire racks. **Yield:** 4 dozen.

Editor's Note: If mint chocolate chips are not available, place 2 cups (12 ounces) semisweet chocolate chips and 1/4 teaspoon peppermint extract in a plastic bag; seal and toss to coat. Allow chips to stand for 24-48 hours.

Almond Butter Cookies

Lynne Romyn, Fayetteville, North Carolina

I came up with this cookie recipe as a way to capture a butter cake popular in my husband's native Netherlands. Almond paste and butter make each melt-in-your-mouth morsel irresistible.

- 1/2 cup butter, softened
- 1/2 cup shortening
-   6 ounces almond paste
- 1-1/3 cups sugar
-   1 egg
-   2 cups all-purpose flour
-   1 teaspoon baking soda

In a large bowl, cream butter, shortening, almond paste and sugar until light and fluffy. Beat in egg. Combine flour and baking soda; gradually add to the creamed mixture.

Roll into 1-1/4-in. balls. Place 2 in. apart on ungreased baking sheets. Bake at 400° for 8-10 minutes or until lightly browned. Remove to wire racks to cool. **Yield:** 6-1/2 dozen.

Oatmeal Fruit Cookies

Brenda Cline, Cody, Wyoming

I've been using this recipe for more than 30 years, so I don't have to tell you how much my family likes it! Whole wheat flour and oats make these crisp yet chewy cookies a hearty around-the-clock snack.

- 1 cup butter, softened
- 1 cup sugar
- 1 cup packed brown sugar
- 2 eggs
- 1 teaspoon vanilla extract
- 4 cups old-fashioned oats
- 1 cup whole wheat flour
- 1 teaspoon baking soda
- 1/2 teaspoon salt

- 1/2 teaspoon ground cinnamon
-   1 cup raisins
-   1 cup chopped walnuts
-   1 cup flaked coconut
-   1 cup chopped dates

In a large bowl, cream butter and sugars until light and fluffy. Add eggs, one at a time, beating well after each addition. Beat in vanilla. Combine the oats, flour, baking soda, salt and cinnamon; gradually add to the creamed mixture and mix well. Stir in the raisins, walnuts, coconut and dates.

Roll into 1-1/2-in. balls. Place 2 in. apart on ungreased baking sheets. Bake at 325° for 14-16 minutes or until edges are firm. Remove to wire racks to cool. **Yield:** about 3-1/2 dozen.

White Chocolate-Cranberry Biscotti

Brenda Keith, Talent, Oregon

The original version of this recipe was handed down from my great-aunt. Through the years, my mother and I have tried different flavor combinations...this is a favorite for all.

- 1/2 cup butter, softened
-   1 cup sugar
-   4 eggs
-   1 teaspoon vanilla extract
-   3 cups all-purpose flour
-   1 tablespoon baking powder
- 3/4 cup dried cranberries
- 3/4 cup vanilla *or* white chips

In a large bowl, cream butter and sugar until light and fluffy. Add eggs, one at a time, beating well after each addition. Beat in vanilla. Combine flour and baking powder; gradually add to creamed mixture and mix well. Stir in cranberries and vanilla chips. Divide dough into three portions.

On ungreased baking sheets, shape each portion into a 10-in. x 2-in. rectangle. Bake at 350° for 20-25 minutes or until lightly browned. Cool for 5 minutes.

Transfer to a cutting board; cut diagonally with a serrated knife into 1-in. slices. Place cut side down on ungreased baking sheets. Bake for 15-20 minutes or until golden brown. Remove to wire racks to cool. Store in an airtight container. **Yield:** 2-1/2 dozen.

About Biscotti Biscotti (bee-skawt-tee) is an Italian cookie that is baked twice. First it's baked as a loaf and cut into individual cookies. Then the cookies are baked producing a dry, crunchy cookie that goes great with coffee.

Big Soft Ginger Cookies

Barbara Heinze, Boise, Idaho

These nicely spiced soft cookies are perfect for folks who like the flavor of ginger but don't care for crunchy gingersnaps.

3/4	cup butter, softened
1	cup sugar
1	egg
1/4	cup molasses
2-1/4	cups all-purpose flour
2	teaspoons ground ginger
1	teaspoon baking soda
3/4	teaspoon cinnamon
1/2	teaspoon ground cloves
1/4	teaspoon salt

Additional sugar

In a large bowl, cream butter and sugar until light and fluffy. Beat in egg and molasses. Combine the flour, ginger, baking soda, cinnamon, cloves and salt; gradually add to the creamed mixture and mix well.

Roll into 1-1/2-in. balls, then roll in sugar. Place 2 in. apart on ungreased baking sheets. Bake at 350° for 10-12 minutes or until puffy and lightly browned. Remove to wire racks to cool. **Yield:** 2-1/2 dozen.

Shaping Cookies Cookies bake more evenly if all the cookies on the baking sheet are the same size. To make the 1-1/2-inch ball of dough called for in the Big Soft Ginger Cookies, use about a 1 tablespoon of dough per cookie.

Tea Cakes

Doris McGough, Dothan, Alabama

I've baked many batches of different cookies through the years, but family and friends tell me these are the best. The simple buttery flavor appeals to all.

- 1 cup butter, softened
- 1-1/2 cups sugar
- 3 eggs
- 1 tablespoon vanilla extract
- 3 cups all-purpose flour
- 1 tablespoon baking powder
- 1/4 teaspoon salt

In a large bowl, cream butter and sugar until light and fluffy. Add eggs, one at a time, beating well after each addition. Beat in vanilla. Combine the flour, baking powder and salt; gradually add to the creamed mixture (the dough will be soft).

Drop by teaspoonfuls 2 in. apart onto greased baking sheets. Bake at 375° for 7-8 minutes or until the edges are golden brown. Remove to wire racks to cool. **Yield:** 9 dozen.

Buttery Sugar Cookies

Cynthia Olson, Springfield, Illinois

It's a good thing this recipe makes a big batch because no one can stop eating just one! These crisp cookies truly do melt in your mouth.

- 2 cups butter, softened
- 2 cups sugar
- 3 eggs
- 5 tablespoons milk
- 1 teaspoon vanilla extract
- 6-1/2 cups all-purpose flour
- 1 teaspoon baking powder
- 1 teaspoon baking soda
- 1 teaspoon salt

Additional sugar

Walnut halves *or* raisins, optional

In a large bowl, cream butter and sugar until light and fluffy. Add eggs, one at a time, beating well after each addition. Beat in milk and vanilla. Combine the flour, baking powder, baking soda and salt; gradually add to the creamed mixture and mix well. Cover and refrigerate for 1 hour or until easy to handle.

On a lightly floured surface, roll out to 1/4-in. thickness. Cut with floured 2-1/2-in. cookie cutters. Place 1 in. apart on greased baking sheets. Sprinkle with sugar; place a walnut or raisin in the center of each if desired.

Bake at 350° for 8-10 minutes or until lightly browned. Remove to wire racks to cool. **Yield:** about 11-1/2 dozen.

Marmalade Chews

Shirleene Wilkins, Lake Placid, Florida

I live in the heart of citrus country and think this cookie really captures that area's flavor. Orange marmalade, juice and peel give the cookie and frosting a delightful taste.

- 1/4 cup shortening
- 1/2 cup sugar
- 1 egg
- 1-1/2 cups all-purpose flour
- 1/4 teaspoon baking soda
- 1/4 teaspoon salt
- 1/2 cup orange marmalade
- 1/2 cup chopped pecans, optional

FROSTING:
- 2 cups confectioners' sugar
- 2 tablespoons butter, melted
- 1 teaspoon grated orange peel
- 2 to 3 tablespoons orange juice

In a large bowl, cream shortening and sugar until light and fluffy. Beat in egg. Combine the flour, baking soda and salt; gradually add to the creamed mixture and mix well. Stir in marmalade and pecans if desired.

Drop by heaping teaspoonfuls 2 in. apart onto greased baking sheets. Bake at 350° for 10-15 minutes or until golden brown. Remove to wire racks to cool.

In a small bowl, combine the confectioners' sugar, butter and orange peel until blended. Add enough orange juice to achieve spreading consistency. Frost cooled cookies. **Yield:** about 4-1/2 dozen.

Lemon Dreams

Karen Scaglione, Nanuet, New York

A buttery cookie with a luscious lemon filling is simply hard to resist. Every time I serve these elegant, delectable cookies, I'm asked for the recipe.

      1 cup butter, softened
    1/3 cup confectioners' sugar
      1 teaspoon vanilla extract
  1-2/3 cups all-purpose flour
FILLING:
    2/3 cup sugar
  1-1/2 teaspoons cornstarch
    1/4 teaspoon salt
      3 tablespoons lemon juice
      1 egg, beaten
      1 tablespoon butter, melted
      1 teaspoon grated lemon peel
Confectioners' sugar, optional

In a small bowl, cream butter and confectioners' sugar until light and fluffy. Beat in vanilla. Gradually add flour and mix well. Cover and refrigerate for 30 minutes or until easy to handle.

Roll into 1-in. balls. Place 2 in. apart on ungreased baking sheets. Using the end of a wooden spoon handle, make an indentation in the center of each.

Bake at 350° for 12-14 minutes or until lightly browned. Remove to wire racks to cool.

For filling, in a large saucepan, combine the sugar, cornstarch and salt. Stir in lemon juice until smooth. Cook and stir over medium-high heat until thickened and bubbly. Reduce heat to low; cook and stir for 2 minutes longer. Remove from the heat. Stir a small amount of hot filling into egg; return all to the pan, stirring constantly. Bring to a gentle boil; cook and stir for 2 minutes. Remove from the heat; gently stir in butter and lemon peel. Cool.

Spoon 1/2 teaspoonful into each cookie. Dust with confectioners' sugar if desired. **Yield:** 3 dozen.

Frosted Molasses Cookies

Sarah Byler, Harrisville, Pennsylvania

If my family knows I've baked these cookies, they're sure to gobble them up in a hurry.

      1 cup butter, softened
      1 cup sugar
      3 egg yolks
      1 cup molasses
    1/2 cup water
      5 cups all-purpose flour
      3 teaspoons baking soda
  1-1/2 teaspoons ground cinnamon
      1 teaspoon baking powder
FROSTING:
  1-1/2 cups sugar
      3 egg whites
    1/4 cup water
      1 cup confectioners' sugar

In a large bowl, cream butter and sugar until light and fluffy. Beat in the egg yolks, molasses and water. Combine the flour, baking soda, cinnamon and baking powder; gradually add to creamed mixture and mix well. Cover and refrigerate for 2 hours or until easy to handle.

On a lightly floured surface, roll out dough to 1/8-in. thickness. Cut with a floured 2-1/2-in. round cookie cutter. Place 1 in. apart on ungreased baking sheets. Bake at 375° for 8-10 minutes or until edges are firm. Remove to wire racks to cool.

For frosting, combine the sugar, egg whites and water in a small heavy saucepan over low heat. With a hand mixer, beat on low speed for 1 minute. Continue beating on low over low heat until frosting reaches 160°, about 8-10 minutes. Pour into a large bowl; add confectioners' sugar. Beat on high until frosting forms stiff peaks, about 7 minutes. Frost cookies. Let stand until dry. **Yield:** 8 dozen.

Editor's Note: A stand mixer is recommended for beating the frosting after it reaches 160°.

Mint Wafers

Barrie Citrowske, Canby, Minnesota

I enjoy nibbling on these cookies with a cup of tea or coffee for a midday treat. For even more mint flavor, use mint chocolate chips instead of semisweet.

1	cup butter, softened
3/4	cup sugar
1	egg
1/4	teaspoon peppermint extract
2-1/4	cups all-purpose flour
1/2	teaspoon salt
1	cup (6 ounces) semisweet chocolate chips
4	teaspoons shortening

In a large bowl, cream butter and sugar until light and fluffy. Beat in egg and extract. Combine flour and salt; gradually add to the creamed mixture and mix well. Shape into two 8-in. rolls; wrap each in plastic wrap. Refrigerated for 3 hours or until firm.

Unwrap and cut into 1/4-in. slices. Place 1 in. apart on ungreased baking sheets. Bake at 350° for 9-10 minutes or until the edges begin to brown. Remove to wire racks to cool completely.

In a microwave, melt chocolate and shortening; stir until smooth. Spread or drizzle over the cooled cookies. **Yield:** about 6 dozen.

Editor's Note: If mint chocolate chips are not available, place 1 cup semisweet chocolate chips and 1/8 teaspoon peppermint extract in a plastic bag; seal and toss to coat. Allow chips to stand for 24-48 hours.

Potato Chip Crunchies

Dorothy Buiter, Worth, Illinois

I usually have all sorts of baked goodies waiting for my family when they come home for the holidays. No matter how fancy the other cookies are, these are usually the first to go. Maybe it's the salty-sweet combination that they like so much.

- 2 cups butter, softened
- 1-1/2 cups sugar
- 1 egg
- 1 teaspoon vanilla extract
- 4 cups all-purpose flour
- 1 cup crushed potato chips
- 1 cup chopped pecans

In a large bowl, cream butter and sugar until light and fluffy. Beat in egg and vanilla. Gradually add flour and mix well. Fold in the potato chips and pecans.

Drop by tablespoonfuls 1-1/2 in. apart onto ungreased baking sheets. Flatten with a fork. Bake at 350° for 12-14 minutes or until golden brown. Remove to wire racks to cool. **Yield:** 8 dozen.

Hearty Whole Wheat Cookies

Lynore Derkson, Airdrie, Alberta

My grandchildren would do just about anything for one of these cookies. Since they're made with oats and whole wheat flour, I don't mind them nibbling on them.

- 1 cup butter, softened
- 2 cups packed brown sugar
- 3 eggs
- 3 tablespoons half-and-half cream
- 2 teaspoons vanilla extract
- 2 cups quick-cooking oats
- 2 cups whole wheat flour
- 1 teaspoon baking powder
- 1 teaspoon baking soda
- 1/2 teaspoon salt
- 1 package (12 ounces) miniature semisweet chocolate chips
- 2 cups coarsely chopped peanuts

In a large bowl, cream butter and brown sugar until light and fluffy. Add eggs, one at a time, beating well after each addition. Beat in the cream and vanilla.

In a blender or food processor, process oats until finely ground. Combine the ground oats, flour, baking powder, baking soda and salt; gradually add to the creamed mixture and mix well. Stir in chocolate chips and peanuts.

Drop by tablespoonfuls 1-1/2 in. apart onto ungreased baking sheets. Bake at 350° for 10-12 minutes or until golden brown. Remove to wire racks to cool. **Yield:** 6 dozen.

Chocolate Zucchini Cookies

Tina Lunt, Bass Harbor, Maine

This recipe started out as a plain zucchini cookie. But over the years, I added nuts and chocolate chips. These soft cookies never make it to the cookie jar!

- 1 cup butter, softened
- 2 cups sugar
- 2 eggs
- 4 cups all-purpose flour
- 2 teaspoons baking soda
- 2 teaspoons ground cinnamon
- 1 teaspoon salt
- 1 teaspoon ground nutmeg
- 1 teaspoon ground cloves
- 2 cups finely shredded zucchini
- 1 cup chopped nuts
- 1/2 cup semisweet chocolate chips

In a large bowl, cream butter and sugar until light and fluffy. Add the eggs, one at a time, beating well after each addition. Combine the flour, baking soda, cinnamon, salt, nutmeg and cloves; gradually add to the creamed mixture and mix well. Stir in the zucchini, nuts and chocolate chips.

Drop by tablespoonfuls 3 in. apart onto ungreased baking sheets. Bake at 375° for 10-12 minutes or until lightly browned. Remove to wire racks to cool. **Yield:** 8 dozen.

Buttery Walnut Cutouts

Grance Simons, Orange City, Florida

Chopped walnuts add flavor and crunch to a typical butter cookie plus give them a pretty golden color.

- 1 cup butter, softened
- 3/4 cup sugar
- 1 egg
- 1 teaspoon vanilla extract
- 2-1/2 cups all-purpose flour
- 2 teaspoons baking powder
- 1/2 teaspoon salt
- 1 cup finely chopped walnuts

In a large bowl, cream butter and sugar until light and fluffy. Beat in egg and vanilla. Combine the flour, baking powder and salt; gradually add to creamed mixture and mix well. Stir in walnuts. Cover and refrigerate for 1 hour or until easy to handle.

On a floured surface, roll out to 1/8-in. thickness. Cut with floured 2-in. cookie cutters. Place 1 in. apart on ungreased baking sheets. Bake at 375° for 6-8 minutes or until edges are golden brown. Remove to wire racks to cool. **Yield:** 4 dozen.

Surprise Crinkles

Lola Fensky, Moundridge, Kansas

I created this recipe by trial and error using many different kinds of candy. Milky Ways were the secret surprise my family liked best.

1	cup shortening
1/2	cup butter, softened
2	cups packed brown sugar
1	cup sugar
3	eggs
1-1/2	teaspoons vanilla extract
4-1/4	cups all-purpose flour
1-1/2	teaspoons baking soda
1/4	teaspoon ground cinnamon
1/8	teaspoon salt
2	packages (14 ounces *each*) fun-size Milky Way candy bars

In a large bowl, cream the shortening, butter and sugars until light and fluffy. Add eggs, one at a time, beating well after each addition. Beat in vanilla. Combine the flour, baking soda, cinnamon and salt; gradually add to the creamed mixture and mix well.

Roll into 1-1/2-in. balls. Cut each candy bar into fourths; push one portion into the center of each ball, completely covering candy with dough. Place 2 in. apart on ungreased baking sheets.

Bake at 350° for 12-14 minutes or until golden brown and surface cracks. Remove to wire racks to cool. **Yield:** 9 dozen.

Caramel Pecan Treasures

Glenda MacEachern, Crown Point, Indiana

Fancy-looking cookies like these may take some time to prepare, but family and friends will surely be impressed! No one can resist the shortbread cookie, caramel filling and melted chocolate top sprinkled with pecans.

1	cup butter, softened
3/4	cup packed brown sugar
1	teaspoon vanilla extract
1-3/4	cups all-purpose flour
1/2	teaspoon baking powder
30	caramels, halved and flattened
2	cups (12 ounces) semisweet chocolate chips
1	tablespoon shortening
1/2	cup finely chopped pecans

In a large bowl, cream butter and brown sugar until light and fluffy. Beat in vanilla. Combine flour and baking powder; gradually add to creamed mixture and mix well.

Roll into 1-in. balls. Place 2 in. apart on greased baking sheets; flatten slightly. Bake at 325° for 12-15 minutes or until golden brown. Remove to wire racks to cool.

Place a half-caramel on each cookie. Melt the chocolate chips and shortening; drizzle over cookies. Sprinkle with pecans. Let stand until firm. **Yield:** 5 dozen.

Shortbread Cutouts

Jean Henderson, Montgomery, Texas

I found this recipe in a magazine over 30 years ago and have made the cutouts for Christmas ever since. Four ingredients make them an oh-so-simple recipe to whip up during the hectic holidays.

1 cup butter, softened
1/2 cup sugar
2-1/2 cups all-purpose flour
Colored sugar, optional

In a large bowl, cream butter and sugar until light and fluffy. Gradually add flour and mix well. Divide dough in half.

On a lightly floured surface, roll out each portion to 1/4-in. thickness. Cut with floured 2-in. to 3-in. cookie cutters.

Place 1 in. apart on ungreased baking sheets. Sprinkle with colored sugar if desired. Bake at 300° for 20-25 minutes until lightly browned. Remove to wire racks to cool. **Yield:** about 2 dozen.

White Chocolate Nut Crackles

Joyce Gething, Pampa, Texas

An aunt and I baked a similar cookie often when I was growing up. Through the years, I added the macadamia nuts and white chocolate chips. My family and co-workers love it when I make these.

- 1/2 cup butter, softened
- 1/2 cup shortening
- 1/2 cup sugar
- 1/2 cup packed brown sugar
- 1 egg
- 1 teaspoon vanilla extract
- 2 cups all-purpose flour
- 1 teaspoon baking soda
- 1 teaspoon cream of tartar
- 1/2 teaspoon salt
- 6 squares (1 ounce *each*) white baking chocolate, coarsely chopped
- 1/2 cup coarsely chopped macadamia nuts, toasted

Additional sugar

In a large bowl, cream the butter, shortening and sugars until light and fluffy. Beat in the egg and vanilla. Combine the flour, baking soda, cream of tartar and salt; gradually add to the creamed mixture and mix well. Stir in chocolate and nuts. Cover and refrigerate for 1 hour or until easy to handle.

Roll into 1-in. balls. Dip each ball halfway in water, then in additional sugar. Place sugar side up 2 in. apart on ungreased baking sheets; flatten slightly. Bake at 400° for 8-10 minutes or until golden brown. Remove to wire racks to cool. **Yield:** 5-1/2 dozen.

Frosted Ginger Cookies

Barbara Larson, Minneapolis, Minnesota

A glossy white frosting gives these cookies just the right amount of sweetness. My grandmother shared the recipe with me as part of a wedding shower gift.

- 1 cup shortening
- 1 cup molasses
- 3 cups all-purpose flour
- 2 teaspoons baking soda
- 1 teaspoon salt
- 1/2 teaspoon ground ginger
- 1/4 teaspoon ground nutmeg
- 1/4 teaspoon ground cloves

FROSTING:
- 3/4 cup water
- 1 envelope unflavored gelatin
- 3/4 cup sugar
- 3/4 cup confectioners' sugar
- 1 teaspoon baking powder
- 1 teaspoon vanilla extract

In a large bowl, combine shortening and molasses. Combine the flour, baking soda, salt, ginger, nutmeg and cloves; gradually add to the molasses mixture. Cover and refrigerate for 2 hours or until easy to handle.

On a lightly floured surface, roll out to 1/4-in. thickness. Cut with floured 3-in. cookie cutters. Place 1 in. apart on ungreased baking sheets. Bake at 350° for 8-10 minutes or until edges are firm. Remove to wire racks to cool.

For frosting, in a small saucepan, combine water and gelatin; let stand for 5 minutes to soften. Stir in sugar; bring to a boil. Reduce heat; stir in confectioners' sugar.

Transfer to a small bowl; beat until foamy. Add baking powder and vanilla; beat on high speed for 5-8 minutes or until thickened. Decorate cookies with frosting. **Yield:** about 4-1/2 dozen.

Cranberry Lemon Sandwiches

Patricia Michalski, Oswego, New York

I bake cookies all year long, so my friends and family call me the Cookie Lady! Whenever I bake these for Christmas, I make three batches...one to keep at home for my husband and two to give as gifts.

- 1 cup butter
- 1 cup shortening
- 1 cup sugar
- 1 cup confectioners' sugar
- 2 eggs
- 2 teaspoons vanilla extract
- 4 cups all-purpose flour
- 1 teaspoon cream of tartar
- 1 teaspoon grated lemon peel
- 1/2 teaspoon salt
- 3/4 cup dried cranberries

FILLING:
- 2/3 cup butter, softened
- 2-3/4 cups confectioners' sugar
- 1/4 cup milk
- 1-1/4 teaspoons grated lemon peel

In a large bowl, cream the butter, shortening and sugars until light and fluffy. Add eggs, one at a time, beating well after each addition. Beat in vanilla. Combine the flour, cream of tartar, lemon peel and salt; gradually add to the creamed mixture and mix well. Stir in cranberries. Cover and refrigerate for 2 hours or until easy to handle.

Roll into 1-in. balls. Place 2 in. apart on ungreased baking sheets. Flatten with a glass dipped in sugar. Bake at 350° for 12-14 minutes or until edges are lightly browned. Remove to wire racks to cool.

In a small bowl, combine the filling ingredients; beat until smooth. Spread on the bottoms of half of the cookies; top with remaining cookies. **Yield:** about 4-1/2 dozen.

Ginger Nut Crisps

Dellene Love, Hood River, Oregon

The only problem with these cookies is that it's hard to eat just one! I came up with this recipe when my mother shared a large supply of ginger. We love these spice cookies.

- 1 cup butter, softened
- 1 cup sugar
- 3/4 cup honey
- 3 cups all-purpose flour
- 1 cup whole wheat flour
- 1 tablespoon ground cinnamon
- 1 tablespoon ground cloves
- 2 to 3 teaspoons ground ginger
- 1-1/2 teaspoons baking soda
- 1 teaspoon salt
- 1-1/2 cups finely chopped pecans *or* almonds

In a large bowl, cream butter and sugar until light and fluffy. Beat in honey. Combine the flours, cinnamon, cloves, ginger, baking soda and salt; gradually add to the creamed mixture and mix well. Stir in nuts. Shape into two 11-in. rolls; wrap each in plastic wrap. Refrigerate for 3 hours or until firm.

Unwrap and cut into 1/4-in. slices. Place 2 in. apart on ungreased baking sheets. Bake at 375° for 8-11 minutes or until firm. Remove to wire racks to cool. **Yield:** 6 dozen.

Frosted Raisin Creams

Kay Strain, Norwalk, Iowa

These old-fashioned raisin spice cookies bring back fond memories of Mom whipping up a batch in her kitchen. The down-home aroma as they bake is a wonderful way to welcome family home.

- 1 cup raisins
- 1-1/4 cups boiling water
- 1 cup butter, softened
- 1-1/2 cups sugar
- 2 eggs
- 3 cups all-purpose flour
- 2 tablespoons ground cinnamon
- 1 teaspoon baking soda
- 1/4 teaspoon salt
- 1/2 cup chopped walnuts
- FROSTING:
- 1/2 cup packed brown sugar
- 1/2 hot milk
- 4-1/2 cups confectioners' sugar

Place raisins in a bowl. Add boiling water; let stand for 5 minutes. Drain, reserving 1 cup liquid; set the raisins and liquid aside.

In a large bowl, cream butter and sugar until light and fluffy. Add eggs, one at a time, beating well after each addition. Combine the flour, cinnamon, baking soda and salt; add to the creamed mixture alternately with reserved

liquid, beating well after each addition. Stir in walnuts and reserved raisins.

Drop by teaspoonfuls 2 in. apart onto ungreased baking sheets. Bake at 350° for 12-15 minutes or until lightly browned. Cool for 1 minute before removing to wire racks to cool completely.

For frosting, whisk brown sugar and milk until sugar is melted. Beat in confectioners' sugar until smooth. Frost cookies. **Yield:** about 9 dozen.

Lemon Cutouts

Bonnie Lytle, Coal Township, Pennsylvania

Grated lemon peel adds a refreshing flavor that makes these cookies stand out from other butter cookies.

- 1 cup butter, softened
- 1-1/4 cups sugar
- 2 eggs
- 2 teaspoons vanilla extract
- 3-1/2 cups all-purpose flour
- 2 teaspoons baking powder
- 1/2 teaspoon grated lemon peel
- Colored sugars

In a large bowl, cream butter and sugar until light and fluffy. Add eggs, one at a time, beating well after each addition. Beat in vanilla. Combine the flour, baking powder and lemon peel; gradually add to the creamed mixture and mix well. Cover and refrigerate for 1 hour or until easy to handle.

On a lightly floured surface, roll out to 1/8-in. thickness. Cut with floured 2-1/2-in. cookie cutters. Place 1 in. apart on ungreased baking sheets. Sprinkle with colored sugars. Bake at 350° for 8-10 minutes or until golden brown. Remove to wire racks to cool. **Yield:** about 6 dozen.

Crisp Peppermint Patties

Deborah Kay Collins, Mansfield, Ohio

Mint lovers will delight in every bite of these crisp cookies. These cookies not only taste fantastic, they're attractive as well.

    1   cup butter-flavored shortening
  1/2   cup sugar
  1/2   cup packed brown sugar
    2   eggs
    1   package (12 ounces) chocolate-covered peppermint
        patties, melted and cooled
    1   teaspoon vanilla extract
2-1/3   cups all-purpose flour
    1   teaspoon baking soda
  1/2   teaspoon salt

In a large bowl, cream shortening and sugars until light and fluffy. Beat in the eggs, melted peppermint patties and vanilla. Combine the flour, baking soda and salt; gradually add to creamed mixture and mix well. Cover and refrigerate for 30 minutes or until easy to handle.

Drop by rounded teaspoonfuls 2 in. apart onto ungreased baking sheets. Bake at 375° for 8-10 minutes or until the surface cracks. Cool for 1-2 minutes before removing to wire racks. **Yield:** 5 dozen.

Storing Cookies Cookies should always be completely cooled and icings should be completely dry before storing. Store crisp cookies separately from soft cookies and strong-flavored cookies separately from delicate-flavored ones.

Caramel Swirls

Jan Smith, Star, Texas

In my opinion, cookies are the best dessert to make and to eat! With a crisp outside and chewy caramel filling, these are definitely one of my favorites.

- 1 cup butter, softened
- 4 ounces cream cheese, softened
- 1 cup packed brown sugar
- 1 egg yolk
- 1 teaspoon maple flavoring
- 2-3/4 cups all-purpose flour

FILLING:

- 30 caramels
- 2 packages (3 ounces *each*) cream cheese, softened

In a large bowl, cream the butter, cream cheese and brown sugar until light and fluffy. Beat in egg yolk and maple flavoring. Gradually add flour and mix well. Refrigerate for 2 hours or until easy to handle.

In a small saucepan or microwave-safe bowl, melt caramels; stir until smooth. Stir in cream cheese until blended; set aside. Divide dough in half. Roll each portion between waxed paper to 1/4-in. thickness. Spread caramel mixture over dough to within 1/2 in. of the edges. Roll up tightly jelly-roll style, starting with a long side. Wrap rolls in plastic wrap; refrigerate for 4 hours or until firm.

Unwrap and cut into 1/4-in. slices. Place 1 in. apart on greased baking sheets. Bake at 350° for 12-14 minutes or until golden brown. Remove to wire racks to cool. **Yield:** 6-1/2 dozen.

Almond Cherry Biscotti

Marilyn Reid, Cherry Creek, New York

I love baking all kinds of cookies, but since I'm Italian, biscotti is at the top of my list. I remember nibbling on these as a child each Christmas.

- 2 cups all-purpose flour
- 1 cup sugar
- 1/2 teaspoon salt
- 1/2 teaspoon baking powder
- 1/4 cup cold butter
- 2 eggs
- 1 tablespoon milk
- 1/2 teaspoon vanilla extract
- 1 cup chopped almonds
- 1 cup halved candied cherries

In a large bowl, combine flour, sugar, salt and baking powder. Cut in the butter until mixture resembles coarse crumbs.

In another bowl, whisk the eggs, milk and vanilla; stir into flour mixture until blended. Stir in almonds and cherries (dough will be crumbly).

Divide dough in half; shape into two balls. On an ungreased baking sheet, shape each half into a 10-in. x 2-1/2-in. rectangle.

Bake at 350° for 30-35 minutes or until golden brown. Carefully remove to wire racks; cool for 20 minutes. Transfer to a cutting board; cut diagonally with a sharp knife into 3/4-in. slices. Place cut side down on ungreased baking sheets.

Bake for 15 minutes or until firm. Remove to wire racks to cool. Store in an airtight container. **Yield:** 2 dozen.

Buttercups

Alice Le Duc, Cedarburg, Wisconsin

These cookies began as simple holiday cutouts. One day I decided to make them with a brown butter filling. Sometimes I'll fill the centers with melted chocolate.

- 1 cup butter, softened
- 1-1/2 cups confectioners' sugar
- 1 egg
- 1 teaspoon vanilla extract
- 2-1/2 cups all-purpose flour

FILLING:
- 1/4 cup butter, cubed
- 1-1/2 cups confectioners' sugar
- 3/4 teaspoon vanilla extract
- 5 tablespoons water
- 1/4 cup raspberry preserves *or* fruit preserves of your choice

In a large bowl, cream butter and sugar until light and fluffy. Beat in egg and vanilla. Gradually add flour and mix well. Divide dough in half; wrap each portion in plastic wrap. Refrigerate for 2 hours or until easy to handle.

On a lightly floured surface, roll out each portion of dough to 1/8-in. thickness. Cut with a floured 2-1/2-in. scalloped cookie cutter. Cut a 1-in. hole in the centers of half of the cookies with a floured cutter.

Place 2 in. apart on ungreased baking sheets. Bake at 375° for 8-10 minutes or until lightly browned. Remove to wire racks to cool.

Heat butter in a small saucepan over medium heat until golden brown, about 7 minutes. Remove from the heat; gradually add the confectioners' sugar, vanilla and enough water to achieve a spreading consistency.

Spread on the bottoms of the solid cookies; top with remaining cookies. Place 1/2 teaspoon preserves in the center of each. **Yield:** 3 dozen.

Frosted Peanut Cookies

Alicia Surma, Tacoma, Washington

Oats, chopped peanuts and peanut butter frosting make this a nice change of pace from a traditional peanut butter cookie. After folks sample these, compliments and recipe requests always follow.

1	cup butter, softened
1-1/2	cups packed brown sugar
2	eggs
1	teaspoon vanilla extract
2	cups all-purpose flour
2	teaspoons baking powder
1	cup quick-cooking oats
1	cup chopped salted peanuts

FROSTING:

1/2	cup peanut butter
3	cups confectioners' sugar
1/3	cup milk

In a large bowl, cream butter and brown sugar until light and fluffy. Beat in eggs and vanilla. Combine flour and baking powder; gradually add to creamed mixture and mix well. Stir in oats and peanuts.

Drop by rounded teaspoonfuls 2 in. apart onto ungreased baking sheets. Bake at 350° for 10-12 minutes or until golden brown. Remove to wire racks to cool.

In a large bowl, beat the frosting ingredients until smooth. Frost cookies. **Yield:** 5 dozen.

Oatmeal Raisin Cookies

Sandi Swartzenberger, Kalispell, Montana

In my small neighborhood, my grandkids and their friends stop by throughout the day. I keep my cookie jar well supplied with these treats.

2	cups butter, softened
2	cups packed brown sugar
1	cup sugar
2	eggs
1/2	cup water
2	teaspoons vanilla extract
6	cups quick-cooking oats
2-1/2	cups all-purpose flour
2	teaspoons salt
2	teaspoons ground cinnamon
1	teaspoon baking soda
2-1/2	cups raisins
2	cups (12 ounces) semisweet chocolate chips
1-1/2	cups chopped walnuts
1	cup flaked coconut

In a large bowl, cream the butter and sugars until light and fluffy. Add eggs, one at a time, beating well after each addition. Beat in water and vanilla. Combine the oats, flour, salt, cinnamon and baking soda; gradually add to creamed mixture and mix well. Transfer to a larger bowl if necessary. Stir in raisins, chips, walnuts and coconut.

Drop by level tablespoonfuls 2 in. apart onto ungreased baking sheets. Bake at 350° for 12-14 minutes or until lightly browned. Remove to wire racks to cool. **Yield:** about 12-1/2 dozen.

Buttery Yeast Spritz

Janet Stucky, Sterling, Illinois

Yeast may be an unusual ingredient for cookies, but the buttery flavor is fabulous. These were my mother's favorite cookies...now I make them for my children and grandchildren.

1	package (1/4 ounce) active dry yeast
2	tablespoons warm water (110° to 115°)
2	cups butter, softened
1	cup sugar
2	egg yolks
4	cups all-purpose flour

In a small bowl, dissolve yeast in water; set aside. In a small bowl, cream butter and sugar until light and fluffy. Beat in egg yolks and yeast mixture. Gradually add flour and mix well.

Using a cookie press fitted with disk of your choice, press dough into desired shapes 1 in. apart onto ungreased baking sheets. Bake at 400° for 7-9 minutes or until lightly browned. Remove to wire racks to cool. **Yield:** 13 dozen.

Apricot-Filled Triangles

Mildred Lorence, Carlisle, Pennsylvania

It's a good thing this recipe makes a big batch because no one can stop eating just one! These crisp, buttery cookies truly do melt in your mouth.

1	pound dried apricots (2-1/2 cups)
1-1/2	cups water
1/2	cup sugar

DOUGH:

2/3	cup shortening
3	tablespoons milk
1-1/3	cups sugar
2	eggs
1	teaspoon lemon extract
4	cups cake flour
2	teaspoons baking powder
1	teaspoon salt

In a small saucepan, cook apricots in water over low heat for 45 minutes or until the water is absorbed and apricots are soft. Cool slightly; transfer to a blender. Cover and process until smooth. Add sugar; cover and process until blended. Set aside.

In a large saucepan over low heat, melt shortening and milk. Remove from the heat; stir in sugar. Add eggs, one at a time, whisking well after each addition. Stir in extract. Combine the flour, baking powder and salt; gradually add to the saucepan and mix well. Cover and refrigerate for 4 hours or until easy to handle.

On a lightly floured surface, roll out to 1/8-in. thickness. Cut with a floured 3-in. round cookie cutter. Place 1 teaspoon apricot filling in the center of each. Bring three edges together over filling, overlapping slightly (a small portion of filling will show in the center); pinch edges gently. Place 1 in. apart on ungreased baking sheets.

Bake at 400° for 8-10 minutes or until golden brown. Remove to wire racks to cool. **Yield:** 6 dozen.

Coconut Macaroons

Naomi Vining, Springdale, Arkansas

This recipe was lost in my files for many, many years before I uncovered it. I decided to make these macaroons for an event at the business my husband and I own, and they were a hit with everyone.

1/2	cup egg whites (about 4)
1/2	teaspoon vanilla extract
1/4	teaspoon salt
1-1/4	cups sugar
3	cups flaked coconut
30	red *or* green candied cherries, halved, optional

In a large bowl, beat the egg whites, vanilla and salt on medium speed until soft peaks form. Gradually add sugar, 1 tablespoon at a time, beating on high until stiff, glossy peaks form and sugar is dissolved, about 6 minutes. Fold in coconut.

Drop by rounded teaspoonfuls 2 in. apart onto lightly greased baking sheets. Top each with a candied cherry half if desired. Bake at 325° for 20-23 minutes or until firm to the touch. Remove to wire racks to cool. Store in an airtight container. **Yield:** 5 dozen.

Toffee Cranberry Crisps

Ann Quaerna, Lake Geneva, Wisconsin

I've had more friends request this recipe than any other cookie recipe I have. The combination of cranberries, chocolate chips and toffee bits is wonderful.

- 1 cup butter, softened
- 3/4 cup sugar
- 3/4 cup packed brown sugar
- 1 egg
- 1 teaspoon vanilla extract
- 1-1/2 cups all-purpose flour
- 1-1/2 cups quick-cooking oats
- 1 teaspoon baking soda
- 1/4 teaspoon salt
- 1 cup dried cranberries
- 1 cup miniature semisweet chocolate chips
- 1 cup English toffee bits *or* almond brickle chips

In a large bowl, cream the butter and sugars until light and fluffy. Beat in egg and vanilla. Combine the flour, oats, baking soda and salt; gradually add to creamed mixture and mix well. Stir in cranberries, chocolate chips and toffee bits. Shape into three 12-in. logs; wrap each in plastic wrap. Refrigerate for 2 hours or until firm.

Unwrap and cut into 1/2-in. slices. Place 2 in. apart on ungreased baking sheets.

Bake at 350° for 8-10 minutes or until golden brown. Remove to wire racks to cool. **Yield:** 5-1/2 dozen.

Lemon Zucchini Drops

Barbara Franklin, Tucson, Arizona

When we lived on the East Coast, a nearby fruit and vegetable stand had a bakery featuring these soft, cake-like cookies. We missed every bite when we moved away, so I developed this recipe.

- 1/2 cup butter, softened
- 1 cup sugar
- 1 egg
- 1 cup finely shredded zucchini
- 1 teaspoon grated lemon peel
- 2 cups all-purpose flour
- 1 teaspoon baking powder
- 1 teaspoon baking soda
- 1 teaspoon ground cinnamon
- 1/2 teaspoon salt
- 1/2 cup raisins
- 1/2 cup chopped walnuts

LEMON GLAZE:
- 2 cups confectioners' sugar
- 2 to 3 tablespoons lemon juice

In a large bowl, cream butter and sugar until light and fluffy. Beat in the egg, zucchini and lemon peel. Combine the flour, baking powder, baking soda, cinnamon and salt; gradually add to the creamed mixture and mix well. Stir in raisins and walnuts.

Drop by tablespoonfuls 3 in. apart onto lightly greased baking sheets. Bake at 375° for 8-10 minutes or until lightly browned. Remove to wire racks to cool.

For glaze, combine sugar and enough lemon juice to achieve a thin spreading consistency. Spread or drizzle over cooled cookies. **Yield:** 3-1/2 dozen.

313

Butterscotch Gingerbread Men

Jane McLean, Birmingham, Alabama

The addition of butterscotch pudding makes these a little different than most gingerbread cutout recipes. The recipe comes from my mother-in-law's files.

- 1/2 cup butter, softened
- 1/2 cup packed brown sugar
- 1 package (3.4 ounces) instant butterscotch pudding mix
- 1 egg
- 1-1/2 cups all-purpose flour
- 1-1/2 teaspoons ground ginger
- 1/2 teaspoon baking soda
- 1/2 teaspoon ground cinnamon

FROSTING:
- 2 cups confectioners' sugar
- 3 tablespoons milk

In a small bowl, cream the butter, brown sugar and pudding mix until light and fluffy. Beat in egg. Combine the flour, ginger, baking soda and cinnamon; gradually add to the creamed mixture and mix well. Cover and refrigerate overnight.

On a lightly floured surface, roll out to 1/8-in. thickness. Cut with a 5-in. gingerbread man cutter. Place 1 in. apart on ungreased baking sheets. Bake at 350° for 8-10 minutes or until edges are golden. Remove to wire racks to cool.

In another small bowl, combine confectioners' sugar and milk until smooth. Decorate cookies with frosting as desired. **Yield:** 1-1/2 dozen.

Swedish Spice Cutouts

Lilly Decker, Clancy, Montana

My sister, Judithh Landgren of White Sulphur Springs, Montana, brought this recipe with her when she came to the United States from Sweden in 1928.

- 1-1/2 cups butter, softened
- 1-3/4 cups packed dark brown sugar
- 1 egg
- 2/3 cup dark corn syrup
- 1/4 cup molasses
- 4-1/2 cups all-purpose flour
- 1-1/4 teaspoons ground cinnamon
- 1 teaspoon baking soda
- 3/4 teaspoon ground cloves

Slivered almonds, optional
Frosting of your choice, optional

In a large bowl, cream butter and brown sugar until light and fluffy. Beat in the egg, corn syrup and molasses. Combine the flour, cinnamon, baking soda and cloves; gradually add to creamed mixture and mix well. Cover and refrigerate for 4 hours or until easy to handle.

On a lightly floured surface, roll dough to 1/8-in. thickness. Cut with floured 2-1/2-in. cookie cutters. Place 1 in. apart on ungreased baking sheets. Top with almonds if desired or leave plain.

Bake at 375° for 8-10 minutes or until edges are lightly browned. Remove to wire racks to cool. Frost plain cookies if desired. **Yield:** about 10 dozen.

Cranberry Crisps

Sandy Furches, Lake City, Florida

I developed this recipe after sampling a similar cookie while traveling in North Carolina. These pretty cookies keep well in the freezer, so I always have some on hand for midday munching.

- 1 cup butter-flavored shortening
- 1 cup sugar
- 1 cup packed brown sugar
- 2 eggs
- 2 teaspoons vanilla extract
- 2-1/2 cups old-fashioned oats
- 2 cups all-purpose flour
- 1 teaspoon baking soda
- 1 teaspoon ground cinnamon
- 1/2 teaspoon salt
- 1/2 teaspoon baking powder
- 1-1/3 cups dried cranberries
- 1 cup coarsely chopped walnuts

In a large bowl, cream shortening and sugars until light and fluffy. Add eggs, one at a time, beating well after each addition. Beat in vanilla. Combine the oats, flour, baking soda, cinnamon, salt and baking powder; gradually add to the creamed mixture and mix well. Stir in the cranberries and walnuts.

Drop by tablespoonfuls 2 in. apart onto lightly greased baking sheets. Bake at 350° for 12-14 minutes or until lightly browned. Remove to wire racks to cool. **Yield:** 5 dozen.

Oatmeal Molasses Crisps

Jori Schellenberger, Everett, Washington

In Amish and Mennonite homes, from-scratch cooking is guaranteed delicious. So when I found this recipe in an Amish cookbook, I knew I had to try it. It's become a favorite of our family as well as the folks at our church fellowship.

2-1/2 cups butter, softened
5 cups sugar
4 eggs
1/3 cup dark molasses
3 teaspoons vanilla extract
4-1/3 cups all-purpose flour
4 teaspoons baking powder
3 teaspoons ground cinnamon
2 teaspoons salt
1 teaspoon baking soda
4-3/4 cups old-fashioned oats
2 cups finely chopped pecans

In a large bowl, cream butter and sugar until light and fluffy. Add eggs, one at a time, beating well after each addition. Beat in molasses and vanilla. Combine the flour, baking powder, cinnamon, salt and baking soda; gradually add to the creamed mixture and mix well. Transfer to a larger bowl if necessary. Stir in oats and pecans.

Drop by tablespoonfuls 2 in. apart onto greased baking sheets. Bake at 375° for 8-10 minutes or until edges are firm. Cool for 3 minutes before removing to wire racks. **Yield:** 15 dozen.

Calypso Cups

Mrs. Frank Kaczmarek, Steubenville, Ohio

These are great cookies to prepare for parties throughout the year. I simply tint the frosting for the occasion—red for Valentine's Day, pastel colors for baby showers and green for Christmas.

- 1 cup butter, softened
- 2 packages (3 ounces *each*) cream cheese, softened
- 2 cups all-purpose flour

FILLING:
- 1/2 cup flaked coconut
- 1/2 cup sugar
- 1-1/2 teaspoons cornstarch
- 1 can (8 ounces) crushed pineapple, undrained
- 1 egg

FROSTING:
- 2 cups confectioners' sugar
- 1/2 cup shortening
- 1 teaspoon vanilla extract
- 3 to 4 tablespoons milk

Finely chopped walnuts and/*or* additional flaked coconut, optional

In a large bowl, beat butter and cream cheese until smooth. Gradually add flour and mix well. Cover and refrigerate for 1 hour or until easy to handle.

Roll into 1-in. balls. Press onto the bottom and up the sides of greased miniature muffin cups. Combine the filling ingredients; spoon into cups. Bake at 350° for 15-20 minutes or until edges are lightly browned. Cool in pans on wire racks.

For frosting, combine the sugar, shortening and vanilla until smooth; add enough milk to achieve spreading consistency. Remove cooled cups from pans. Frost; sprinkle with walnuts and additional flaked coconut if desired. **Yield:** 4 dozen.

Chocolate Marshmallow Meltaways

Joanna Swartley, Harrisonburg, Virginia

Kids are thrilled to find a marshmallow hidden under this cookie's cocoa frosting. I enjoyed these cookies as a child, and now my own family loves them, too.

- 1/2 cup butter-flavored shortening
- 3/4 cup sugar
- 1 egg
- 1/4 cup milk
- 1 teaspoon vanilla extract
- 1-3/4 cups all-purpose flour
- 1/2 cup baking cocoa
- 1/2 teaspoon salt
- 1/2 teaspoon baking soda
- 18 large marshmallows, halved

FROSTING:
- 3 tablespoons butter, softened
- 3 cups confectioners' sugar
- 3 tablespoons baking cocoa
- 1/8 teaspoon salt
- 4 to 6 tablespoons milk

In a large bowl, cream shortening and sugar until light and fluffy. Beat in the egg, milk and vanilla. Combine the flour, cocoa, salt and baking soda; gradually add to creamed mixture and mix well.

Drop by tablespoonfuls 2 in. apart onto ungreased baking sheets. Bake at 350° for 8 minutes. Press a marshmallow half, cut side down, onto each cookie; bake 2 minutes longer. Remove to wire racks to cool.

In a small bowl, beat the butter, confectioners' sugar, cocoa and salt until smooth. Add enough milk to achieve a spreading consistency. Frost cookies. **Yield:** 3 dozen.

Ambrosia Bites

Arlene Steinwart, Grand Island, Nebraska

These chewy oatmeal cookies are packed with the refreshing flavors of orange and lemon, plus dates, raisins and coconut. When our children, grandchildren and great-grandchildren ask me to make Grandma's Cookies, these are the ones they're referring to.

- 1 cup butter, softened
- 1 cup sugar
- 1 cup packed brown sugar
- 2 eggs
- 1 tablespoon grated lemon peel
- 1 tablespoon grated orange peel
- 1 teaspoon vanilla extract
- 2 cups all-purpose flour
- 1-1/2 cups quick-cooking oats
- 1-1/2 teaspoons baking soda
- 1 teaspoon baking powder
- 1 teaspoon salt
- 1 cup chopped walnuts
- 1 cup raisins
- 1 cup chopped dates
- 1 cup flaked coconut

In a large bowl, cream butter and sugars until light and fluffy. Beat in the eggs, peels and vanilla. Combine the flour, oats, baking soda, baking powder and salt; gradually add to creamed mixture until well blended. Stir in remaining ingredients.

Drop by heaping tablespoonfuls 3 in. apart onto ungreased baking sheets. Bake at 375° for 8-10 minutes or until golden brown. Remove to wire racks to cool. **Yield:** 6 dozen.

Chocolate Chip Cookie Pops

Silretta Graves, Park Forest, Illinois

My family prefers milk chocolate to dark or semisweet chocolate, so I created this recipe. Baking the pops on a stick makes them fun, but the cookies are just as delicious by themselves.

- 2 cups butter, softened
- 1-1/2 cups sugar
- 1-1/2 cups packed brown sugar
- 3 eggs
- 3 teaspoons vanilla extract
- 4-3/4 cups all-purpose flour
- 1-1/2 teaspoons baking soda
- 1 teaspoon salt
- 3 cups milk chocolate chips
- 2 cups chopped pecans
- 12 dozen Popsicle sticks

In a large bowl, cream butter and sugars until light and fluffy. Add eggs, one at a time, beating well after each addition. Beat in vanilla. Combine the flour, baking soda and salt; gradually add to creamed mixture and mix well. Transfer to a larger bowl if necessary. Stir in chocolate chips and pecans.

Drop by rounded teaspoonfuls 3 in. apart onto ungreased baking sheets. Insert a wooden stick into each cookie if desired. Bake at 375° for 10-12 minutes or until lightly browned. Cool for 1 minute before removing to wire racks. **Yield:** about 12 dozen.

Baking Classics | Cookies

Fancy Peanut Butter Cookies

Janet Hooper, Emporium, Pennsylvania

I always received compliments on my moist and chewy peanut butter cookies. But I wondered how to make them even more special, and I decided to decorate them!

- 1 cup shortening
- 1 cup peanut butter
- 1 cup sugar
- 1 cup packed brown sugar
- 2 eggs
- 1/4 cup milk
- 2 teaspoons vanilla extract
- 3-1/2 cups all-purpose flour
- 2 teaspoons baking soda
- 1 teaspoon salt

FROSTING:
- 1/4 cup butter, softened
- 1/4 cup shortening
- 1/4 cup peanut butter
- 4 cups confectioners' sugar
- 1/4 cup milk
- 1 teaspoon vanilla extract
- Dash salt

ICING:
- 1/2 cup semisweet chocolate chips, melted
- 2 tablespoons milk

In a large bowl, cream the shortening, peanut butter and sugars until light and fluffy. Add eggs, one at a time, beating well after each addition. Beat in milk and vanilla. Combine the flour, baking soda and salt; gradually add to the creamed mixture and mix well.

Roll into 1-in. balls. Place 2 in. apart on ungreased baking sheets. Bake at 375° for 10-12 minutes or until golden brown. Remove to wire racks.

For frosting, in a large bowl, cream the butter, shortening, peanut butter and confectioners' sugar until light and fluffy. Beat in the milk, vanilla and salt until smooth. Frost cookies. Combine icing ingredients; drizzle over frosting. **Yield:** 7-1/2 dozen.

Editor's Note: Reduced-fat or generic brands of peanut butter are not recommended for this recipe.

Nutty Butter Munchies

Zenola Frazier, Tallulah, Louisiana

I developed this recipe for a crisp cookie as a way to satisfy my sweet tooth. Peanuts and pecans are abundant here in Louisiana, so I bake with them often.

1 cup butter, softened
1/2 cup chunky peanut butter
1 cup sugar
1 cup packed brown sugar
3 eggs
1 teaspoon vanilla extract
1/2 teaspoon almond extract
3 cups all-purpose flour
1/2 teaspoon baking soda
1/2 teaspoon salt
1-1/2 cups chopped pecans
1/2 cup salted peanuts

In a large bowl, cream the butter, peanut butter and sugars until light and fluffy. Add eggs, one at a time, beating well after each addition. Beat in extracts. Combine the flour, baking soda and salt; gradually add to the creamed mixture and mix well. Stir in nuts.

Drop by tablespoonfuls 2 in. apart onto greased baking sheets. Flatten with a glass dipped in sugar. Bake at 350° for 10-12 minutes or until the edges are lightly browned. Remove to wire racks to cool. **Yield:** 8-1/2 dozen.

Baking Classics | Cookies

Uniform Drop Cookies To ensure drop cookies bake up to a uniform size, use an ice cream scoop with spring release. A 1-tablespoon-size scoop will give you a 2-inch cookie. Just scoop the dough, then even off the top with a flat-edge metal spatula and release onto a baking sheet.

Apricot Sesame Cookies

Jeanne Allen, Webster, New York

This recipe is a favorite of mine to make for special occasions. The cookies freeze beautifully, so they can conveniently be made ahead of time. Substitute peach, strawberry or raspberry jam if you like.

- 1 cup butter, softened
- 1/2 cup sugar
- 1 teaspoon almond extract
- 2 cups all-purpose flour
- 1/2 teaspoon salt
- 1/4 cup plus 3 tablespoons sesame seeds
- 6 tablespoons apricot jam

In a large bowl, cream butter and sugar until light and fluffy. Beat in extract. Combine flour and salt; gradually add to the creamed mixture and mix well.

Roll into 1-in. balls; roll in sesame seeds. Place 2 in. apart on ungreased baking sheets.

Using the end of a wooden spoon handle, make a 3/8-in.-deep indentation in the center of each ball. Fill with jam. Bake at 400° for 10-12 minutes or until lightly browned. Remove to wire racks to cool. **Yield:** 4 dozen.

Sweet Potato Spice Cookies

Ruth Shaffer, Elizabethville, Pennsylvania

Shredded sweet potatoes, butterscotch chips, pecans, coconut and spices are creatively combined in a one-of-a-kind cookie that always brings rave reviews.

- 3/4 cup butter, softened
- 1 cup sugar
- 1/4 cup packed brown sugar
- 1 egg
- 1 cup finely shredded uncooked sweet potato
- 3 tablespoons orange juice concentrate
- 2 cups all-purpose flour
- 1 teaspoon baking powder
- 1 teaspoon ground cinnamon
- 1/2 teaspoon baking soda
- 1/2 teaspoon salt
- 1/4 teaspoon ground nutmeg
- 1-1/4 cups quick-cooking oats
- 1 cup butterscotch chips
- 1 cup flaked coconut
- 1 cup chopped pecans

In a large bowl, cream butter and sugars until light and fluffy. Beat in the egg, sweet potato and orange juice concentrate. Combine the flour, baking powder, cinnamon, baking soda, salt and nutmeg; gradually add to the creamed mixture and mix well. Stir in remaining ingredients.

Drop by rounded teaspoonfuls 2 in. apart onto greased baking sheets. Bake at 350° for 14-16 minutes or until firm. Remove to wire racks to cool. **Yield:** 7 dozen.

Cream-Filled Chocolate Cookies

Maxine Finn, Emmetsburg, Iowa

I've been baking these cookies for years. My children and grandchildren gobble them up.

- 1 cup butter, softened
- 2 cups sugar
- 2 eggs
- 1 teaspoon vanilla extract
- 3 cups all-purpose flour
- 2/3 cup baking cocoa
- 1 teaspoon baking soda
- 1 teaspoon salt
- 1/2 cup milk

FILLING:
- 1/2 cup butter, softened
- 1-1/2 cups confectioners' sugar
- 1 cup marshmallow creme
- 1 teaspoon vanilla extract

In a large bowl, cream butter and sugar until light and fluffy. Add eggs, one at a time, beating well after each addition. Beat in vanilla. Combine the flour, cocoa, baking soda and salt; add to creamed mixture alternately with milk, beating well after each addition. Refrigerate for at least 2 hours.

Drop by rounded teaspoonfuls 2 in. apart onto greased baking sheets. Bake at 375° for 10-12 minutes or until edges are set. Remove to wire racks to cool.

In a small bowl, combine filling ingredients; beat until smooth. Spread on the bottoms of half of the cookies; top with remaining cookies. Store in the refrigerator. **Yield:** about 4-1/2 dozen.

Toffee Cashew Treasures

Denise Sokolowski, Milwaukee, Wisconsin

After searching for a recipe that combined all my favorites, I decided to create my own cookie. The result is a lacy, crisp cookie that's sure to earn you rave reviews.

- 1 cup butter, softened
- 1 cup sugar
- 1 cup packed brown sugar
- 2 eggs
- 1 teaspoon vanilla extract
- 2 cups all-purpose flour
- 2 cups old-fashioned oats
- 1 teaspoon baking soda
- 1/2 teaspoon baking powder
- 1/2 teaspoon salt
- 1 cup flaked coconut
- 1 cup English toffee bits *or* almond brickle chips
- 1 cup chopped cashews, toasted

In a large bowl, cream butter and sugars until light and fluffy. Add the eggs, one at a time, beating well after each addition. Beat in vanilla. Combine the flour, oats, baking soda, baking powder and salt; gradually add to the creamed mixture and mix well. Stir in the remaining ingredients.

Drop by rounded tablespoonfuls 3 in. apart onto ungreased baking sheets. Bake at 350° for 12-14 minutes or until lightly browned. Cool for 2 minutes before removing to wire racks. **Yield:** about 5 dozen.

Peppermint Snowballs

Susan Bonnstetter, Slayton, Minnesota

The holidays don't begin around our house until a batch of these cookies is baking in the oven. Their wonderful aroma scrumptiously says, "Christmas!"

  1   cup butter, softened
1/2   cup confectioners' sugar
  1   teaspoon vanilla extract
2-1/2 cups all-purpose flour
1/2   cup ground nuts, optional

FILLING:
  2   tablespoons cream cheese, softened
1/2   cup confectioners' sugar
  1   teaspoon milk
  3   tablespoons crushed peppermint candies
  1   drop red food coloring, optional

TOPPING:
1/2   cup crushed peppermint candies
1/2   cup confectioners' sugar

In a large bowl, cream butter and sugar until light and fluffy. Beat in vanilla. Gradually add flour. Stir in nuts if desired. Knead dough until pliable. Cover and refrigerate for 1 hour or until easy to handle.

In small bowl, beat the cream cheese, confectioners' sugar, milk, candy and food coloring if desired.

Roll tablespoonfuls of dough into balls. Using the end of a wooden spoon handle, make a deep indentation in the center of each.

Fill with 1/4 teaspoon filling. Cover with 1/4 teaspoonfuls of dough; seal and reshape into balls. Combine topping ingredients; roll balls in topping.

Place 1 in. apart on ungreased baking sheets. Bake at 350° for 12-14 minutes or until firm. Roll warm cookies in remaining topping; cool on wire racks. **Yield:** 4 dozen.

323

Orange Dreams

Susan Waren, North Manchester, Indiana

A fellow teacher shared this recipe with me. We have several great bakers on our teaching staff, and each of us takes turns bringing special treats to the lounge. These moist, chewy cookies with a pleasant orange flavor are a favorite.

1 cup butter, softened
1/2 cup sugar
1/2 cup packed brown sugar
1 egg
1 tablespoon grated orange peel
2-1/4 cups all-purpose flour
3/4 teaspoon baking soda
1/2 teaspoon salt
1-1/2 cups vanilla *or* white chips

In a large bowl, cream butter and sugars until light and fluffy. Beat in egg and orange peel. Combine the flour, baking soda and salt; gradually add to creamed mixture and mix well. Stir in vanilla chips.

Drop by rounded tablespoonfuls 2 in. apart onto ungreased baking sheets. Bake at 350° for 10-12 minutes or until golden brown. Remove to wire racks to cool. **Yield:** 4-1/2 dozen.

Cloverleaf Cookies

Patricia Gilbert, Kansas City, Missouri

This recipe is a favorite of kids because they get three cookies in one! Combining three different flavors of dough—chocolate chip, peanut butter and chocolate—is a fun and tasty idea.

- 1/2　cup butter, softened
- 1/2　cup shortening
- 3/4　cup packed brown sugar
- 1/2　cup sugar
- 1　egg
- 1-1/2　teaspoons vanilla extract
- 1-3/4　cups all-purpose flour
- 1　teaspoon baking soda
- 1/2　teaspoon salt
- 1/2　cup miniature semisweet chocolate chips
- 1/4　cup chunky peanut butter
- 1　square (1 ounce) unsweetened chocolate, melted and cooled

In a large bowl, cream butter, shortening and sugars until light and fluffy. Beat in egg and vanilla. Combine the flour, baking soda and salt; gradually add to the creamed mixture and mix well.

Divide dough into thirds. Add the chocolate chips to one portion, peanut butter to another and melted chocolate to the third portion. Cover and chill for 2 hours or until firm.

Roll 1/2 teaspoonfuls of dough into balls. For each cookie, place three balls (one of each dough) with edges touching on ungreased baking sheets to form a cloverleaf.

Place cookies 2 in. apart. Bake at 350° for 7-9 minutes or until golden brown. Cool for 1 minute before removing to wire racks. **Yield:** 5 dozen.

Apple Doodles

Cecilia Lorraine Ruiz, Sunnyvale, California

I changed an apple cake recipe into a recipe for these cookies. It's a nice way to feature fall's delicious produce.

- 2/3　cup butter-flavored shortening
- 1　cup sugar
- 1　egg
- 1　teaspoon vanilla extract
- 2　cups all-purpose flour
- 2-1/4　teaspoons ground cinnamon
- 1　teaspoon baking powder
- 1　teaspoon baking soda
- 1/2　teaspoon salt
- 1　cup finely diced peeled tart apple
- 3/4　cup chopped walnuts, optional

In a large bowl, cream shortening and sugar until light and fluffy. Beat in egg and vanilla. Combine the flour, cinnamon, baking powder, baking soda and salt; stir half into the creamed mixture. Stir in the apple, walnuts if desired and remaining flour mixture.

Drop by heaping teaspoonfuls 3 in. apart onto lightly greased baking sheets. Bake at 375° for 13-15 minutes or until golden brown. Remove to wire racks to cool. **Yield:** 3-1/2 dozen.

Fruit 'n' Spice Rounds

Allison Bell, Helena, Montana

While looking for a way to use an abundance of dates I had on hand, I came across this recipe. With raisins and walnuts—and a delectable lemon glaze—these quickly became a family favorite.

- 1 cup butter, softened
- 1-1/2 cups sugar
- 3 eggs
- 3 cups all-purpose flour
- 2 teaspoons ground cinnamon
- 1 teaspoon baking soda
- 1 teaspoon ground cloves
- 1 teaspoon ground nutmeg
- 1-1/2 cups finely chopped dates
- 1 cup finely chopped raisins
- 1 cup finely chopped walnuts

GLAZE:
- 2 cups confectioners' sugar
- 2 tablespoons lemon juice
- 2 tablespoons water

In a large bowl, cream butter and sugar until light and fluffy. Add eggs, one at a time, beating well after each addition. Combine the flour, cinnamon, baking soda, cloves and nutmeg; gradually add to the creamed mixture. Stir in the dates, raisins and walnuts. Cover and refrigerate for 2 hours or until easy to handle.

On a floured surface, roll out to 1/4-in. thickness. Cut with a floured 2-1/2-in. round cookie cutter. Place 1 in. apart on greased baking sheets.

Bake at 375° for 10-12 minutes. Remove to wire racks. Meanwhile, combine glaze ingredients until smooth; brush over warm cookies. **Yield:** 5 dozen.

Monster Cookies

Dolores DeMarco, Hammonton, New Jersey

These big crisp cookies are packed with lots of irresistible ingredients, so they appeal to everyone. When you put a plate of these cookies on the table, they disappear fast.

- 2 cups butter, softened
- 2 cups sugar
- 2 cups packed brown sugar
- 4 eggs
- 4 teaspoons vanilla extract
- 3 cups all-purpose flour
- 2 teaspoons baking powder
- 1 teaspoon baking soda
- 4 cups quick-cooking oats
- 4 cups crisp rice cereal
- 2 cups flaked coconut
- 2 cups (12 ounces) semisweet chocolate chips
- 2 cups coarsely chopped walnuts

In a large bowl, cream the butter and sugars until light and fluffy. Add eggs, one at a time, beating well after each addition. Beat in vanilla. Combine the flour, baking powder and baking soda; gradually add to the creamed mixture and mix well. Transfer to a larger bowl if necessary. Stir in the remaining ingredients.

Drop by heaping tablespoonfuls 3 in. apart onto lightly greased baking sheets. Bake at 350° for 10-12 minutes or until golden brown. Remove to wire racks to cool. **Yield:** 8 dozen.

Lemon Drop Cookies

Pat Zimmerman, Midland, Texas

After visiting my sister, she gave us a care package for the trip home. Tucked inside were these delightful cookies. Crushed lemon drop candies and grated lemon peel lend to the refreshing taste.

- 1/2 cup butter, softened
- 3/4 cup sugar
- 1 egg
- 1 tablespoon half-and-half cream
- 1 teaspoon grated lemon peel
- 1-1/2 cups all-purpose flour
- 1/2 cup finely crushed lemon drops
- 1 teaspoon baking powder
- 1/4 teaspoon salt

In a large bowl, cream butter and sugar until light and fluffy. Beat in the egg, cream and lemon peel. Combine the flour, lemon drops, baking powder and salt; gradually add to the creamed mixture and mix well.

Drop by rounded teaspoonfuls 3 in. apart onto greased baking sheets. Bake at 350° for 8-10 minutes or until edges are lightly browned. Cool for 2 minutes before removing to wire racks. **Yield:** about 3-1/2 dozen.

Almond-Tipped Shortbread Fingers

Cindy Sifford, Mt. Zion, Illinois

My husband enjoys these cookies so much that he usually can't wait until they're set to start eating them. If you'd like, try dipping them into melted semisweet chocolate and chopped pecans.

- 1 cup butter, softened
- 3/4 cup packed brown sugar
- 2 teaspoons vanilla extract
- 2 cups all-purpose flour
- 6 squares (1 ounce *each*) white baking chocolate
- 1-1/4 cups chopped almonds

In a large bowl, cream butter and brown sugar until light and fluffy. Beat in vanilla. Gradually add flour. Shape 1/2 cupfuls of dough into 1/2-in.-thick logs. Cut logs into 2-in. pieces.

Place 2 in. apart on ungreased baking sheets. Bake at 325° for 15-17 minutes or until lightly browned. Remove to wire racks to cool.

In a microwave, melt white chocolate at 30% power; stir until smooth. Dip one end of each cookie into chocolate, then into almonds. Place on waxed paper to set. **Yield:** 4 dozen.

Almond Jelly Cookies

Laraine Hadley, Moretown, Vermont

My mother-in-law used to send these wonderful cookies in her special care packages to our family. We could hardly wait to open the box and dig in!

1-1/2   cups butter, softened
     1   cup sugar
1-1/2   cups ground almonds
     1   teaspoon vanilla extract
2-1/2   cups all-purpose flour
   1/2   teaspoon salt
     1   cup jelly *or* jam of your choice

In a large bowl, cream butter and sugar until light and fluffy. Add almonds and vanilla; mix well. Combine flour and salt; gradually add to the creamed mixture until blended. Refrigerate for 2 hours or until easy to handle.

On a lightly floured surface, roll out half of the dough to 1/8-in. thickness. Cut with a 2-in. round cookie cutter. Repeat with remaining dough, using a 2-in. doughnut cutter so the center is out of each cookie.

Place 1 in. apart on ungreased baking sheets. Bake at 350° for 10-12 minutes or until edges are lightly browned. Remove to wire racks to cool.

Spread 1/2 teaspoon of the jelly over the bottom of the solid cookies; place cookies with cutout center over jelly. **Yield:** 5 dozen.

Triple Chocolate Caramel Cookies

Colleen Jennings, Freeburg, Illinois

I love caramel, chocolate and pecans together. While I had recipes for cake, cheesecake and candy that feature this combination, I didn't have one for cookies. So I came up with this recipe.

1-1/2 cups butter, softened
1 cup sugar
1 egg
1 teaspoon vanilla extract
3 cups all-purpose flour
1/2 cup baking cocoa
1 package (12 ounces) miniature semisweet chocolate chips
1 cup chopped pecans, toasted
1 bottle (12-1/2 ounces) caramel ice cream topping
4 to 6 ounces dark chocolate candy coating, melted

In a large bowl, cream butter and sugar until light and fluffy. Beat in egg and vanilla. Combine flour and cocoa; gradually add to the creamed mixture and mix well. Stir in chocolate chips and pecans.

Roll into 1-in. balls. Place 2 in. apart on ungreased baking sheets. Using the end of a wooden spoon handle, make a 3/8- to 1/2-in.-deep indentation in the center of each ball. Smooth any cracks. Fill each indentation half full with caramel topping.

Bake at 350° for 15-18 minutes or until caramel is very bubbly and cookies are set. Cool for 5 minutes before removing to wire racks. Drizzle cooled cookies with candy coating. **Yield:** 6 dozen.

Dutch Treats

Ava Rexrode, Blue Grass, Virginia

I was born and raised in Holland, where we used almond paste quite often in our baking. I created this recipe to capture the outstanding flavors of home.

1 cup butter, softened
2 packages (3 ounces *each*) cream cheese, softened
2 cups all-purpose flour
FILLING:
3 eggs
1 cup sugar
1 can (8 ounces) almond paste, cut into cubes
Sliced almonds

In a large bowl, cream butter and cream cheese until light and fluffy. Gradually add the flour. Cover and refrigerate for 1 hour or until easy to handle.

Roll into 1-in. balls. Press dough onto the bottom and up the sides of ungreased miniature muffin cups; set aside.

For filling, in a small bowl, beat eggs until foamy. Add sugar until blended. Beat in the almond paste. Spoon a rounded teaspoonful into each cup; top each with three almond slices.

Bake at 325° for 25-30 minutes or until lightly browned and filling is set. Cool for 10 minutes before removing to wire racks. **Yield:** about 10 dozen.

Cherry Snowballs

Evy Adams, West Seneca, New York

A juicy maraschino cherry is the pleasant surprise tucked inside these festive cookies. My mother clipped this recipe out of the newspaper many years ago.

    1   cup butter, softened
    1/2 cup confectioners' sugar
    1   tablespoon water
    1   teaspoon vanilla extract
    2   cups all-purpose flour
    1   cup quick-cooking oats
    1/2 teaspoon salt
    36   maraschino cherries, well drained
COATING:
    2   cups confectioners' sugar
    1/4 to 1/3 cup milk
    2   cups flaked coconut, finely chopped

In a large bowl, cream butter and sugar until light and fluffy. Beat in water and vanilla. Combine the flour, oats and salt; gradually add to the creamed mixture and mix well.

Shape a tablespoonful of dough around each cherry, forming a ball. Place 2 in. apart on ungreased baking sheets. Bake at 350° for 18-20 minutes or until bottoms are browned. Remove to wire racks to cool.

In a small bowl, combine the confectioners' sugar and enough milk to achieve smooth dipping consistency. Dip cookies, then roll in coconut. Place on waxed paper; let stand until set. **Yield:** 3 dozen.

Mocha-Pecan Butter Balls

Kathleen Pruitt, Hoopeston, Illinois

When I was a little girl, one of my mother's co-workers always gave us tins of assorted Christmas cookies. These were the ones I reached for first.

    2/3 cup butter, softened
    1   package (3 ounces) cream cheese, softened
    2/3 cup instant chocolate drink mix
    1/3 cup confectioners' sugar
    2   teaspoons vanilla extract
    1   teaspoon instant coffee granules
    1-3/4 cups all-purpose flour
    1/4 teaspoon salt
    1   cup finely chopped pecans
Additional confectioners' sugar

In a large bowl, cream the butter and cream cheese until light and fluffy. Beat in the drink mix, sugar, vanilla and coffee granules. Combine the flour and salt; gradually add to creamed mixture and mix well. Stir in pecans. Cover and refrigerate for 1 hour or until easy to handle.

Roll into 1-in. balls. Place 1 in. apart on ungreased baking sheets. Bake at 350° for 15-18 minutes or until firm. Cool on pan for 1-2 minutes. Roll warm cookies in additional confectioners' sugar; cool on wire racks. **Yield:** 4 dozen.

Almond Oatmeal Cutouts

Martha Dahlman, Regina, Saskatchewan

Almond gives these cutout oatmeal cookies added flavor. The dough is slightly sticky, so roll out the dough between pieces of waxed paper.

    1/2 cup butter, softened
    1/2 cup shortening
    3/4 cup sugar
    2   teaspoons almond extract
    1-3/4 cups all-purpose flour
    1-1/4 cups old-fashioned oats

In a large bowl, cream the butter, shortening and sugar until light and fluffy. Beat in extract. Combine flour and oats; gradually add to the creamed mixture.

Roll out between waxed paper to 1/4-in. thickness. Cut with floured 2-1/2-in. cookie cutters dipped in flour.

Place 1 in. apart on ungreased baking sheets. Bake at 350° for 12-15 minutes or until lightly browned. Remove to wire racks to cool. **Yield:** 2-1/2 dozen.

English Tea Cakes

Beverly Christian, Fort Worth, Texas

These unique cookies are baked in muffin cups, giving them a perfectly round shape. I sometimes omit the pecans and decorate the cookies for holidays.

    2   cups butter, softened
    1   cup sugar
    2   teaspoons vanilla extract
    4   cups all-purpose flour
   60   walnut *or* pecan halves, toasted

In a large bowl, cream butter and sugar until light and fluffy. Beat in vanilla. Gradually add flour and mix well. Drop by heaping tablespoonfuls into greased miniature muffin cups; flatten slightly. Press a walnut half into the center of each.

Bake at 350° for 10-12 minutes or until edges are lightly browned. Cool for 2 minutes before removing from pans to wire racks. **Yield:** 5 dozen.

Fudge-Filled Sandies

Jeanette Ray, Lindenhurst, Illinois

I dream of one day owning a cookie shop. Until then, I'll delight friends and family with my homemade concoctions. These cookies are like pecan sandies, but I've added a touch of delicious chocolate.

- 1 cup butter, softened
- 3/4 cup confectioners' sugar
- 1 teaspoon vanilla extract
- 2 cups all-purpose flour
- 1 cup finely chopped pecans

Additional confectioners' sugar

FILLING:

- 3/4 cup semisweet chocolate chips
- 1 tablespoon shortening
- 2 tablespoons light corn syrup
- 1 tablespoon water

In a large bowl, cream butter and confectioners' sugar until light and fluffy. Beat in vanilla. Combine flour and pecans; gradually add to creamed mixture and mix well.

Roll into 1-in. balls. Place 1 in. apart on ungreased baking sheets. Using the end of a wooden spoon handle, make an indentation in the center of each.

Bake at 325° for 18-20 minutes or until lightly browned. Roll warm cookies in additional confectioners' sugar; cool on wire racks.

In a microwave, melt chocolate chips and shortening; stir until smooth. Stir in the corn syrup and water. Spoon into cooled cookies. **Yield:** 4 dozen.

Sugar Cookie Slices

Lonna Peterman, New Port Richey, Florida

My husband's great-aunt gave me this recipe. They slice nicely and are easier to make than traditional cutout sugar cookies.

- 1-1/2 cups butter, softened
- 1-1/2 cups sugar
- 1/2 teaspoon vanilla extract
- 3 cups all-purpose flour
- 1 teaspoon baking soda
- 1/2 teaspoon salt

In a large bowl, cream butter and sugar until light and fluffy. Beat in vanilla. Combine the flour, baking soda and salt; gradually add to the creamed mixture and mix well. Shape into two 8-in. rolls; wrap each in plastic wrap. Refrigerate for 4 hours or until firm.

Unwrap and cut into 1/4-in. slices. Place 2 in. apart on ungreased baking sheets. Bake at 350° for 12-14 minutes or until set (do not brown). Remove to wire racks to cool. **Yield:** 5 dozen.

Coffee Almond Crisps

Sarah Benthien, Wauwatosa, Wisconsin

The blend of coffee, cinnamon and toasted almonds has made my cookies a favorite for over 50 years. These crispy treats make good coffee "dunking" cookies.

- 1 cup shortening
- 2 cups packed brown sugar
- 2 eggs
- 1/2 cup brewed coffee, room temperature
- 3-1/2 cups all-purpose flour
- 1 teaspoon baking soda
- 1 teaspoon salt
- 1-1/2 teaspoons ground cinnamon, *divided*
- 1 cup chopped almonds, toasted
- 3 tablespoons sugar

In a large bowl, cream shortening and brown sugar until light and fluffy. Add eggs, one at a time, beating well after each addition. Beat in coffee. Combine the flour, baking soda, salt and 1 teaspoon of cinnamon; gradually add to the creamed mixture and mix well. Stir in almonds.

Drop by rounded teaspoonfuls 2 in. apart onto ungreased baking sheets. Combine sugar and remaining cinnamon; sprinkle over cookies. Flatten slightly.

Bake at 375° for 10-12 minutes or until firm. Remove to wire racks to cool. **Yield:** 6 dozen.

Double Butterscotch Cookies

Beverly Duncan, Lakeville, Ohio

This old-fashioned cookie can also be made with miniature chocolate chips or coconut in place of the toffee bits.

- 1/2 cup butter, softened
- 1/2 cup shortening
- 4 cups packed brown sugar
- 4 eggs
- 1 tablespoon vanilla extract
- 6 cups all-purpose flour
- 3 teaspoons baking soda
- 3 teaspoons cream of tartar
- 1 teaspoon salt
- 1 package English toffee bits (10 ounces) *or* almond brickle chips (7-1/2 ounces)
- 1 cup finely chopped pecans

In a large bowl, cream the butter, shortening and brown sugar until light and fluffy. Add eggs, one at a time, beating well after each addition. Beat in vanilla. Combine the flour, baking soda, cream of tartar and salt; gradually add to the creamed mixture and mix well. Stir in toffee bits and pecans. Shape into three 14-in. rolls; wrap each in plastic wrap. Refrigerate for 4 hours or until firm.

Unwrap and cut into 1/2-in. slices. Place 2 in. apart on greased baking sheets. Bake at 375° for 9-11 minutes or until lightly browned. Cool for 1-2 minutes before removing from pans to wire racks to cool completely. **Yield:** about 7 dozen.

pg. 356

Brownies

pg. 344

pg. 339

pg. 355

Raspberry Truffle Brownies

Leslie Knicl, Mahomet, Illinois

On the outside, these look like traditional brownies. When people bite in, though, are they surprised! It's almost like eating a rich chocolate candy.

- 1/2 cup butter, cubed
- 1-1/4 cups semisweet chocolate chips
- 2 eggs
- 3/4 cup packed brown sugar
- 1 teaspoon instant coffee granules
- 2 tablespoons water
- 3/4 cup all-purpose flour
- 1/2 teaspoon baking powder

FILLING:
- 1 cup (6 ounces) semisweet chocolate chips
- 1 package (8 ounces) cream cheese, softened
- 1/4 cup confectioners' sugar
- 1/3 cup seedless red raspberry jam

GLAZE:
- 1/4 cup semisweet chocolate chips
- 1 teaspoon shortening

In a microwave, melt butter and chocolate chips; stir until smooth. Cool slightly. In a large mixing bowl, beat eggs and brown sugar until blended. Dissolve coffee crystals in water; add to egg mixture. Beat in chocolate until well blended. Combine flour and baking powder; gradually add into chocolate mixture.

Spread in a greased 9-in. square baking pan. Bake at 350° for 30-35 minutes or until brownies test done. Cool on a wire rack.

For filling, in a microwave, melt chocolate chips; stir until smooth. Cool. In a small mixing bowl, beat cream cheese and confectioners' sugar until smooth. Beat in jam. Stir in melted chocolate; spread over cooled brownies.

For glaze, in a microwave, melt chocolate chips and shortening; stir until smooth. Drizzle over filling. Chill before cutting into bars. Store in the refrigerator. **Yield:** about 5 dozen.

Favorite Cake Brownies

Margaret Harris, Edgecomb, Maine

If you prefer cake-like brownies instead of the fudgy sort, you'll adore this recipe. Topped with confectioners' sugar and a chocolate drizzle, they can't be beat.

- 1/4 cup butter
- 2/3 cup sugar
- 1/4 cup baking cocoa
- 1 egg white
- 1/3 cup fat-free milk
- 1/2 teaspoon vanilla extract
- 3/4 cup all-purpose flour
- 1/4 teaspoon baking powder
- 1/4 teaspoon baking soda
- 1/3 cup chopped nuts
- 1 teaspoon confectioners' sugar

TOPPING:

- 1/2 cup confectioners' sugar
- 1 tablespoon baking cocoa
- 1 tablespoon fat-free milk
- 1/4 teaspoon vanilla extract

In a large saucepan, melt butter; remove from the heat. Stir in sugar and cocoa until smooth. Add the egg white, milk and vanilla; stir just until blended. Combine flour, baking powder and baking soda; stir into chocolate mixture just until blended. Stir in nuts.

Pour into a 9-in. square baking pan coated with cooking spray. Bake at 350° for 16-18 minutes or until a toothpick inserted near the center comes out clean. Cool on a wire rack. Dust with confectioners' sugar.

In a small bowl, combine topping ingredients until smooth. Drizzle over brownies. Cut into bars. **Yield:** 16 brownies.

Blonde Brownies

Anne Weiler, Philadelphia, Pennsylvania

My family has enjoyed these bars as a potluck dessert, brown-bag treat and anytime snack many times throughout the years. Butterscotch or peanut butter chips can be used in place of the chocolate chips.

- 1/4 cup butter-flavored shortening
- 1-1/2 cups packed brown sugar
- 2 eggs
- 1/2 teaspoon vanilla extract
- 1 cup all-purpose flour
- 1-1/2 teaspoons baking powder
- 1/2 teaspoon salt
- 1 cup chopped walnuts
- 1/2 cup semisweet chocolate chips

In a large mixing bowl, cream shortening and brown sugar until light and fluffy. Add eggs, one at a time, beating well after each addition. Beat in vanilla. Combine flour, baking powder and salt; gradually add to the creamed mixture and mix well. Stir in nuts and chocolate chips.

Spread into a greased 11-in. x 7-in. x 2-in. baking pan. Bake at 350° for 25-30 minutes or until a toothpick inserted near the center comes out clean. Cool on wire rack. Cut into bars. **Yield:** 2 dozen.

Hazelnut Brownies

Becki Strader, Kennewick, Washington

I created these deep chocolate brownies by combining several recipes. After they cooled, I divided them up and put them in the freezer or we would have eaten the entire pan! They're now a family favorite.

- 1 cup butter, melted
- 2 cups sugar
- 4 eggs
- 2 teaspoons vanilla extract
- 1 cup all-purpose flour
- 3/4 cup baking cocoa
- 1/2 teaspoon baking powder
- 1/4 teaspoon salt
- 1/2 cup chopped hazelnuts

FROSTING:

- 2 cups (12 ounces) semisweet chocolate chips
- 1 cup heavy whipping cream *or* refrigerated hazelnut nondairy creamer
- 2 tablespoons butter
- 1/2 cup coarsely chopped hazelnuts

In a large mixing bowl, combine the butter and sugar until light and fluffy. Add eggs, one at a time, beating well after each addition. Beat in vanilla. Combine the flour, cocoa, baking powder and salt; gradually add to butter mixture. Fold in hazelnuts.

Spread into a greased 13-in. x 9-in. x 2-in. baking pan. Bake at 350° for 30-35 minutes or until a toothpick inserted near the center comes out clean. Cool on a wire rack.

For frosting, in a microwave, melt chips and cream until chips are melted; stir until smooth. Stir in butter until melted. Cover and refrigerate for 30 minutes or until frosting achieves spreading consistency, stirring several times. Frost brownies. Sprinkle with hazelnuts. Cut into bars. **Yield:** 2 dozen.

Candy Bar Brownies

Sharon Evans, Rockwell, Iowa

Two kinds of candy bars are baked into these brownies making them an extra-special treat.

- 3/4 cup butter, melted
- 2 cups sugar
- 4 eggs
- 2 teaspoons vanilla extract
- 1-1/2 cups all-purpose flour
- 1/3 cup baking cocoa
- 1/2 teaspoon baking powder
- 1/4 teaspoon salt
- 4 Snickers bars (2.07 ounces *each*), cut into 1/4-inch pieces
- 3 plain milk chocolate candy bars (1.55 ounces *each*), coarsely chopped

In a large bowl, combine the butter, sugar, eggs and vanilla. In a small bowl, combine the flour, cocoa, baking powder and salt; set aside 1/4 cup. Stir remaining dry ingredients into the egg mixture until well combined. Toss Snickers pieces with reserved flour mixture; stir into batter.

Transfer to a greased 13-in. x 9-in. x 2-in. baking pan. Sprinkle with milk chocolate candy bar pieces. Bake at 350° for 30-35 minutes or until a toothpick inserted near the center comes out clean (do not overbake). Cool on a wire rack. Chill before cutting into bars. **Yield:** 3 dozen.

Caramel Macadamia Nut Brownies

Jamie Bursell, Juneau, Alaska

One bite and you'll agree this is the most delectable brownie you'll ever sink your teeth into. Eat it with a fork to enjoy every last morsel of chocolate, caramel and nuts.

- 1 teaspoon plus 3/4 cup butter, *divided*
- 3 squares (1 ounce *each*) unsweetened chocolate
- 3 eggs
- 1-1/2 cups packed brown sugar
- 2 teaspoons vanilla extract
- 3/4 cup all-purpose flour
- 1/4 teaspoon baking soda

CARAMEL LAYER:
- 3/4 cup sugar
- 3 tablespoons water
- 1/4 cup heavy whipping cream
- 2 tablespoons butter

TOPPING:
- 1-1/2 cups semisweet chocolate chips
- 1 cup milk chocolate chips
- 1 jar (3-1/2 ounces) macadamia nuts, coarsely chopped

Line a 9-in. square baking pan with foil; grease the foil with 1 teaspoon butter and set aside. In a microwave-safe bowl, melt chocolate and remaining butter; stir until smooth. Cool for 10 minutes.

In a large bowl, beat eggs and brown sugar until blended; beat in chocolate mixture and vanilla. Combine flour and baking soda; gradually add to chocolate mixture.

Pour into prepared pan. Bake at 325° for 40 minutes or until a toothpick inserted near the center comes out with moist crumbs (do not overbake). Cool on a wire rack.

For caramel layer, in a large heavy saucepan, combine sugar and water. Cook and stir over medium heat for 4-5 minutes or until sugar is dissolved. Cook over medium-high heat without stirring until syrup is golden, about 5 minutes; remove from the heat.

In a small saucepan, heat cream over low heat until small bubbles form around edge of pan. Gradually stir cream into syrup (mixture will boil up). Cook and stir over low heat until blended. Stir in butter until melted. Remove from the heat; cool slightly.

Pour over brownies to within 1/4 in. of edges. Sprinkle with chips and nuts. Bake at 325° for 5 minutes (do not let chips melt completely). Cool completely on a wire rack. Refrigerate for 4 hours. Lift out of the pan; remove foil. Cut into bars. **Yield:** 20 brownies.

Peanut Butter Brownies

Margaret McNeil, Memphis, Tennessee

The combination of chocolate and peanut butter makes these brownies a real crowd-pleaser. They're so good, they won a ribbon at our local fair.

    3 eggs
    1 cup butter, melted
    2 teaspoons vanilla extract
    2 cups sugar
1-1/4 cups all-purpose flour
  3/4 cup baking cocoa
  1/2 teaspoon baking powder
  1/4 teaspoon salt
    1 cup milk chocolate chips
FILLING:
    2 packages (8 ounces *each*) cream cheese, softened
  1/2 cup creamy peanut butter
  1/4 cup sugar
    1 egg
    2 tablespoons milk

In a large mixing bowl, beat the eggs, butter and vanilla until smooth. Combine the sugar, flour, cocoa, baking powder and salt; gradually add to egg mixture. Stir in chocolate chips. Set aside 1 cup for topping. Spread remaining batter into a greased 13-in. x 9-in. x 2-in. baking pan.

In a small mixing bowl, beat the cream cheese, peanut butter and sugar until smooth. Beat in egg and milk on low just until combined. Carefully spread over batter. Drop reserved batter by tablespoonfuls over filling. Cut through batter with a knife to swirl.

Bake at 350° for 35-40 minutes or until a toothpick inserted in the center comes out clean. Cool on a wire rack. Chill until serving. **Yield:** 3 dozen.

Editor's Note: Reduced-fat or generic brands of peanut butter are not recommended for this recipe.

Double-Decker Brownies

Heather Hooker, Belmont, Ontario

With two taste-tempting layers and a savory frosting, no one will be able to eat just one of these brownies!

CHOCOLATE LAYER:
- 2 eggs, lightly beaten
- 1 cup sugar
- 3/4 cup all-purpose flour
- 1/2 cup chopped walnuts
- Dash salt
- 1/2 cup butter, melted
- 1/4 cup baking cocoa

BUTTERSCOTCH LAYER:
- 1/2 cup butter, softened
- 1-1/2 cups packed brown sugar
- 2 eggs
- 2 teaspoons vanilla extract
- 1-1/2 cups all-purpose flour
- 1/4 teaspoon salt
- 1/2 cup chopped walnuts

FROSTING:
- 1/4 cup butter, cubed
- 1/2 cup packed brown sugar
- 3 tablespoons milk
- 1-1/2 cups confectioners' sugar, sifted
- 1/3 cup semisweet chocolate chips
- 1/3 cup butterscotch chips
- 1 tablespoon shortening

In a large bowl, combine the eggs, sugar, flour, walnuts and salt. In another bowl, stir butter and cocoa until smooth; stir into egg mixture until blended. Pour into a greased 13-in. x 9-in. x 2-in. baking pan; set aside.

For butterscotch layer, in a large bowl, cream butter and brown sugar until light and fluffy. Beat in eggs and vanilla. Stir in the flour, salt and walnuts.

Spoon over chocolate layer. Bake at 350° for 30-35 minutes or until brownies begin to pull away from sides of pan. Cool on a wire rack.

For frosting, in a small saucepan, combine the butter, brown sugar and milk; bring to a boil and boil for 2 minutes. Remove from the heat; stir in confectioners' sugar until smooth. Quickly spread over brownies.

In a microwave, melt chocolate chips, butterscotch chips and shortening; stir until smooth. Drizzle over frosting. **Yield:** 3 dozen.

Banana Cocoa Brownies

Rebecca Luginbill, Pandora, Ohio

Banana pairs great with chocolate, making these treats an all-time favorite in my home. I hope you enjoy them as much as we do.

- 1 cup quick-cooking oats
- 1 cup boiling water
- 4 egg whites
- 1-1/2 cups mashed ripe bananas (about 3 medium)
- 3/4 cup packed brown sugar
- 1/2 cup sugar
- 2 tablespoons canola oil
- 1 teaspoon vanilla extract
- 1 cup all-purpose flour
- 1/4 cup baking cocoa
- 1 teaspoon baking soda
- 1/2 teaspoon salt

In a small bowl, combine oats and boiling water; let stand for 5 minutes. In a large bowl, beat the egg whites, bananas, sugars, oil and vanilla until blended. Combine the flour, cocoa, baking soda and salt; gradually add to creamed mixture. Stir in the oat mixture.

Spread into a 13-in. x 9-in. x 2-in. pan coated with cooking spray. Bake at 350° for 20-25 minutes or until a toothpick inserted near the center comes out clean (do not overbake). Cool on a wire rack. Cut into bars. **Yield:** 4 dozen.

Saucepan Brownies

Dorelene Doddridge, Kirk, Colorado

Preparing a brownie batter in a saucepan with biscuit mix may sound odd, but it sure cuts down on prep time. You won't believe the delicious results.

- 1 cup (6 ounces) semisweet chocolate chips
- 1/4 cup butter, cubed
- 2 cups biscuit/baking mix
- 1 can (14 ounces) sweetened condensed milk
- 1 egg, lightly beaten
- 1 cup chopped walnuts

In a microwave, melt chocolate chips and butter; stir until smooth. Cool slightly. Stir in the biscuit mix, milk and egg until blended. Add nuts.

Pour into a greased 13-in. x 9-in. x 2-in. baking pan. Bake at 350° for 25 minutes. **Yield:** 2-1/2 dozen.

Keeping Brownies Store most brownies in an airtight container at room temperature. Brownies with a pudding layer, cream cheese or other perishable ingredients should be stored in the refrigerator.

Moist Cake Brownies

Louise Stacey, Dane, Wisconsin

These brownies have been in my recipe collection since I was 9 years old. I've added to and altered the recipe over the years, and now I think it has the perfect amount of everything, including semisweet and milk chocolate chips and pecans. My husband and son love them.

- 2/3 cup butter, cubed
- 3/4 cup baking cocoa
- 1/4 cup canola oil
- 2 cups sugar
- 4 eggs
- 2 teaspoons vanilla extract
- 1-1/2 cups all-purpose flour
- 1 teaspoon baking powder
- 1 teaspoon salt
- 2/3 cup semisweet chocolate chips
- 1/2 cup milk chocolate chips
- 1 cup coarsely chopped pecans

Confectioners' sugar

Pecan halves, toasted, optional

Melt butter in a large saucepan. Whisk in cocoa and oil until smooth. Cook and stir over low heat until cocoa is blended. Transfer to a large bowl; stir in sugar. Add eggs, one at a time, beating well after each addition. Stir in vanilla. Combine the flour, baking powder and salt; gradually add to cocoa mixture. Stir in the chocolate chips and pecans.

Spread into a greased 13-in. x 9-in. x 2-in. baking pan. Bake at 350° for 25-30 minutes or until a toothpick inserted near the center comes out clean. Cool in pan on a wire rack. Dust with confectioners' sugar. Garnish with pecan halves if desired. Cut into bars. **Yield:** 2 dozen.

Cheesecake Brownies

James Harris, Columbus, Georgia

German chocolate cake mix and chopped nuts make a delicious change-of-pace crust for these brownies. Featuring a terrific cheesecake topping, the dessert is tough to beat.

- 1 package (18-1/4 ounces) German chocolate cake mix
- 1 egg, lightly beaten
- 1/2 cup butter, melted
- 1 cup chopped nuts

TOPPING:
- 1 package (8 ounces) cream cheese, softened
- 1 cup sugar
- 2 eggs, lightly beaten
- 1 teaspoon vanilla extract

In a large mixing bowl, beat the cake mix, egg, butter and nuts until well blended. Press into a greased 13-in. x 9-in. x 2-in. baking pan; set aside.

In small bowl, beat cream cheese, sugar, eggs and vanilla until smooth. Carefully spread over batter.

Bake at 350° for 30 to 35 minutes or until golden brown. Cool on a wire rack. Cut into bars. Store in the refrigerator. **Yield:** 2 dozen.

Rocky Road Brownies

Rita Lenes, Kent, Washington

Anyone who likes rocky road ice cream will like these moist, fudgy brownies loaded with goodies. They're great for children's parties or bake sales.

- 3/4 cup butter, cubed
- 4 squares (1 ounce *each*) unsweetened chocolate

- 4 eggs
- 2 cups sugar
- 1 teaspoon vanilla extract
- 1 cup all-purpose flour
- 2 cups miniature marshmallows
- 1 cup (6 ounces) semisweet chocolate chips
- 1 cup chopped walnuts

In a microwave, melt butter and chocolate; stir until smooth. Cool for 10 minutes.

In a large mixing bowl, beat the eggs, sugar and vanilla until blended. Stir in chocolate mixture. Gradually add flour until well blended.

Spread into a greased 13-in. x 9-in. x 2-in. baking pan. Bake at 350° for 25-30 minutes or until a toothpick inserted near the center comes out clean. Sprinkle with the marshmallows, chocolate chips and walnuts; bake 4 minutes longer. Cool in pan on a wire rack. Cut into bars. **Yield:** 2 dozen.

Almond Macaroon Brownies

Jayme Goffin, Crown Point, Indiana

Even when we were in the middle of remodeling our old farmhouse, I made time to bake at least three times a week. This is a little fancier brownie that's great for guests.

- 6 squares (1 ounce *each*) semisweet chocolate
- 1/2 cup butter
- 2/3 cup sugar
- 2 eggs
- 1 teaspoon vanilla extract
- 1 cup all-purpose flour
- 1/3 cup chopped almonds

TOPPING:
- 1 package (3 ounces) cream cheese, softened
- 1/3 cup sugar
- 1 egg
- 1 tablespoon all-purpose flour
- 1 cup flaked coconut
- 1/3 cup chopped almonds
- 16 whole almonds
- 1 square (1 ounce) semisweet chocolate, melted

In a microwave, melt chocolate and butter; stir until smooth. Whisk in the sugar, eggs and vanilla until smooth. Add flour and chopped almonds. Spread into a greased 8-in. square baking dish.

In a large bowl, beat the cream cheese, sugar, egg and flour until smooth. Stir in coconut and chopped almonds. Spread over brownie layer. Evenly place whole almonds over topping.

Bake at 350° for 35-40 minutes until a toothpick inserted near the center comes out with moist crumbs (do not overbake). Cool on a wire rack. Drizzle with melted chocolate. Cut into bars. **Yield:** 16 brownies.

Mocha Mousse Brownies

Stacy Waller, Eagan, Minnesota

Chocolate is one of my favorite foods, and these dark chocolate goodies are the perfect pairing of coffee-flavored mousse and fudge brownie.

 2/3 cup semisweet chocolate chips
 1/2 cup butter
   1 cup plus 2 tablespoons sugar
   2 eggs
 1/4 cup hot water
   2 tablespoons instant coffee granules
 1/2 cup all-purpose flour
 1/2 cup baking cocoa
   1 teaspoon baking powder
MOCHA MOUSSE:
   1 package (3 ounces) cream cheese, softened
 1/4 cup sweetened condensed milk
 1/2 cup semisweet chocolate chips, melted
   1 envelope unflavored gelatin
 1/4 cup cold water
   2 tablespoons instant coffee granules
   1 cup heavy whipping cream

In a saucepan over low heat, melt the chips and butter over low heat; stir until smooth. Pour into a large bowl. Beat in sugar until smooth. Add eggs, one at a time, beating well after each addition. Combine hot water and coffee granules; add to chocolate mixture. Combine the flour, cocoa and baking powder; gradually beat into chocolate mixture.

Spread into a greased 13-in. x 9-in. x 2-in. baking pan. Bake at 350° for 15-20 minutes or until a toothpick inserted near the center comes out clean (brownies will be thin). Cool on a wire rack.

For mousse, in a small bowl, beat cream cheese until smooth; beat in milk and melted chips. In a small saucepan, sprinkle gelatin over cold water; let stand for 1 minute. Cook and stir over low heat until gelatin is dissolved. Remove from the heat; stir in coffee granules until dissolved.

In another small bowl, beat whipping cream until slightly thickened. Beat in gelatin. Fold into cream cheese mixture. Spread over brownies. Cover and refrigerate for 3 hours or until set. Cut into squares. Store in the refrigerator. **Yield:** 2 dozen.

343

Creamy Cashew Brownies

Karen Wagner, Danville, Illinois

My sister-in-law dubbed me the "dessert queen" because of treats like this that I take to our family get-togethers. The brownies have a fudge-like texture and a rich cream cheese topping. Cashews and a hot fudge swirl make them special.

> 1 package fudge brownie mix (13-inch x 9-inch pan size)
> 1/3 cup water
> 1/4 cup canola oil
> 1 egg
> 1 cup (6 ounces) semisweet chocolate chips
> TOPPING:
> 2 packages (8 ounces *each*) cream cheese, softened
> 1-1/2 cups confectioners' sugar
> 1 teaspoon vanilla extract
> 1 cup salted cashews, coarsely chopped
> 1/2 cup hot fudge ice cream topping, warmed

In a large bowl, combine the brownie mix, water, oil and egg. Stir in chips. Spread into a greased 13-in. x 9-in. x 2-in. baking pan.

Bake at 350° for 25-27 minutes or until a toothpick inserted near the center comes out clean (do not overbake). Cool on a wire rack.

For topping, in a large bowl, beat the cream cheese, confectioners' sugar and vanilla until smooth. Spread over brownies. Sprinkle with cashews; drizzle with hot fudge topping. Refrigerate before cutting into bars. Store in the refrigerator. **Yield:** 2 dozen.

Easy PB Brownies

Kathy Crow, Payson, Arizona

Dressing up a boxed cake mix with peanut butter and melted chocolate chips is the secret to this super-easy recipe. My daughter, Delleen, got this recipe from co-workers and then shared it with me.

- 1 package (18-1/4 ounces) chocolate cake mix
- 1/3 cup canola oil
- 1 egg
- 1 can (14 ounces) sweetened condensed milk
- 2 cups (12 ounces) semisweet chocolate chips, melted
- 1/2 cup peanut butter
- 1 teaspoon vanilla extract

In a bowl, combine the cake mix, oil and egg until crumbly. Set aside 1 cup for topping. Firmly press remaining mixture into a greased 13-in. x 9-in. x 2-in. baking pan; set aside.

In a bowl, combine the milk, chocolate chips, peanut butter and vanilla until smooth. Spread over crust. Sprinkle with reserved crumb mixture.

Bake at 350° for 25-30 minutes or until brownies pull away from the pan. Cool on a wire rack. Cut into bars. **Yield:** 4-1/2 dozen.

Chocolate Bliss Brownies

Juanita Lou Williams, Enid, Oklahoma

I first tried these at a brunch and begged the hostess for the recipe. Sometimes I'll eliminate the frosting and just sprinkle the top with confectioners' sugar.

- 1/2 cup butter, softened
- 1 cup sugar
- 4 eggs
- 1 can (16 ounces) chocolate syrup
- 1 cup all-purpose flour
- 1 teaspoon salt
- 1 cup chopped nuts

FROSTING:
- 6 tablespoons butter, cubed
- 1-1/2 cups sugar
- 1/3 cup milk
- 1/2 cup semisweet chocolate chips

In a large bowl, cream the butter and sugar until light and fluffy. Add eggs, one at a time, beating well after each addition. Add chocolate syrup. Combine flour and salt; gradually add to creamed mixture until blended. Stir in nuts.

Pour into a greased 13-in. x 9-in. x 2-in. baking pan. Bake at 350° for 25-30 minutes or until a toothpick inserted near the center comes out clean (brownies may appear moist). Cool on a wire rack.

In a small saucepan, melt butter. Add sugar and milk. Bring to a boil; boil for 30 seconds. Remove from the heat. Add the chips; stir until melted. Beat until frosting reaches spreading consistency. Frost cooled brownies; cut into bars. **Yield:** 4-1/2 dozen.

Nutty Fudgy Brownies

Dorothy Scalzitti, Stanwood, Washington

I love to cook and look forward to spending quality time with my young son in the kitchen. This is one recipe I'll be sure to share with him when he gets older.

- 2 cups sugar
- 3/4 cup baking cocoa
- 1/2 teaspoon baking soda
- 2/3 cup vegetable oil, *divided*
- 1/2 cup boiling water
- 1-1/3 cups all-purpose flour
- 1 teaspoon vanilla extract
- 1/4 teaspoon salt
- 2 eggs
- 1 cup chopped walnuts

In a bowl, combine the sugar, cocoa and baking soda. Add 1/3 cup oil and water; beat until smooth. Beat in the flour, vanilla, salt, eggs and remaining oil. Stir in the walnuts.

Spread into a greased 13-in. x 9-in. x 2-in. baking pan. Bake at 350° for 35-40 minutes or until a toothpick inserted near the center comes out clean. Cool on a wire rack. Cut into bars. **Yield:** 6 dozen.

Three-Layer Chocolate Brownies

Billie Hopkins, Enterprise, Oregon

I often serve these hearty, cake-like brownies with a fork for easier eating. The oatmeal crust, rich filling and chocolate frosting make them a hit wherever I take them.

- 1 cup quick-cooking oats
- 1/2 cup packed brown sugar
- 1/3 cup all-purpose flour
- 1/4 teaspoon baking soda
- 1/4 teaspoon salt
- 1/4 cup butter, melted

FILLING:
- 1/2 cup butter
- 2 squares (1 ounce *each*) semisweet chocolate
- 1 cup sugar
- 2 eggs, beaten
- 1/4 cup milk
- 2 teaspoons vanilla extract
- 2/3 cup all-purpose flour
- 1/4 teaspoon baking soda
- 1/4 teaspoon salt

FROSTING:
- 3 tablespoons butter, softened
- 1 square (1 ounce) unsweetened chocolate, melted
- 1 cup confectioners' sugar
- 1 tablespoon milk
- 3/4 teaspoon vanilla extract

In a small mixing bowl, combine the oats, brown sugar, flour, baking soda, salt and butter; beat on low speed until blended. Press into a greased 9-in. square baking pan. Bake at 350° for 10 minutes.

Meanwhile, in a saucepan, melt butter and chocolate over low heat; stir until smooth. Remove from the heat; stir in the sugar, eggs, milk and vanilla. Combine the flour, baking soda and salt; gradually stir into the chocolate mixture until smooth. Pour over crust.

Bake for 35-40 minutes or until the top springs back when lightly touched. Cool on wire rack.

In a bowl, combine frosting ingredients; beat until smooth. Frost cooled brownies. Cut into bars. **Yield:** 1-1/2 dozen.

Fudgy Mint Squares

Heather Campbell, Lawrence, Kansas

We've had this recipe since I was in junior high school. No one can resist the fudgy brownie base, cool minty cheesecake filling and luscious chocolate glaze in these mouthwatering bars.

- 10 tablespoons butter, softened, *divided*
- 3 squares (1 ounce *each*) unsweetened chocolate, chopped
- 3 eggs

- 1-1/2 cups sugar
- 2 teaspoons vanilla extract
- 1 cup all-purpose flour
- 1 package (8 ounces) cream cheese, softened
- 1 tablespoon cornstarch
- 1 can (14 ounces) sweetened condensed milk
- 1 teaspoon peppermint extract
- 4 drops green food coloring, optional
- 1 cup (6 ounces) semisweet chocolate chips
- 1/2 cup heavy whipping cream

In a microwave, melt 8 tablespoons of the butter and unsweetened chocolate; stir until smooth. Cool slightly. In a small bowl, beat 2 eggs, sugar and vanilla. Beat in chocolate mixture until blended. Gradually add in flour.

Spread into a greased 13-in. x 9-in. x 2-in. baking pan. Bake at 350° for 15-20 minutes or until top is set.

In a large bowl, beat cream cheese and remaining butter until smooth. Add cornstarch; beat until smooth. Gradually beat in milk and remaining egg. Beat in extract and food coloring if desired.

Pour over crust. Bake for 15-20 minutes or until center is almost set. Cool on a wire rack.

In a small heavy saucepan, combine chocolate chips and cream. Cook and stir over medium heat until chips are melted. Cool for 30 minutes or until lukewarm, stirring occasionally. Pour over cream cheese layer. Chill for 2 hours or until set. Cut into bars. Store in the refrigerator. **Yield:** about 4 dozen.

Frosted Cookie Brownies

Alicia French, Crestline, California

Years ago, my children and I came up with these bars by combining two of their favorite treats. With a crisp cookie crust and a fluffy frosting, these brownies are the most requested dessert at our house.

- 1 tube (18 ounces) refrigerated chocolate chip cookie dough
- 3 cups miniature marshmallows
- 2 cups (12 ounces) semisweet chocolate chips
- 1 cup butter, cubed
- 4 eggs
- 2 teaspoons vanilla extract
- 1 cup all-purpose flour
- 1/2 teaspoon baking powder
- 1/4 teaspoon salt
- 1 cup chopped walnuts

FROSTING:

- 2 cups miniature marshmallows
- 6 tablespoons milk
- 1/4 cup butter, softened
- 2 squares (1 ounce *each*) unsweetened chocolate
- 3 cups confectioners' sugar

Press cookie dough into a greased 13-in. x 9-in. x 2-in. baking pan. Bake at 350° for 10 minutes.

Meanwhile, in a saucepan, combine the marshmallows, chips and butter; cook and stir over low heat until melted and smooth. Transfer to a large bowl; cool. Beat in eggs and vanilla. Combine the flour, baking powder and salt; stir into marshmallow mixture. Stir in nuts.

Spread over cookie crust. Bake for 30-35 minutes or until a toothpick inserted near the center comes out clean. Cool on a wire rack.

For frosting, in a small saucepan, combine the marshmallows, milk, butter and chocolate. Cook and stir over low heat until smooth. Remove from the heat; beat in confectioners' sugar until smooth. Frost brownies. Cut into bars. **Yield:** 15 servings.

Marbling Batters To marble batters, spoon one batter in a random pattern over the other batter. Gently cut through the batters with a knife to swirl. Be careful not to overdo it, or the two batters will blend together and you will lose the effect.

Mocha Brownies

Suzanne Strocsher, Bothell, Washington

My husband doesn't drink coffee, but he loves the taste of these delightful brownies.

> 1 package fudge brownie mix (13-inch x 9-inch pan size)
> 1/2 cup water
> 1/4 cup canola oil
> 1 egg
> 2 teaspoons instant coffee granules
> 1 teaspoon vanilla extract

FILLING:

> 1/4 cup butter, softened
> 1/2 cup packed brown sugar
> 1 egg
> 2 teaspoons instant coffee granules
> 1 teaspoon vanilla extract
> 1 cup chopped walnuts
> 3/4 cup semisweet chocolate chips

ICING:

> 1/2 cup semisweet chocolate chips
> 1 tablespoon butter
> 1/4 teaspoon instant coffee granules
> 1 to 2 teaspoons milk

In a large bowl, combine the brownie mix, water, oil, egg, coffee granules and vanilla. Spread into a greased 13-in. x 9-in. x 2-in. baking pan. Bake at 350° for 30-35 minutes or until a toothpick inserted near the center comes out clean (do not overbake).

Meanwhile, in a small bowl, cream butter and sugar until light and fluffy. Beat in the egg, coffee and vanilla until well blended. Stir in walnuts and chocolate chips. Spread over brownies. Bake at 350° for 17 minutes or until set. Cool on a wire rack.

For icing, in a small saucepan melt the chocolate chips and butter over low heat, stirring constantly. Whisk in coffee granules and enough milk to reach a drizzling consistency. Drizzle over warm brownies. Cool before cutting into bars. **Yield:** 3 dozen.

Cream Cheese Swirl Brownies

Heidi Johnson, Worland, Wyoming

I'm a chocolate lover, and this treat has satisfied my cravings many times. No one guesses the brownies are light because their chewy texture and rich chocolate flavor can't be beat. My family requests them often.

> 3 eggs
> 6 tablespoons butter, softened
> 1 cup sugar, *divided*
> 3 teaspoons vanilla extract
> 1/2 cup all-purpose flour
> 1/4 cup baking cocoa
> 1 package (8 ounces) reduced-fat cream cheese

Separate two eggs, putting each white in a separate bowl (discard yolks or save for another use); set aside. In a small bowl, beat butter and 3/4 cup sugar until crumbly. Beat in the whole egg, one egg white and vanilla until well combined. Combine flour and cocoa; gradually add to egg mixture until blended. Pour into a 9-in. square baking pan coated with cooking spray; set aside.

In a small bowl, beat cream cheese and remaining sugar until smooth. Beat in the second egg white.

Drop by rounded tablespoonfuls over the batter; cut through batter with a knife to swirl. Bake at 350° for 25-30 minutes or until set and edges pull away from sides of pan. Cool on a wire rack. **Yield:** 1 dozen.

Out-of-This-World Brownies

Jeannette Haley, Council, Idaho

For company and every time there is a local bake sale, I bake a batch of these fabulous brownies. Most everyone who tastes them says, "Yum! These are the best brownies I have ever eaten!" My cooking background came from my mother. Just watching her helped educate me in the "ways of the kitchen."

- 1 cup butter, softened
- 2 cups sugar
- 4 eggs
- 2 teaspoons vanilla extract
- 2 cups all-purpose flour
- 1/4 cup plus 3 tablespoons baking cocoa
- 1/8 teaspoon salt

BROWN BUTTER FROSTING:
- 1/2 cup butter
- 4 cups confectioners' sugar
- 1/4 cup plus 2 teaspoons half-and-half cream
- 2 teaspoons vanilla extract

GLAZE:
- 1 square (1 ounce) unsweetened chocolate
- 1 tablespoon butter

In a large bowl, cream butter and sugar until light and fluffy. Add eggs, one at a time, beating well after each addition. Beat in vanilla. Combine the flour, cocoa and salt; gradually add to the creamed mixture.

Spread into an ungreased 13-in. x 9-in. x 2-in. baking pan. Bake at 350° for 25-30 minutes or until a toothpick inserted near the center comes out clean (do not overbake). Cool on wire rack.

For frosting, in a heavy saucepan, cook and stir butter over medium heat for 5-7 minutes or until golden brown. Pour into a bowl; beat in the confectioners' sugar, cream and vanilla. Frost cooled brownies.

For glaze, in a microwave, melt chocolate and butter; stir until smooth. Drizzle over the frosting. Cut into bars. **Yield:** 3 dozen.

Triple-Chocolate Brownie Squares

Kathy Fannoun, Brooklyn Park, Minnesota

Featuring a chocolate-pudding layer, a frosting of whipped topping and chocolate chips, these refrigerator brownies simply can't be beat.

- 1 package reduced-fat brownie mix (13-inch x 9-inch pan size)
- 1-1/2 cups fat-free milk
- 1 package (1.4 ounces) sugar-free instant chocolate pudding mix
- 1/4 cup fat-free hot fudge ice cream topping
- 1/4 cup plus 1 tablespoon miniature semisweet chocolate chips, *divided*
- 4 cups frozen fat-free whipped topping, thawed, *divided*

Prepare and bake brownies according to package directions, using a 13-in. x 9-in. x 2-in. baking pan coated with cooking spray. Cool on a wire rack.

Meanwhile, in a large mixing bowl, whisk milk and pudding mix for 2 minutes; let stand for 2 minutes or until soft-set. Beat in fudge topping until blended.

In a microwave, melt 1/4 cup chocolate chips; stir until smooth. Beat into pudding mixture. Fold in 2 cups whipped topping. Spread over cooled brownies. Cover and refrigerate until the pudding is set. Spread with the remaining whipped topping. Sprinkle with the remaining chocolate chips. **Yield:** 15 servings.

Fast Fudgy Brownies

Mary Sprick, New Haven, Missouri

For from-scratch brownies that don't tax your kitchen time, consider my super-easy treat. Loaded with chocolate and cherry flavor, they're popular in my house.

- 1 cup canola oil
- 4 eggs
- 1 teaspoon vanilla extract
- 2 cups sugar
- 1-1/3 cups all-purpose flour
- 1/2 cup baking cocoa
- 1 teaspoon salt
- 1 cup (6 ounces) semisweet chocolate chips
- 1/2 cup chopped maraschino cherries *or* nuts, optional

In a large bowl, beat the oil, eggs and vanilla on medium speed for 1 minute. Combine the sugar, flour, cocoa and salt; gradually add to egg mixture just until blended. Stir in chocolate chips and cherries.

Pour into a greased 13-in. x 9-in. x 2-in. baking pan. Bake at 350° for 30-35 minutes or until a toothpick inserted near the center comes out with moist crumbs (do not overbake). Cool on a wire rack. Cut into bars. **Yield:** 2 dozen.

Caramel Cashew Brownies

Judy High, Berryville, Arkansas

I always have my eye out for a good recipe, like the one for these marvelous golden brownies. It's hard to eat just one!

- 18 caramels
- 1/3 cup butter
- 2 tablespoons milk
- 3/4 cup sugar
- 2 eggs
- 1/2 teaspoon vanilla extract
- 1 cup all-purpose flour
- 1/2 teaspoon baking powder
- 1/4 teaspoon salt
- 1 cup chopped salted cashews

In a large saucepan, cook and stir the caramels, butter and milk over low heat until the caramels are melted and mixture is smooth. Remove from the heat. Add the sugar; stir until smooth.

In a small bowl, combine the eggs and vanilla; stir into caramel mixture. In a bowl, combine the flour, baking powder and salt; stir into the caramel mixture until blended. Fold in cashews.

Transfer to a greased 9-in. square baking pan. Bake at 350° for 24-28 minutes or until a toothpick inserted near the center comes out clean. Cool on a wire rack. Cut into bars. **Yield:** 25 brownies.

Jack-o'-Lantern Brownies

Flo Burtnett, Gage, Oklahoma

Hosting a Halloween party? Use a cookie cutter to easily cut these homemade chocolate brownies into pumpkin shapes, then give them personality with orange, black and green frosting. Our grandchildren think these are great.

3/4	cup butter
1-1/2	cups sugar
3	eggs
1-1/2	teaspoons vanilla extract
3/4	cup all-purpose flour
1/2	cup baking cocoa
1/2	teaspoon baking powder
1/4	teaspoon salt
1	can (16 ounces) vanilla frosting

Orange paste food coloring
Green and black decorating gel
Candy corn and milk chocolate M&M's, optional

In a large bowl, cream the butter and sugar until light and fluffy. Beat in eggs and vanilla. Combine the flour, cocoa, baking powder and salt; gradually add to the creamed mixture.

Line a greased 13-in. x 9-in. x 2-in. baking pan with waxed paper; grease the paper. Spread batter evenly in pan. Bake at 350° for 18-22 minutes or until brownies begin to pull away from sides of pan. Cool on a wire rack.

Run a knife around the edge of pan. Invert brownies onto a work surface and remove waxed paper. Cut brownies with a 3-in. pumpkin cookie cutter, leaving at least 1/8 in. between each shape. (Discard the scraps or save for another use.)

Tint frosting with orange food coloring; frost brownies. Use green gel to create the pumpkin stems and black gel and candy corn and M&M's to decorate the faces if desired. **Yield:** about 1 dozen.

Very Chocolate Brownies

Jan Mock, Dillon, Montana

These brownies have chocolate chips and melted chocolate in the batter, making them doubly delicious. It's a crowd-pleasing treat I can always count on.

- 2/3 cup butter
- 1-1/2 cups sugar
- 1/4 cup water
- 4 cups (24 ounces) semisweet chocolate chips, *divided*
- 2 teaspoons vanilla extract
- 4 eggs
- 1-1/2 cups all-purpose flour
- 1/2 teaspoon baking soda
- 1/2 teaspoon salt

In a large heavy saucepan, bring butter, sugar and water to a boil, stirring constantly. Remove from the heat. Stir in 2 cups of chocolate chips until melted; cool slightly. Beat in vanilla. Cool.

In a large mixing bowl, beat eggs. Gradually add chocolate mixture until blended. Combine the flour, baking soda and salt; gradually add to chocolate mixture and mix well. Stir in remaining chocolate chips.

Spread into a greased 13-in. x 9-in. x 2-in. baking pan. Bake at 325° for 35-40 minutes or until a toothpick inserted near the center comes out clean. Cool on a wire rack. Cut into bars. **Yield:** 3 dozen.

Cappuccino Cake Brownies

Mary Houchin, Lebanon, Illinois

If you like your sweets with a cup of coffee, this recipe is for you! These no-nut brownies combine a mild coffee flavor with the richness of semisweet chocolate chips. They're a quick and easy dessert or anytime treat at our house.

- 1 tablespoon instant coffee granules
- 2 teaspoons boiling water
- 1 cup (6 ounces) semisweet chocolate chips
- 1/4 cup butter, softened
- 1/2 cup sugar
- 2 eggs
- 1/2 cup all-purpose flour
- 1/4 teaspoon ground cinnamon

In a small bowl, dissolve coffee in water; set aside. In a microwave, melt chocolate chips; stir until smooth. In a small bowl, cream butter and sugar until light and fluffy. Beat in the eggs, melted chocolate and coffee mixture. Combine flour and cinnamon; gradually add to creamed mixture until blended.

Pour into a greased 8-in. square baking dish. Bake at 350° for 25-30 minutes or until a toothpick inserted near the center comes out clean. Cool on a wire rack. Cut into squares. **Yield:** 16 bars.

Friendship Brownies

Travis Burkholder, Middleburg, Pennsylvania

Layered in a jar, this brownie mix is the perfect gift to give friends and family during the holidays.

BROWNIE MIX:
- 1 cup plus 2 tablespoons all-purpose flour
- 2/3 cup packed brown sugar
- 3/4 teaspoon salt
- 2/3 cup sugar
- 1 teaspoon baking powder
- 1/3 cup baking cocoa
- 1/2 cup semisweet chocolate chips
- 1/2 cup chopped walnuts

ADDITIONAL INGREDIENTS:
- 3 eggs
- 2/3 cup canola oil
- 1 teaspoon vanilla extract

Pour the flour into a 1-qt. glass container with a tight-fitting lid. Layer with the brown sugar, salt, sugar, baking powder, cocoa, chocolate chips and nuts (do not mix). Cover and store in a cool, dry place for up to 6 months.

To prepare brownies: In a large bowl, beat the eggs, oil and vanilla. Stir in the brownie mix until well combined.

Spread into a greased 9-in. square baking pan. Bake at 350° for 34-38 minutes or until a toothpick inserted near the center comes out clean. Cool on a wire rack. Cut into bars. **Yield:** 16 brownies.

Raspberry Crunch Brownies

Rita Winterberger, Huson, Montana

These rich and flavorful brownies with nut-like crunch prove that desserts don't have to be full of fat to be splendid.

- 1/4 cup canola oil
- 1-1/4 cups sugar
- 4 egg whites
- 1 cup all-purpose flour
- 2/3 cup baking cocoa
- 1/2 teaspoon baking powder
- 1/4 teaspoon salt
- 1-1/2 teaspoons vanilla extract
- 1/4 cup raspberry jam
- 2 tablespoons Grape-Nuts cereal

In a large mixing bowl, beat oil and sugar until blended. Beat in egg whites. Combine the flour, cocoa, baking powder and salt; gradually add to sugar mixture just until moistened. Stir in vanilla. (Batter will be thick.)

Coat a 9-in. square pan with cooking spray. Spread batter into pan. Bake at 350° for 20 to 25 minutes or until a toothpick inserted in the center comes out clean. Cool for 10 minutes on a wire rack. Spread with jam and sprinkle with Grape-Nuts if desired. Cool completely. Cut into bars. **Yield:** 2 dozen.

Gift-Wrapped Brownies

Dopris Roots, Big Timber, Montana

With bright green and red frosting "ribbon" piped on top, these chocolaty "packages" are a pretty addition to any holiday gathering. They'll make a sweet gift for everyone on your Christmas list!

- 1/2 cup shortening
- 4 squares (1 ounce *each*) semisweet baking chocolate
- 3 eggs
- 1 cup sugar
- 2 teaspoons vanilla extract, *divided*
- 1/2 cup all-purpose flour
- 1/2 cup chopped nuts
- 1/2 teaspoon salt
- 1/2 teaspoon baking powder
- 2 cups confectioners' sugar
- 1/4 cup heavy whipping cream

Red and green food coloring

In a microwave, melt shortening and chocolate; stir until smooth. Set aside. In a large mixing bowl, beat eggs, sugar and 1 teaspoon vanilla. Gradually add the flour, nuts, salt, baking powder and chocolate mixture.

Pour into a greased 8-in. square baking dish. Bake at 350° for 20-25 minutes or until a toothpick inserted near the center comes out clean. Cool on a wire rack. Cut into 2-in. x 1-in. rectangles; remove from pan.

In a large mixing bowl, beat the confectioners' sugar, cream and remaining vanilla until smooth; set half aside. Spread remaining frosting over top of brownies. Tint half of the reserved frosting red and half green.

Cut a small hole in the corner of two plastic or pastry bags; fill one bag with red frosting and one with green. Insert pastry tip if desired. To decorate, pipe ribbon and bows on brownies or create designs of your choice. **Yield:** 2-1/2 dozen.

Macadamia Chip Brownies

Lucile Cline, Wichita, Kansas

With two kinds of chocolate, plus the macadamia nuts, there's no need to frost these scrumptious bars! I like to make them for special occasions. I'm a retired home economist and love to bake for fun and relaxation. Often, I share goodies with friends and families at our local Ronald McDonald House.

- 1/3 cup butter
- 4 squares (1 ounce *each*) white baking chocolate
- 2 eggs
- 1 cup sugar
- 1 teaspoon vanilla extract
- 1 cup all-purpose flour
- 1/4 teaspoon salt
- 1/2 cup chopped macadamia nuts
- 1/2 cup milk chocolate chips

In a saucepan, melt butter and white chocolate over low heat; stir until smooth. Remove from the heat. Cool slightly.

In a large bowl, beat eggs and sugar. Add chocolate mixture and vanilla. Combine flour and salt; gradually add to chocolate mixture. Stir in nuts and chocolate chips.

Pour into a greased 9-in. square baking pan. Bake at 325° for 30-35 minutes or until top is lightly browned. Cool on a wire rack. Cut into bars. **Yield:** 1-1/2 dozen.

Valentine Brownies

Susan Ohlendorf, Austin, Texas

I found a fun way to show my loved ones how much they mean to me. I prepare brownies from a mix, cut a heart shape out of each one and fill the center with homemade frosting. Our grandson loves to eat the little heart-shaped brownies that are left over.

- 1 package fudge brownie mix (13-inch x 9-inch pan size)
- 1/2 cup butter, softened
- 1-1/2 cups confectioners' sugar
- 1/4 teaspoon vanilla extract
- 1/4 cup baking cocoa

Prepare and bake brownie mix according to package directions for fudge-like brownies. Cool completely on a wire rack.

Meanwhile, in a small bowl, cream the butter, confectioners' sugar and vanilla until light and fluffy. Place in a heavy-duty resealable plastic bag; cut a small hole in a corner of bag. Set aside.

Line a baking sheet with waxed paper. Dust with cocoa; set aside. Cut brownies into 15 rectangles. Using a 1-1/2-in. heart-shaped cookie cutter, cut out a heart from the center of each brownie. Reserve cutout centers for another use. Place brownies on prepared baking sheet. Pipe frosting into centers of brownies. **Yield:** 15 brownies.

Layered Brownie Cookies

Amy Corey, Monticello, Maine

Graham crackers are sandwiched between a brownie base and chocolate chip cookie top in these terrific treats. My mother made these bar cookies for us, and now I make them for my children.

- 3/4 cup butter, softened
- 1 cup sugar
- 2 eggs
- 1 teaspoon vanilla extract
- 1-3/4 cups all-purpose flour
- 1 teaspoon salt
- 1 teaspoon baking soda
- 1/3 cup milk
- 1 square (1 ounces) semisweet chocolate, melted
- 3/4 cup chopped walnuts
- 9 whole graham crackers
- 3/4 cup semisweet chocolate chips

In a large bowl, cream butter and sugar until light and fluffy. Add eggs, one at a time, beating well after each addition. Beat in vanilla. Combine the flour, salt and baking soda; add to the creamed mixture alternately with milk, beating well after each addition.

Remove a third of the batter to another bowl; stir in melted chocolate. Fold in walnuts. Spread into a greased 13-in. x 9-in. x 2-in. baking pan. Arrange graham crackers over top.

Add chocolate chips to remaining batter. Drop by spoonfuls over graham crackers and spread evenly. Bake at 375° for 20-25 minutes or until top springs back when lightly touched. Cool on a wire rack. Cut into bars. **Yield:** 2 dozen.

Two-Tone Fudge Brownies

Rebecca Kays, Klamath Falls, Oregon

These moist, fudgy brownies have a scrumptious topping that tastes just like chocolate chip cookie dough! Everyone loves these brownies...and they make a big batch.

 1 cup (6 ounces) semisweet chocolate chips
 1/2 cup butter, softened
 1 cup sugar
 3 eggs
 1 teaspoon vanilla extract
 1-1/4 cups all-purpose flour
 1/4 teaspoon baking soda
 3/4 cup chopped walnuts
COOKIE DOUGH LAYER:
 1/2 cup butter, softened
 1/2 cup packed brown sugar
 1/4 cup sugar
 3 tablespoons milk
 1 teaspoon vanilla extract
 1 cup all-purpose flour
 1 cup (6 ounces) semisweet chocolate chips

In a microwave, melt chocolate chips; stir until smooth. Cool slightly. In a large mixing bowl, cream butter and sugar until light and fluffy. Beat in eggs and vanilla. Stir in melted chocolate. Combine flour and baking soda; gradually add to batter. Stir in walnuts.

Spread into a greased 13-in. x 9-in. x 2-in. baking pan. Bake at 350° for 16-22 minutes or until a toothpick inserted near the center comes out clean. Cool on a wire rack.

For cookie dough layer, in a small bowl, cream butter and sugars until light and fluffy. Beat in milk and vanilla. Gradually add flour. Stir in chocolate chips. Drop by tablespoonfuls over cooled brownies; carefully spread over top. Cut into squares. Store in the refrigerator. **Yield:** 4 dozen.

Black Walnut Brownies

Catherine Berra Bleem, Walsh, Illinois

It takes only a handful of ingredients to help me bake up these treats in no time. The black walnuts are a great change of pace, but feel free to use whatever variety of nut your family enjoys most.

 1 cup sugar
 1/4 cup canola oil
 2 eggs
 1 teaspoon vanilla extract
 1/2 cup all-purpose flour
 2 tablespoons baking cocoa
 1/2 teaspoon salt
 1/2 cup chopped black walnuts

In a small bowl, beat sugar and oil until blended. Beat in eggs and vanilla. Combine the flour, cocoa and salt; gradually add to sugar mixture until well blended. Stir in the walnuts.

Pour into a greased 8-in. square baking dish. Bake at 350° for 30-35 minutes or until a toothpick comes out clean. Cool on a wire rack. Cut into bars. **Yield:** 16 servings.

Snow Flurry Brownies

Sherry Olson, Boulder, Colorado

These brownies are the best dessert in my recipe box. I've even prepared them on the spur of the moment while company was over for dinner. They take just minutes to mix up, and generate many compliments.

 1 cup sugar
 1/2 cup butter, melted
 2 eggs
 1/2 teaspoon vanilla extract
 2/3 cup all-purpose flour
 1/2 cup baking cocoa
 1/2 teaspoon baking powder
 1/2 teaspoon salt
 1/2 cup vanilla *or* white chips
 1/2 cup chopped macadamia nuts *or* almonds

In a large bowl, whisk together the sugar, butter, eggs and vanilla. Combine the flour, cocoa, baking powder and salt; add to sugar mixture until well blended. Stir in vanilla chips and nuts.

Spread into a greased 8-in. square baking dish. Bake at 350° for 25-30 minutes or until a toothpick inserted near the center comes out with moist crumbs (do not overbake). Cool on a wire rack. Cut into diamond shapes if desired. **Yield:** 16 brownies.

pg. 363

Bars

pg. 367

pg. 383

pg. 376

Chocolate Chip Marshmallow Bars

Sara Yoder, Apple Creek, Ohio

With marshmallows and chocolate chips, these melt-in-your-mouth bars appeal to kids of all ages. They disappear fast wherever I take them.

- 1 cup shortening
- 3/4 cup sugar
- 3/4 cup packed brown sugar
- 2 eggs
- 1 teaspoon vanilla extract
- 2-1/4 cups all-purpose flour
- 1 teaspoon baking soda
- 1 teaspoon salt
- 2 cups miniature marshmallows
- 1-1/2 cups semisweet chocolate chips
- 3/4 cup chopped walnuts

In a large bowl, cream shortening and sugars until light and fluffy. Add eggs, one at a time, beating well after each addition. Beat in vanilla. Combine the flour, baking soda and salt; gradually add to creamed mixture and mix well. Stir in the marshmallows, chips and walnuts.

Spread into a greased 13-in. x 9-in. x 2-in. baking pan. Bake at 350° for 25-30 minutes or until golden brown. Cool on a wire rack. Cut into bars. **Yield:** 3 dozen.

Orange Slice Bars

Elaine Norton, Sandusky, Michigan

These tasty bars are a portable way to satisfy a sweet tooth.

- 1 pound orange candy slices, cut into 1/8-inch strips
- 6 tablespoons hot water

- 1/2 cup butter, softened
- 2-1/4 cups packed brown sugar
- 4 eggs
- 1 teaspoon vanilla extract
- 2-1/2 cups all-purpose flour
- 2 teaspoons baking powder
- 1/2 teaspoon salt
- 1/2 cup chopped walnuts
  Confectioners' sugar

In a large bowl, combine candy and water. Cover and refrigerate overnight; drain well and set aside.

In a large bowl, cream butter and brown sugar until light and fluffy. Add eggs, one at a time, beating well after each. Beat in vanilla. Combine the flour, baking powder and salt; gradually add to creamed mixture and mix well. Fold in walnuts and candy.

Spread into a greased 15-in. x 10-in. x 1-in. baking pan. Bake at 350° for 25-30 minutes or until golden brown. Cool on a wire rack. Dust with confectioners' sugar. Cut into bars. **Yield:** about 4 dozen.

Peanut Butter Caramel Bars

Lee Ann Karnowski, Stevens Point, Wisconsin

When my husband, Bob, and our three sons sit down to dinner, they ask, "What's for dessert?" I have a happy group of guys when I report that these rich bars are on the menu. They're chock-full of yummy ingredients.

- 1 package (18-1/4 ounces) yellow cake mix
- 1/2 cup butter, softened
- 1 egg
- 20 miniature peanut butter cups, chopped
- 2 tablespoons cornstarch
- 1 jar (12-1/4 ounces) caramel ice cream topping
- 1/4 cup peanut butter
- 1/2 cup salted peanuts
  TOPPING:
- 1 can (16 ounces) milk chocolate frosting
- 1/2 cup chopped salted peanuts

In a large bowl, combine the cake mix, butter and egg; beat until no longer crumbly, about 3 minutes. Stir in the peanut butter cups.

Press into a greased 13-in. x 9-in. x 2-in. baking pan. Bake at 350° for 18-22 minutes or until lightly browned.

Meanwhile, in a large saucepan, combine the cornstarch, caramel topping and peanut butter; stir until smooth. Cook over low heat for about 25-27 minutes or until mixture comes to a boil,; stirring occasionally. Remove from the heat; stir in peanuts.

Spread evenly over warm crust. Bake 6-7 minutes longer or until almost set. Cool completely on a wire rack. Spread with frosting; sprinkle with peanuts. Cover and refrigerate for at least 1 hour before cutting into bars. Store in the refrigerator. **Yield:** about 3 dozen.

Peaches 'n' Cream Bars

Hubert Scott, Cockeysville, Maryland

If you like peach pie, you'll love these easy-to-make bars with a crunchy almond topping.

- 1 tube (8 ounces) refrigerated crescent rolls
- 1 package (8 ounces) cream cheese, softened
- 1/2 cup sugar
- 1/4 teaspoon almond extract
- 1 can (21 ounces) peach pie filling
- 1/2 cup all-purpose flour
- 1/4 cup packed brown sugar
- 3 tablespoons cold butter
- 1/2 cup sliced almonds

Unroll crescent dough into one long rectangle. Press onto the bottom and slightly up the sides of a greased 13-in. x 9-in. x 2-in. baking pan; seal perforations. Bake at 375° for 5 minutes. Cool completely on a wire rack.

In a large bowl, beat the cream cheese, sugar and extract until smooth. Spread over crust. Spoon pie filling over cream cheese layer. In a small bowl, combine flour and brown sugar. Cut in butter until mixture resembles coarse crumbs. Stir in nuts; sprinkle over peach filling.

Bake at 375° for 25-28 minutes or until edges are golden brown. Cool for 1 hour on a wire rack. Cut into bars. Store in the refrigerator. **Yield:** about 2 dozen.

Lime Cooler Bars

Dorothy Anderson, Ottawa, Kansas

These delectable bars are very popular at my house and are guaranteed to get a thumbs-up approval from your gang, too. Lime juice puts a tangy twist on these tantalizing bars, offering a burst of citrus flavor in every mouthwatering bite.

2-1/2 cups all-purpose flour, *divided*
  1/2 cup confectioners' sugar
  3/4 cup cold butter, cubed
    4 eggs
    2 cups sugar
  1/3 cup lime juice
  1/2 teaspoon grated lime peel
  1/2 teaspoon baking powder
Additional confectioners' sugar

In a large bowl, combine 2 cups flour and confectioners' sugar; cut in butter until mixture resembles coarse crumbs. Pat into a greased 13-in. x 9-in. x 2-in. baking pan. Bake at 350° for 20 minutes or until lightly browned.

In a large bowl, whisk the eggs, sugar, lime juice and peel until frothy. Combine the baking powder and remaining flour; whisk in egg mixture. Pour over hot crust.

Bake for 20-25 minutes or until light golden brown. Cool on a wire rack. Dust with confectioners' sugar. Cut into squares. **Yield:** 3 dozen.

Baking Classics | Bars

Pumpkin Cheesecake Bars

Agnes Jasa, Malabar, Florida

This recipe caught my eye and was extremely popular at the annual Christmas party. It's a great dessert for fall.

- 1 cup all-purpose flour
- 1/3 cup packed brown sugar
- 5 tablespoons cold butter
- 1 cup finely chopped pecans
- 1 package (8 ounces) cream cheese, softened
- 3/4 cup sugar
- 1/2 cup canned pumpkin
- 2 eggs
- 1 teaspoon vanilla extract
- 1-1/2 teaspoons ground cinnamon
- 1 teaspoon ground allspice

In a large bowl, combine flour and brown sugar. Cut in butter until crumbly. Stir in pecans; set aside 3/4 cup for topping.

Press remaining crumb mixture into a greased 8-in. square baking pan. Bake at 350° for 15 minutes or until edges are lightly browned. Cool on a wire rack.

In a large bowl, beat cream cheese and sugar until smooth. Beat in the pumpkin, eggs, vanilla, cinnamon and allspice. Pour over crust. Sprinkle with reserved crumb mixture.

Bake for 30-35 minutes or until golden brown. Cool on a wire rack. Cut into bars. Store in the refrigerator. **Yield:** 16 bars.

Apricot Oat Bars

Dorothy Myrick, Kent, Washington

With an oat-filled crust and golden crumb topping, these apricot-filled bars are sweet and chewy. Snackers just can't resist my fruity treats.

- 1 cup quick-cooking oats
- 1 cup all-purpose flour
- 2/3 cup packed brown sugar
- 1/4 teaspoon baking soda
- 1/4 teaspoon salt
- 1/4 cup canola oil
- 3 tablespoons unsweetened apple juice
- 1 jar (10 ounces) apricot spreadable fruit

In a large bowl, combine the oats, flour, brown sugar, baking soda and salt. Add oil and apple juice; stir until moistened. Set aside 1/2 cup for topping.

Press remaining oat mixture into an 11-in. x 7-in. x 2-in. baking pan coated with cooking spray. Spread the apricot fruit spread to within 1/4 in. of edges. Sprinkle with reserved oat mixture. Bake at 325° for 30-35 minutes or until golden brown. **Yield:** 16 bars.

Chewy Walnut Bars

Nancy Tuschak, Vacaville, California

Since they need just four ingredients and one mixing bowl, I often whip up a batch of these family-favorite bars. I'm thanked "mmmm-many" times over!

- 2-1/3 cups packed brown sugar
- 2 cups biscuit/baking mix
- 4 eggs
- 2 cups chopped walnuts

In a large bowl, combine brown sugar and biscuit mix. Beat in eggs until well blended. Fold in walnuts.

Pour into a greased 13-in. x 9-in. x 2-in. baking pan. Bake at 350° for 30-35 minutes or until golden brown. Cool on wire rack. Cut into bars. **Yield:** about 3 dozen.

Raspberry Delights

Georgiana Hagman, Louisville, Kentucky

These attractive bars have a rich, buttery crust holding the sweet jam topping. They're a big favorite on my Christmas cookie trays.

- 1 cup butter, softened
- 1 cup sugar
- 2 egg yolks
- 2 cups all-purpose flour
- 1 cup coarsely ground pecans
- 1 cup raspberry jam

In a large bowl, cream butter and sugar until light and fluffy. Beat in egg yolks. Gradually add flour and mix well. Stir in the pecans.

Spread half into a lightly greased 13-in. x 9-in. x 2-in. baking pan. Top with jam. Drop remaining dough by teaspoonfuls over jam.

Bake at 350° for 25-30 minutes or until top is golden brown. Cool on a wire rack. Cut into bars. **Yield:** 3 dozen.

Caramel Pecan Bars

Emma Manning, Crossett, Arkansas

This recipe won first place at a cookie contest held where I work. These rich bars really capture the flavor of pecan pie.

    1   cup butter, cubed
2-1/4   cups packed brown sugar
    2   eggs
    2   teaspoons vanilla extract
1-1/2   cups all-purpose flour
    2   teaspoons baking powder
    2   cups chopped pecans
Confectioners' sugar, optional

In a large saucepan, heat butter and brown sugar over medium heat until sugar is dissolved. In a small bowl, beat the eggs, vanilla and butter mixture. Combine flour and baking powder; gradually add to the butter mixture and mix well. Stir in pecans.

Spread into a greased 13-in. x 9-in. x 2-in. baking pan. Bake at 350° for 20-25 minutes or until a toothpick inserted near the center comes out with moist crumbs and edges are crisp. Cool on a wire rack. Dust with confectioners' sugar if desired. Cut into bars. **Yield:** 4 dozen.

Teddy Carrot Bars

Susan Schuller, Brainerd, Minnesota

I was sure to point out to the mother-to-be and shower guests that these yummy bars include two jars of baby food! Decorating them with purchased Teddy Grahams took very little time and conveniently carried out the theme.

1-1/4   cups all-purpose flour
    1   cup sugar
    1   teaspoon baking soda
    1   teaspoon ground cinnamon
  1/2   teaspoon salt
    1   jar (4 ounces) carrot baby food
    1   package (7 ounces) applesauce baby food
    2   eggs
    2   tablespoons canola oil
CREAM CHEESE FROSTING:
    1   package (3 ounces) cream cheese, softened
    1   teaspoon vanilla extract
    2   to 2-1/2 cups confectioners' sugar
    1   to 3 teaspoons milk
   24   cinnamon-flavored bear-shaped graham crackers

In a large bowl, combine the flour, sugar, baking soda, cinnamon and salt. In a bowl, combine the baby foods, eggs and oil; add to dry ingredients just until blended.

Pour into a greased 13-in. x 9-in. x 2-in. baking pan. Bake at 350° for 20-25 minutes or until a toothpick inserted near the center comes out clean. Cool completely on a wire rack. Cut into bars.

For frosting, in a large bowl, beat cream cheese and vanilla until smooth. Gradually add confectioners' sugar. Add enough to milk to achieve desired consistency. Place a dollop of frosting on each bar; top with a bear-shaped graham cracker. Store in the refrigerator. **Yield:** 2 dozen.

Spiced Apple Bars

Evelyn Winchester, Hilton, New York

Chopped walnuts and hearty oats make these moist apple and cinnamon squares especially tasty.

  1/2   cup butter, softened
    1   cup sugar
    2   eggs
    1   cup all-purpose flour
    1   cup quick-cooking oats
    1   tablespoon baking cocoa
    1   teaspoon baking powder
    1   teaspoon ground cinnamon
  1/2   teaspoon baking soda
  1/2   teaspoon salt
  1/2   teaspoon ground nutmeg
  1/4   teaspoon ground cloves
1-1/2   cups diced peeled tart apple
  1/2   cup chopped walnuts
Confectioners' sugar

In a large bowl, cream butter and sugar until light and fluffy. Add the eggs, one at a time, beating well after each addition. Combine the flour, oats, cocoa, baking powder, cinnamon, baking soda, salt, nutmeg and cloves; gradually add to creamed mixture and mix well. Stir in apple and nuts.

Spread into a greased 13-in. x 9-in. x 2-in. baking pan. Bake at 375° for 20-25 minutes or until a toothpick comes out clean. Cool on a wire rack. Dust with confectioners' sugar. Cut into bars. **Yield:** about 2-1/2 dozen.

Walnut Cookie Strips

June Grimm, San Rafael, California

This recipe is a classic in our home. It will be enjoyed by both kids and adults in your kitchen, too.

- 1/2 cup all-purpose flour
- 1/8 teaspoon salt
- 1/4 cup cold butter, cubed

FILLING:

- 1 egg
- 3/4 cup packed brown sugar
- 2 tablespoons all-purpose flour
- 1/2 teaspoon vanilla extract
- 1/8 teaspoon baking powder
- 1/2 cup chopped walnuts
- 1/4 cup flaked coconut

FROSTING:

- 3/4 cup confectioners' sugar
- 1 tablespoon butter, softened
- 1 tablespoon orange juice
- 1/2 teaspoon lemon juice
- 1/4 cup chopped walnuts

In a small bowl, combine flour and salt; cut in butter until crumbly. Press into a greased 9-in. x 5-in. x 3-in. loaf pan. Bake at 350° for 15 minutes or until lightly browned.

Meanwhile, in a small bowl, beat egg. Beat in the brown sugar, flour, vanilla and baking powder. Stir in nuts and coconut. Pour over hot crust. Bake 15 minutes longer or until set. Cool completely on a wire rack.

For frosting, in another small bowl, beat the confectioners' sugar, butter and juices until smooth. Spread over filling; sprinkle with nuts. Cover and refrigerate for 1-2 hours or until frosting is set. Cut into strips. Store in the refrigerator. **Yield:** 2 dozen.

Baking Classics | Bars

Oatmeal Date Bars

Elnora Hamel, Greenville, Illinois

I've been making these bars for a very long time. I remember my dad saying they were the best he ever tasted. Use your food processor to easily grind the oats.

- 2 cups quick-cooking oats
- 3/4 cup shortening
- 1/2 cup sugar
- 2 cups all-purpose flour
- 1 teaspoon baking soda
- 1/2 teaspoon salt
- 1/2 cup buttermilk

FILLING:
- 3 cups chopped dates (about 1 pound)
- 1 cup sugar
- 1 cup water
- 1 to 2 tablespoons lemon juice, optional

GLAZE:
- 1-1/2 cups confectioners' sugar
- 1/8 teaspoon salt
- 1 teaspoon vanilla extract
- 3 tablespoons milk

Place oats in a food processor. Cover and process until finely ground; set aside. In a large bowl, cream shortening and sugar until light and fluffy. Combine the oats, flour, baking soda and salt; add to creamed mixture alternately with buttermilk, beating well after each addition.

Divide dough in half. On a lightly floured surface, roll half of dough to fit the bottom and up the sides of a greased 13-in. x 9-in. x 2-in. baking pan. Transfer to pan; set aside.

In a large saucepan, combine the dates, sugar, water and lemon juice if desired; bring to a boil. Cool for 10 minutes.

Spread over crust. Roll remaining dough to fit pan; place over filling and seal edges. Bake at 400° for 15-20 minutes or until crust is golden brown. Combine glaze ingredients; spread over bars while warm. Cool on a wire rack before cutting into bars. **Yield:** 3 dozen.

Blueberry Oat Bars

Deena Hubler, Jasper, Indiana

Oats add crunch to the tasty crust and crumbly topping of these fruity bars. I often bake them for church parties. Men especially love them.

- 1-1/2 cups all-purpose flour
- 1-1/2 cups quick-cooking oats
- 1-1/2 cups sugar, *divided*
- 1/2 teaspoon baking soda
- 3/4 cup cold butter
- 2 cups fresh *or* frozen blueberries
- 2 tablespoons cornstarch
- 2 tablespoons lemon juice

In a large bowl, combine the flour, oats, 1 cup sugar and baking soda. Cut in the butter until mixture resembles coarse crumbs. Reserve 2 cups for the topping. Press remaining crumb mixture into a greased 13-in. x 9-in. x 2-in. baking pan; set aside.

In a large saucepan, combine the blueberries, cornstarch, lemon juice and remaining sugar. Bring to a boil; cook and stir for 2 minutes or until thickened.

Spread evenly over the crust. Sprinkle with the reserved crumb mixture. Bake at 375° for 25 minutes or until lightly browned. Cool on a wire rack. Cut into bars. **Yield:** 2-1/2 to 3 dozen.

Lemon Graham Squares

Janis Plourde, Smooth Rock Falls, Ontario

My Aunt Jackie brought these lemon bars to every family gathering. They're my favorite lemon dessert. The crispy top and bottom offer a nice texture.

- 1 can (14 ounces) sweetened condensed milk
- 1/2 cup lemon juice
- 1-1/2 cups graham cracker crumbs (about 24 squares)
- 3/4 cup all-purpose flour
- 1/3 cup packed brown sugar
- 1/2 teaspoon baking powder

Dash salt
- 1/2 cup butter, melted

In a small bowl, combine milk and lemon juice; set aside. In a large bowl, combine the cracker crumbs, flour, brown sugar, baking powder and salt. Stir in butter until crumbly.

Press half of the crumb mixture into a greased 9-in. square baking pan. Pour lemon mixture over crust; sprinkle with remaining crumbs. Bake at 375° for 20-25 minutes or until lightly browned. Cool on a wire rack. Cut into bars. Store in the refrigerator. **Yield:** 3 dozen.

Toffee Nut Squares

Anna Marie Cobb, Pearland, Texas

My mother passed along this yummy recipe. Her soft but chewy bars are packed with brown sugar, coconut and nuts and are a hit at any party.

- 1/2　cup butter, softened
- 1/2　cup packed brown sugar
- 1　cup all-purpose flour
- 1/4　cup heavy whipping cream

FILLING:
- 1　cup packed brown sugar
- 2　eggs
- 1　teaspoon vanilla extract
- 2　tablespoons all-purpose flour
- 1　teaspoon baking powder
- 1/4　teaspoon salt
- 1　cup flaked coconut
- 1　cup chopped nuts

In a large bowl, cream the butter and brown sugar until light and fluffy. Gradually add flour. Add cream, 1 tablespoon at a time, until a soft dough forms. Press into an ungreased 9-in. square baking pan. Bake at 350° for 15 minutes.

Meanwhile, in a small bowl, beat the brown sugar, eggs and vanilla until blended. Combine the flour, baking powder and salt; gradually add to mixture. Stir in coconut and nuts.

Spread over crust. Bake for 25-20 minutes or until a toothpick inserted near the center comes out clean. Cool on a wire rack. Cut into squares before cutting. **Yield:** about 1-1/2 dozen.

Double Chocolate Bars

Nancy Clark, Zeigler, Illinois

A friend brought these fudgy bars a few years ago to tempt me with yet another chocolate treat. They are simple to make...and cleanup is a breeze! They're very rich, though, so be sure to cut them into bite-size pieces.

- 1　package (16 ounces) cream-filled chocolate sandwich cookies, crushed
- 3/4　cup butter, melted
- 1　can (14 ounces) sweetened condensed milk
- 2　cups (12 ounces) miniature semisweet chocolate chips, *divided*

Combine cookie crumbs and butter; pat onto the bottom of an ungreased 13-in. x 9-in. x 2-in. baking pan. Cover and microwave milk and 1 cup chocolate chips until chips are melted; stir until smooth.

Pour over crust. Sprinkle with remaining chips. Bake at 350° for 10-12 minutes or until chips begin to melt but do not lose their shape. Cool on a wire rack. Cut into bars. **Yield:** about 4 dozen.

Strawberry Oatmeal Bars

Flo Burtnett, Gage, Oklahoma

Their fruity filling and fluffy coconut topping make these bars truly one of a kind. They really dress up my trays of Christmas goodies.

- 1-1/4　cups all-purpose flour
- 1-1/4　cups quick-cooking oats
- 1/2　cup sugar
- 1/2　teaspoon baking powder
- 1/4　teaspoon salt
- 3/4　cup butter, melted
- 2　teaspoons vanilla extract
- 1　cup strawberry preserves
- 1/2　cup flaked coconut

In a bowl, combine the flour, oats, sugar, baking powder and salt. Add butter and vanilla; stir until crumbly. Set aside 1 cup. Press remaining crumb mixture evenly into an ungreased 13-in. x 9-in. x 2-in. baking pan. Spread the preserves over crust. Combine coconut and reserved crumb mixture; sprinkle over preserves.

Bake at 350° for 25-30 minutes or until coconut is lightly browned. Cool on a wire rack. Cut into bars. **Yield:** 3 dozen.

Peanut Mallow Bars

Claudia Ruiss, Massapequa, New York

Searching for the perfect combination of salty and sweet sensations? Well, look no further! Salted peanuts and rich caramel topping join marshmallow creme and brown sugar in these irresistible, chewy bars.

    1   cup chopped salted peanuts
    3/4 cup all-purpose flour
    3/4 cup quick-cooking oats
    2/3 cup packed brown sugar
    1/2 teaspoon salt
    1/2 teaspoon baking soda
    1   egg, lightly beaten
    1/3 cup cold butter

TOPPING:
    1   jar (7 ounces) marshmallow creme
    2/3 cup caramel ice cream topping
    1-3/4 cups salted peanuts

In a large bowl, combine the peanuts, flour, oats, sugar, salt and baking soda; stir in the egg. Cut in butter until crumbly. Press into a greased 13-in. x 9-in. x 2-in. baking pan. Bake at 350° for 8-10 minutes or until lightly browned.

Spoon marshmallow creme over hot crust; carefully spread evenly. Drizzle with the caramel topping; sprinkle with peanuts. Bake for 15-20 minutes or until lightly browned. Cool on a wire rack. Cut into bars. **Yield:** 3 dozen.

Cherry Bars

Jane Kamp, Grand Rapids, Michigan

Want something simple to satisfy a large group? Try these festive, fruit-filled bars. With their pretty color from cherry pie filling and subtle almond flavor, they're destined to become one of your most requested goodies.

    1 cup butter, softened
    2 cups sugar
    4 eggs
    1 teaspoon vanilla extract
  1/4 teaspoon almond extract
    3 cups all-purpose flour
    1 teaspoon salt
    2 cans (21 ounces *each*) cherry pie filling

GLAZE:
    1 cup confectioners' sugar
  1/2 teaspoon vanilla extract
  1/2 teaspoon almond extract
    2 to 3 tablespoons milk

In a large bowl, cream butter and sugar until light and fluffy. Add eggs, one at a time, beating well after each addition. Beat in the extracts. Combine flour and salt; gradually add to the creamed mixture just until combined.

Spread 3 cups batter into a greased 15-in. x 10-in. x 1-in. baking pan. Spread with pie filling. Drop the remaining batter by teaspoonfuls over filling.

Bake at 350° for 30-35 minutes or until a toothpick comes out clean. Cool on a wire rack. Combine the glaze ingredients; drizzle over the top. Cut into bars. **Yield:** 5 dozen.

Gooey Chip Bars

Beatriz Boggs, Delray Beach, Florida

I can satisfy a sweet tooth in a jiffy with my chewy, chocolaty bars. You'll never believe how easy they are to assemble.

- 2 cups graham cracker crumbs
- 1 can (14 ounces) sweetened condensed milk
- 1 cup (6 ounces) semisweet chocolate chips, *divided*
- 1/2 cup chopped walnuts *or* pecans, optional

In a large bowl, combine cracker crumbs and milk. Stir in 1/2 cup chocolate chips and nuts if desired (batter will be very thick).

Pat onto the bottom of a well-greased 8-in. square baking dish. Sprinkle with remaining chocolate chips. Bake at 350° for 20-25 minutes or until golden brown. Cool on a wire rack. Cut into bars. **Yield:** 1-1/2 dozen.

Fruit 'n' Nut Spice Bars

Loretta Dunn, Lyons, Oregon

These bars are chock-full of flavor from honey, spices, walnuts and chips. Plus they're topped off with a drizzle of vanilla glaze.

- 3/4 cup chopped maraschino cherries
- 2-1/4 cups all-purpose flour, *divided*
- 1 package (8 ounces) cream cheese, softened
- 1/2 cup butter, softened
- 1-1/2 cups packed brown sugar
- 1 egg
- 1/4 cup honey
- 1-1/2 teaspoons baking powder
- 1 teaspoon salt
- 1 teaspoon ground cinnamon
- 1 teaspoon ground nutmeg
- 1 cup chopped walnuts
- 3/4 cup miniature chocolate chips
- 1-1/3 cups confectioners' sugar
- 2 tablespoons milk
- 1/4 teaspoon vanilla extract

In a small bowl, toss cherries with 1/4 cup flour; set aside. In a large bowl, beat cream cheese, butter and brown sugar until smooth. Beat in egg and honey. Combine the baking powder, salt, cinnamon, nutmeg and remaining flour; add to creamed mixture and mix well. Stir in the nuts, chocolate chips and reserved cherries.

Spread into a greased 15-in. x 10-in. x 1-in. baking pan. Bake at 350° for 30-35 minutes or until golden brown. In a small bowl, combine the confectioners' sugar, milk and vanilla until smooth; drizzle over warm bars. Cool on a wire rack for 1 hour. Cut into bars. Store in the refrigerator. **Yield:** 4 dozen.

Rustic Nut Bars

Barbara Driscoll, West Allis, Wisconsin

Everyone will munch with joy when they bite into these chewy, gooey bars. They'll love the shortbread-like crust and the wildly nutty topping.

- 1 tablespoon plus 3/4 cup cold butter, *divided*
- 2-1/3 cups all-purpose flour
- 1/2 cup sugar
- 1/2 teaspoon baking powder
- 1/2 teaspoon salt
- 1 egg, lightly beaten

TOPPING:
- 2/3 cup honey
- 1/2 cup packed brown sugar
- 1/4 teaspoon salt
- 6 tablespoons butter, cubed
- 2 tablespoons heavy whipping cream
- 1 cup chopped hazelnuts, toasted
- 1 cup roasted salted almonds
- 1 cup salted cashews, toasted
- 1 cup pistachios, toasted

Line a 13-in. x 9-in. x 2-in. baking pan with foil; grease the foil with 1 tablespoon butter. Set aside.

In a large bowl, combine flour, sugar, baking powder and salt; cut in remaining butter until mixture resembles coarse crumbs. Stir in egg until blended (mixture will be dry).

Press firmly onto the bottom of prepared pan. Bake at 375° for 18-20 minutes or until edges are golden brown. Cool on a wire rack.

In a large heavy saucepan, bring the honey, brown sugar and salt to a boil over medium heat until sugar is smooth, stirring often. Boil without stirring for 2 minutes. Add butter and cream. Bring to a boil; cook and stir for 1 minute or until smooth. Remove from the heat; stir in the hazelnuts, almonds, cashews and pistachios. Spread over crust.

Bake at 375° for 15-20 minutes or until topping is bubbly. Cool completely on a wire rack. Using foil, lift bars out of pan. Discard foil; cut into squares. **Yield:** about 3 dozen.

Marbled Chocolate Cheesecake Bars

Jean Komlos, Plymouth, Michigan

Chocolate and cream cheese are swirled in these yummy bars to create a sensation that's sure to please your sweet tooth…and fool it at the same time! This dessert tastes so rich, it's hard to believe it's on the lighter side.

- 3/4 cup water
- 1/3 cup butter
- 1-1/2 squares (1-1/2 ounces) unsweetened chocolate
- 2 cups all-purpose flour
- 1-1/2 cups packed brown sugar
- 1 teaspoon baking soda
- 1/2 teaspoon salt
- 1 egg
- 1 egg white
- 1/2 cup reduced-fat sour cream

CREAM CHEESE MIXTURE:
- 1 package (8 ounces) reduced-fat cream cheese
- 1/3 cup sugar
- 1 egg white
- 1 tablespoon vanilla extract
- 1 cup (6 ounces) miniature semisweet chocolate chips

In a small saucepan, combine the water, butter and chocolate. Cook and stir over low heat until melted; stir until smooth. Cool.

In a large bowl, combine the flour, brown sugar, baking soda and salt. Beat in the egg, egg white and sour cream on low speed just until combined. Beat in chocolate mixture until smooth. In another bowl, beat the cream cheese, sugar, egg white and vanilla until smooth; set aside.

Spread chocolate batter into a 15-in. x 10-in. x 1-in. baking pan coated with cooking spray. Drop the cream cheese mixture by tablespoonfuls over batter; cut through batter with a knife to swirl. Sprinkle with chocolate chips.

Bake at 375° for 20-25 minutes or until a toothpick inserted near the center comes out clean. Cool on a wire rack. **Yield:** about 4 dozen.

Windmill Cookie Bars

Edna Hoffman, Hebron, Indiana

When I went to my grandma's house as a child, she was often baking Dutch windmill cookies. Like her cookies, my bars feature crisp slivered almonds.

- 1 cup butter, softened
- 1 cup sugar
- 1 egg, *separated*
- 2 cups all-purpose flour
- 1 teaspoon ground cinnamon
- 1/4 teaspoon baking soda
- 1 cup slivered almonds

In a large bowl, cream butter and sugar until light and fluffy. Beat in egg yolk. Combine the flour, cinnamon and baking soda; gradually add to creamed mixture and mix well.

Press into a greased 15-in. x 10-in. x 1-in. baking pan. Beat the egg white; brush over dough. Sprinkle with almonds.

Bake at 350° for 20-25 minutes or until a toothpick inserted near the center comes out clean. Cool on a wire rack for 5 minutes; cut into bars. Cool completely. **Yield:** 2-1/2 dozen.

Coconut Granola Bars

Maria Cade, Fort Rock, Oregon

These quick-to-fix bars are wholesome and delicious. I sometimes make them for bake sales.

- 3/4 cup packed brown sugar
- 2/3 cup peanut butter
- 1/2 cup corn syrup
- 1/2 cup butter, melted
- 2 teaspoons vanilla extract
- 3 cups old-fashioned oats
- 1 cup (6 ounces) semisweet chocolate chips
- 1/2 cup flaked coconut
- 1/2 cup sunflower kernels
- 1/3 cup toasted wheat germ
- 2 teaspoons sesame seeds

In a large bowl, combine the brown sugar, peanut butter, corn syrup, butter and vanilla. Combine the remaining ingredients; add to peanut butter mixture and stir to coat. Press into two greased 13-in. x 9-in. x 2-in. baking pans.

Bake at 350° for 25-30 minutes or until golden brown. Cool on wire racks. Cut into bars. **Yield:** 3 dozen.

Blueberry Lattice Bars

Debbie Ayers, Baileyville, Maine

Since our area has an annual blueberry festival, my daughters and I are always looking for great new berry recipes to enter in the cooking contest. These lovely, yummy bars won a blue ribbon one year.

    1   cup butter, softened
  1/2   cup sugar
    1   egg
  1/2   teaspoon vanilla extract
2-3/4   cups all-purpose flour
  1/4   teaspoon salt
FILLING:
    1   cup sugar
    3   tablespoons cornstarch
    3   cups fresh *or* frozen blueberries

In a large bowl, cream butter and sugar until light and fluffy. Beat in egg. Beat in vanilla. Combine flour and salt; gradually add to creamed mixture and mix until well blended. Cover and refrigerate for 2 hours.

Meanwhile, in a small saucepan, combine the sugar and cornstarch. Add blueberries. Bring to a boil; cook and stir for 2 minutes or until thickened.

Roll two-thirds of the dough into a 14-in. x 10-in. rectangle. Place in a greased 13-in. x 9-in. x 2-in. baking dish. Top with filling. Roll out remaining dough to 1/4-in. thickness. Cut into 1/2-in.-wide strips; make a lattice crust over filling.

Bake at 375° for 30-35 minutes or until top is golden brown. Cool on a wire rack. Cut into bars. **Yield:** 2 dozen.

Storing Bars Most bars can be stored directly in the pan. Just cover the pan with foil or slip into a large plastic bag and store at room temperature. If the bars were made with perishable ingredients, such as cream cheese, they should be stored in the refrigerator.

Chocolate Oatmeal Bars

Mary Ann Meredith, Pittsford, Michigan

I made this dessert for eight ladies who recently stayed at our bed-and-breakfast, and they just raved about it. An oat crust is topped with chocolate and peanut butter, then sprinkled with crushed toffee candy bars.

- 1/3 cup butter, softened
- 1 cup packed brown sugar
- 1/3 cup corn syrup
- 1 teaspoon vanilla extract
- 4 cups quick-cooking oats
- 1 package (11-1/2 ounces) milk chocolate chips
- 2/3 cup chunky peanut butter
- 4 Heath candy bars (1.4 ounces *each*), crushed

In a large bowl, cream the butter and brown sugar until light and fluffy. Beat in corn syrup and vanilla. Stir in oats; press into a greased 13-in. x 9-in. x 2-in. baking pan.

Bake at 350° for 12-15 minutes or until golden brown. Cool on a wire rack.

In a microwave, melt chocolate chips and peanut butter; stir until smooth. Spread over cooled bars. Sprinkle with the crushed candy bars. Chill until set. Cut into bars. **Yield:** 3 dozen.

Glazed Persimmon Bars

Delores Leach, Penn Valley, California

For a tasty change of pace, give persimmon flavored brownies a try. They are a wonderful way to take a break during the day. Persimmons are an excellent source of vitamins A and C and are rich in fiber. They star in these dessert bars along with dates and nuts.

- 1 cup mashed ripe persimmon pulp
- 1 cup sugar
- 1/2 cup canola oil
- 1 egg
- 1-1/2 teaspoons lemon juice
- 1-3/4 cups all-purpose flour
- 1 teaspoon baking soda
- 1 teaspoon salt
- 1 teaspoon ground cinnamon
- 1 teaspoon ground nutmeg
- 1/4 teaspoon ground cloves, optional
- 1-1/2 cups chopped dates *or* raisins
- 1 cup chopped nuts
GLAZE:
- 1 cup confectioners' sugar
- 2 tablespoons lemon juice

In a large bowl, combine the persimmon, sugar, oil, egg and lemon juice. Combine the flour, baking soda, salt and spices; add to sugar mixture. Stir in dates and nuts.

Spread into a greased 15-in. x 10-in. x 1-in. baking pan. Bake at 350° for 20-25 minutes or until a toothpick inserted near the center comes out clean. Cool in pan on a wire rack.

Combine glaze ingredients; spread over bars. Cut into bars. Store in the refrigerator. **Yield:** about 4 dozen.

Pear Custard Bars

Jeannette Nord, San Juan Capistrano, California

When I take this crowd-pleasing treat to a potluck, I come home with an empty pan every time.

- 1/2 cup butter, softened
- 1/3 cup sugar
- 1/4 teaspoon vanilla extract
- 3/4 cup all-purpose flour
- 2/3 cup chopped macadamia nuts
FILLING/TOPPING:
- 1 package (8 ounces) cream cheese, softened
- 1/2 cup sugar
- 1 egg
- 1/2 teaspoon vanilla extract
- 1 can (15-1/4 ounces) pear halves, drained
- 1/2 teaspoon sugar
- 1/2 teaspoon ground cinnamon

In a large bowl, cream butter and sugar until light and fluffy. Beat in vanilla. Gradually add flour to creamed mixture and mix well. Stir in the nuts.

Press into a greased 8-in. square baking dish. Bake at 350° for 20 minutes or until lightly browned. Cool on a wire rack.

In a small bowl, beat cream cheese until smooth. Beat in the sugar, egg and vanilla. Pour over crust. Cut pears into 1/8-in. slices; arrange in a single layer over filling. Combine sugar and cinnamon; sprinkle over pears.

Bake at 375° for 28-30 minutes (center will be soft set and will become firmer upon cooling). Cool on a wire rack for 45 minutes.

Cover and refrigerate for at least 2 hours before cutting into bars. Store in the refrigerator. **Yield:** 16 bars.

Lime Coconut Bars

Mary Jane Jones, Williamstown, West Virginia

I found this dessert in my mother's recipe collection. I like to garnish them with whipped cream and lime.

- 3/4 cup finely crushed crisp sugar cookies
- 3 tablespoons cold butter
- 2-1/4 cups flaked coconut

FILLING:
- 1/4 cup butter, softened
- 3/4 cup sugar
- 1/2 cup lime juice
- 4-1/2 teaspoons yellow cornmeal

Dash salt
- 4 egg yolks
- 1 teaspoon grated lime peel

Confectioners' sugar

Place the crushed cookies in a bowl. Cut in butter until mixture resembles coarse crumbs. Stir in coconut; set aside 1 cup for topping. Press the remaining mixture into a greased 8-in. baking dish. Bake at 350° for 13-15 minutes or until golden brown.

Meanwhile, for filling, combine the butter, sugar, lime juice, cornmeal and salt in a heavy saucepan. Cook and stir over low heat until sugar is dissolved and cornmeal is softened, about 10 minutes. Remove from the heat.

In a small bowl, lightly beat the egg yolks. Stir a small amount of hot lime mixture into the yolks; return all to the pan, stirring constantly. Cook and stir until a thermometer reads 160° and mixture coats the back of a metal spoon, about 20 minutes. Remove from the heat; stir in lime peel.

Pour over the crust; sprinkle with reserved coconut mixture. Bake at 350° for 18-20 minutes or until golden brown. Cool completely on a wire rack. Dust with confectioners' sugar. Cut into bars. **Yield:** 16 bars.

Editor's Note: The cornmeal is used as a thickener in the filling.

Chocolate Caramel Bars

Judy Broody, Oak Forest, Illinois

These bars have a delightful combination of chocolate, caramel and walnuts. I often rely on bar cookies for their ease of preparation.

- 1/2 cup butter, softened
- 1 cup packed brown sugar
- 2 cups all-purpose flour

CARAMEL LAYER:
- 1/3 cup butter, cubed
- 1/2 cup packed brown sugar
- 1 cup chopped walnuts

TOPPING:
- 1-1/2 cups semisweet chocolate chips

In a large bowl, cream butter and brown sugar until light and fluffy. Gradually add flour until well combined. Press into a greased 13-in. x 9-in. x 2-in. baking pan; set aside.

In a large saucepan, combine butter and brown sugar. Bring to a boil; cook for 1 minute. Stir in walnuts. Spread over crust.

Bake at 350° for 16-18 minutes or until set. Immediately sprinkle with chocolate chips. Allow chips to soften for a few minutes, then spread over caramel layer. Cool on a wire rack. Cut into bars. **Yield:** 3 dozen.

Cheesecake Dreams

Barbara Allstrand, Oceanside, California

These bars are a dream not only because of their creamy filling but they're so simple to make. Cheesecake lovers can't eat just one!

- 1 cup all-purpose flour
- 1/3 cup packed brown sugar
- 1/2 cup chopped pecans
- 1/3 cup butter, melted

FILLING:
- 1 package (8 ounces) cream cheese, softened
- 1/4 cup sugar
- 1 egg
- 2 tablespoons milk
- 1 tablespoon lemon juice
- 1 teaspoon vanilla extract

In a large bowl, combine the flour, brown sugar and pecans. Stir in butter until crumbly. Set aside 1/3 cup for topping. Press remaining mixture into a greased 8-in. square baking dish. Bake at 350° for 12-15 minutes or until lightly browned.

Meanwhile, in a large bowl, beat cream cheese and sugar until smooth. Beat in the egg, milk, lemon juice and vanilla. Pour over crust; sprinkle with reserved pecan mixture.

Bake for 20-25 minutes or until firm. Cool on a wire rack. Cut into 16 squares, then cut each square in half diagonally. Store in the refrigerator. **Yield:** 32 bars.

Raspberry Citrus Bars

Ruby Nelson, Naumelle, Arkansas

This recipe was an instant hit with my family when I first made it. The combination of raspberries, lemon juice and orange peel gives it a unique taste.

1	cup butter, softened
3/4	cup confectioners' sugar
2-1/4	cups all-purpose flour, *divided*
4	eggs
1-1/2	cups sugar
1/3	cup lemon juice
2	tablespoons grated orange peel
1	teaspoon baking powder
1-1/2	cups unsweetened raspberries

In a large bowl, cream the butter and confectioners' sugar until light and fluffy. Gradually add 2 cups flour just until combined.

Press mixture into a greased 13-in. x 9-in. x 2-in. baking pan. Bake at 350° for 20 minutes or until lightly browned.

Meanwhile, in a large bowl, beat the eggs, sugar, lemon juice and orange peel. Combine the baking powder and remaining flour; gradually add to egg mixture. Sprinkle raspberries over the crust. Pour filling over the berries.

Bake for 30-35 minutes or until lightly browned and filling is set. Cool on a wire rack. Cut into bars. Store in the refrigerator. **Yield:** 12-15 servings.

Apricot Bars

Kim Gilliland, Simi Valley, California

These moist bars have a great flavor. Everyone in my family loves them, and I get lots of requests for the recipe.

- 2/3 cup dried apricots
- 1/2 cup water
- 1/2 cup butter, softened
- 1/4 cup confectioners' sugar
- 1-1/3 cups all-purpose flour, *divided*
- 2 eggs
- 1 cup packed brown sugar
- 1/2 teaspoon baking powder
- 1/4 teaspoon salt
- 1/2 teaspoon vanilla extract
- 1/2 cup chopped walnuts

Additional confectioners' sugar

In a small saucepan, cook apricots in water over medium heat for 10 minutes or until softened. Drain, cool and chop; set aside.

In a large bowl, cream butter and confectioners' sugar until light and fluffy. Gradually add 1 cup flour until well blended.

Press into a greased 8-in. square baking dish. Bake at 350° for 20 minutes or until lightly browned.

Meanwhile, in a small bowl, beat eggs and brown sugar until blended. In another small bowl, combine the baking powder, salt, and remaining flour; gradually add to egg mixture. Beat in the vanilla. Stir in the apricots and nuts. Pour over crust.

Bake at 350° for 30 minutes or until set. Cool on wire rack. Dust with confectioners' sugar. Cut into bars. Store in the refrigerator. **Yield:** 16 bars.

Fruitcake Squares

Nora Seaton, McLean, Virginia

My family prefers these scrumptious squares to the larger, more traditional fruitcake. Since they're so quick and simple to make, I always include several batches in my annual Christmas baking spree.

- 6 tablespoons butter, melted
- 4 cups crushed vanilla wafers (about 120 wafers)
- 1 cup pecan halves
- 3/4 cup chopped dates
- 3/4 cup chopped mixed candied fruit
- 1/2 cup chopped candied pineapple
- 1 can (14 ounces) sweetened condensed milk
- 1 teaspoon vanilla extract

Pour butter into a 15-in. x 10-in. x 1-in. baking pan. Sprinkle with wafer crumbs. Arrange pecans and fruit over crumbs; press down gently. Combine milk and vanilla; pour evenly over fruit.

Bake at 350° for 20-25 minutes or until lightly browned. Cool on a wire rack. Cut into bars. **Yield:** about 3 dozen.

Crispy Date Bars

Anna Sheehan, Spokane, Washington

I bake these chewy bars around the holidays because they are a nice-sized batch for my family. Plus, they keep well in the refrigerator, so I can make them when it's convenient.

- 1 cup all-purpose flour
- 1/2 cup packed brown sugar
- 1/2 cup cold butter

FILLING:
- 1 cup chopped dates
- 1/2 cup sugar
- 1/2 cup butter
- 1 egg, beaten
- 2 cups crisp rice cereal
- 1 cup chopped nuts
- 1 teaspoon vanilla extract

FROSTING:
- 1 package (3 ounces) cream cheese, softened
- 2 cups confectioners' sugar
- 1/2 teaspoon vanilla extract

In a large bowl, combine the flour and sugar; cut in butter until crumbly. Press into a greased 9-in. square baking pan. Bake at 375° for 10-12 minutes or until golden brown.

Meanwhile, in a heavy saucepan, combine the dates, sugar and butter; bring to a boil. Reduce heat; cook and stir for 3 minutes. Add 1/2 cup hot mixture to egg; return all to the pan. Bring to a gentle boil. Remove from the heat; stir in the cereal, nuts and vanilla. Spread over crust. Cool on a wire rack.

In a small bowl, combine frosting ingredients; beat until creamy. Frost bars. Cut into bars. Store in the refrigerator. **Yield:** 2 dozen.

Dusting with Confectioners' Sugar To achieve a light coating of confectioners' sugar over the top of bars, brownies, cakes or other desserts, place some confectioners' sugar in a small fine mesh strainer. Tap the rim of the strainer gently as you move it over the top of the dessert.

Peppermint Oat Bars

Connie Major Williams, Dexter, Michigan

These bars were a hit with my brother-in-law. Peppermint, oatmeal and chocolate chips are a terrific combination.

- 1 cup all-purpose flour
- 1/2 cup quick-cooking oats
- 1/3 cup sugar
- 1/3 cup butter, melted
- 1/3 cup chopped walnuts
- 4 ounces cream cheese, softened
- 1 egg
- 1/2 teaspoon vanilla extract
- 1/3 cup semisweet chocolate chips
- 1/3 to 1/2 cup crushed peppermint candies

In a large bowl, combine the flour, oats, sugar and butter. Stir in walnuts (mixture will be crumbly). Set aside 3/4 cup for topping.

Press the remaining mixture into a greased 9-in. square baking pan. Bake at 350° for 10-12 minutes or until lightly browned. Cool on a wire rack.

In a large bowl, beat cream cheese until fluffy. Beat in egg and vanilla. Stir in chocolate chips and peppermint candies.

Pour over crust; sprinkle with reserved crumb mixture. Bake at 350° for 20-22 minutes or until lightly browned. Cool on a wire rack. Cut into bars. Store in refrigerator. **Yield:** about 1-1/2 dozen.

Classic Lemon Bars

Melissa Mosness, Loveland, Colorado

Looking for old-fashioned taste without a lot of effort? Give my lemony bars a try. You'll be amazed at how quickly they come together.

- 1/2 cup butter, softened
- 1/4 cup sugar
- 1 cup all-purpose flour

FILLING:

- 3/4 cup sugar
- 2 eggs
- 3 tablespoons lemon juice
- 2 tablespoons all-purpose flour
- 1/4 teaspoon baking powder

Confectioners' sugar

In a small bowl, cream butter and sugar until light and fluffy; gradually beat in flour until blended.

Press into an ungreased 8-in. square baking dish. Bake at 350° for 15-20 minutes or until edges are lightly browned.

For filling, in a small bowl, beat the sugar, eggs, lemon juice, flour and baking powder until frothy. Pour over crust.

Bake for 10-15 minutes or until set and lightly browned. Cool on a wire rack. Sprinkle with confectioners' sugar. Cut into squares. **Yield:** 9 servings.

Peanut Butter 'n' Chocolate Bars

Debra Rowley, Hattiesburg, Mississippi

This is my most requested recipe. I sometimes replace the chocolate or peanut butter chips with butterscotch chips.

- 1 cup butter, softened
- 3/4 cup sugar
- 3/4 cup packed brown sugar
- 2 eggs
- 1 teaspoon vanilla extract
- 2-1/4 cups all-purpose flour
- 1 teaspoon baking soda
- 1/4 teaspoon salt
- 1-1/4 cups semisweet chocolate chips
- 1-1/4 cups peanut butter chips

In a large bowl, cream butter and sugars until light and fluffy. Add the eggs, one at a time, beating well after each addition. Beat in vanilla. Combine the flour, baking soda and salt; gradually add to creamed mixture and mix well. Stir in chips.

Spread into a greased 15-in. x 10-in. x 1-in. baking pan. Bake at 375° for 20-25 minutes or until a toothpick inserted near the center comes out clean. Cool on a wire rack. Cut into bars. **Yield:** about 4 dozen.

Scotch Shortbread Bars

Jane Hodge, West End, North Carolina

It was at my bridal shower in the 60's that I first sampled these pretty bars. Now each time I make them, I'm reminded of that happy occasion.

- 1 cup butter, softened
- 1/2 cup confectioners' sugar
- 2 cups all-purpose flour
- 1/4 teaspoon baking powder
- 1/4 teaspoon salt

Additional confectioners' sugar

In a large mixing bowl, cream butter and sugar until light and fluffy. Combine the flour, baking powder and salt; gradually add to the creamed mixture and mix well.

Spread into an ungreased 11-in. x 7-in. x 2-in. baking pan. Prick several times with a fork. Bake at 350° for 20-22 minutes or until edges begin to brown. Dust with confectioners' sugar. Cool on a wire rack. Cut into bars. **Yield:** 2 dozen.

Spice Cake Bars

Dena Hayden, Vassar, Michigan

Whenever I went to Grandmother's, she served these flavorful bars, topped with creamy frosting. Today, I do the same for our grandchildren, who also like the treats.

- 1 cup butter, softened
- 1 cup sugar
- 1 egg
- 1 cup molasses
- 1 cup hot water
- 3 cups all-purpose flour
- 2 teaspoons ground ginger
- 2 teaspoons ground allspice
- 1 teaspoon baking soda
- 1 teaspoon ground cloves

FROSTING:

- 1/2 cup shortening
- 1/2 cup butter, softened
- 2 to 3 teaspoons lemon juice
- 4 cups confectioners' sugar

In a large bowl, cream butter and sugar until light and fluffy. Beat in egg. Beat in molasses and water until blended. Combine the flour, ginger, allspice, baking soda and cloves; gradually add to the creamed mixture.

Pour into a greased 15-in. x 10-in. x 1-in. baking pan. Bake at 375° for 18-22 minutes or until a toothpick inserted near the center comes out clean. Cool on wire rack.

Meanwhile, in a small bowl, beat shortening, butter and lemon juice until smooth. Beat in sugar until light and fluffy; frost top. Cut into bars. Frost bars. **Yield:** about 2 dozen.

Cranberry Walnut Bars

Sylvia Gidwani, Milford, New Jersey

This recipe was given to me by a friend. My family enjoys these bars as is or topped with ice cream.

1/4 cup butter, softened
1/2 cup sugar
1/2 cup packed brown sugar
  1 egg
  1 teaspoon vanilla extract
1-1/4 cups all-purpose flour
  1 teaspoon baking powder
1/4 teaspoon salt
1/4 teaspoon ground cinnamon
  1 cup chopped fresh *or* frozen cranberries
1/2 cup chopped walnuts

In a large bowl, cream butter and sugars until light and fluffy. Beat in egg and vanilla. Combine the flour, baking powder, salt and cinnamon; gradually add to creamed mixture. Fold in cranberries and walnuts.

Spread into a greased 9-in. square baking pan. Bake at 350° for 30-35 minutes or until a toothpick inserted near the center comes out clean. Cool on a wire rack. Cut into bars. **Yield:** 1-1/2 dozen.

Coconut Raspberry Bars

Amanda Denton, Barre, Vermont

While mixing a batch of plain bars, I was inspired to add raspberry preserves and flaked coconut to the dough...and wound up with these yummy treats, now a family favorite.

    3/4 cup butter, softened
      1 cup sugar
      1 egg
    1/2 teaspoon vanilla extract
      2 cups all-purpose flour
    1/4 teaspoon baking powder
      2 cups flaked coconut, *divided*
    1/2 cup chopped walnuts
      1 jar (12 ounces) raspberry preserves
      1 cup vanilla *or* white chips

In a large bowl, cream butter and sugar until light and fluffy. Beat in egg and vanilla. Combine flour and baking powder; gradually add to the creamed mixture. Stir in 1-1/4 cups coconut and the walnuts.

Press three-fourths of the dough into a greased 13-in. x 9-in. x 2-in. baking pan. Spread with preserves. Sprinkle with chips and remaining coconut. Crumble remaining dough over the top; press lightly.

Bake at 350° for 30-35 minutes or until golden brown. Cool on a wire rack. Cut into squares. **Yield:** 3 dozen.

Frosted Cherry Nut Bars

Christine Carter, Corinth, Vermont

Cherries, nuts and chocolate chips peek out of these bars, making them impossible for folks to stop at trying just one. With their pretty look, they're especially nice to have on hand during the holidays.

    1/2 cup butter, softened
    1/2 cup sugar
    1/2 cup packed brown sugar
      2 eggs
      1 teaspoon vanilla extract
      2 cups all-purpose flour
  1-1/2 teaspoons baking powder
    1/2 teaspoon salt
    3/4 cup milk
      1 cup mixed nuts, coarsely chopped
      1 cup halved maraschino cherries
      1 cup (6 ounces) semisweet chocolate chips
FROSTING:
    1/4 cup butter
      2 cups confectioners' sugar
      2 tablespoons milk
    1/2 teaspoon vanilla extract

In a large bowl, cream the butter and sugars until light and fluffy. Add eggs, one at a time, beating well after each addition. Beat in the vanilla. Combine the flour, baking powder and salt; add to creamed mixture alternately with milk, beating well after each addition. Stir in the nuts, cherries and chocolate chips.

Spread into a greased 15-in. x 10-in. x 1-in. baking pan. Bake at 325° for 25-30 minutes or until golden brown.

Meanwhile, in a small heavy saucepan, cook butter over medium heat for 5-7 minutes or until golden brown. Pour into a large bowl; beat in the confectioners' sugar, milk and vanilla. Frost warm bars. Cool on a wire rack before cutting into bars. **Yield:** about 6 dozen.

German Chocolate Bars

Jennifer Sharp, Murfreesboro, Tennessee

My mom gave me this recipe at Christmas when I wanted to make something different for gifts. The chewy bars can be cut into larger pieces, but they're very rich.

      1 package (18-1/4 ounces) German chocolate cake mix
    2/3 cup cold butter
      1 cup (6 ounces) semisweet chocolate chips
      1 can (15 ounces) coconut-pecan frosting
    1/4 cup milk

Place cake mix in a large bowl; cut in butter until crumbly. Press 2-1/2 cups into a greased 13-in. x 9-in. x 2-in. baking pan. Bake at 350° for 10 minutes; immediately sprinkle with chocolate chips. Drop frosting by tablespoonfuls over the chips.

Stir milk into the remaining crumb mixture; drop by teaspoonfuls over top. Bake 25-30 minutes longer or until bubbly around the edges and top is cracked. Cool on a wire rack. Refrigerate for 4 hours before cutting into bars. **Yield:** 4 dozen.

Golden M&M's Bars

Martha Haseman, Hinckley, Illinois

Our family loves to take drives, and I often bring these bars along for snacking in the car.

- 1/2 cup butter, softened
- 3/4 cup sugar
- 3/4 cup packed brown sugar
- 2 eggs
- 2 teaspoons vanilla extract
- 1-1/2 cups all-purpose flour
- 1 teaspoon baking powder
- 1/2 teaspoon salt
- 1 cup vanilla *or* white chips
- 1-3/4 cups plain M&M's, *divided*

In a large bowl, cream butter and sugars until light and fluffy. Beat in eggs and vanilla. Combine the flour, baking powder and salt; gradually add to the creamed mixture. Stir in chips and 1 cup of M&M's.

Spoon into a greased 13-in. x 9-in. x 2-in. baking pan; spread evenly in pan. Sprinkle with the remaining M&M's. Bake at 350° for 25-30 minutes or until golden brown. Cool on a wire rack. Cut into bars. **Yield:** 2 dozen.

Sour Cream Raisin Squares

Leona Eash, McConnelsville, Ohio

My aunt shared this recipe with me, and my family has always enjoyed it. I love to make these bars for friends who visit or for giving away as gifts.

- 1 cup butter, softened
- 1 cup packed brown sugar
- 2 cups all-purpose flour
- 2 cups quick-cooking oats
- 1 teaspoon baking powder
- 1 teaspoon baking soda
- 1/8 teaspoon salt

FILLING:
- 4 egg yolks
- 2 cups (16 ounces) sour cream
- 1-1/2 cups raisins
- 1 cup sugar
- 1 tablespoon cornstarch

In a large bowl, cream the butter and brown sugar until light and fluffy. Combine the flour, oats, baking powder, baking soda and salt; gradually add to creamed mixture (mixture will be crumbly).

Set aside 2 cups; pat remaining crumbs into a greased 13-in. x 9-in. x 2-in. baking pan. Bake at 350° for 15 minutes. Cool.

Meanwhile, in a small saucepan, combine all the filling ingredients. Bring to a boil; cook and stir for 5-8 minutes. Pour over crust; sprinkle with reserved crumbs. Bake 15 minutes longer. **Yield:** 12-16 servings.

Toffee Bars

Ruth Burrus, Zionsville, Indiana

These shortbread bars have the taste of toffee without the hassle of making candy. They're an attractive addition to any cookie tray.

- 1 cup butter, softened
- 1 cup packed brown sugar
- 1 egg yolk
- 1 teaspoon vanilla extract
- 2 cups all-purpose flour
- 1/4 teaspoon salt
- 6 milk chocolate candy bars (1.55 ounces *each*)
- 1/2 cup finely chopped pecans

In a large bowl, cream butter and brown sugar until light and fluffy. Beat in egg yolk and vanilla. Gradually add flour and salt, beating until smooth.

Press into a greased 15-in. x 10-in. x 1-in. baking pan. Bake at 350° for 17-19 minutes or until light golden brown. Immediately place chocolate bars on top; bake 1 minute longer. Spread melted chocolate over bars; sprinkle with pecans. **Yield:** about 4 dozen.

Peanut Butter-Honey Bars

Janet Hamacher, La Moille, Illinois

If you're in a hurry in the morning, just one of these bars with a glass of milk gets you started on the right foot.

- 1/2 cup peanut butter
- 2 eggs, lightly beaten
- 1/4 cup honey
- 2/3 cup nonfat dry milk powder
- 3 cups fruit and fiber cereal (any flavor)

In a large bowl, combine the peanut butter, eggs and honey until smooth. Stir in milk powder. Add cereal; toss to coat.

Spread in a greased 8-in. square baking dish. Bake at 325° for 20 minutes (mixture may look damp). Cool on a wire rack. Cut into bars. Store in the refrigerator. **Yield:** 6 servings.

Editor's Note: Reduced-fat or generic brands of peanut butter are not recommended for this recipe.

Evenly Baked Bars When pouring batter into the pan or pressing the crust into the pan, make sure the corners are evenly filled. If one corner is thinner than the others, it will overbake before the rest of the pan is even done.

Frosted Peanut Butter Fingers

Leah Gallington, Corona, California

I first learned about these quick crowd-pleasers from a next-door neighbor when I sniffed the delightful aroma of a batch baking. Topped with extra peanut butter and chocolate frosting, the chewy bars are a delight!

  1 cup butter, softened
1-1/2 cups packed brown sugar
  1 cup sugar
2-1/2 cups creamy peanut butter, *divided*
  1 egg
1-1/2 teaspoons vanilla extract
2-1/2 cups quick-cooking oats
  2 cups all-purpose flour
  1 teaspoon baking soda
1/2 teaspoon salt

CHOCOLATE FROSTING:
  6 tablespoons butter, softened
  4 cups confectioners' sugar
1/2 cup baking cocoa
  1 teaspoon vanilla extract
  6 to 8 tablespoons milk

In a large bowl, cream butter and sugars until light and fluffy. Beat in 1 cup peanut butter, egg and vanilla. Combine the oats, flour, baking soda and salt; gradually add to creamed mixture and mix well.

Spread into a greased 15-in. x 10-in. x 1-in. baking pan. Bake at 350° for 13-17 minutes or until golden brown. Cool slightly on a wire rack, about 12 minutes. Spread with remaining peanut butter. Cool completely.

In a large bowl, beat the butter, confectioners' sugar, cocoa, vanilla and enough milk to achieve spreading consistency. Spread over peanut butter. Cut into bars. **Yield:** about 3 dozen.

Editor's Note: Reduced-fat or generic brands of peanut butter are not recommended for this recipe.

Coconut Cranberry Bars

Dolly McDonald, Edmonton, Alberta

I begged a neighbor for the recipe after tasting these yummy bars at a coffee she hosted. The colors make them real eye-pleasers, too!

1-1/2   cups graham cracker crumbs (about 24 squares)
  1/2   cup butter, melted
1-1/2   cups vanilla *or* white chips
1-1/2   cups dried cranberries

1   can (14 ounces) sweetened condensed milk
1   cup flaked coconut
1   cup pecan halves

In a small bowl, combine cracker crumbs and butter until crumbly; press into a greased 13-in. x 9-in. x 2-in. baking pan. In a large bowl, combine the remaining ingredients.

Gently spread over crust. Bake at 350° for 25-28 minutes or until edges are golden brown. Cool on a wire rack. Cut into bars. **Yield:** 3 dozen.

Remove Bars Easily from Pan To pop bars out of the pan without any fuss, line the pan with foil. First cut a piece of foil that is larger than the pan. Turn the pan upside down and mold the foil around the bottom and sides of the pan. Turn the pan right side up and insert the foil, allowing the edges to hang over the pan. Grease foil if recipe directs to grease the pan. Bake and cool as directed. After the bars are completely cooled, lift out of the pan using the foil.

Cinnamon Raisin Bars

Nancy Rohr, St. Louis, Missouri

Although these bars keep well, they don't last long with my husband around. As soon as the house fills with their wonderful aroma, he comes running into the kitchen looking for a sample!

- 1/2 cup butter, softened
- 1 cup packed brown sugar
- 2 tablespoons water
- 1-1/2 cups all-purpose flour
- 1-1/2 cups quick-cooking oats
- 1/2 teaspoon baking soda
- 1/2 teaspoon salt

RAISIN FILLING:
- 1/4 cup sugar
- 1 tablespoon cornstarch
- 1 cup water
- 2 cups raisins

ICING:
- 1 cup confectioners' sugar
- 1/4 teaspoon ground cinnamon
- 1 to 2 tablespoons milk

In a large bowl, cream butter and brown sugar until light and fluffy. Stir in water. Combine the flour, oats, baking soda and salt; add to creamed mixture. Beat until crumbly. Firmly press half into a greased 13-in. x 9-in. x 2-in. baking pan; set the remaining oat mixture aside.

In a small saucepan, combine the sugar, cornstarch and water until smooth; stir in raisins. Bring to a boil. Reduce heat; cook and stir over medium heat until thickened. Cool to room temperature; spread over crust.

Top with reserved oat mixture; gently press down. Bake at 350° for 30-35 minutes or until golden brown. Cool on a wire rack.

In a small bowl, combine the confectioners' sugar and cinnamon; stir in enough milk to reach drizzling consistency. Drizzle over bars. Cut and store in an airtight container. **Yield:** about 3 dozen.

Honey Pecan Triangles

Debbie Fogel, East Berne, New York

These tasty bars have all the goodness of pecan pie. They're enough to serve to a large crowd and are always a big hit.

- 2 teaspoons plus 1/2 cup butter, softened, *divided*
- 1/2 cup packed brown sugar
- 1 egg yolk
- 1-1/2 cups all-purpose flour

TOPPING:
- 1 cup packed brown sugar
- 1/2 cup butter
- 1/4 cup honey
- 1/2 cup heavy whipping cream
- 4 cups chopped pecans

Line a 13-in. x 9-in. x 2-in. baking pan with foil; butter the foil with 2 teaspoons butter. Set aside. In a large bowl, cream remaining butter and brown sugar until light and fluffy. Beat in egg yolk until blended. Gradually add flour.

Press into prepared pan. Bake at 350° for 15 minutes or until golden brown.

Meanwhile, in a large saucepan, combine the brown sugar, butter and honey. Bring to a boil over medium heat; cook and stir for 3 minutes. Remove from the heat; stir in cream and pecans. Pour over crust. Bake for 30 minutes longer or until hot and bubbly. Cool completely on a wire rack.

Use foil to lift the bars out of the pan and place on a cutting board. Carefully remove foil. Cut into 24 bars; cut each in half diagonally. **Yield:** 4 dozen.

Peppermint Chocolate Bars

Christine Harrell, Chester, Virginia

I received this treasured recipe from a dear friend. The frosting and topping makes these thin bars eye-catching.

- 1/2 cup butter
- 2 squares (1 ounce *each*) unsweetened chocolate
- 2 eggs
- 1 cup sugar
- 2 teaspoons vanilla extract
- 1/2 cup all-purpose flour
- 1/2 teaspoon salt
- 1/2 cup chopped pecans *or* walnuts

FROSTING:
- 1/4 cup butter, softened
- 2 cups confectioners' sugar
- 1 teaspoon peppermint extract
- 3 to 4 tablespoons heavy whipping cream

TOPPING:
- 1 square (1 ounce) semisweet chocolate
- 1 tablespoon butter

In a microwave, melt butter and chocolate; stir until smooth. Cool slightly. Meanwhile, in a large bowl, beat the eggs, sugar and vanilla. Add the chocolate mixture and mix well. Combine flour and salt; gradually add to chocolate mixture. Stir in nuts.

Spread into a greased 13-in. x 9-in. x 2-in. baking pan. Bake at 350° for 16-20 minutes or until a toothpick inserted near the center comes out clean. Cool on a wire rack.

In a small bowl, cream butter, confectioners' sugar and extract until light and fluffy. Add enough cream until frosting reaches spreading consistency. Frost cooled bars. Melt chocolate and butter; drizzle over frosting. Cut into bars. **Yield:** 4 dozen.

Merry Cherry Bars

Joan Wood, Shelton, Washington

Flaked coconut and chopped nuts are tasty companions for the maraschino cherries in these festive baked goods. Be sure you add them to your holiday cookie tray.

- 1 cup all-purpose flour
- 3 tablespoons confectioners' sugar
- 1/2 cup cold butter, cubed
- 1 cup sugar
- 1/4 cup all-purpose flour
- 1/2 teaspoon baking powder
- 1/4 teaspoon salt
- 2 eggs, lightly beaten
- 1 teaspoon vanilla extract
- 3/4 cup chopped nuts
- 1/2 cup flaked coconut
- 1/2 cup maraschino cherries, quartered

In a large bowl, combine the flour and confectioners' sugar; cut in butter until the mixture resembles coarse crumbs. Pat into a greased 11-in. x 7-in. x 2-in. baking pan. Bake at 375° for 10 minutes or until the edges are lightly browned. Cool.

In a large bowl, combine the sugar, flour, baking powder and salt. Add eggs and vanilla. Fold in nuts, coconut and cherries; spread over crust.

Bake at 375° for 17-22 minutes or until lightly browned. Cool before cutting. **Yield:** 1-1/2 dozen.

Grandma's Date Bars

Marilyn Reid, Cherry Creek, New York

These nicely textured bars are delicious. It's a good recipe for today's diet awareness, because there's no shortening in it. My great-grandmother, who was born in 1868, made these bars, and the recipe has come down through the generations. Now my children are making them.

- 1 cup sugar
- 1 cup all-purpose flour
- 1 teaspoon baking powder
- 1/2 teaspoon salt
- 1 cup chopped dates
- 1 cup chopped walnuts
- 3 eggs, beaten

Confectioners' sugar

In a large bowl, combine the sugar, flour, baking powder, salt, dates, walnuts and eggs until well blended. Transfer to a greased 8-in. square baking dish.

Bake at 350° for 25 minutes or until a toothpick inserted near the center comes out clean. Cool on a wire rack. Dust with the confectioners' sugar. Cut into squares. **Yield:** 16 servings.

Raisin Cinnamon Bars

Jean Morgan, Roscoe, Illinois

I've been making these simple iced bars for years. They're easy to prepare for dessert or are great in the afternoon as a sweet treat with a cup of hot coffee.

    1/4   cup butter, softened
      1   cup packed brown sugar
      1   egg
    1/2   cup hot brewed coffee
  1-1/2   cups all-purpose flour
      1   teaspoon baking powder
    1/2   teaspoon ground cinnamon
    1/4   teaspoon baking soda
    1/4   teaspoon salt
    1/2   cup raisins
    1/4   cup chopped pecans

ICING:
      1   cup confectioners' sugar
    1/2   teaspoon vanilla extract
      4   to 5 teaspoons water

In a large bowl, combine butter and brown sugar until crumbly, about 2 minutes. Beat in egg. Gradually beat in coffee. Combine the flour, baking powder, cinnamon, baking soda and salt. Gradually add to the coffee mixture until blended. Stir in raisins and pecans.

Transfer to a 13-in. x 9-in. x 2-in. baking pan coated with cooking spray. Bake at 350° for 18-20 minutes or until edges begin to pull away from the sides of the pan and a toothpick inserted near the center comes out clean. Cool on a wire rack for 5 minutes.

Meanwhile for icing, in a small bowl, combine the confectioners' sugar, vanilla and enough water to achieve spreading consistency. Spread over warm bars. Cool completely. Cut into bars. **Yield:** 1-1/2 dozen.

Chocolate Maple Bars

Cathy Schumacher, Alto, Michigan

Use real maple syrup for both the bar and the chocolate-maple frosting. They're sure to disappear quickly.

- 1/2 cup shortening
- 3/4 cup maple syrup
- 1/2 cup sugar
- 3 eggs
- 3 tablespoons milk
- 1 teaspoon vanilla extract
- 1-1/4 cups all-purpose flour
- 1/4 teaspoon baking powder
- 1/4 teaspoon salt
- 1-1/2 squares (1-1/2 ounces) unsweetened chocolate, melted
- 1/2 cup chopped pecans
- 1/2 cup flaked coconut

FROSTING:
- 1/4 cup butter, softened
- 1 cup confectioners' sugar
- 1/2 cup baking cocoa
- 1/2 cup maple syrup
- 1 cup miniature marshmallows

In a large bowl, beat the shortening, syrup and sugar until blended. Beat in the eggs, milk and vanilla. Combine the flour, baking powder and salt; add to sugar mixture and mix well. Remove half of the batter to another bowl.

Combine melted chocolate and pecans; stir into one bowl. Spread into a greased 13-in. x 9-in. x 2-in. baking pan. Add coconut to remaining batter. Spread carefully over the chocolate batter.

Bake at 350° for 25 minutes or until a toothpick inserted near the center comes out clean. Cool completely on a wire rack.

For frosting, in a small bowl, beat butter until smooth. Gradually add the confectioners' sugar and cocoa. Gradually add syrup, beating until smooth. Fold in marshmallows. Frost bars. Cut into bars. **Yield:** 3 dozen.

Frosted Cocoa Bars

Cathryn White, Newark, Delaware

It's nice to have a trusty bar recipe like this when you are short on time. The subtle coffee flavor in the frosting adds a fantastic tasty touch.

- 1-1/4 cups shortening
- 1-1/4 cups packed brown sugar
- 1/2 cup corn syrup
- 1-1/2 teaspoons vanilla extract
- 4 eggs
- 1-1/4 cups all-purpose flour
- 2/3 cup baking cocoa
- 1 teaspoon salt
- FROSTING:
- 1/2 cup butter
- 3 cups confectioners' sugar
- 2 tablespoons brewed coffee
- 1-1/2 teaspoons vanilla extract
- 3 to 4 tablespoons milk

In a large bowl, cream shortening and brown sugar until light and fluffy. Beat in corn syrup and vanilla. Add eggs, one at a time, beating well after each addition. Combine the flour, cocoa and salt; gradually add to creamed mixture and mix well.

Spread into a greased 15-in. x 10-in. x 1-in. baking pan. Bake at 350° for 20-25 minutes or until a toothpick inserted near the center comes out clean. Cool on a wire rack.

In a large heavy saucepan, cook butter over medium heat for 5-7 minutes or until golden brown. Pour into a small bowl; beat in the confectioners' sugar, coffee, vanilla and enough milk until frosting reaches spreading consistency.

Frost cooled brownies. Cover and refrigerate until firm, about 1 hour. Cut into bars. **Yield:** 8 dozen.

Chocolate Chip Oat Bars

Kim Wills, Sagamore Hills, Ohio

I stir up a big panful of these chewy oat squares loaded with nuts and chocolate chips whenever I need a special treat. The sweet bars are simple to make, and they cut cleanly when cool to make serving a breeze.

- 1 cup all-purpose flour
- 1 cup quick-cooking oats
- 3/4 cup packed brown sugar
- 1/2 cup cold butter, cubed
- 1 can (14 ounces) sweetened condensed milk
- 1 cup chopped pecans
- 1 cup (6 ounces) semisweet chocolate chips

In a large bowl, combine the flour, oats and brown sugar. Cut in the butter until crumbly. Press half of the mixture into a greased 13-in. x 9-in. x 2-in. baking pan.

Bake at 350° for 8-10 minutes. Spread condensed milk evenly over the crust. Sprinkle with pecans and chocolate chips. Top with remaining oat mixture and pat lightly. Bake

25-30 minutes longer or until lightly browned. Cool on a wire rack. Cut into bars. **Yield:** about 2-1/2 dozen.

Lemon Shortbread Squares

Janet Sater, Arlington, Virginia

During the Christmas season, I keep homemade cookies available in my office to share with co-workers. These easy-to-prepare squares are always a hit.

- 1/2 cup plus 2 tablespoons butter, softened
- 1/2 cup confectioners' sugar
- 1/2 teaspoon lemon extract
- 1/2 teaspoon vanilla extract
- 1/4 teaspoon grated lemon peel, optional
- 1-1/4 cups all-purpose flour
- 1/2 cup chopped pecans

In a large bowl, cream butter and sugar until light and fluffy. Beat in extracts and lemon peel if desired. Gradually add flour. Mix until dough forms a ball and pulls away from the side of the bowl.

Press into an ungreased 9-in. square baking pan. Score with a sharp knife into 16 squares. Prick each square twice with a fork. Sprinkle with pecans; press firmly into dough.

Bake at 325° for 20-25 minutes or until lightly browned and pecans are toasted. Cool for 5 minutes. Cut along scored lines. Cool completely in pan on a wire rack. Store in an airtight container. **Yield:** 16 squares.

Dream Bars

Hillary Lawson, Plummer, Idaho

These bar cookies are a family favorite and excellent travelers. Wonderfully moist and chewy, they're definite winners with kids of all ages.

CRUST:
- 1 cup all-purpose flour
- 1/2 cup packed brown sugar
- 1/2 cup cold butter, cubed

FILLING:
- 2 eggs, lightly beaten
- 1 cup packed brown sugar
- 1 teaspoon vanilla extract
- 2 tablespoons all-purpose flour
- 1/2 teaspoon salt
- 1 cup flaked coconut
- 1 cup chopped walnuts

In a small bowl, combine flour and brown sugar; cut in butter until crumbly. Pat into a 13-in. x 9-in. x 2-in. baking pan. Bake at 350° for 10 minutes.

Meanwhile, in a large bowl, beat eggs and brown sugar; stir in vanilla. Combine flour and salt; add to egg mixture. Fold in coconut and walnuts. Spread over baked crust. Return to oven and bake 20-25 minutes longer or until golden brown. Cool in pan on a wire rack. Cut into bars. **Yield:** 32 servings.

Caramel-Chocolate Oat Squares

Kellie Ochsner, Newton, Iowa

In the summer, we often have weekend guests who go boating with us. These sweet, chewy bars are the perfect treat to take along. They bake in the microwave so they don't heat up the kitchen.

- 3/4 cup butter, cubed
- 1-1/4 cups all-purpose flour
- 1-1/4 cups quick-cooking oats
- 3/4 cup packed brown sugar
- 1/2 teaspoon baking soda
- 1/4 teaspoon salt
- 24 caramels
- 1/4 cup milk
- 1 cup (6 ounces) semisweet chocolate chips
- 1/2 cup chopped walnuts, optional

In a microwave, heat butter, uncovered, on high for 20-30 seconds or until softened. Combine the flour, oats, brown sugar, baking soda and salt; stir into butter until blended.

Set a third of the mixture aside for topping. Press remaining mixture onto the bottom of an 8-in. square microwave-safe dish. Cook, uncovered, on high for 1-2 minutes or until crust is raised and set (crust will be uneven), rotating a half turn after the first minute.

In a 1-qt. microwave-safe dish, heat the caramels and milk, uncovered, on high for 1 minute or until melted and smooth, stirring once. Sprinkle chips and nuts if desired over crust. Pour caramel mixture over all.

Sprinkle with reserved oat mixture; press down lightly. Microwave, uncovered, on high for 2-3 minutes or until the caramel is bubbly, rotating a quarter turn every minute. Cool before cutting. **Yield:** 16 servings.

Editor's Note: This recipe was tested in a 1,100-watt microwave.

Peanut Jelly Bars

Sonja Blow, Reeds Spring, Missouri

A layer of grape jelly between a peanut-oatmeal crust and topping gives these satisfying bars a taste of a peanut butter and jelly sandwich!

- 3/4 cup butter, softened
- 1 cup packed brown sugar
- 1-1/2 cups all-purpose flour
- 1 teaspoon salt
- 1/2 teaspoon baking soda
- 1-1/2 cups quick-cooking oats
- 1/2 cup chopped salted peanuts
- 1 jar (12 ounces) grape jelly

In a large bowl, cream butter and brown sugar until light and fluffy. Combine the flour, salt and baking soda; gradually add to creamed mixture and mix well. Stir in oats and peanuts (mixture will be crumbly).

Press half of the mixture into a greased 13-in. x 9-in. x 2-in. baking pan. Spread with jelly. Cover with remaining crumb mixture. Bake at 400° for 25 minutes or until golden brown. Cool on a wire rack. Cut into bars. **Yield:** 2 dozen.

Coconut Chip Nut Bars

Judith Strohmeyer, Albrightsville, Pennsylvania

There's something for everyone in these delectable bars, from coconut and chocolate chips to walnuts and toffee. They're popular with kids and adults alike—so make a big batch. You'll be amazed at how fast they vanish!

1-3/4 cups all-purpose flour
  3/4 cup confectioners' sugar
  1/4 cup baking cocoa
1-1/4 cups cold butter, cubed
    1 can (14 ounces) sweetened condensed milk
    2 cups (12 ounces) semisweet chocolate chips, *divided*
    1 teaspoon vanilla extract
    1 cup chopped walnuts
  1/2 cup flaked coconut
  1/2 cup English toffee bits *or* almond brickle chips

In a small bowl, combine the flour, sugar and cocoa. Cut in butter until mixture resembles coarse crumbs. Press firmly into a greased 13-in. x 9-in. x 2-in. baking pan. Bake at 350° for 10 minutes.

Meanwhile, in a small saucepan, combine milk and 1 cup chocolate chips; cook and stir over low heat until smooth and chips are melted. Stir in vanilla.

Pour over crust. Sprinkle with walnuts and remaining chocolate chips. Top with coconut and toffee bits. Gently press down into chocolate layer. Bake at 350° for 18-20 minutes or until firm. Cool on a wire rack. Cut into bars. **Yield:** 3 dozen.

Butterscotch Cashew Bars

Lori Berg, Wentzville, Missouri

I knew these nutty bars were a success when I took them on our annual family vacation. My husband couldn't stop eating them...and my sister-in-law, who is a great cook, asked for the recipe.

    1   cup plus 2 tablespoons butter, softened
    3/4 cup plus 2 tablespoons packed brown sugar
    2-1/2 cups all-purpose flour
    1-3/4 teaspoons salt
TOPPING:
    1   package (10 to 11 ounces) butterscotch chips
    1/2 cup plus 2 tablespoons light corn syrup
    3   tablespoons butter
    2   teaspoons water
    2-1/2 cups salted cashew halves

In a large bowl, cream the butter and brown sugar until light and fluffy. Combine flour and salt; add to creamed mixture just until combined.

Press into a greased 15-in. x 10-in. x 1-in. baking pan. Bake at 350° for 10-12 minutes or until lightly browned.

Meanwhile, in a small saucepan, combine the butterscotch chips, corn syrup, butter and water. Cook and stir over medium heat until chips and butter are melted.

Spread over crust. Sprinkle with cashews; press down lightly. Bake for 11-13 minutes longer or until topping is bubbly and lightly browned. Cool on a wire rack. Cut into bars. **Yield:** 3-1/2 dozen.

Baking Classics | Bars

Rhubarb Dream Bars

Marion Tomlinson, Madison, Wisconsin

Dreaming of a different way to use rhubarb? Try these sweet bars. The shortbread-like crust is topped with rhubarb, walnuts and coconut for delicious results.

- 1-1/4 cups all-purpose flour, *divided*
- 1/3 cup confectioners' sugar
- 1/2 cup cold butter, cubed
- 1-1/4 to 1-1/2 cups sugar
- 2 eggs
- 2 cups diced fresh *or* frozen rhubarb
- 1/2 cup chopped walnuts
- 1/2 cup flaked coconut

In a large bowl, combine 1 cup flour and confectioners' sugar. Cut in the butter until crumbly. Pat into a lightly greased 13-in. x 9-in. x 2-in. baking dish. Bake at 350° for 13-15 minutes or until edges are lightly browned.

In a large bowl, combine sugar and remaining flour. Add eggs. Stir in rhubarb, walnuts and coconut; pour over crust.

Bake 30-35 minutes longer or until set. Cool on a wire rack. Cut into bars. Store in the refrigerator. **Yield:** 2-1/2 to 3 dozen.

Editor's Note: If using frozen rhubarb, measure rhubarb while still frozen, then thaw completely. Drain in a colander, but do not press liquid out.

Pineapple Coconut Squares

Elaine Anderson, New Galilee, Pennsylvania

I don't remember where I got this recipe, but I'm sure glad I have it. The tangy pineapple and flaked coconut give these bars an unbeatable, tropical flair.

- 2 tablespoons butter, melted
- 3 tablespoons sugar
- 1 egg
- 1 cup all-purpose flour
- 1 teaspoon baking powder
- 2 cans (8 ounces *each*) unsweetened crushed pineapple, drained

TOPPING:
- 1 tablespoon butter, melted
- 1 cup sugar
- 2 eggs
- 2 cups flaked coconut

In a large bowl, cream butter and sugar until light and fluffy. Beat in egg. Combine flour and baking powder; stir into creamed mixture. Press into a 9-in. square baking pan coated with cooking spray. Spread pineapple over crust; set aside.

For topping, in a small bowl, beat butter and sugar until blended. Beat in eggs. Stir in coconut. Spread over pineapple. Bake at 325° for 35-40 minutes or until golden brown. Cool on a wire rack. Cut into bars. Store in the refrigerator. **Yield:** 16 servings.

Candy Cereal Treats

Janet Shearer, Jackson, Michigan

These scrumptious bars travel well and are loved by kids of all ages. They're chock-full of great flavor.

- 1/2 cup butter, softened
- 2/3 cup packed brown sugar
- 2 egg yolks
- 1 teaspoon vanilla extract
- 1-1/2 cups all-purpose flour
- 1/2 teaspoon baking powder
- 1/2 teaspoon salt
- 1/4 teaspoon baking soda
- 3 cups miniature marshmallows

TOPPING:
- 2/3 cup corn syrup
- 1/4 cup butter, softened
- 1 package (10 ounces) peanut butter chips
- 2 teaspoons vanilla extract
- 2 cups crisp rice cereal
- 1 cup salted peanuts
- 1 cup milk chocolate M&M's

In a large bowl, cream butter and brown sugar until light and fluffy. Beat in egg yolks and vanilla. Combine the flour, baking powder, salt and baking soda; gradually add to the creamed mixture until mixture resembles coarse crumbs (do not overmix).

Press into a greased 13-in. x 9-in. x 2-in. baking pan. Bake at 350° for 12-14 minutes or until golden brown. Immediately sprinkle with marshmallows; bake 2-3 minutes longer or until marshmallows are puffed. Cool on a wire rack.

For topping, in a large saucepan, combine the corn syrup, butter and peanut butter chips. Cook and stir over medium heat until chips are melted and mixture is smooth. Remove from the heat; stir in the vanilla, cereal, nuts and M&M's. Spread over crust. Cool completely before cutting into bars. **Yield:** 2 dozen.

Index

Alphabetical Index

This handy index lists every recipe in alphabetical order, so you can easily find your favorite recipe.

General Recipe Index

This handy index lists every recipe by food category and/or major ingredient, so you can easily locate recipes that suit your needs.